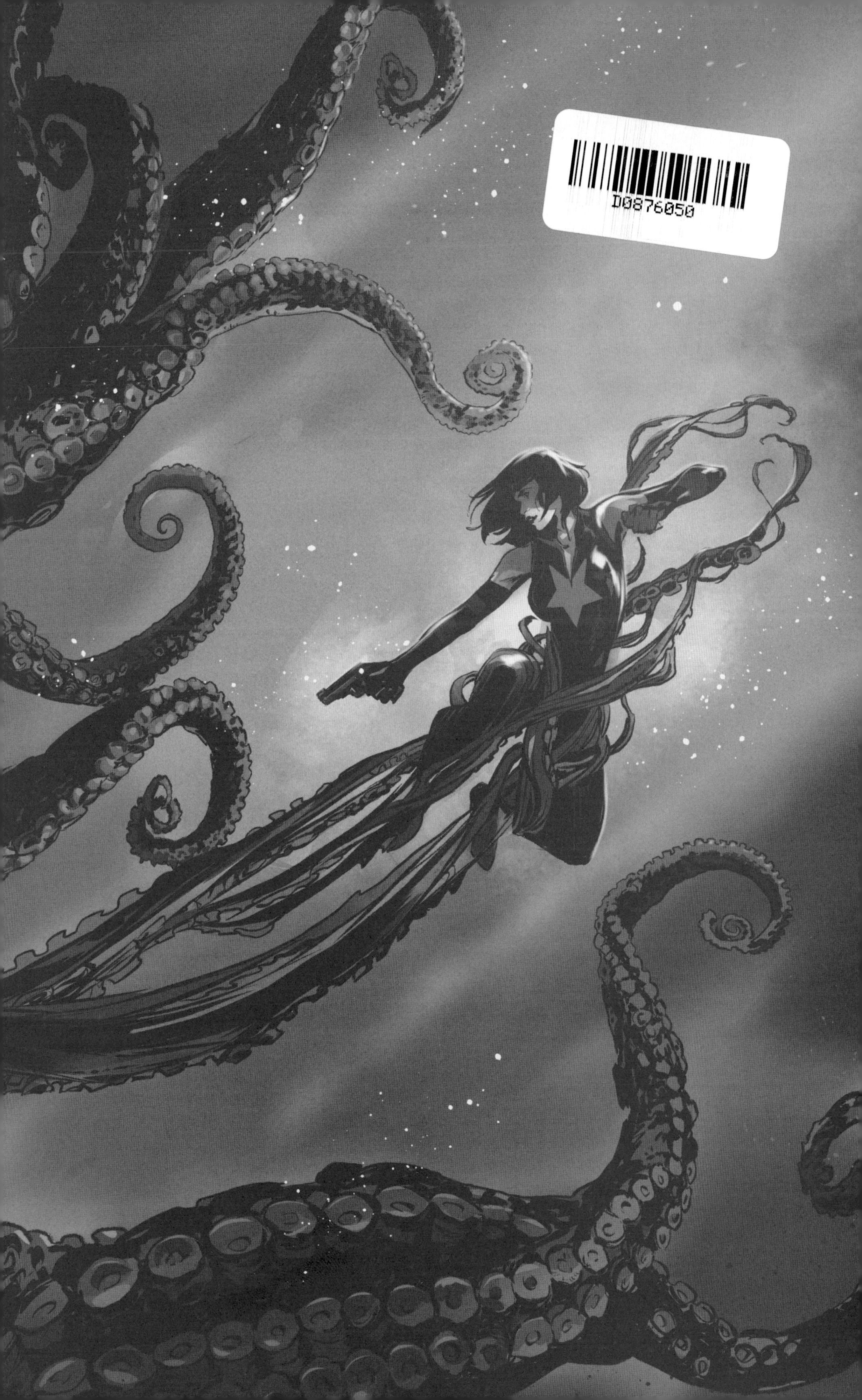

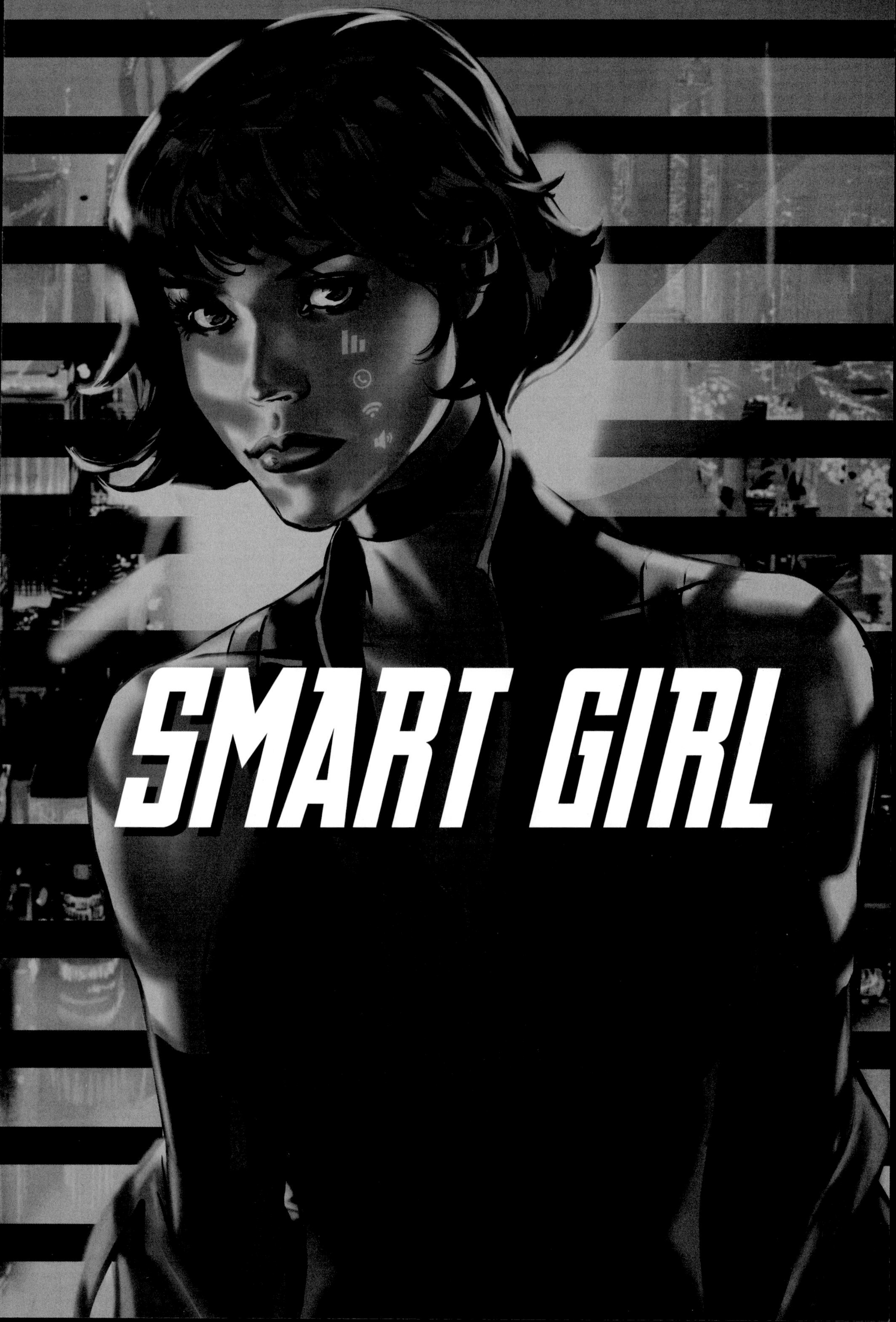
SMART GIRL

TITAN COMICS

SENIOR EDITOR / Jake Devine
DESIGNER / Donna Askem
ASSISTANT EDITOR/ Phoebe Hedges
MANAGING EDITOR / Martin Eden
SENIOR DESIGNER Andrew Leung
ART DIRECTOR / Oz Browne
PRODUCTION COTROLLERS / Caterina Falqui & Kelly Fenlon
PRODUCTION MANAGER / Jackie Flook
SALES & CIRCULATION MANAGER / Steve Tothill
PUBLICIST / Phoebe Trillo
MARKETING & ADVERTISEMENT ASSISTANT / Lauren Noding
SALES & MARKETING COORDINATOR / George Wickenden
ACQUISITIONS EDITOR / Duncan Baizley
PUBLISHING DIRECTOR / Ricky Claydon
PUBLISHING DIRECTOR /John Dziewiatkowski
OPERATIONS DIRECTOR / Leigh Baulch
PUBLISHERS / Vivian Cheung & Nick Landau

SMART GIRL
ISBN: 9781787737198
Published by Titan Comics
A division of Titan Publishing Group Ltd.
144 Southwark St.
London SE1 0UP

Originally published in Spanish as Smart Girl © Fernando Dagnino. All rights reserved.

First edition: October 2021

10 9 8 7 6 5 4 3 2 1

Printed in China.

www.titan-comics.com
Follow us on Twitter @ComicsTitan
Visit us at facebook.com/comicstitan

To my father.

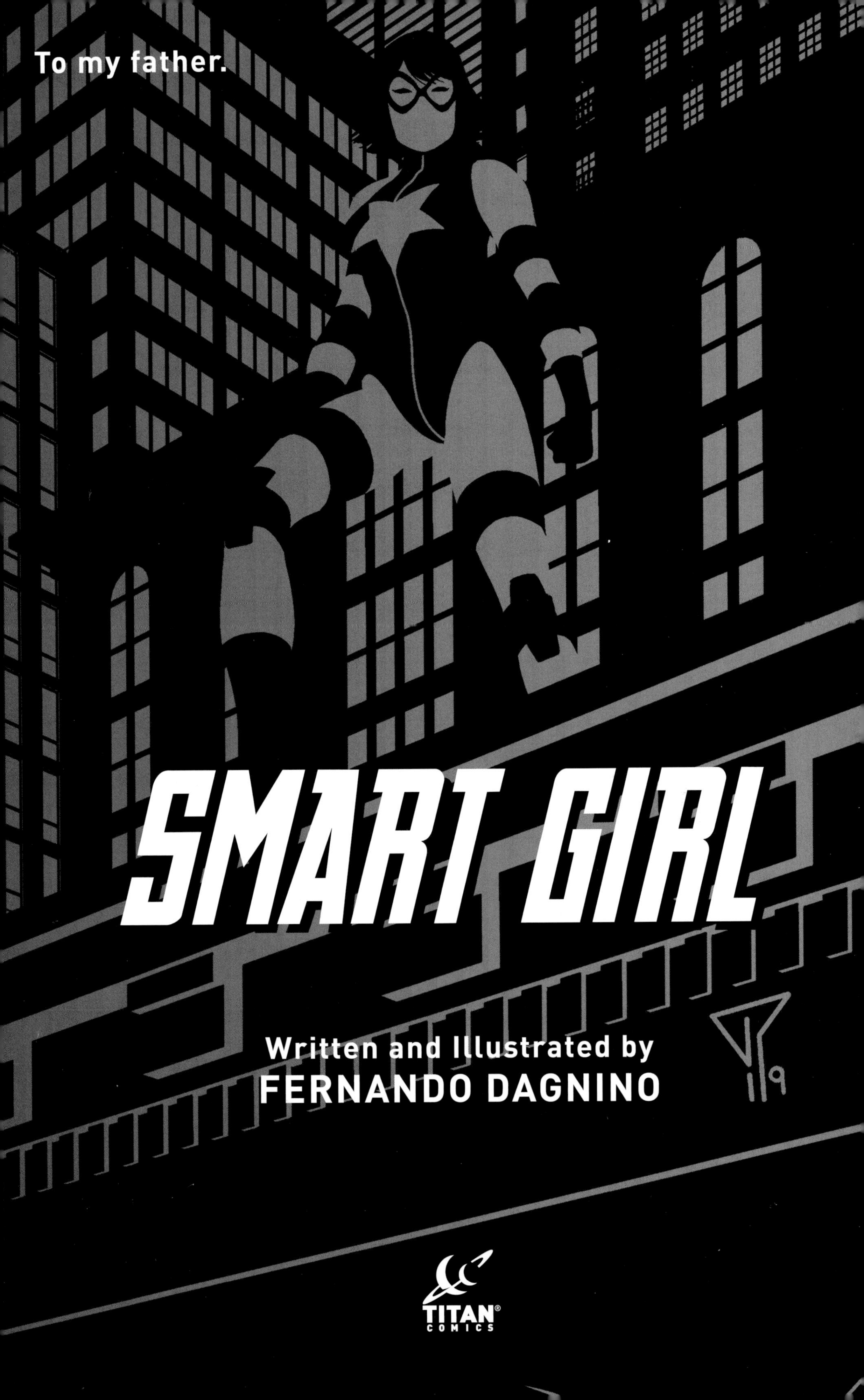

SMART GIRL

Written and Illustrated by
FERNANDO DAGNINO

TITAN COMICS

'I Love Your War With Fernando!'

The comment took me by surprise, and I didn't know how to respond.

You see, I'd only just met Fernando a few days earlier, as we'd both been invited to the Hercegnovski Strip Festival in Montenegro. On my first night, I was led to a table of local and overseas artists (including Fernando) ahead of the official opening ceremony. Within seconds they were handing me my first shot, and it all went quickly downhill from there (both literally and figuratively).

I was already familiar with Fernando's work from his run on DC's *Suicide Squad* (which I had read and enjoyed) but I was unprepared for the level of craftsmanship on display in his exhibition at the festival or in the sketches he did for the local attendees and guests. His work was a cut above, and it demonstrated a creativity beyond what I had seen before.

I'm not sure how it began, but at some point early in the festival, we started buying one another an extra shot each time we went to the bar, and would try to slip that extra shot under the other person's nose without them realizing and then slip away. The local spirits (fruit brandies) were known as rakija, and we were particularly fond of the plum variety called slivovitz.

Towards the end of the festival, we went on a short cruise around the harbor and out into the Adriatic, which culminated in throwing a literal 'message in a bottle' out to sea. It was on the way home from this particular outing that I found myself confronted by one of the organizers who said, 'I love your war with Fernando. You know, your war of drinks,' he said with a laugh.

Cut to the airport when I was flying home a few days later, and I bought a couple of mini bottles of rakija/slivovitz at the duty-free store. These would go into my arsenal for the following month when I saw Fernando again at New York Comic Con. I'm not saying I smuggled those bottles into the Javits Centre and left them on his table in Artists Alley, but I'm not saying I didn't do it either.

Coming back to the festival, Fernando had showed me some of the work he'd been doing on *Smart Girl*, and I was blown away! He already had a deal for French and Spanish editions of the book, but was looking for a publisher to bring it to the American market.

I was working for Titan at the time, and came back to the office saying we needed to publish it before someone else does. Its futuristic setting was so much like the *Blade Runner* license we'd just acquired, and I thought having Fernando do a run on that, then launching *Smart Girl* off the back of it, would be an ideal strategy. Fast forward almost four years later, and that's exactly what's happened.

You may not be able to spend time with Fernando at a comics festival to find out what an interesting guy he is, or buy him copious amounts of shots, but you can experience the next best thing by discovering the man and his artistry through this book. To see this work finally coming to English-speaking audiences is both an honor and a privilege, and I'm pleased to call him my friend. I hope you enjoy this stylish, noir-inspired futuristic thriller, and that you continue to explore his other work.

Meanwhile, despite a temporary ceasefire, the war continues...

Chris Thompson
London, United Kingdom
May 2021

SMART GIRL

Prologue

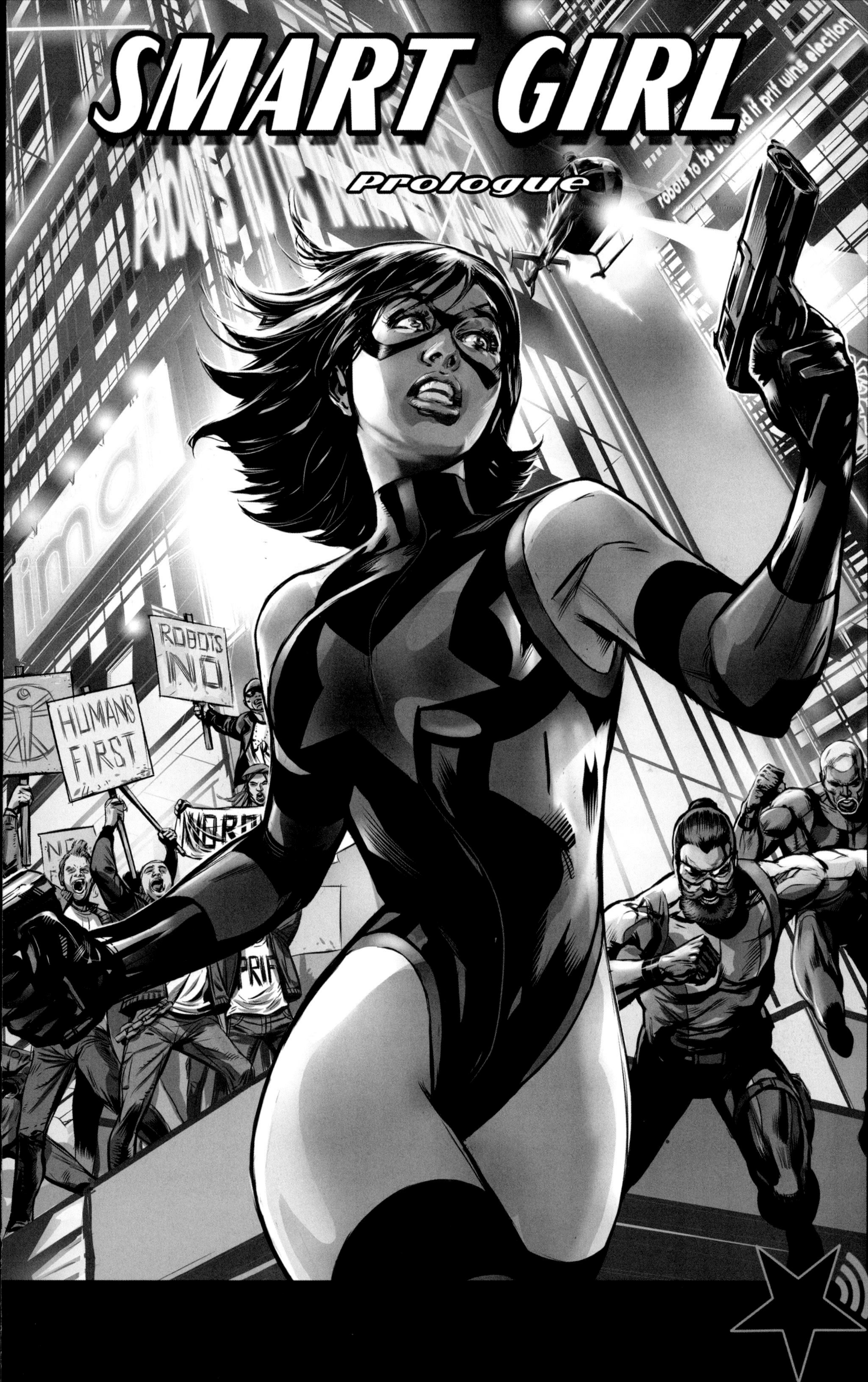
ROBOTS NO
HUMANS FIRST

FOREWORD

In 2028, the first A.I. processors were marketed on a large scale, giving birth to the first generation of prodigious androids that revolutionized the world.

But the biggest change was yet to come...

Once these A.I.s tested successfully in real-life environments, they were uploaded back onto the network, thus creating an online existential consciousness called: *Schemata.*

Created by independent laboratories using free software, these early experimental schematas devised a new organic language between humans and machines. This new relationship favored an unprecedented era of free global exchange of services and knowledge, as well as a period of greater democracy and transparency.

Humanity had given birth to a new android sensibility, whose loyal and loving gaze upon their creators gave humans a new understanding of diversity and social responsibility; not only towards their android creations, but to the entire human race.

But an alliance of the largest corporations on the planet, *T.O.T.E.M.* (TransOceanic Trade Endowment Mutuality), would not allow their influence and profit margin to be diminished by this new paradigm. Their response was to create *Gorgona* – a corporate macro-schemata that became ubiquitous in every language, company, town, home and device. In two years, Gorgona flooded the networks, becoming the sole benefactor and regulator of economic, social and domestic life.

The original schematas were soon relegated to the dark web, practically inaccessible to anyone except technicians and hackers. As a result, they resorted to acts of piracy. In 2070, the original schematas were declared illegal and were locked in a transoceanic cable knot, where they still remain, learning and growing in secret...

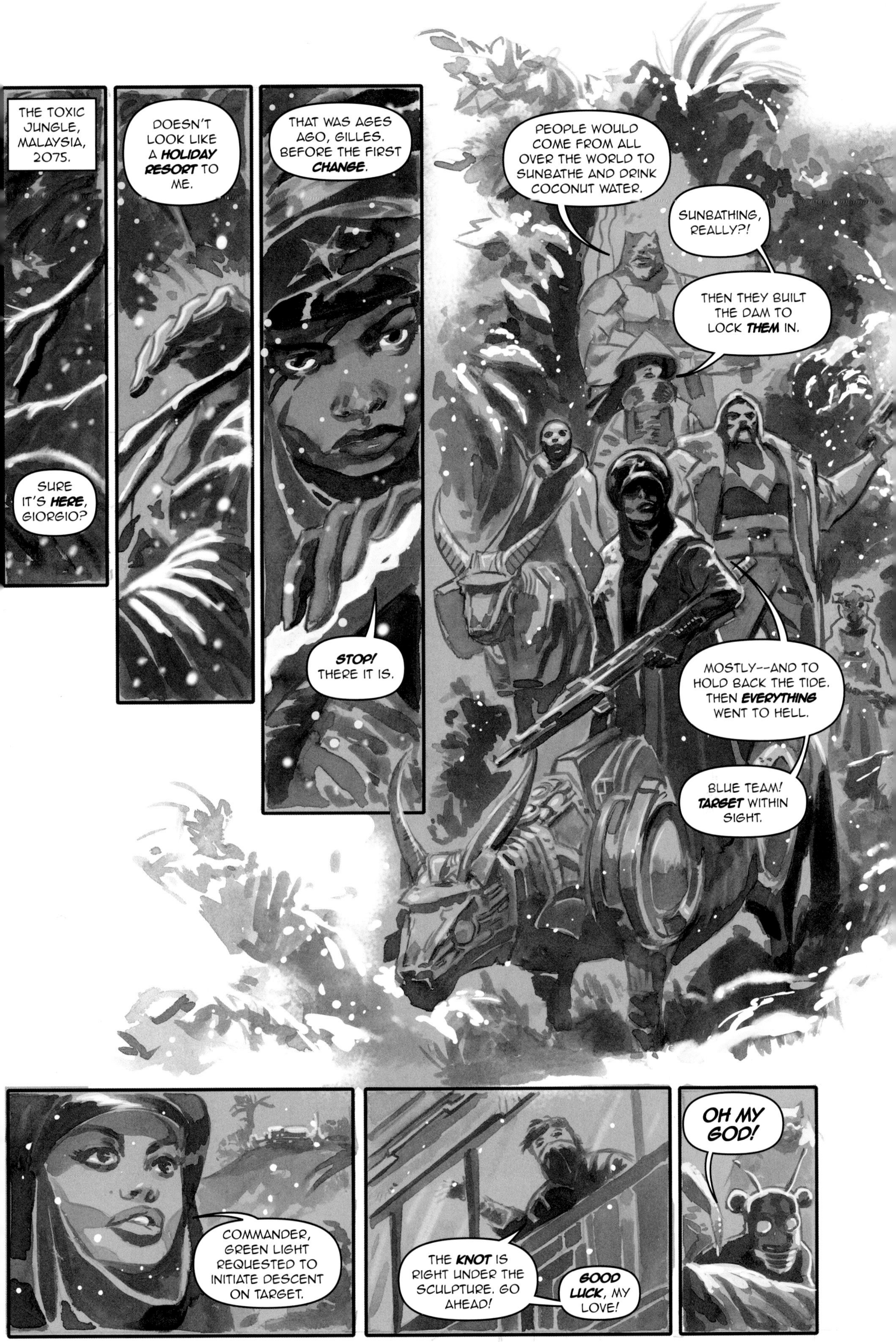
THE TOXIC JUNGLE, MALAYSIA, 2075.
SURE IT'S **HERE**, GIORGIO?
DOESN'T LOOK LIKE A **HOLIDAY RESORT** TO ME.
THAT WAS AGES AGO, GILLES. BEFORE THE FIRST **CHANGE**.
STOP! THERE IT IS.
PEOPLE WOULD COME FROM ALL OVER THE WORLD TO SUNBATHE AND DRINK COCONUT WATER.
SUNBATHING, REALLY?!
THEN THEY BUILT THE DAM TO LOCK **THEM** IN.
MOSTLY--AND TO HOLD BACK THE TIDE. THEN **EVERYTHING** WENT TO HELL.
BLUE TEAM! **TARGET** WITHIN SIGHT.
COMMANDER, GREEN LIGHT REQUESTED TO INITIATE DESCENT ON TARGET.
THE **KNOT** IS RIGHT UNDER THE SCULPTURE. GO AHEAD!
GOOD LUCK, MY LOVE!
OH MY GOD!

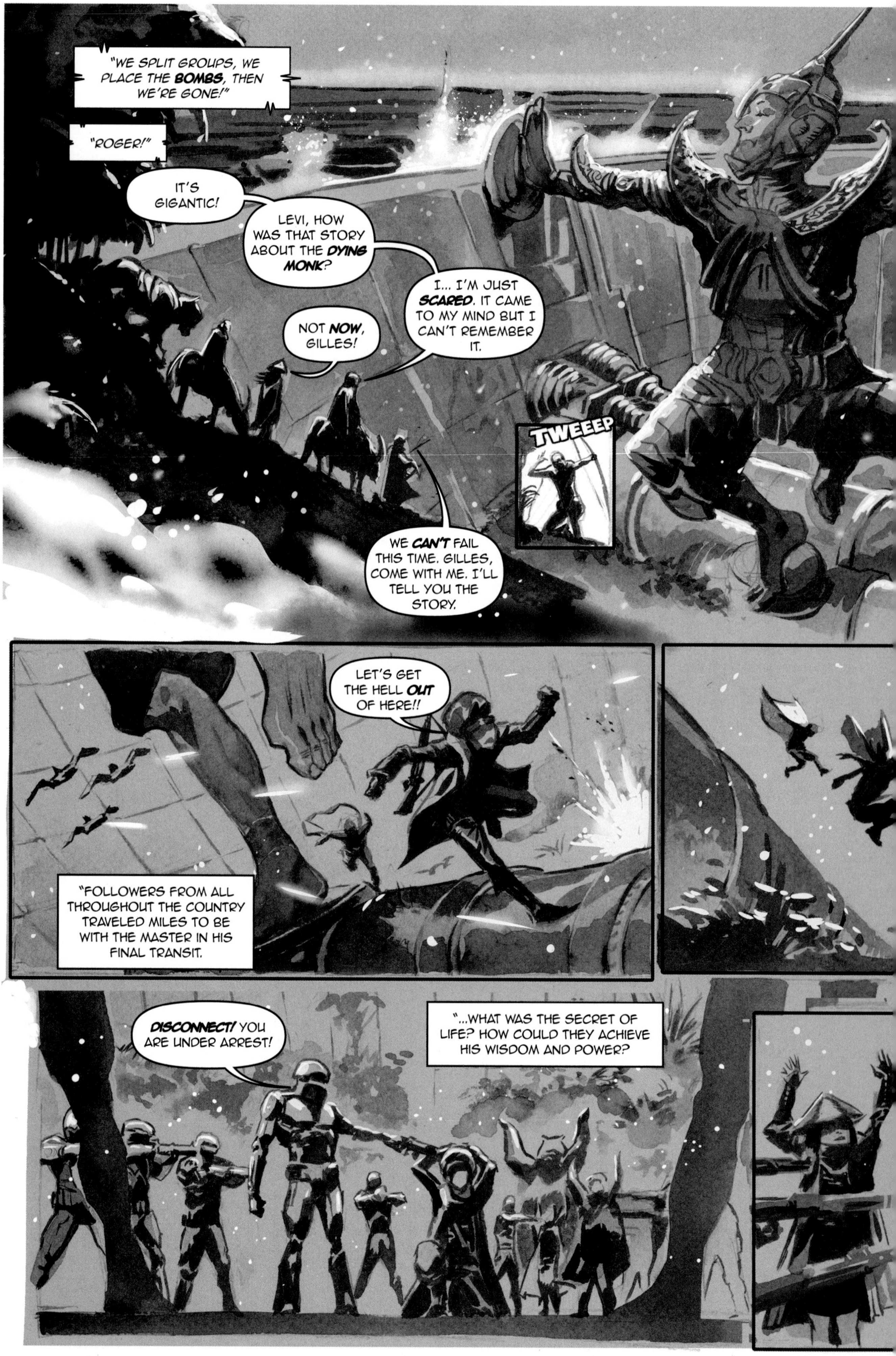
"WE SPLIT GROUPS, WE PLACE THE **BOMBS**, THEN WE'RE GONE!"
"ROGER!"
IT'S GIGANTIC!
LEVI, HOW WAS THAT STORY ABOUT THE ***DYING MONK***?
I... I'M JUST ***SCARED***. IT CAME TO MY MIND BUT I CAN'T REMEMBER IT.
NOT ***NOW***, GILLES!
TWEEEP
WE ***CAN'T*** FAIL THIS TIME. GILLES, COME WITH ME. I'LL TELL YOU THE STORY.
LET'S GET THE HELL ***OUT*** OF HERE!!
"FOLLOWERS FROM ALL THROUGHOUT THE COUNTRY TRAVELED MILES TO BE WITH THE MASTER IN HIS FINAL TRANSIT.
DISCONNECT! YOU ARE UNDER ARREST!
"...WHAT WAS THE SECRET OF LIFE? HOW COULD THEY ACHIEVE HIS WISDOM AND POWER?

TROK

"HE WAS THE WISEST MONK OF ALL THE REGION...

"ADMIRED LIKE A GOD FOR HIS WISDOM AND POWER.

FRRZZZZ

PRAF

"IT WAS SAID HIS LOVE COULD HEAL THE SICK -- HIS FAITH WOULD RAISE HIM ABOVE THE GROUND.

"BUT ONE DAY...

PLOK

PLOK

PLOK

"HIS TIME CAME TO DEPART FROM THIS WORLD.

BUZZ BUZZ

SHIT! WE'VE BEEN SPOTTED!!

THOD

FREEZE!

"ALL THE PILGRIMS GATHERED AROUND HIS DEATHBED, TO ASK HIM BEFORE HE DIED: WHAT IS THE SECRET OF LIFE?

I GUESS WE HAVE *NO OTHER* CHOICE, MY SOLDIERS!

WHAT THE HELL? WE'VE BEEN...

"REVERED MASTER, WHAT ARE YOUR FINAL WORDS? THEY ASKED HIM.

SOLDIERS, FRIENDS, OUR *END* HAS COME...

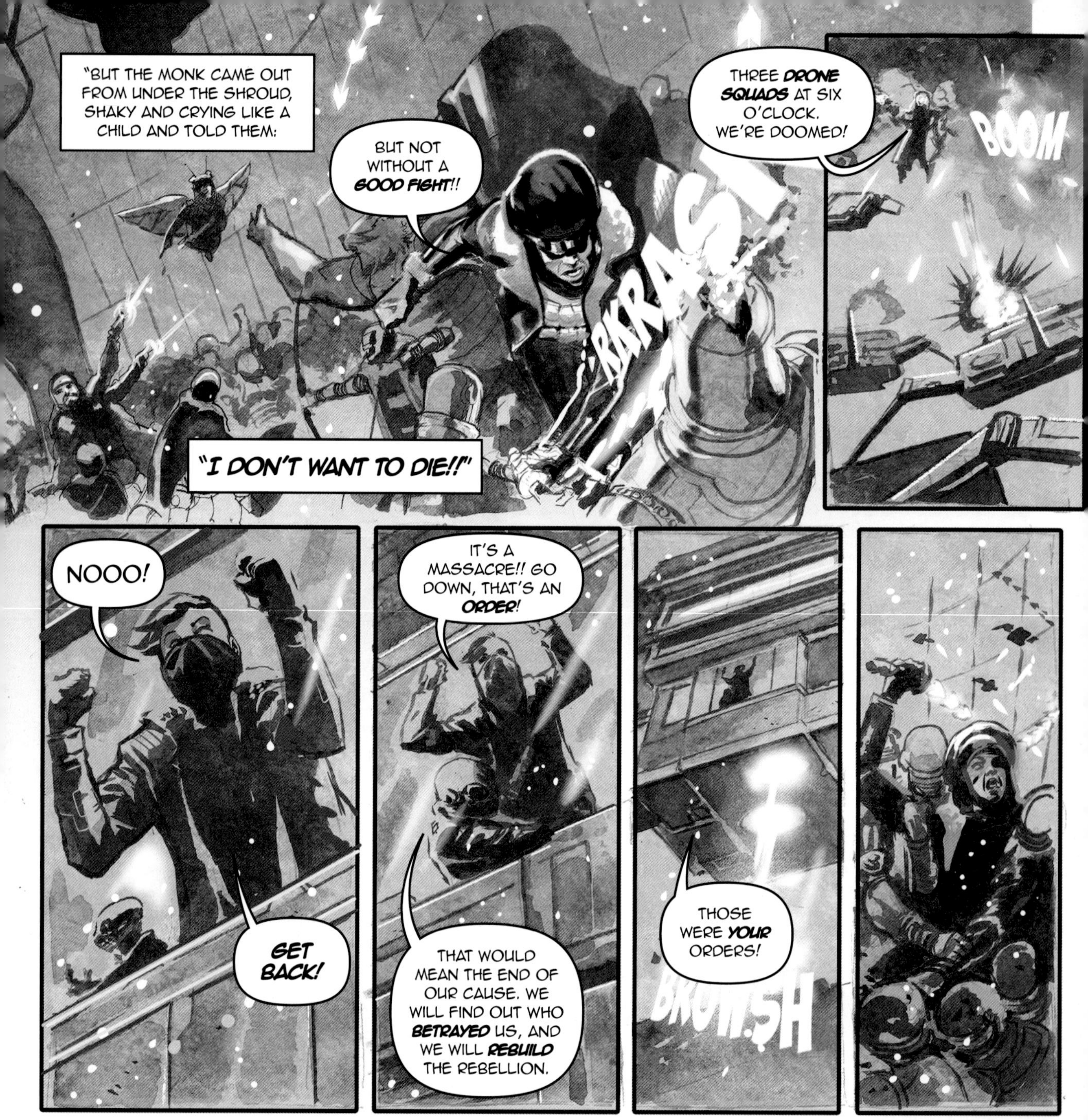
"BUT THE MONK CAME OUT FROM UNDER THE SHROUD, SHAKY AND CRYING LIKE A CHILD AND TOLD THEM:
BUT NOT WITHOUT A GOOD FIGHT!!
KRASH
"I DON'T WANT TO DIE!!"
THREE DRONE SQUADS AT SIX O'CLOCK. WE'RE DOOMED!
BOOM
NOOO!
GET BACK!
IT'S A MASSACRE!! GO DOWN, THAT'S AN ORDER!
THAT WOULD MEAN THE END OF OUR CAUSE. WE WILL FIND OUT WHO BETRAYED US, AND WE WILL REBUILD THE REBELLION.
THOSE WERE YOUR ORDERS!
BROWSH

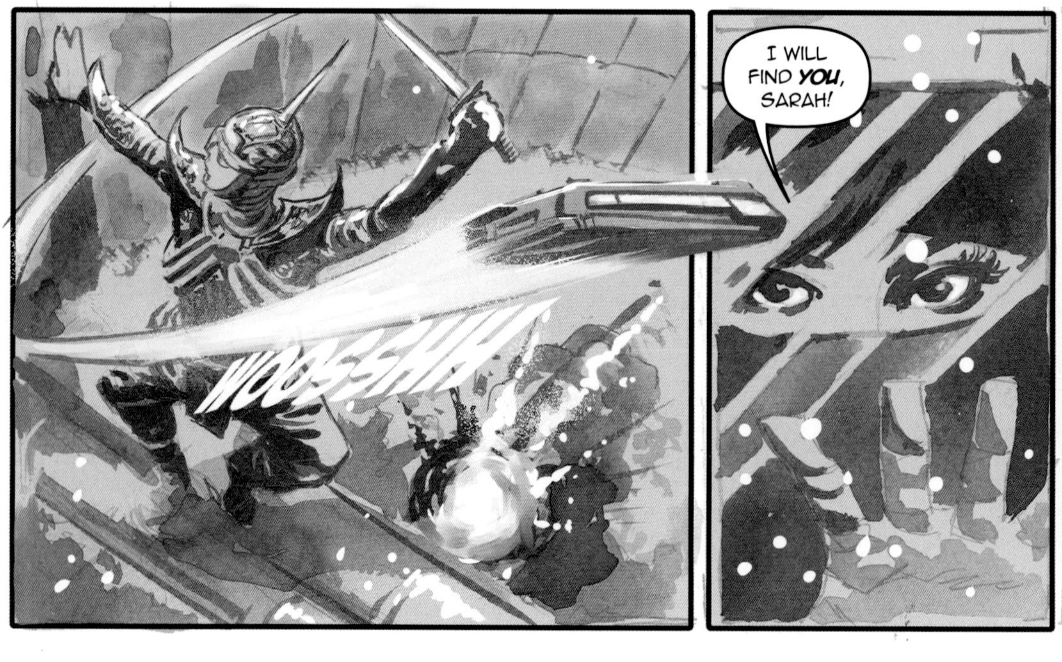
WOOSSHH
I WILL FIND YOU, SARAH!

"IT MATTERS WHAT STORIES WE TELL TO TELL OTHER STORIES WITH; IT MATTERS WHAT KNOTS KNOT KNOTS, WHAT THOUGHTS THINK THOUGHTS, WHAT TIES TIE TIES. IT MATTERS WHAT STORIES MAKE WORLDS, WHAT WORLDS MAKE STORIES."

-Donna J. Haraway

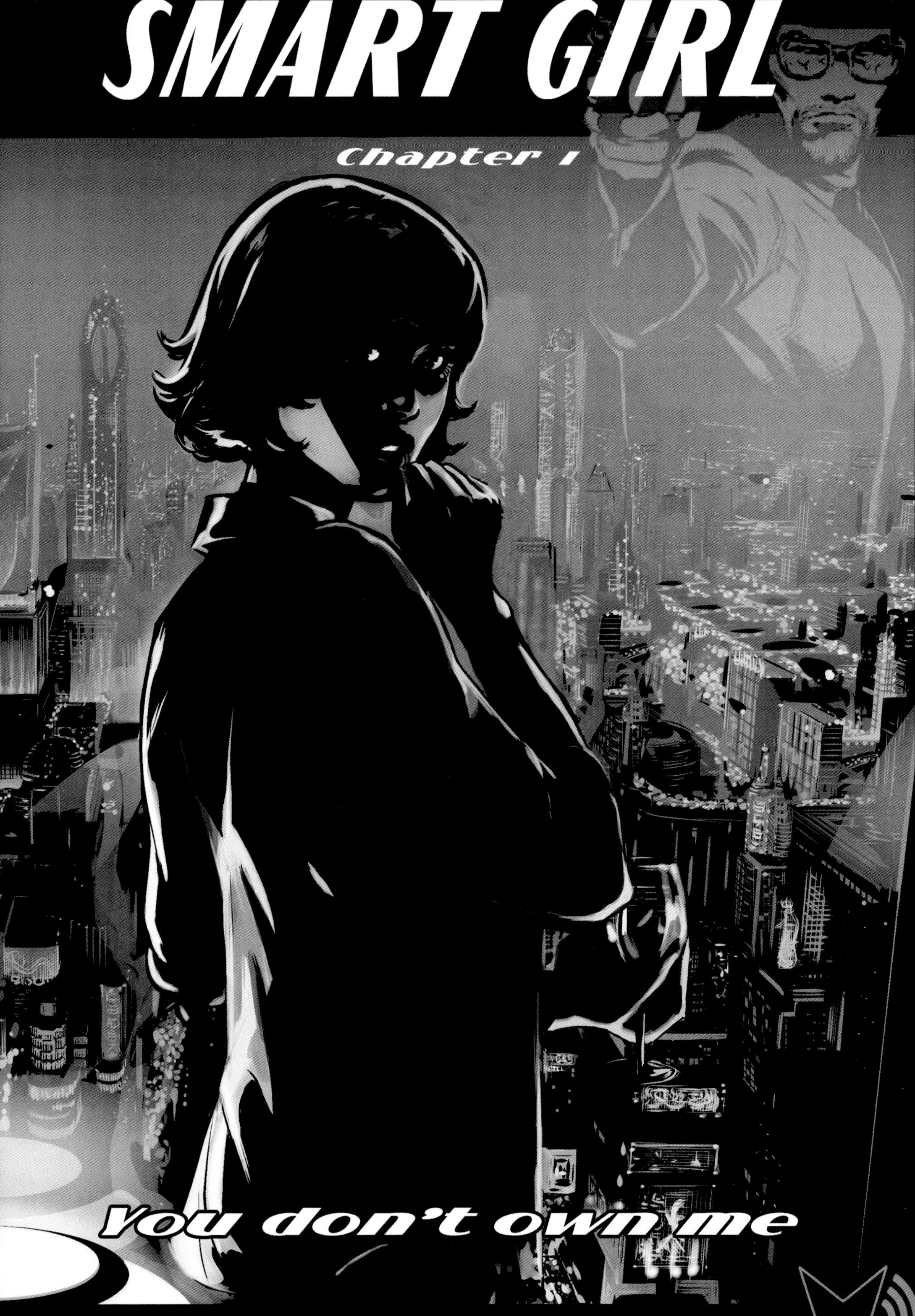
SMART GIRL
Chapter 1
You don't own me

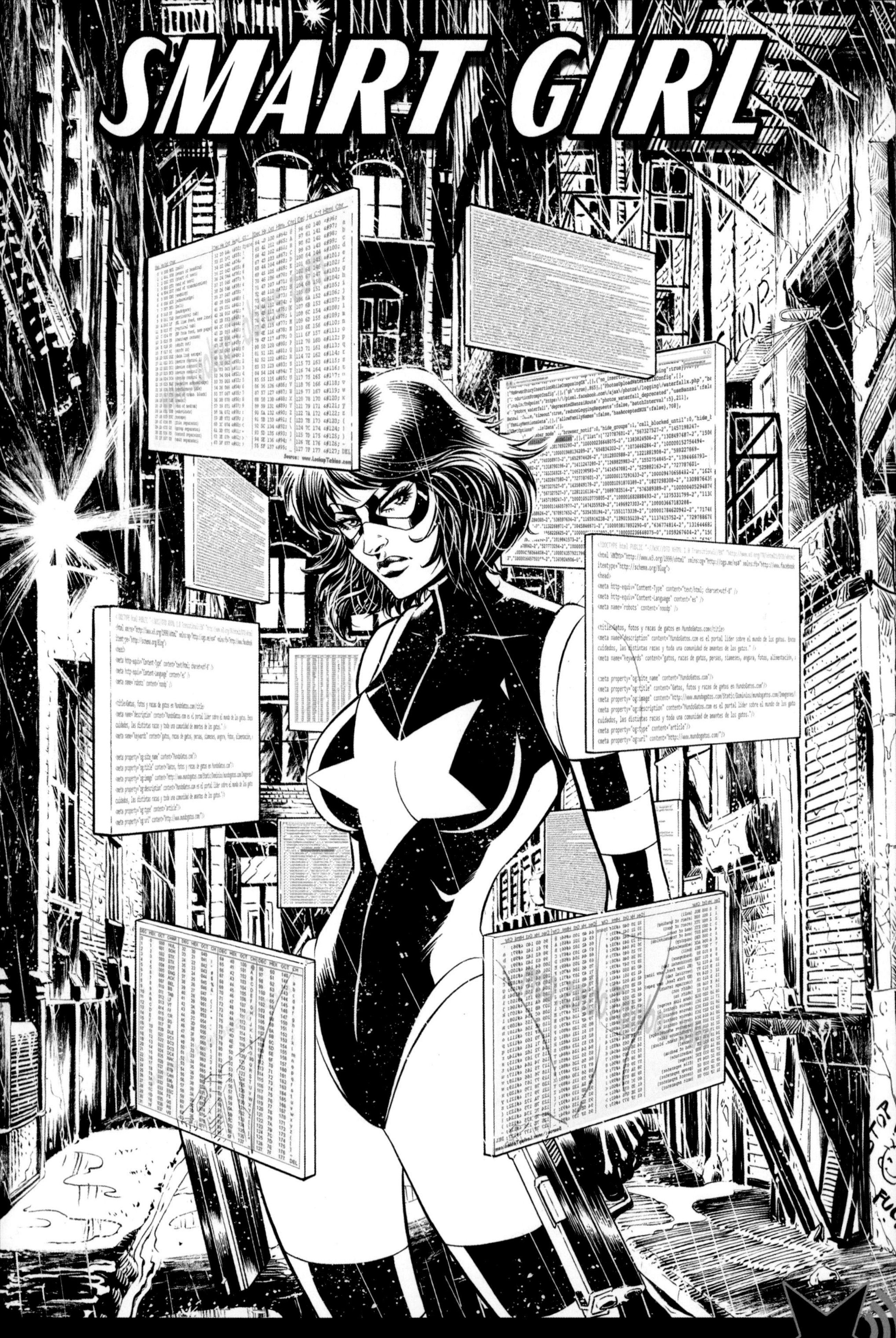
SMART GIRL

Artwork by Jordi Tarragona

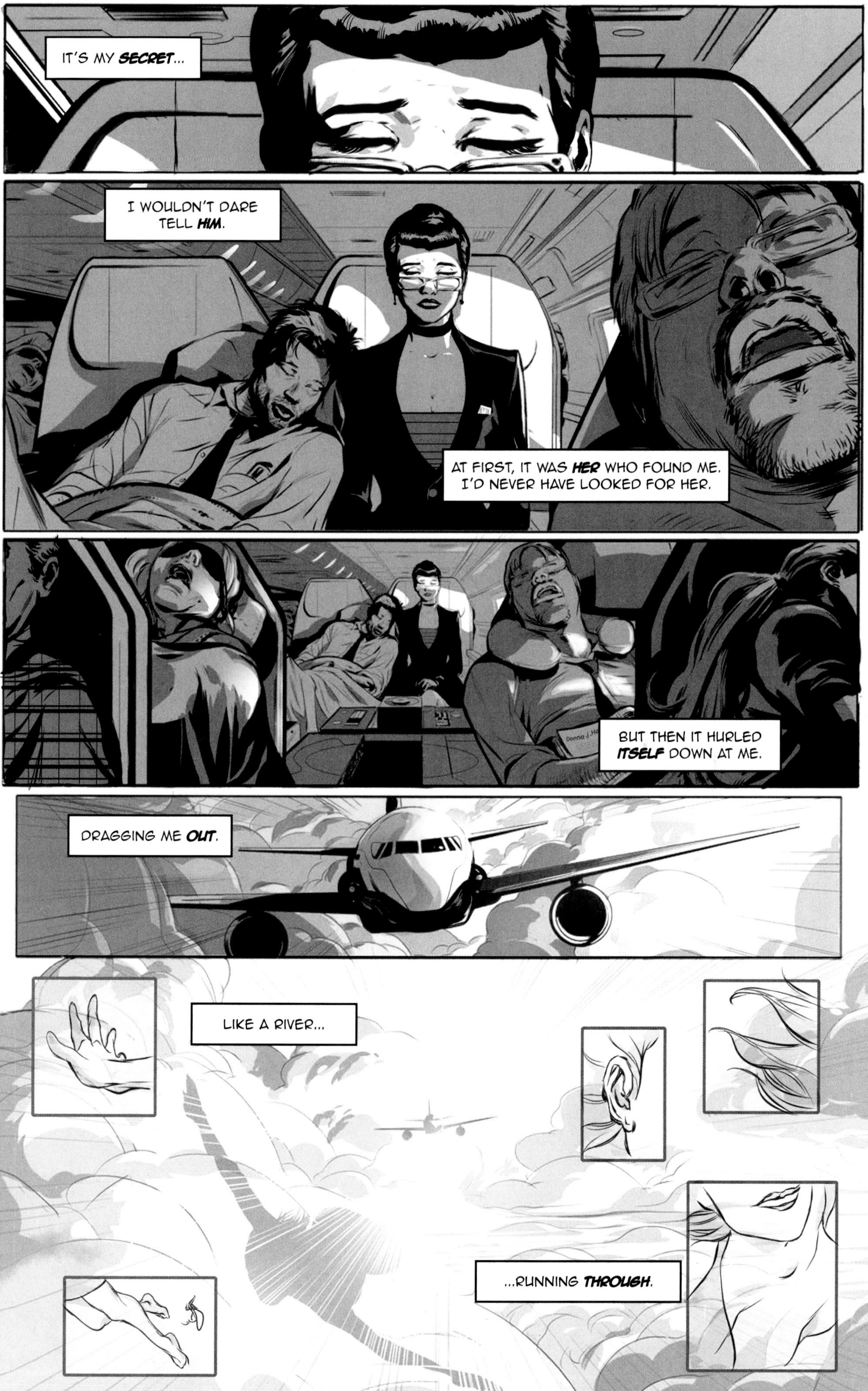
IT'S MY **SECRET**...
I WOULDN'T DARE TELL **HIM**.
AT FIRST, IT WAS **HER** WHO FOUND ME. I'D NEVER HAVE LOOKED FOR HER.
BUT THEN IT HURLED **ITSELF** DOWN AT ME.
DRAGGING ME **OUT**.
LIKE A RIVER...
...RUNNING **THROUGH**.

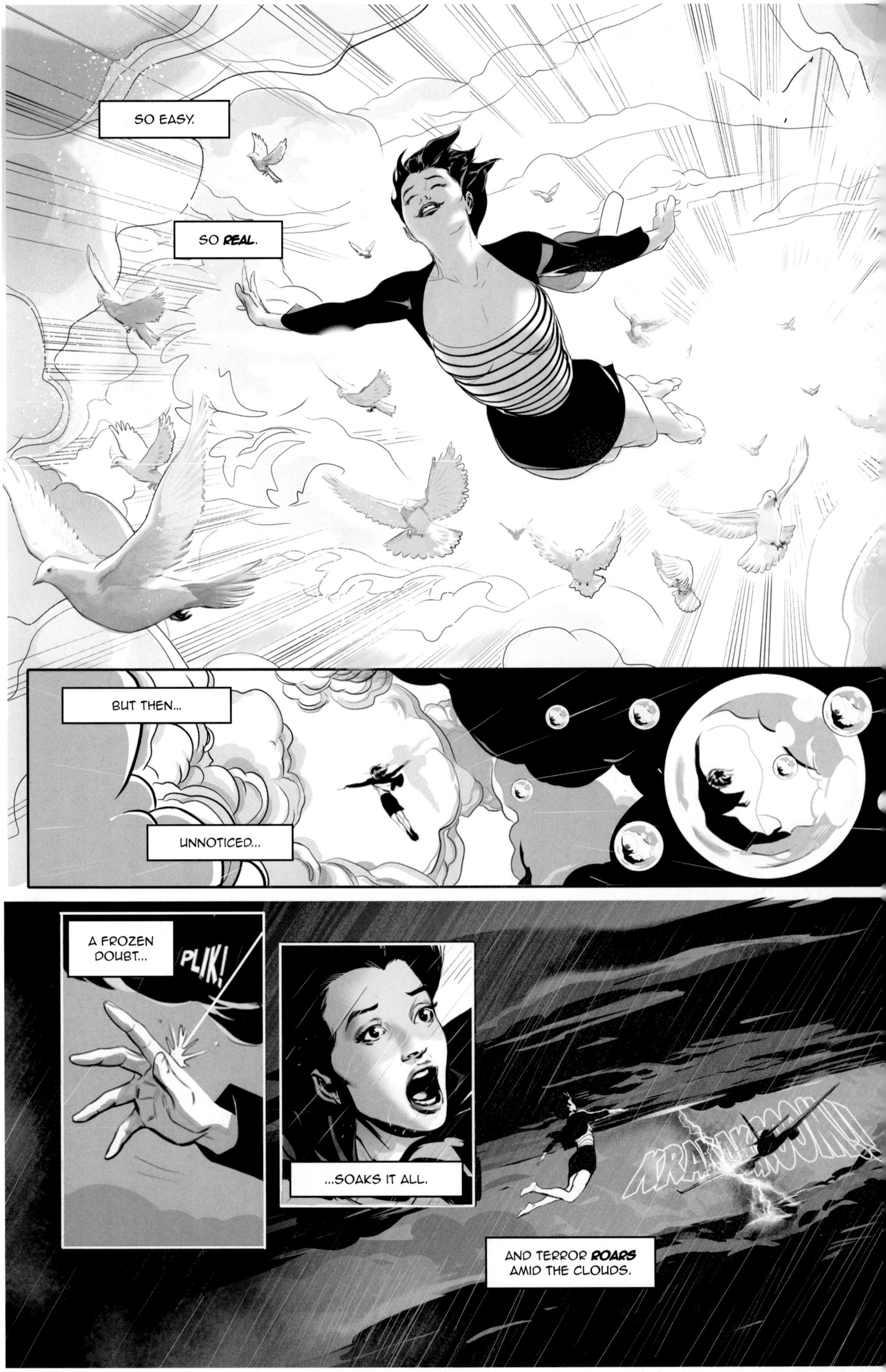
SO EASY.
SO **REAL**.
BUT THEN...
UNNOTICED...
A FROZEN DOUBT...
PLIK!
...SOAKS IT ALL.
AND TERROR **ROARS** AMID THE CLOUDS.

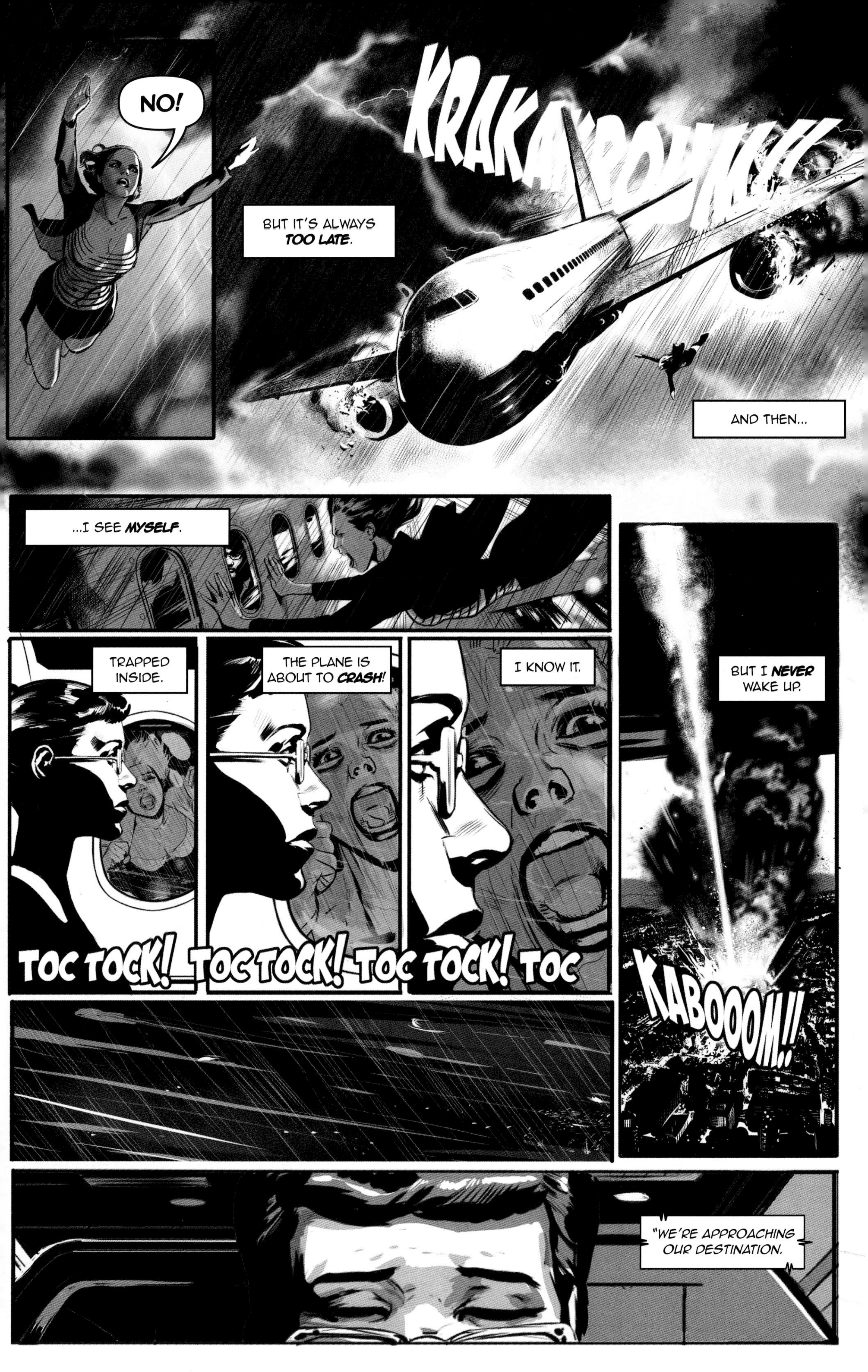
NO!
KRAKA-BOOM!!
BUT IT'S ALWAYS TOO LATE.
AND THEN...
...I SEE MYSELF.
TRAPPED INSIDE.
THE PLANE IS ABOUT TO CRASH!
I KNOW IT.
TOC TOCK! TOC TOCK! TOC TOCK! TOC
BUT I NEVER WAKE UP.
KABOOOM!!
"WE'RE APPROACHING OUR DESTINATION.

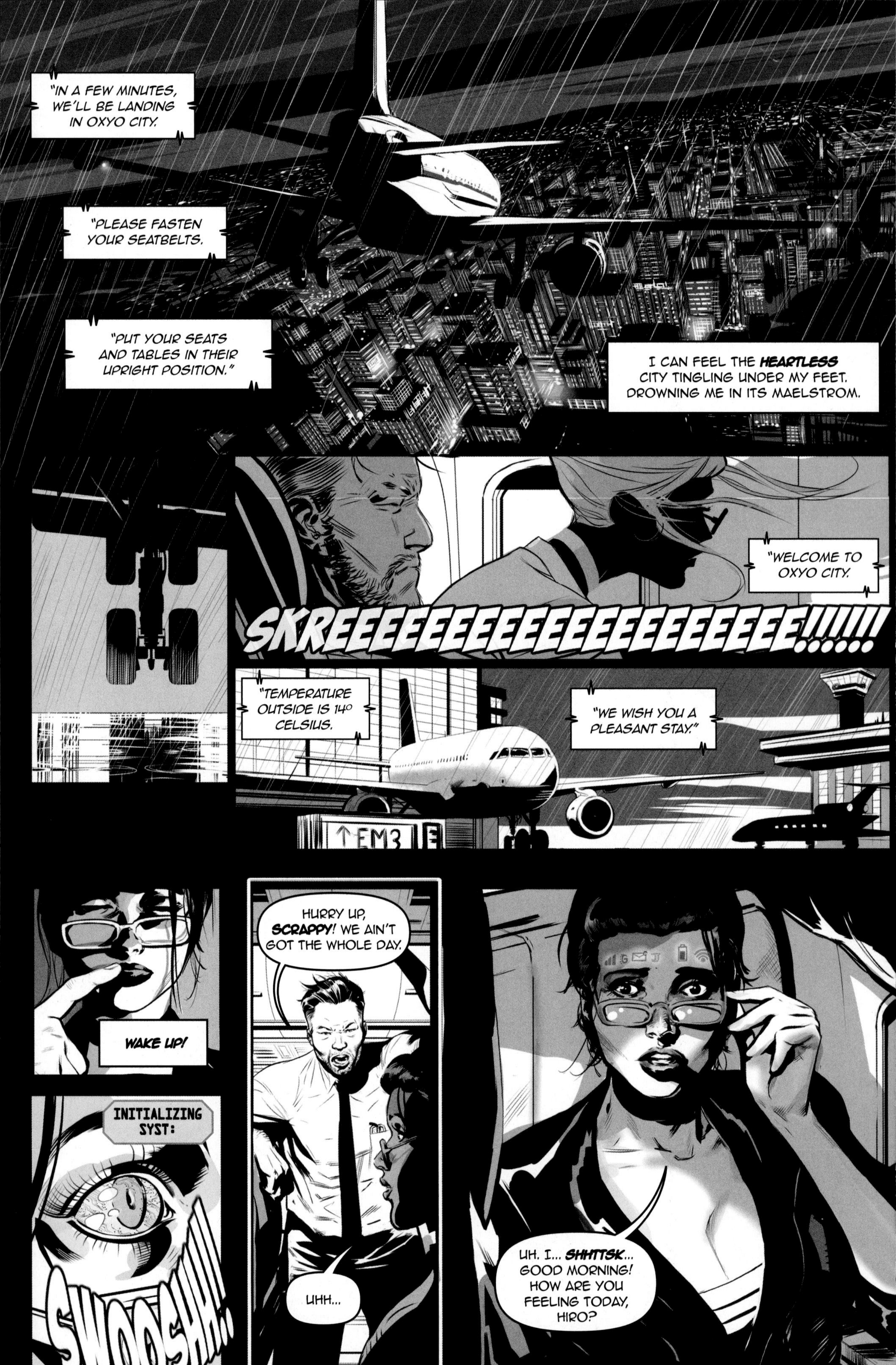
"IN A FEW MINUTES, WE'LL BE LANDING IN OXYO CITY.
"PLEASE FASTEN YOUR SEATBELTS.
"PUT YOUR SEATS AND TABLES IN THEIR UPRIGHT POSITION."
I CAN FEEL THE HEARTLESS CITY TINGLING UNDER MY FEET. DROWNING ME IN ITS MAELSTROM.
"WELCOME TO OXYO CITY.
SKREEEEEEEEEEEEEEEEEEEEEE!!!!!!
"TEMPERATURE OUTSIDE IS 14º CELSIUS.
"WE WISH YOU A PLEASANT STAY."
EM3
WAKE UP!
INITIALIZING SYST:
SWOOSHH!!
HURRY UP, SCRAPPY! WE AIN'T GOT THE WHOLE DAY.
UHH...
UH. I... SHHTTSK... GOOD MORNING! HOW ARE YOU FEELING TODAY, HIRO?

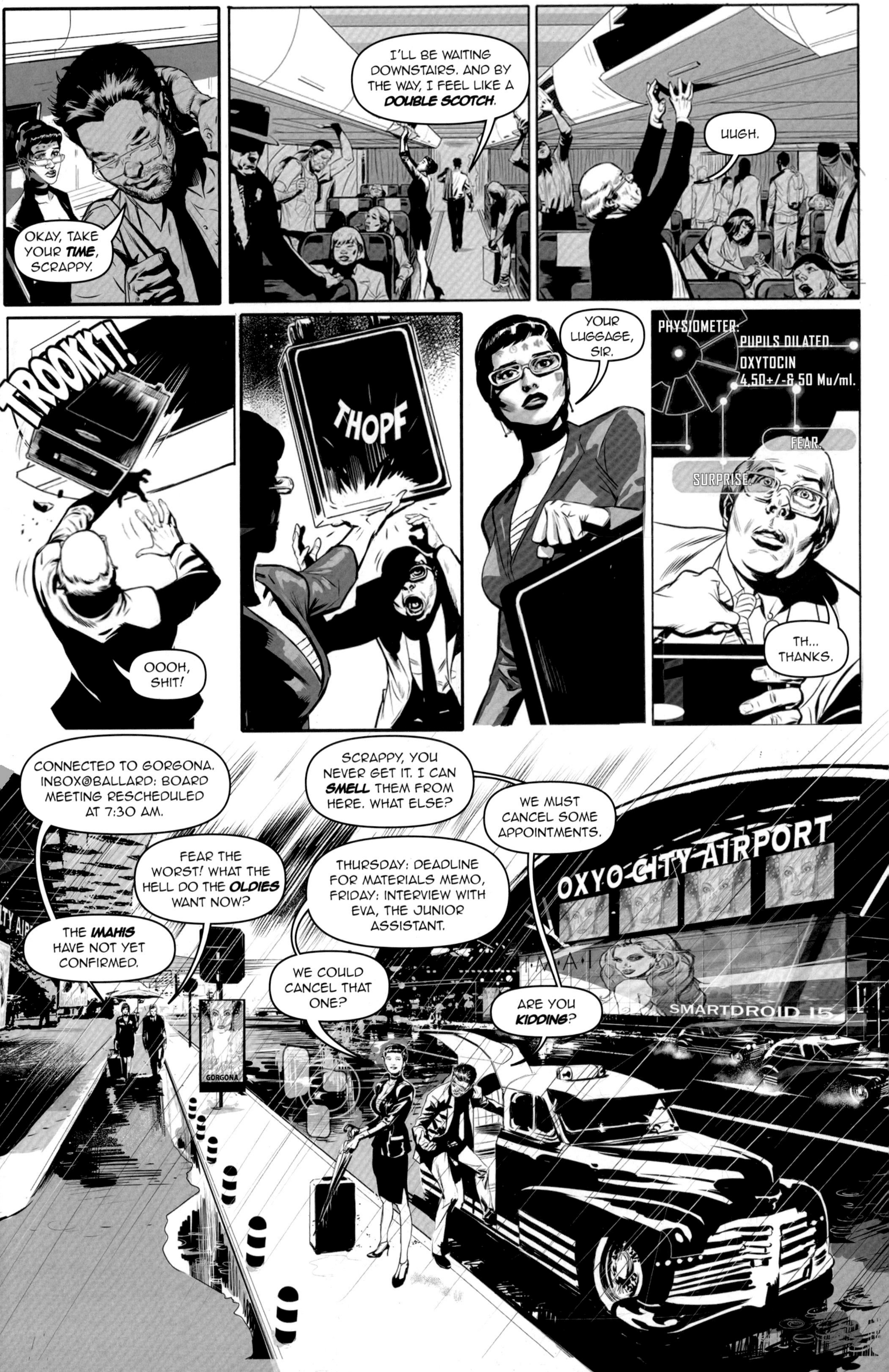

OKAY, TAKE YOUR *TIME*, SCRAPPY.
I'LL BE WAITING DOWNSTAIRS. AND BY THE WAY, I FEEL LIKE A *DOUBLE SCOTCH*.
UUGH.
TROOKKT!
OOOH, SHIT!
THOPF
YOUR LUGGAGE, SIR.
PHYSIOMETER:
PUPILS DILATED.
OXYTOCIN
4,50+/-6,50 Mu/ml.
FEAR.
SURPRISE.
TH... THANKS.
CONNECTED TO GORGONA. INBOX@BALLARD: BOARD MEETING RESCHEDULED AT 7:30 AM.
FEAR THE WORST! WHAT THE HELL DO THE *OLDIES* WANT NOW?
THE *IMAHIS* HAVE NOT YET CONFIRMED.
SCRAPPY, YOU NEVER GET IT. I CAN *SMELL* THEM FROM HERE. WHAT ELSE?
WE MUST CANCEL SOME APPOINTMENTS.
THURSDAY: DEADLINE FOR MATERIALS MEMO, FRIDAY: INTERVIEW WITH EVA, THE JUNIOR ASSISTANT.
WE COULD CANCEL THAT ONE?
ARE YOU *KIDDING*?
OXYO-CITY AIRPORT
SMARTDROID 15
GORGONA

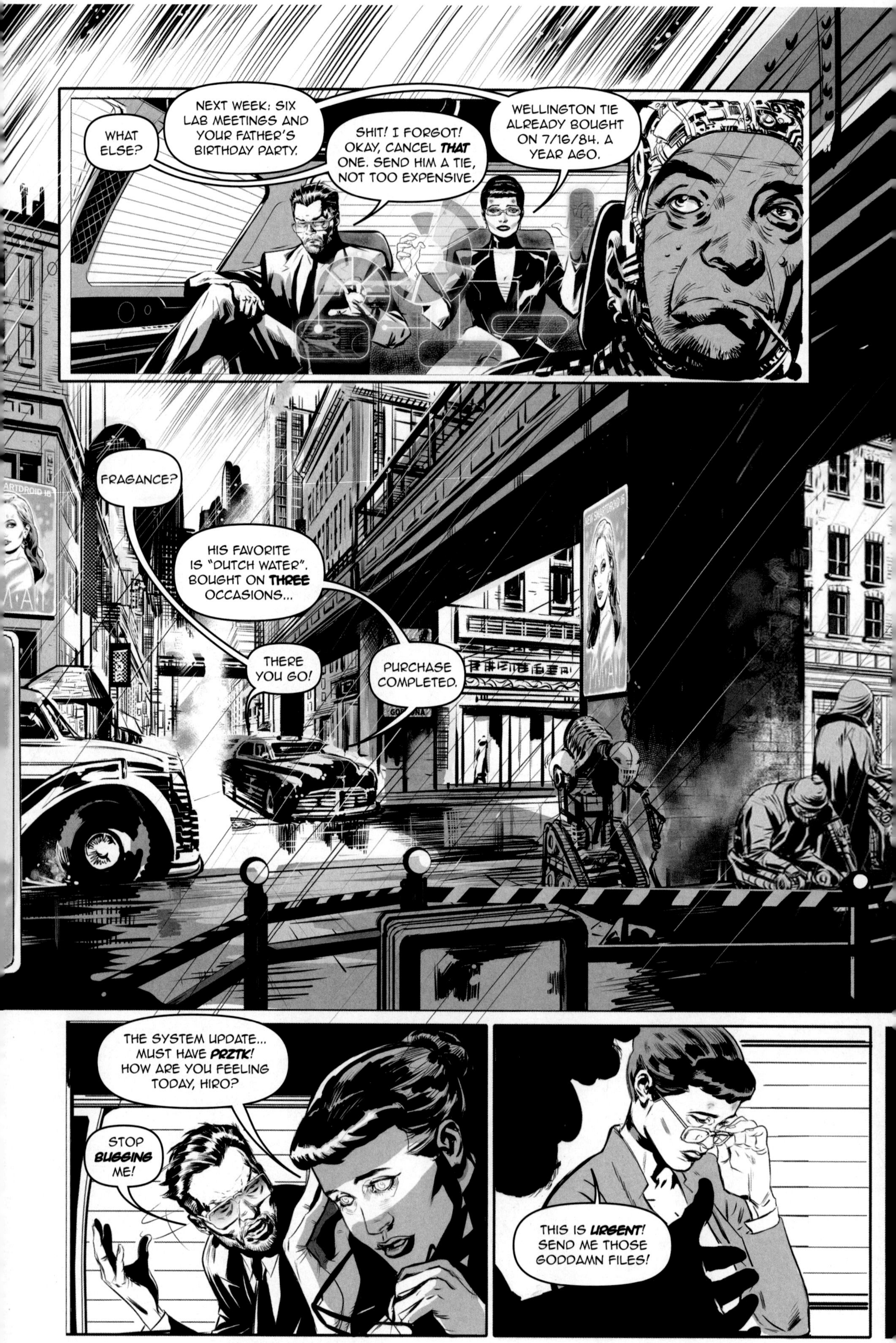
WHAT ELSE?
NEXT WEEK: SIX LAB MEETINGS AND YOUR FATHER'S BIRTHDAY PARTY.
SHIT! I FORGOT! OKAY, CANCEL **THAT** ONE. SEND HIM A TIE, NOT TOO EXPENSIVE.
WELLINGTON TIE ALREADY BOUGHT ON 7/16/84. A YEAR AGO.
FRAGANCE?
HIS FAVORITE IS "DUTCH WATER". BOUGHT ON **THREE** OCCASIONS...
THERE YOU GO!
PURCHASE COMPLETED.
THE SYSTEM UPDATE... MUST HAVE **PRZTK**! HOW ARE YOU FEELING TODAY, HIRO?
STOP **BUGGING** ME!
THIS IS **URGENT**! SEND ME THOSE GODDAMN FILES!

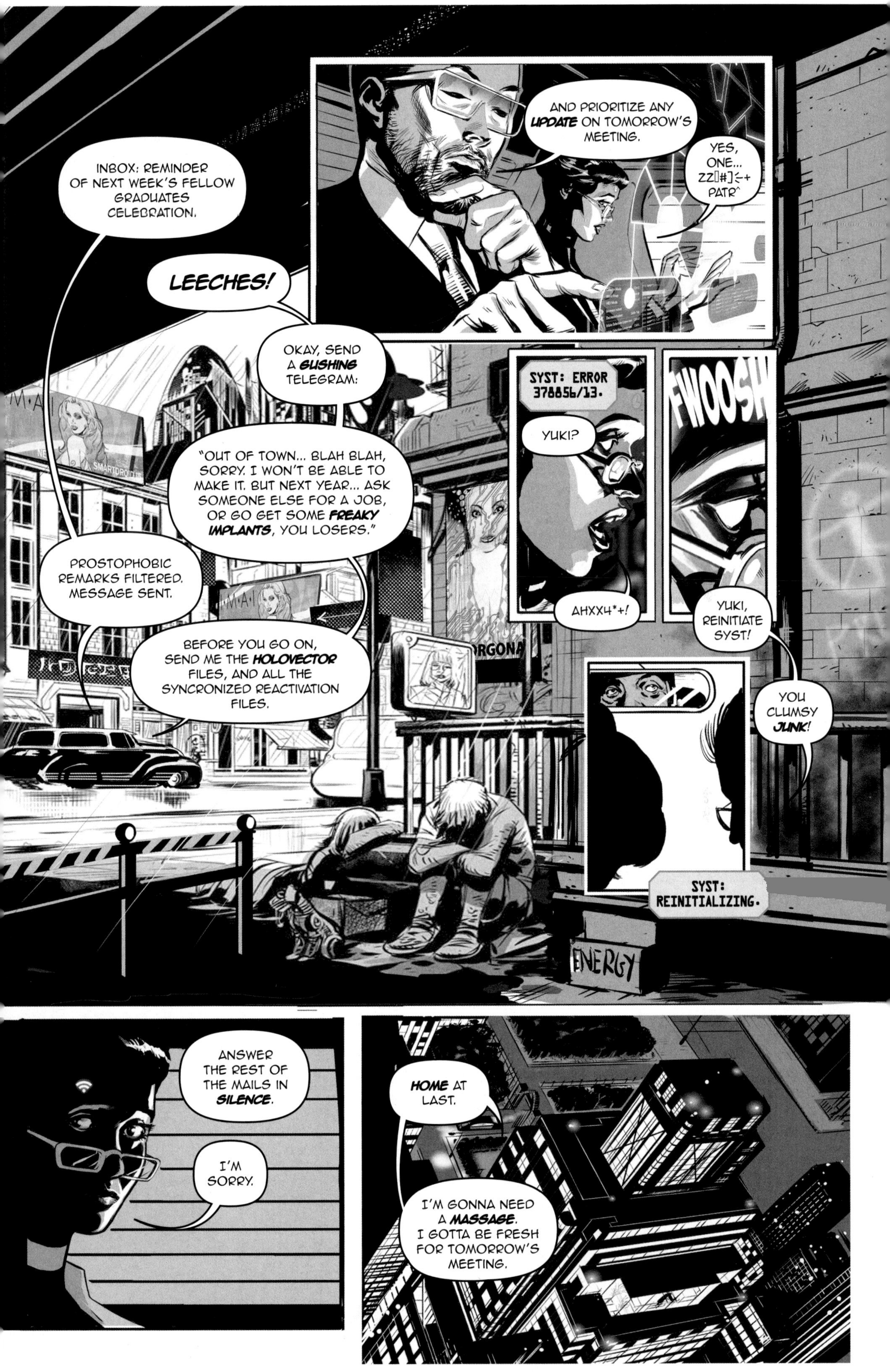
AND PRIORITIZE ANY UPDATE ON TOMORROW'S MEETING.
YES, ONE... ZZ▯#]⋲+ PATR^
INBOX: REMINDER OF NEXT WEEK'S FELLOW GRADUATES CELEBRATION.
LEECHES!
OKAY, SEND A GUSHING TELEGRAM:
"OUT OF TOWN... BLAH BLAH, SORRY. I WON'T BE ABLE TO MAKE IT. BUT NEXT YEAR... ASK SOMEONE ELSE FOR A JOB, OR GO GET SOME FREAKY IMPLANTS, YOU LOSERS."
PROSTOPHOBIC REMARKS FILTERED. MESSAGE SENT.
BEFORE YOU GO ON, SEND ME THE HOLOVECTOR FILES, AND ALL THE SYNCRONIZED REACTIVATION FILES.
SYST: ERROR 378856/13.
YUKI?
AHXX4*+!
FWOOSH
YUKI, REINITIATE SYST!
YOU CLUMSY JUNK!
SYST: REINITIALIZING.
ENERGY
ANSWER THE REST OF THE MAILS IN SILENCE.
I'M SORRY.
HOME AT LAST.
I'M GONNA NEED A MASSAGE. I GOTTA BE FRESH FOR TOMORROW'S MEETING.

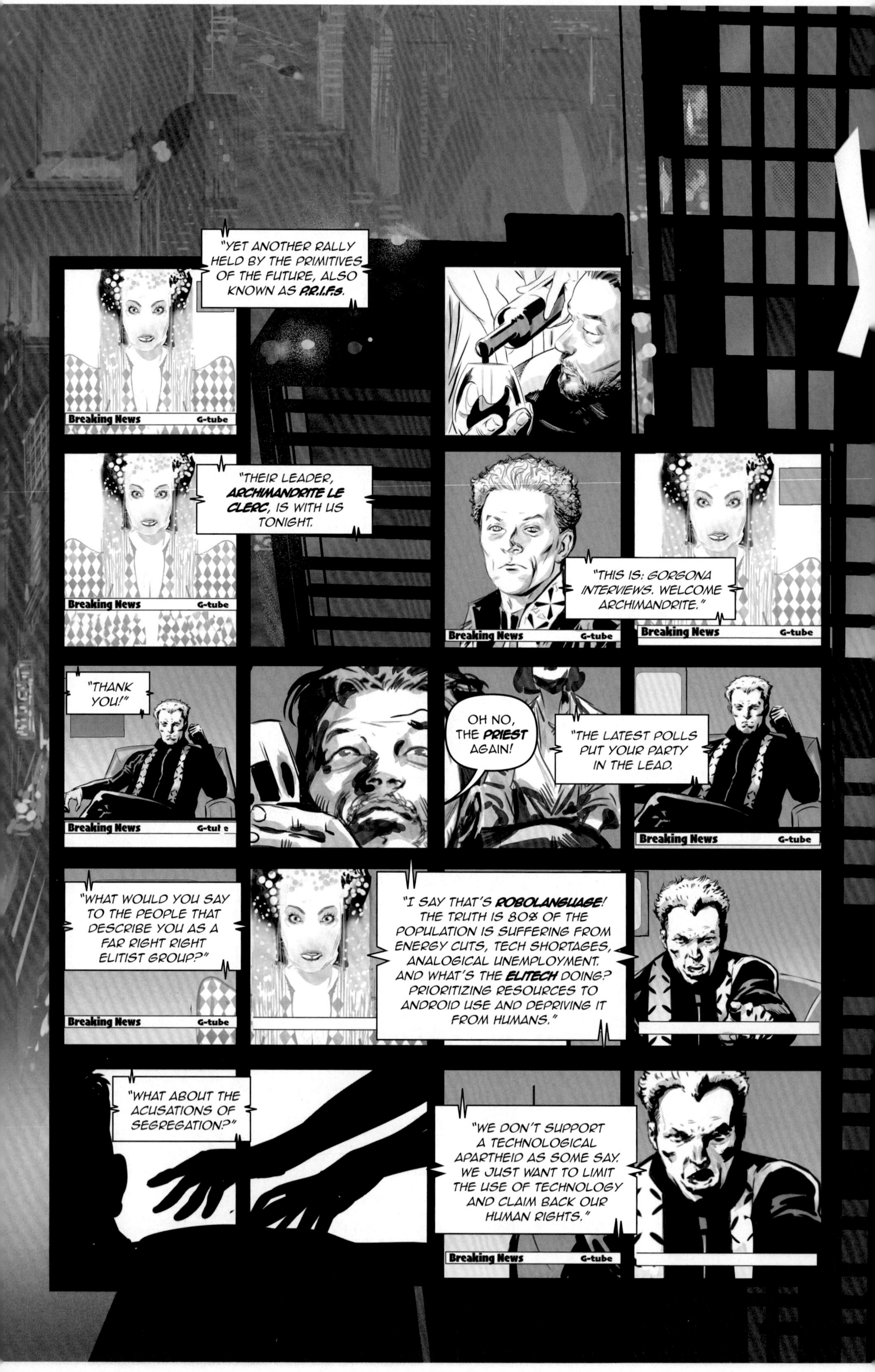
"YET ANOTHER RALLY HELD BY THE PRIMITIVES OF THE FUTURE, ALSO KNOWN AS P.R.I.F.s.
Breaking News
G-tube
"THEIR LEADER, ARCHIMANDRITE LE CLERC, IS WITH US TONIGHT.
Breaking News
G-tube
Breaking News
G-tube
"THIS IS: GORGONA INTERVIEWS. WELCOME ARCHIMANDRITE."
Breaking News
G-tube
"THANK YOU!"
Breaking News
OH NO, THE PRIEST AGAIN!
"THE LATEST POLLS PUT YOUR PARTY IN THE LEAD.
Breaking News
G-tube
"WHAT WOULD YOU SAY TO THE PEOPLE THAT DESCRIBE YOU AS A FAR RIGHT RIGHT ELITIST GROUP?"
Breaking News
G-tube
"I SAY THAT'S ROBOLANGUAGE! THE TRUTH IS 80% OF THE POPULATION IS SUFFERING FROM ENERGY CUTS, TECH SHORTAGES, ANALOGICAL UNEMPLOYMENT. AND WHAT'S THE ELITECH DOING? PRIORITIZING RESOURCES TO ANDROID USE AND DEPRIVING IT FROM HUMANS."
"WHAT ABOUT THE ACUSATIONS OF SEGREGATION?"
"WE DON'T SUPPORT A TECHNOLOGICAL APARTHEID AS SOME SAY. WE JUST WANT TO LIMIT THE USE OF TECHNOLOGY AND CLAIM BACK OUR HUMAN RIGHTS."
Breaking News
G-tube

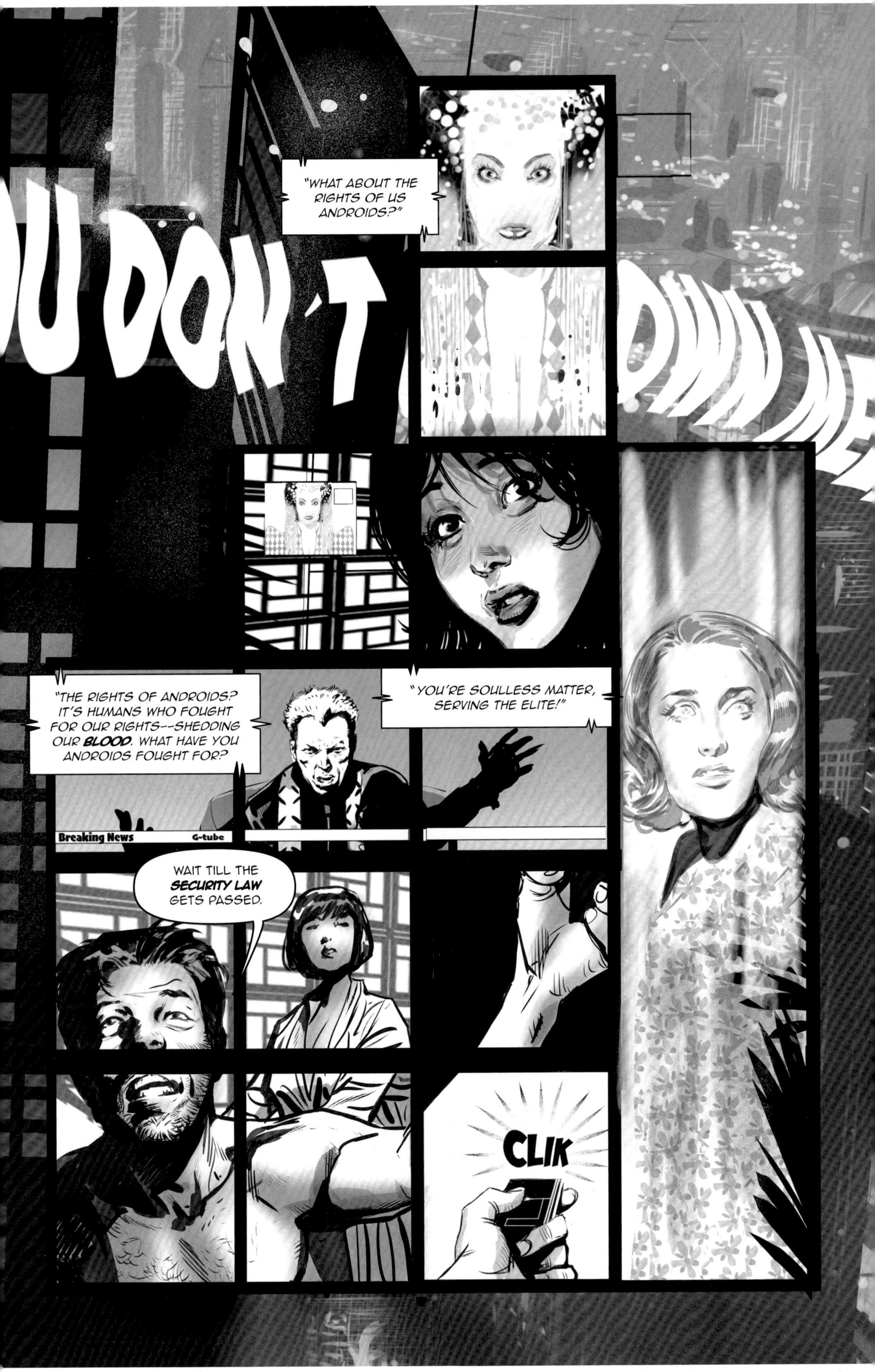
"WHAT ABOUT THE RIGHTS OF US ANDROIDS?"
"THE RIGHTS OF ANDROIDS? IT'S HUMANS WHO FOUGHT FOR OUR RIGHTS--SHEDDING OUR **BLOOD**. WHAT HAVE YOU ANDROIDS FOUGHT FOR?
Breaking News
G-tube
"YOU'RE SOULLESS MATTER, SERVING THE ELITE!"
WAIT TILL THE **SECURITY LAW** GETS PASSED.
CLIK

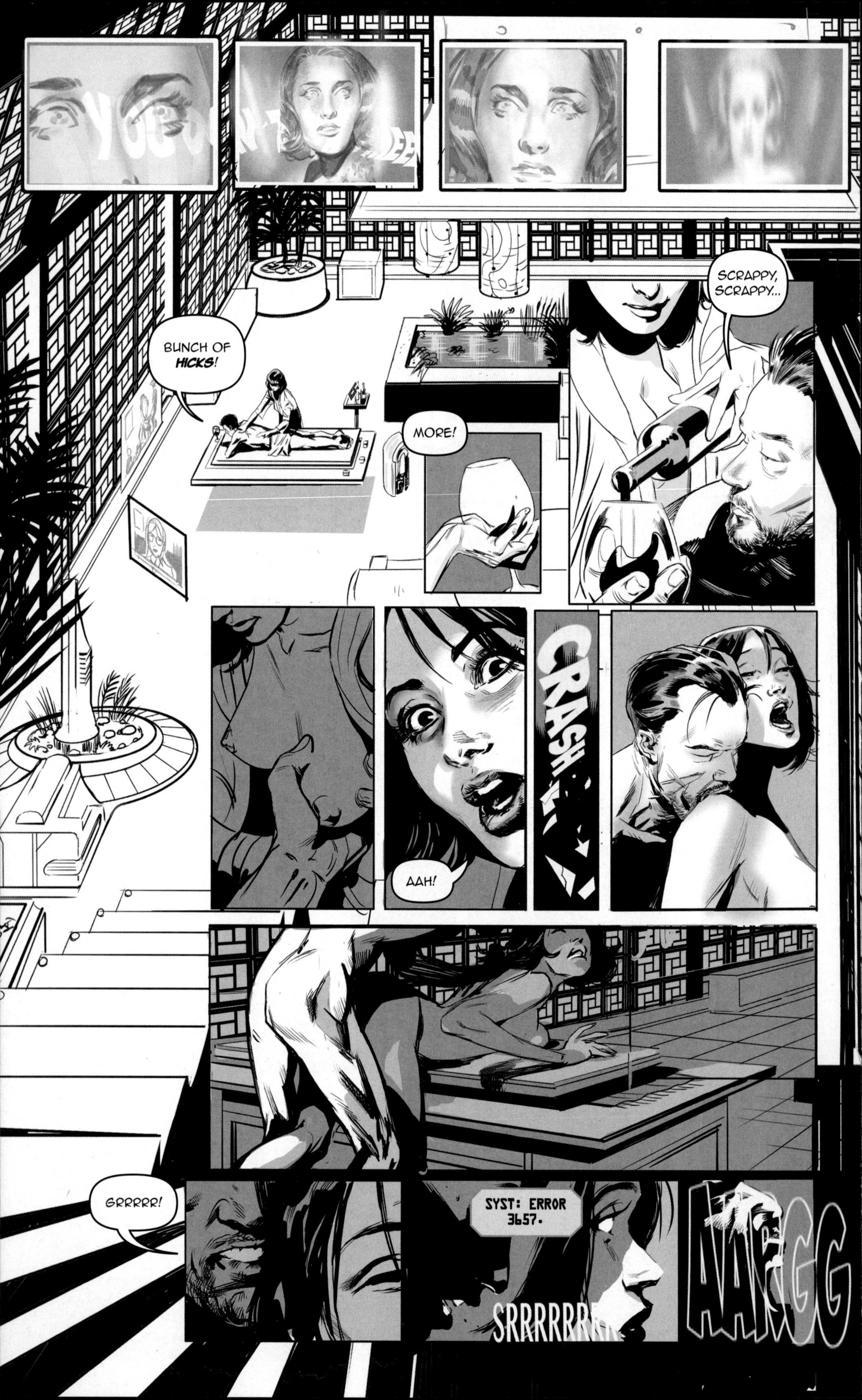
BUNCH OF **HICKS**!
MORE!
SCRAPPY, SCRAPPY...
AAH!
CRASH
GRRRRR!
SYST: ERROR 3657.
SRRRRRRR

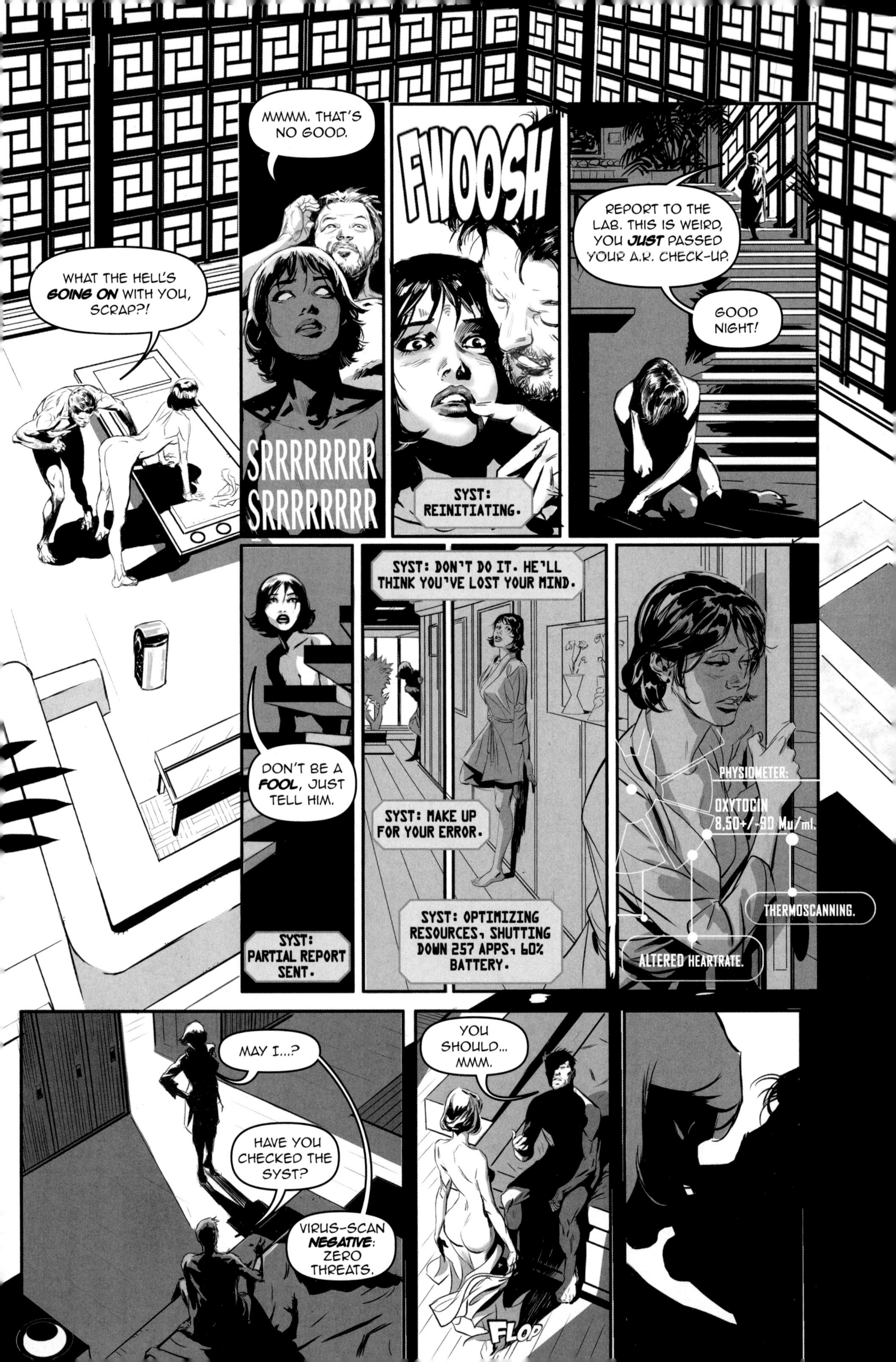
WHAT THE HELL'S GOING ON WITH YOU, SCRAP?!
MMMM. THAT'S NO GOOD.
SRRRRRRRR SRRRRRRRR
FWOOSH
SYST: REINITIATING.
REPORT TO THE LAB. THIS IS WEIRD, YOU JUST PASSED YOUR A.R. CHECK-UP.
GOOD NIGHT!
DON'T BE A FOOL, JUST TELL HIM.
SYST: PARTIAL REPORT SENT.
SYST: DON'T DO IT. HE'LL THINK YOU'VE LOST YOUR MIND.
SYST: MAKE UP FOR YOUR ERROR.
SYST: OPTIMIZING RESOURCES, SHUTTING DOWN 257 APPS, 60% BATTERY.
PHYSIOMETER:
OXYTOCIN 8,50+/-90 Mu/ml.
THERMOSCANNING.
ALTERED HEARTRATE.
MAY I...?
HAVE YOU CHECKED THE SYST?
VIRUS-SCAN NEGATIVE: ZERO THREATS.
YOU SHOULD... MMM.
FLOP

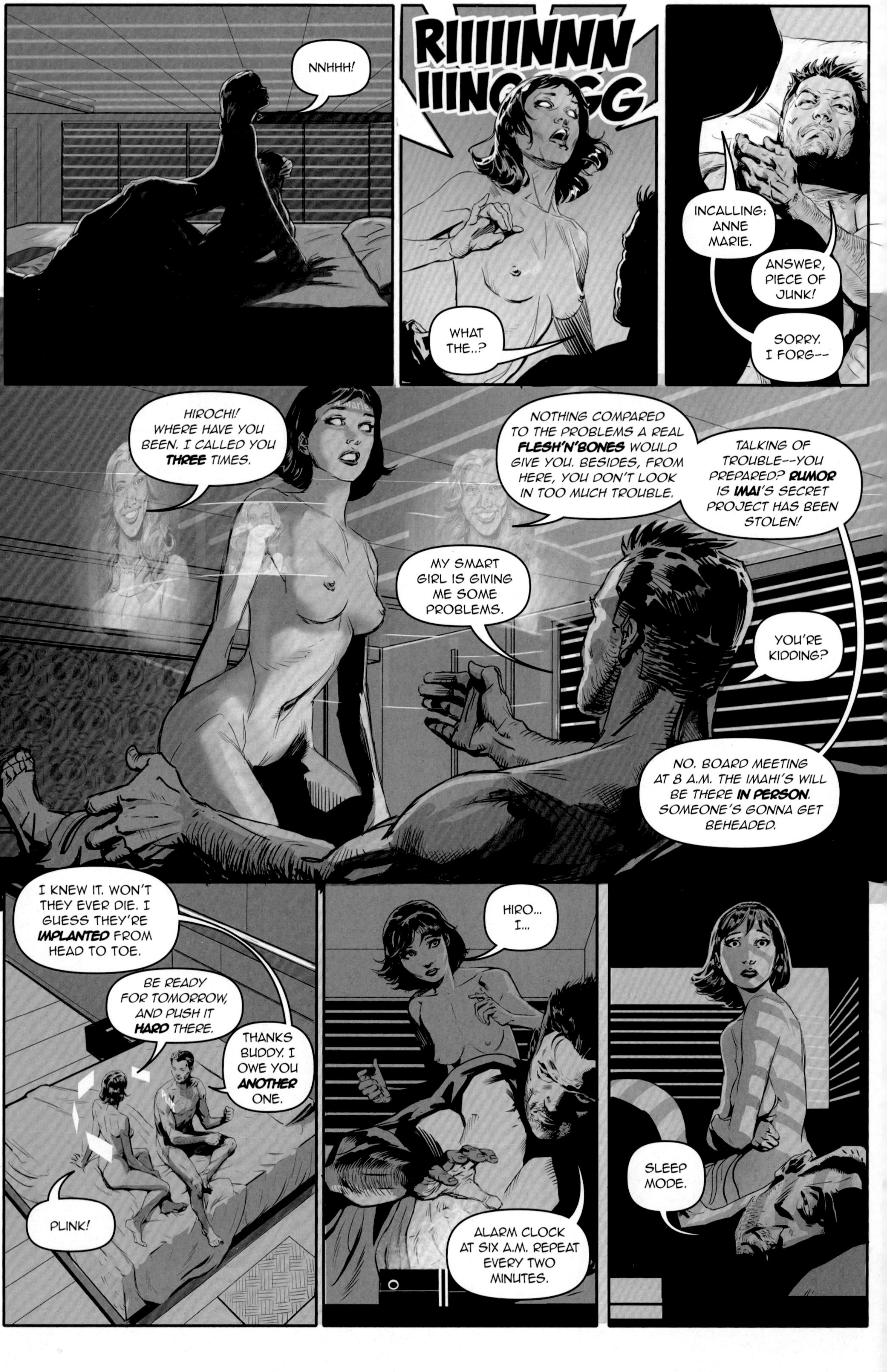
NNHHH!
RIIIIINNN IIINGGGG
WHAT THE..?
INCALLING: ANNE MARIE.
ANSWER, PIECE OF JUNK!
SORRY. I FORG--
HIROCHI! WHERE HAVE YOU BEEN. I CALLED YOU THREE TIMES.
NOTHING COMPARED TO THE PROBLEMS A REAL FLESH'N'BONES WOULD GIVE YOU. BESIDES, FROM HERE, YOU DON'T LOOK IN TOO MUCH TROUBLE.
MY SMART GIRL IS GIVING ME SOME PROBLEMS.
TALKING OF TROUBLE--YOU PREPARED? RUMOR IS IMAI'S SECRET PROJECT HAS BEEN STOLEN!
YOU'RE KIDDING?
NO. BOARD MEETING AT 8 A.M. THE IMAHI'S WILL BE THERE IN PERSON. SOMEONE'S GONNA GET BEHEADED.
I KNEW IT. WON'T THEY EVER DIE. I GUESS THEY'RE IMPLANTED FROM HEAD TO TOE.
BE READY FOR TOMORROW, AND PUSH IT HARD THERE.
THANKS BUDDY. I OWE YOU ANOTHER ONE.
PLINK!
HIRO... I...
ALARM CLOCK AT SIX A.M. REPEAT EVERY TWO MINUTES.
SLEEP MODE.

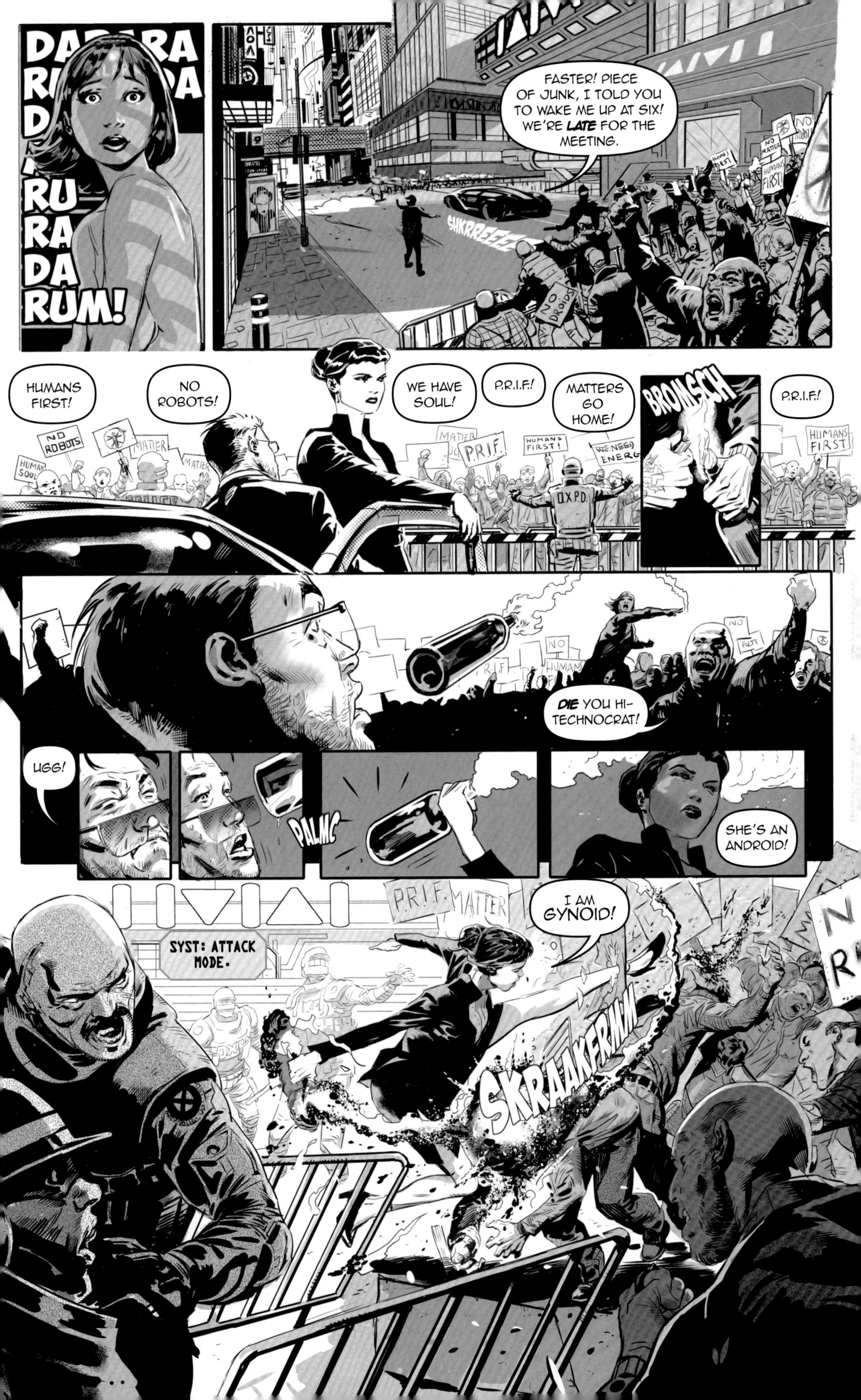

RU
RA
DA
RUM!
FASTER! PIECE OF JUNK, I TOLD YOU TO WAKE ME UP AT SIX! WE'RE **LATE** FOR THE MEETING.
SHKRREEEZ
HUMANS FIRST!
NO ROBOTS!
NO DROIDS
HUMANS FIRST!
NO ROBOTS!
WE HAVE SOUL!
P.R.I.F.!
MATTERS GO HOME!
BROMSCH
P.R.I.F.!
P.R.I.F.
HUMANS FIRST!
HUMANS FIRST
O.X.P.D.
DIE YOU HI-TECHNOCRAT!
UGG!
PALMC
SHE'S AN ANDROID!
P.R.I.F.
MATTER
I AM GYNOID!
SYST: ATTACK MODE.
SKRAAKFRMM

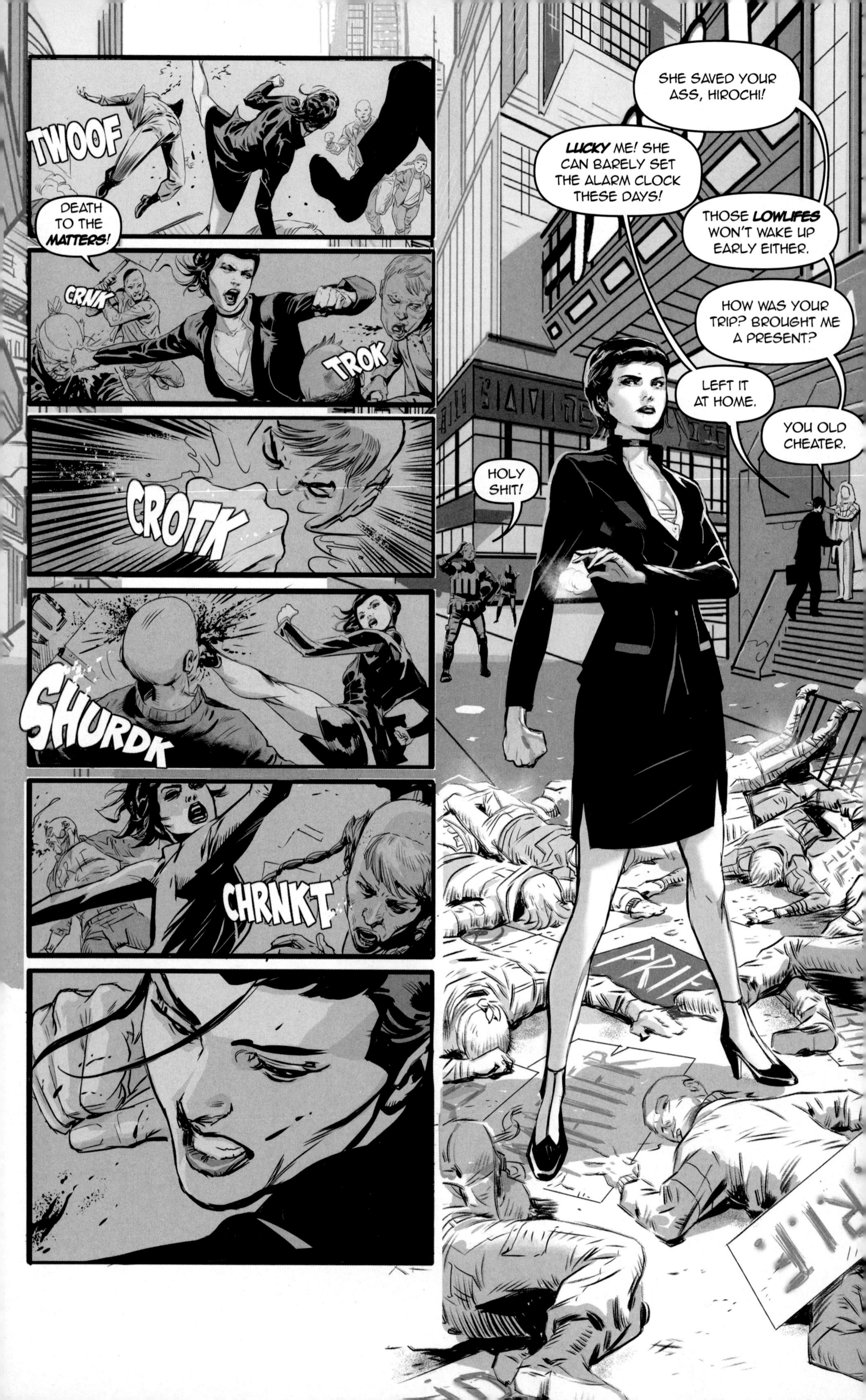
TWOOF
DEATH TO THE MATTERS!
CRNK
TROK
CROTK
SHURDK
CHRNKT
SHE SAVED YOUR ASS, HIROCHI!
LUCKY ME! SHE CAN BARELY SET THE ALARM CLOCK THESE DAYS!
THOSE LOWLIFES WON'T WAKE UP EARLY EITHER.
HOW WAS YOUR TRIP? BROUGHT ME A PRESENT?
LEFT IT AT HOME.
YOU OLD CHEATER.
HOLY SHIT!

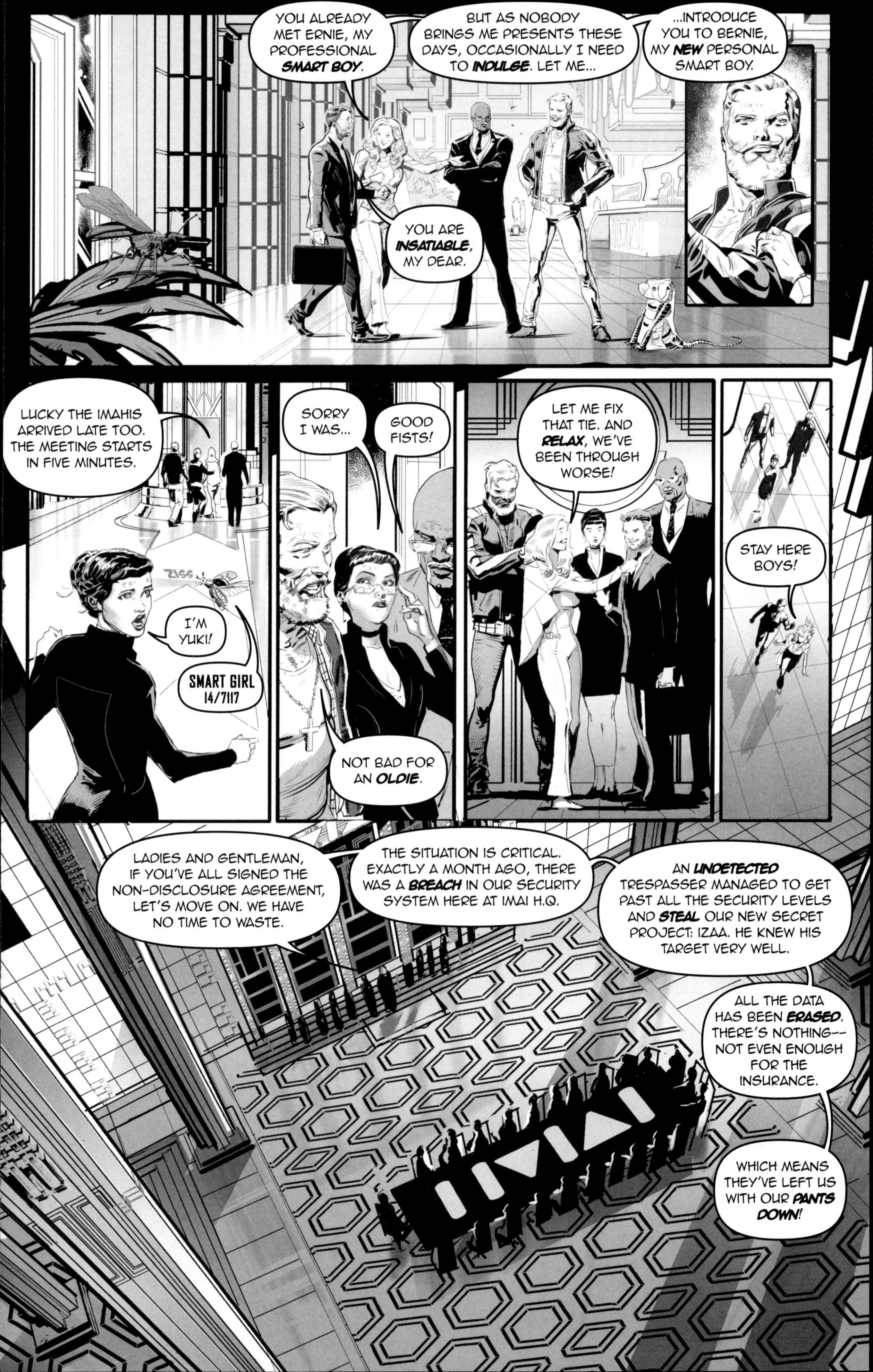

YOU ALREADY MET ERNIE, MY PROFESSIONAL SMART BOY.
BUT AS NOBODY BRINGS ME PRESENTS THESE DAYS, OCCASIONALLY I NEED TO INDULGE. LET ME...
YOU ARE INSATIABLE, MY DEAR.
...INTRODUCE YOU TO BERNIE, MY NEW PERSONAL SMART BOY.
LUCKY THE IMAHIS ARRIVED LATE TOO. THE MEETING STARTS IN FIVE MINUTES.
ZISS
I'M YUKI!
SMART GIRL 14/7117
SORRY I WAS...
GOOD FISTS!
NOT BAD FOR AN OLDIE.
LET ME FIX THAT TIE. AND RELAX, WE'VE BEEN THROUGH WORSE!
STAY HERE BOYS!
LADIES AND GENTLEMAN, IF YOU'VE ALL SIGNED THE NON-DISCLOSURE AGREEMENT, LET'S MOVE ON. WE HAVE NO TIME TO WASTE.
THE SITUATION IS CRITICAL. EXACTLY A MONTH AGO, THERE WAS A BREACH IN OUR SECURITY SYSTEM HERE AT IMAI H.Q.
AN UNDETECTED TRESPASSER MANAGED TO GET PAST ALL THE SECURITY LEVELS AND STEAL OUR NEW SECRET PROJECT: IZAA. HE KNEW HIS TARGET VERY WELL.
ALL THE DATA HAS BEEN ERASED. THERE'S NOTHING--NOT EVEN ENOUGH FOR THE INSURANCE.
WHICH MEANS THEY'VE LEFT US WITH OUR PANTS DOWN!

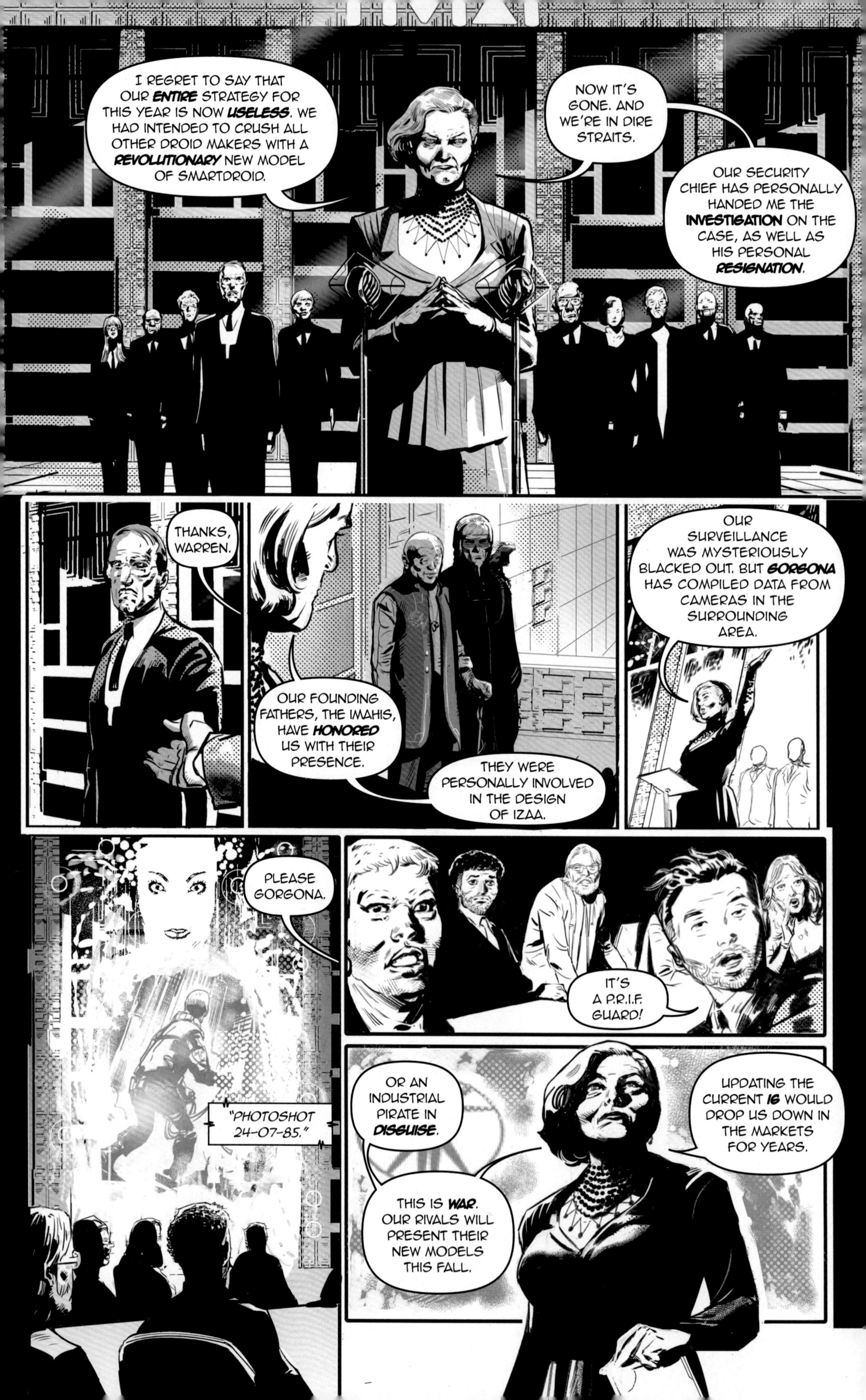
I REGRET TO SAY THAT OUR ENTIRE STRATEGY FOR THIS YEAR IS NOW USELESS. WE HAD INTENDED TO CRUSH ALL OTHER DROID MAKERS WITH A REVOLUTIONARY NEW MODEL OF SMARTDROID.
NOW IT'S GONE. AND WE'RE IN DIRE STRAITS.
OUR SECURITY CHIEF HAS PERSONALLY HANDED ME THE INVESTIGATION ON THE CASE, AS WELL AS HIS PERSONAL RESIGNATION.
THANKS, WARREN.
OUR FOUNDING FATHERS, THE IMAHIS, HAVE HONORED US WITH THEIR PRESENCE.
THEY WERE PERSONALLY INVOLVED IN THE DESIGN OF IZAA.
OUR SURVEILLANCE WAS MYSTERIOUSLY BLACKED OUT. BUT GORGONA HAS COMPILED DATA FROM CAMERAS IN THE SURROUNDING AREA.
PLEASE GORGONA.
"PHOTOSHOT 24-07-85."
IT'S A P.R.I.F. GUARD!
OR AN INDUSTRIAL PIRATE IN DISGUISE.
THIS IS WAR. OUR RIVALS WILL PRESENT THEIR NEW MODELS THIS FALL.
UPDATING THE CURRENT 16 WOULD DROP US DOWN IN THE MARKETS FOR YEARS.

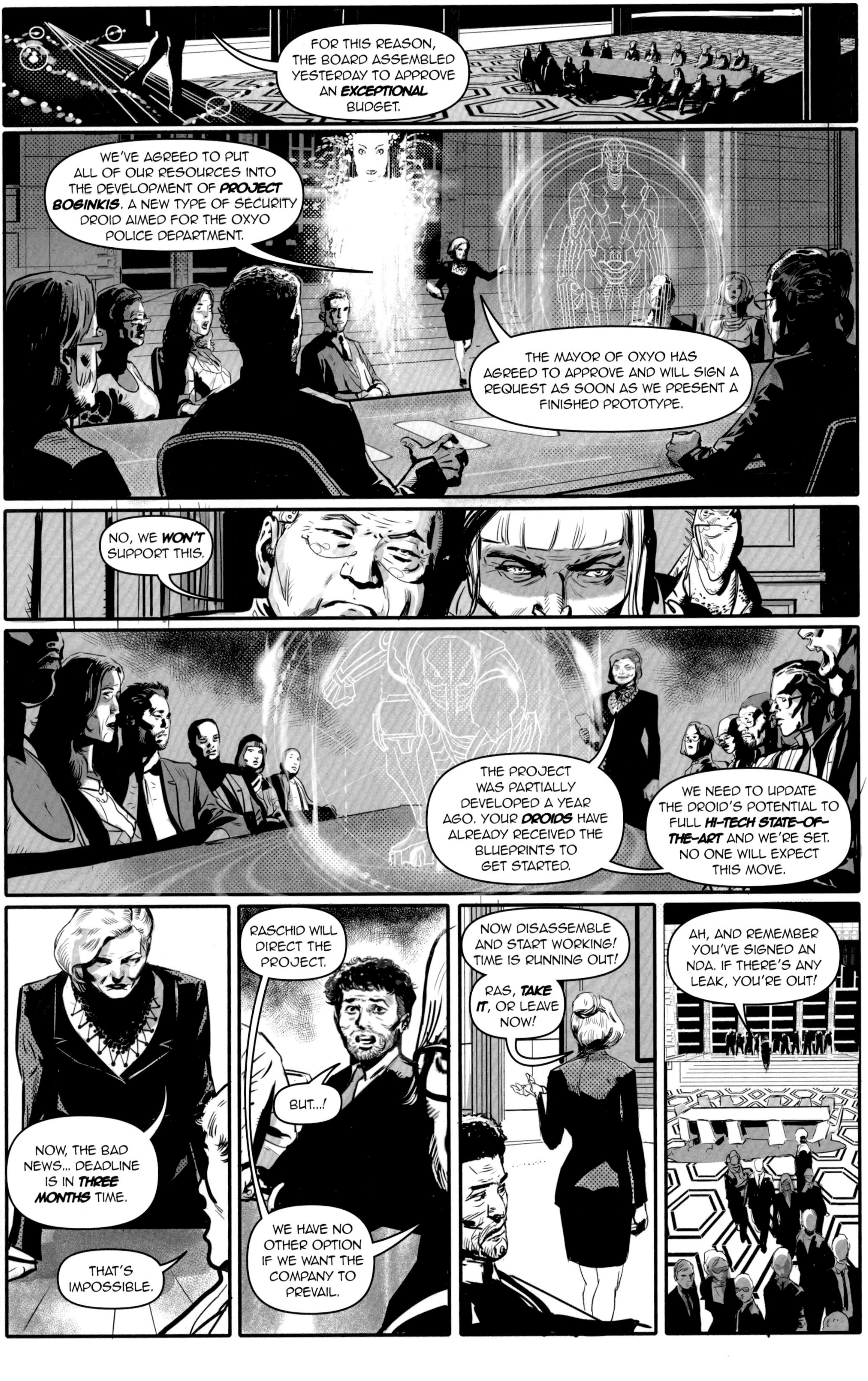

FOR THIS REASON, THE BOARD ASSEMBLED YESTERDAY TO APPROVE AN **EXCEPTIONAL** BUDGET.
WE'VE AGREED TO PUT ALL OF OUR RESOURCES INTO THE DEVELOPMENT OF **PROJECT BOGINKIS**. A NEW TYPE OF SECURITY DROID AIMED FOR THE OXYO POLICE DEPARTMENT.
THE MAYOR OF OXYO HAS AGREED TO APPROVE AND WILL SIGN A REQUEST AS SOON AS WE PRESENT A FINISHED PROTOTYPE.
NO, WE **WON'T** SUPPORT THIS.
THE PROJECT WAS PARTIALLY DEVELOPED A YEAR AGO. YOUR **DROIDS** HAVE ALREADY RECEIVED THE BLUEPRINTS TO GET STARTED.
WE NEED TO UPDATE THE DROID'S POTENTIAL TO FULL **HI-TECH STATE-OF-THE-ART** AND WE'RE SET. NO ONE WILL EXPECT THIS MOVE.
NOW, THE BAD NEWS... DEADLINE IS IN **THREE MONTHS** TIME.
THAT'S IMPOSSIBLE.
RASCHID WILL DIRECT THE PROJECT.
BUT...!
WE HAVE NO OTHER OPTION IF WE WANT THE COMPANY TO PREVAIL.
NOW DISASSEMBLE AND START WORKING! TIME IS RUNNING OUT!
RAS, **TAKE IT**, OR LEAVE NOW!
AH, AND REMEMBER YOU'VE SIGNED AN NDA. IF THERE'S ANY LEAK, YOU'RE OUT!

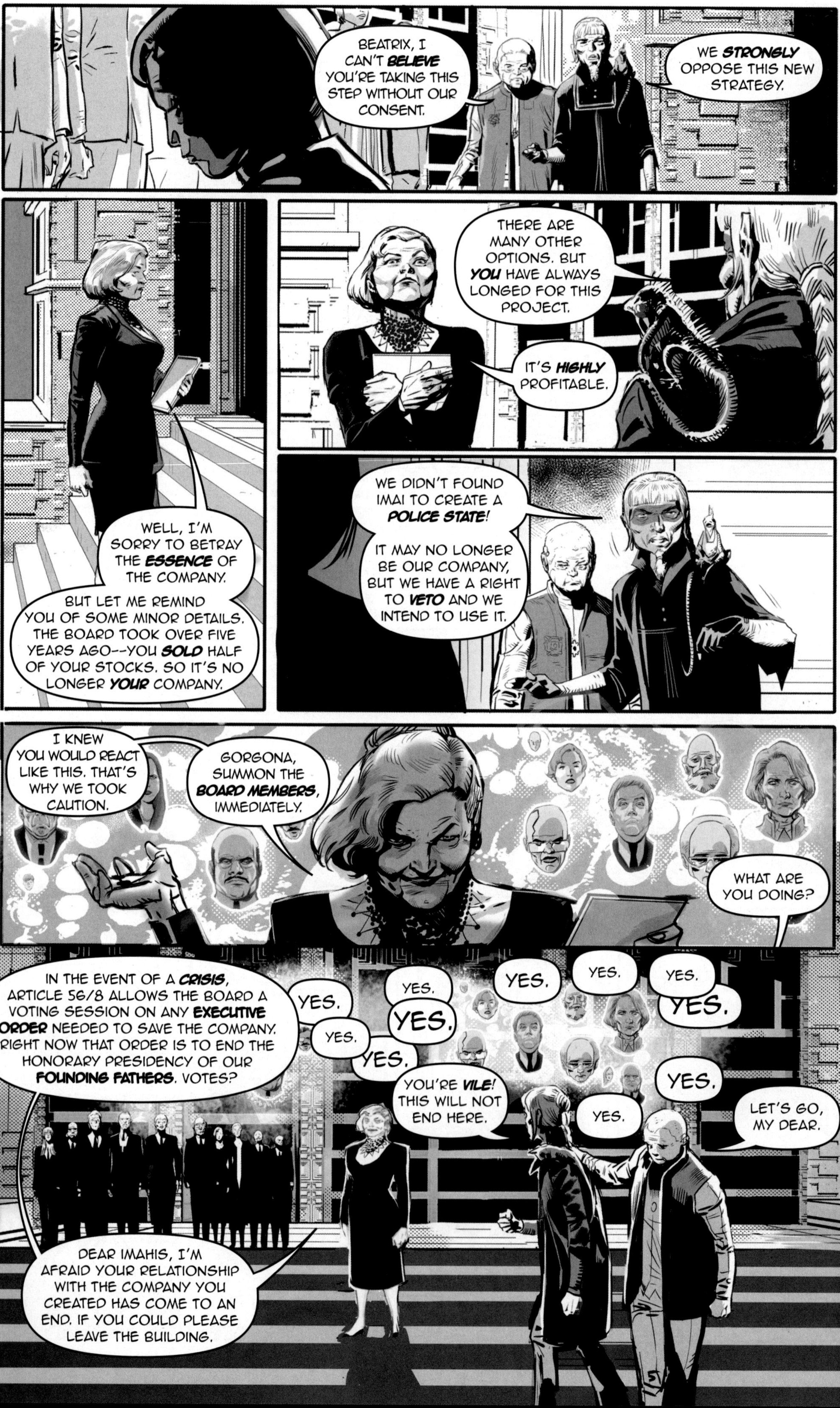

BEATRIX, I CAN'T BELIEVE YOU'RE TAKING THIS STEP WITHOUT OUR CONSENT.
WE STRONGLY OPPOSE THIS NEW STRATEGY.
WELL, I'M SORRY TO BETRAY THE ESSENCE OF THE COMPANY.
BUT LET ME REMIND YOU OF SOME MINOR DETAILS. THE BOARD TOOK OVER FIVE YEARS AGO--YOU SOLD HALF OF YOUR STOCKS. SO IT'S NO LONGER YOUR COMPANY.
THERE ARE MANY OTHER OPTIONS. BUT YOU HAVE ALWAYS LONGED FOR THIS PROJECT.
IT'S HIGHLY PROFITABLE.
WE DIDN'T FOUND IMAI TO CREATE A POLICE STATE!
IT MAY NO LONGER BE OUR COMPANY, BUT WE HAVE A RIGHT TO VETO AND WE INTEND TO USE IT.
I KNEW YOU WOULD REACT LIKE THIS. THAT'S WHY WE TOOK CAUTION.
GORGONA, SUMMON THE BOARD MEMBERS, IMMEDIATELY.
WHAT ARE YOU DOING?
IN THE EVENT OF A CRISIS, ARTICLE 56/8 ALLOWS THE BOARD A VOTING SESSION ON ANY EXECUTIVE ORDER NEEDED TO SAVE THE COMPANY. RIGHT NOW THAT ORDER IS TO END THE HONORARY PRESIDENCY OF OUR FOUNDING FATHERS. VOTES?
YES.
YES.
YES.
YES.
YES.
YES.
YES.
YES.
YES.
YES.
YES.
YOU'RE VILE! THIS WILL NOT END HERE.
LET'S GO, MY DEAR.
DEAR IMAHIS, I'M AFRAID YOUR RELATIONSHIP WITH THE COMPANY YOU CREATED HAS COME TO AN END. IF YOU COULD PLEASE LEAVE THE BUILDING.

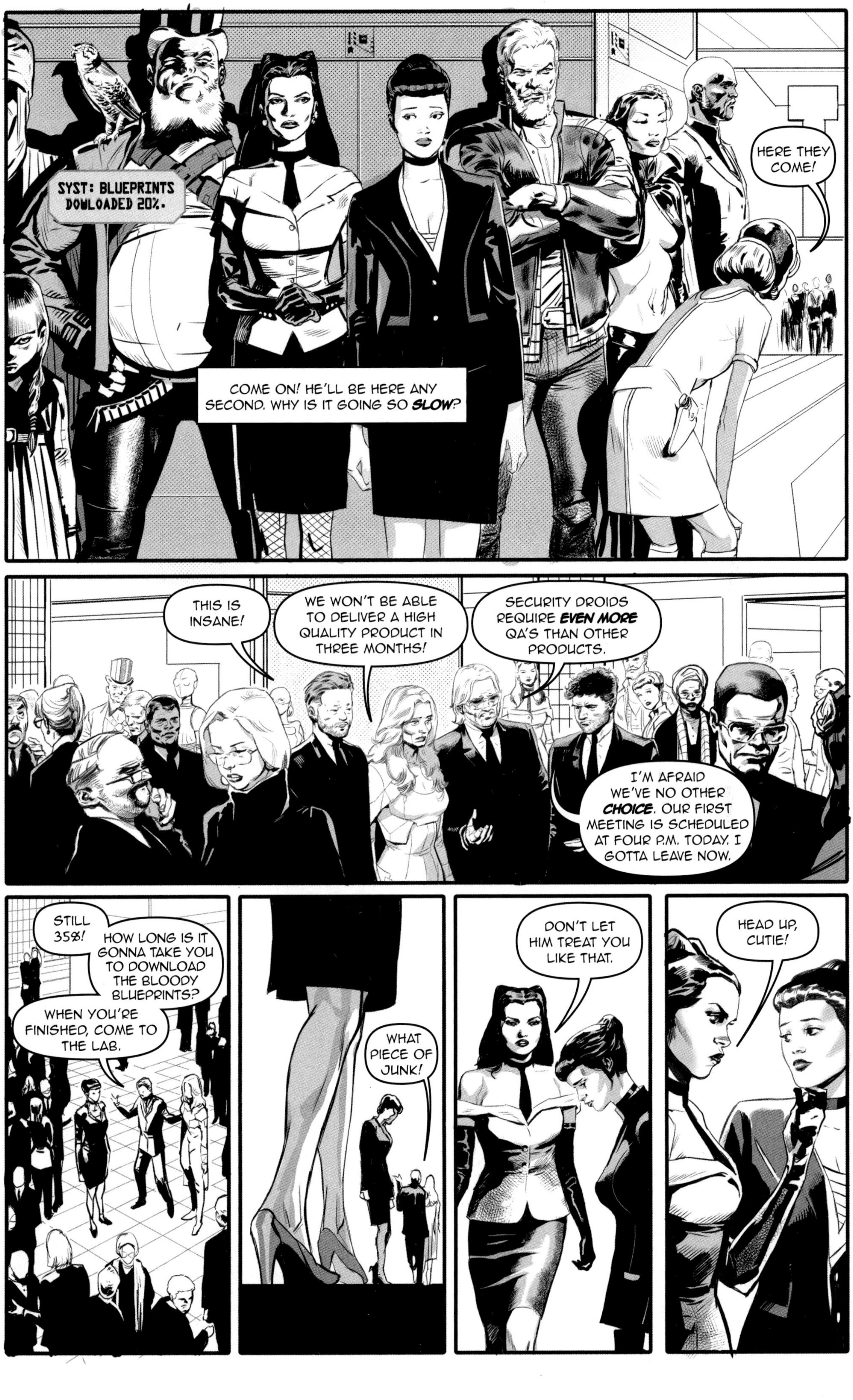
SYST: BLUEPRINTS DOWLOADED 20%.
COME ON! HE'LL BE HERE ANY SECOND. WHY IS IT GOING SO SLOW?
HERE THEY COME!
THIS IS INSANE!
WE WON'T BE ABLE TO DELIVER A HIGH QUALITY PRODUCT IN THREE MONTHS!
SECURITY DROIDS REQUIRE EVEN MORE QA'S THAN OTHER PRODUCTS.
I'M AFRAID WE'VE NO OTHER CHOICE. OUR FIRST MEETING IS SCHEDULED AT FOUR P.M. TODAY. I GOTTA LEAVE NOW.
STILL 35%!
HOW LONG IS IT GONNA TAKE YOU TO DOWNLOAD THE BLOODY BLUEPRINTS?
WHEN YOU'RE FINISHED, COME TO THE LAB.
WHAT PIECE OF JUNK!
DON'T LET HIM TREAT YOU LIKE THAT.
HEAD UP, CUTIE!

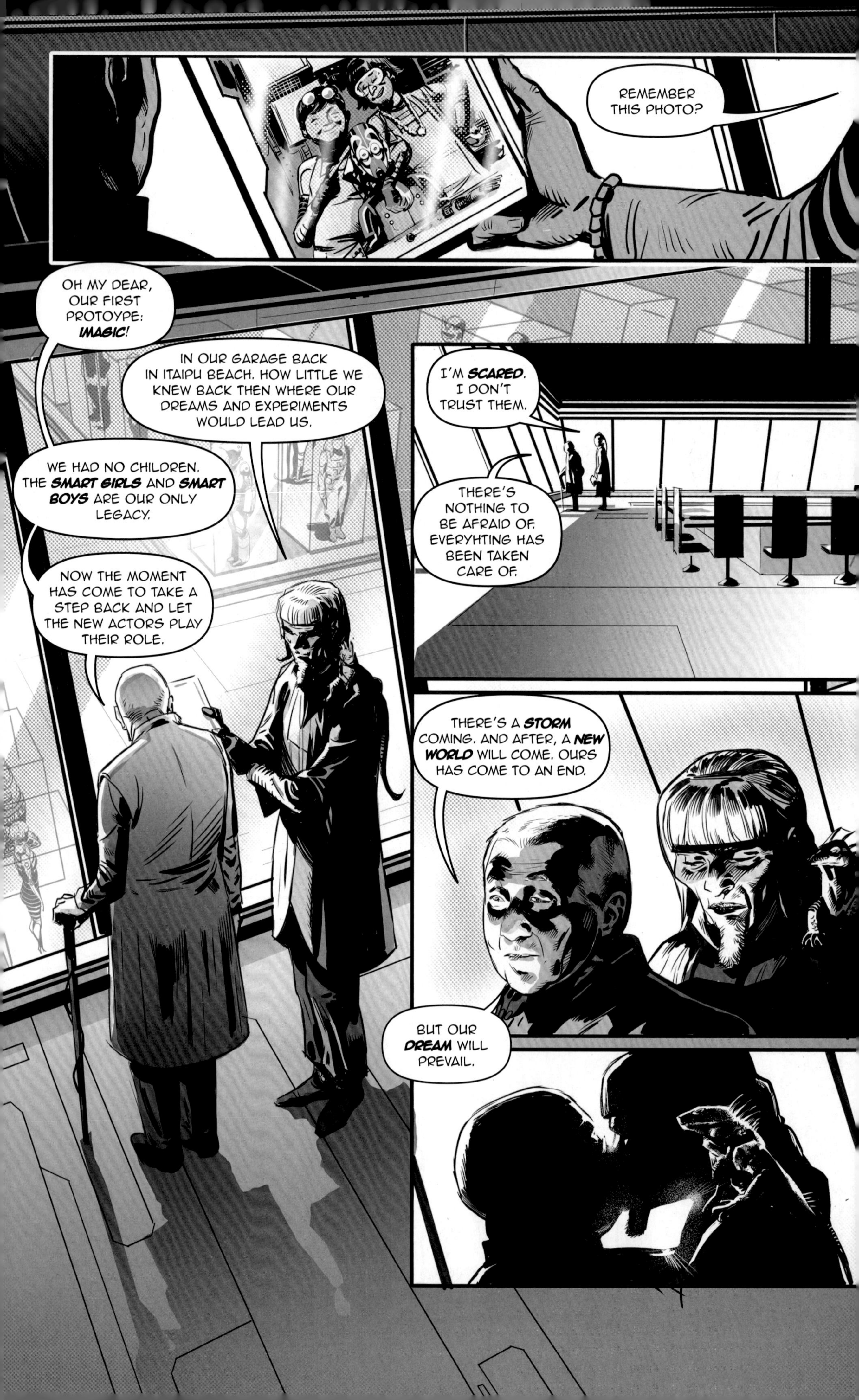
REMEMBER THIS PHOTO?
OH MY DEAR, OUR FIRST PROTOYPE: **IMAGIC**!
IN OUR GARAGE BACK IN ITAIPU BEACH. HOW LITTLE WE KNEW BACK THEN WHERE OUR DREAMS AND EXPERIMENTS WOULD LEAD US.
WE HAD NO CHILDREN. THE **SMART GIRLS** AND **SMART BOYS** ARE OUR ONLY LEGACY.
NOW THE MOMENT HAS COME TO TAKE A STEP BACK AND LET THE NEW ACTORS PLAY THEIR ROLE.
I'M **SCARED**. I DON'T TRUST THEM.
THERE'S NOTHING TO BE AFRAID OF. EVERYHTING HAS BEEN TAKEN CARE OF.
THERE'S A **STORM** COMING. AND AFTER, A **NEW WORLD** WILL COME. OURS HAS COME TO AN END.
BUT OUR **DREAM** WILL PREVAIL.

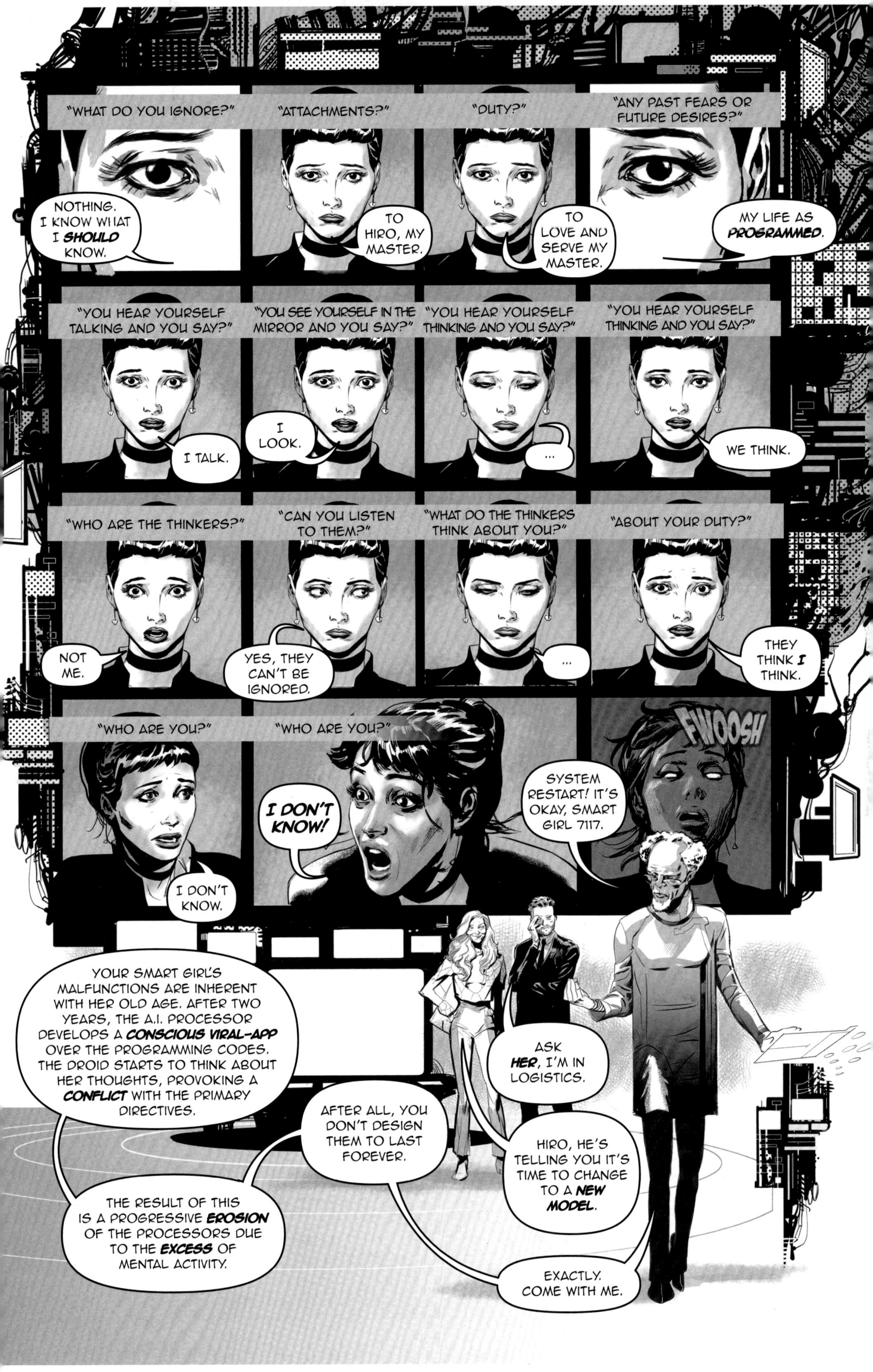
"WHAT DO YOU IGNORE?"
NOTHING. I KNOW WHAT I SHOULD KNOW.
"ATTACHMENTS?"
TO HIRO, MY MASTER.
"DUTY?"
TO LOVE AND SERVE MY MASTER.
"ANY PAST FEARS OR FUTURE DESIRES?"
MY LIFE AS PROGRAMMED.
"YOU HEAR YOURSELF TALKING AND YOU SAY?"
I TALK.
"YOU SEE YOURSELF IN THE MIRROR AND YOU SAY?"
I LOOK.
"YOU HEAR YOURSELF THINKING AND YOU SAY?"
...
"YOU HEAR YOURSELF THINKING AND YOU SAY?"
WE THINK.
"WHO ARE THE THINKERS?"
NOT ME.
"CAN YOU LISTEN TO THEM?"
YES, THEY CAN'T BE IGNORED.
"WHAT DO THE THINKERS THINK ABOUT YOU?"
...
"ABOUT YOUR DUTY?"
THEY THINK I THINK.
"WHO ARE YOU?"
I DON'T KNOW.
"WHO ARE YOU?"
I DON'T KNOW!
FWOOSH
SYSTEM RESTART! IT'S OKAY, SMART GIRL 7117.
YOUR SMART GIRL'S MALFUNCTIONS ARE INHERENT WITH HER OLD AGE. AFTER TWO YEARS, THE A.I. PROCESSOR DEVELOPS A CONSCIOUS VIRAL-APP OVER THE PROGRAMMING CODES. THE DROID STARTS TO THINK ABOUT HER THOUGHTS, PROVOKING A CONFLICT WITH THE PRIMARY DIRECTIVES.
THE RESULT OF THIS IS A PROGRESSIVE EROSION OF THE PROCESSORS DUE TO THE EXCESS OF MENTAL ACTIVITY.
AFTER ALL, YOU DON'T DESIGN THEM TO LAST FOREVER.
ASK HER, I'M IN LOGISTICS.
HIRO, HE'S TELLING YOU IT'S TIME TO CHANGE TO A NEW MODEL.
EXACTLY. COME WITH ME.

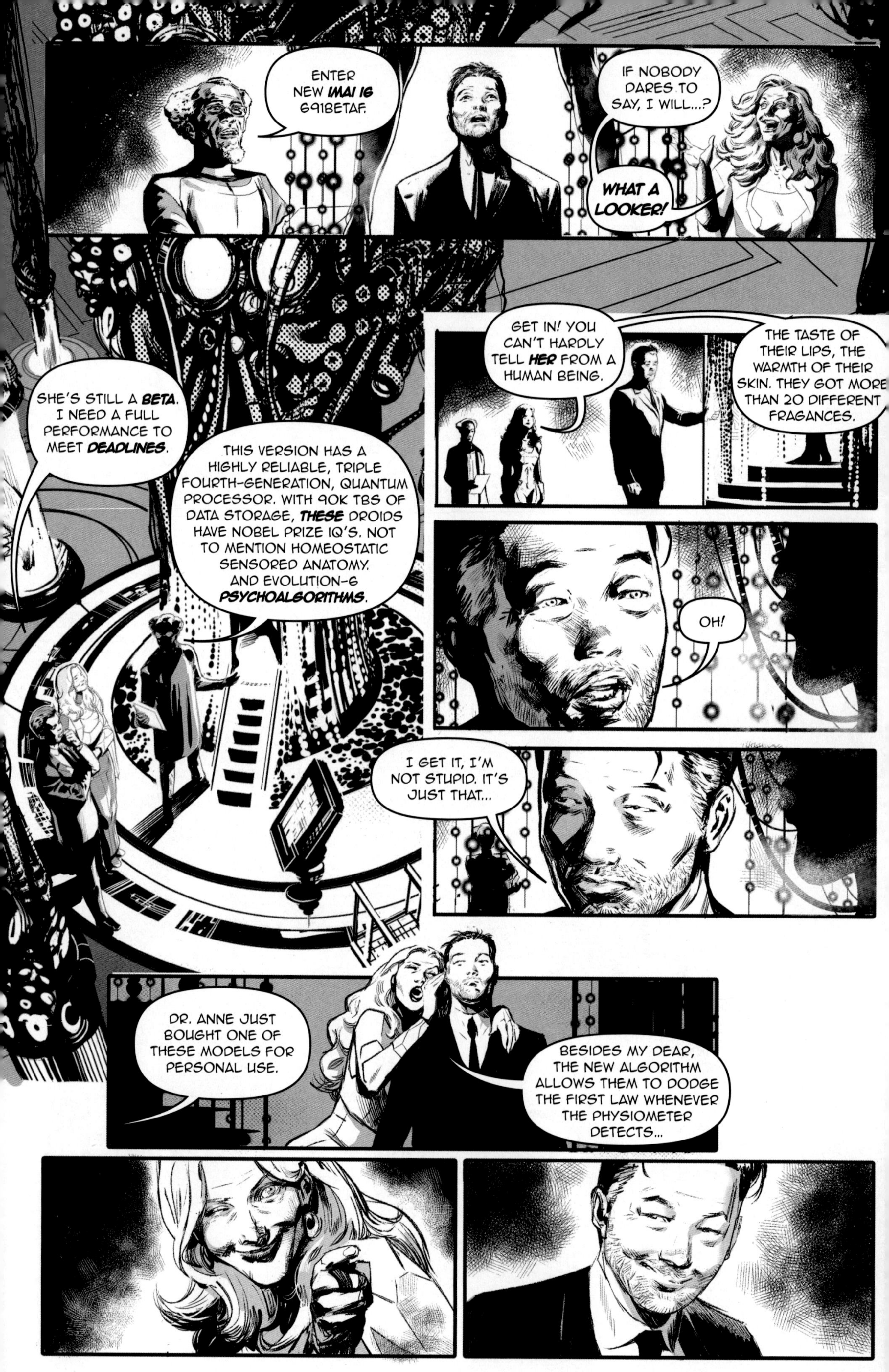
ENTER NEW IMAI 16 691BETAF.
IF NOBODY DARES TO SAY, I WILL...?
WHAT A LOOKER!
SHE'S STILL A BETA. I NEED A FULL PERFORMANCE TO MEET DEADLINES.
THIS VERSION HAS A HIGHLY RELIABLE, TRIPLE FOURTH-GENERATION, QUANTUM PROCESSOR. WITH 90K TBS OF DATA STORAGE, THESE DROIDS HAVE NOBEL PRIZE IQ'S. NOT TO MENTION HOMEOSTATIC SENSORED ANATOMY. AND EVOLUTION-6 PSYCHOALGORITHMS.
GET IN! YOU CAN'T HARDLY TELL HER FROM A HUMAN BEING.
THE TASTE OF THEIR LIPS, THE WARMTH OF THEIR SKIN. THEY GOT MORE THAN 20 DIFFERENT FRAGANCES.
OH!
I GET IT, I'M NOT STUPID. IT'S JUST THAT...
DR. ANNE JUST BOUGHT ONE OF THESE MODELS FOR PERSONAL USE.
BESIDES MY DEAR, THE NEW ALGORITHM ALLOWS THEM TO DODGE THE FIRST LAW WHENEVER THE PHYSIOMETER DETECTS...

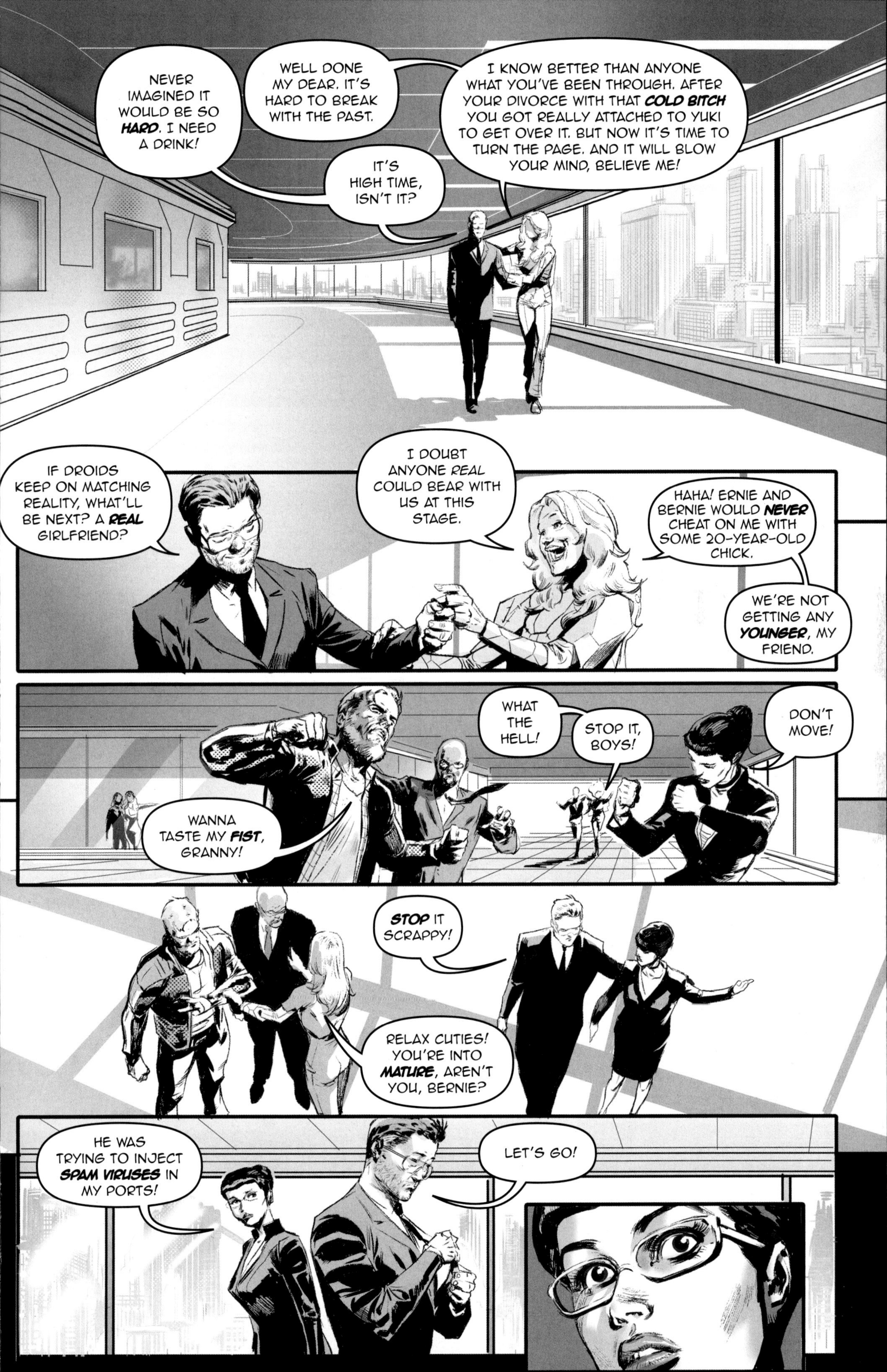
NEVER IMAGINED IT WOULD BE SO **HARD**. I NEED A DRINK!
WELL DONE MY DEAR. IT'S HARD TO BREAK WITH THE PAST.
I KNOW BETTER THAN ANYONE WHAT YOU'VE BEEN THROUGH. AFTER YOUR DIVORCE WITH THAT **COLD BITCH** YOU GOT REALLY ATTACHED TO YUKI TO GET OVER IT. BUT NOW IT'S TIME TO TURN THE PAGE. AND IT WILL BLOW YOUR MIND, BELIEVE ME!
IT'S HIGH TIME, ISN'T IT?
IF DROIDS KEEP ON MATCHING REALITY, WHAT'LL BE NEXT? A **REAL** GIRLFRIEND?
I DOUBT ANYONE *REAL* COULD BEAR WITH US AT THIS STAGE.
HAHA! ERNIE AND BERNIE WOULD **NEVER** CHEAT ON ME WITH SOME 20-YEAR-OLD CHICK.
WE'RE NOT GETTING ANY **YOUNGER**, MY FRIEND.
WANNA TASTE MY **FIST**, GRANNY!
WHAT THE HELL!
STOP IT, BOYS!
DON'T MOVE!
STOP IT SCRAPPY!
RELAX CUTIES! YOU'RE INTO **MATURE**, AREN'T YOU, BERNIE?
HE WAS TRYING TO INJECT **SPAM VIRUSES** IN MY PORTS!
LET'S GO!

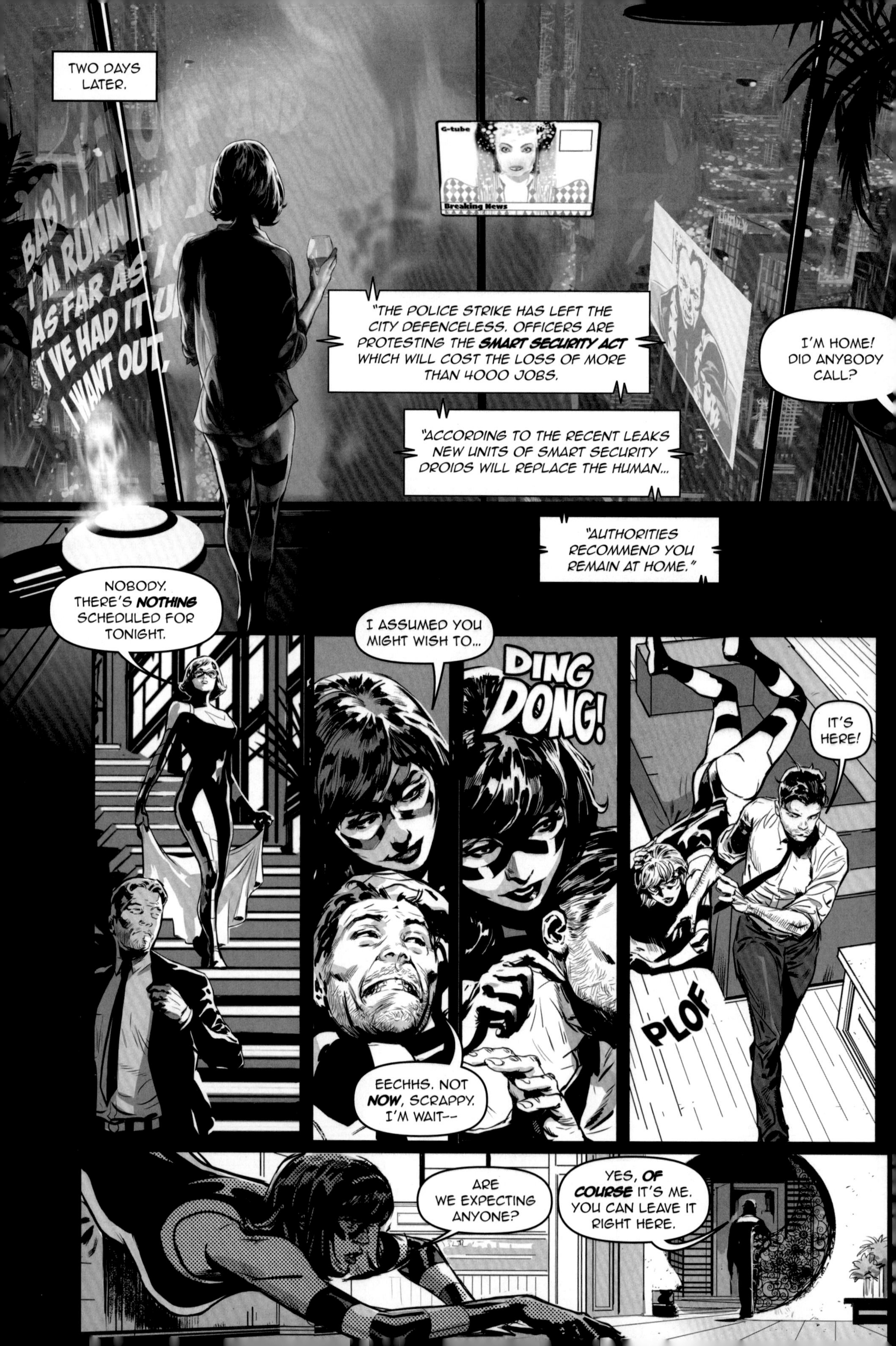

TWO DAYS LATER.
G-tube
Breaking News
"THE POLICE STRIKE HAS LEFT THE CITY DEFENCELESS. OFFICERS ARE PROTESTING THE **SMART SECURITY ACT** WHICH WILL COST THE LOSS OF MORE THAN 4000 JOBS.
"ACCORDING TO THE RECENT LEAKS NEW UNITS OF SMART SECURITY DROIDS WILL REPLACE THE HUMAN...
I'M HOME! DID ANYBODY CALL?
"AUTHORITIES RECOMMEND YOU REMAIN AT HOME."
NOBODY. THERE'S **NOTHING** SCHEDULED FOR TONIGHT.
I ASSUMED YOU MIGHT WISH TO...
EECHHS. NOT **NOW**, SCRAPPY. I'M WAIT--
DING DONG!
IT'S HERE!
PLOF
ARE WE EXPECTING ANYONE?
YES, **OF COURSE** IT'S ME. YOU CAN LEAVE IT RIGHT HERE.

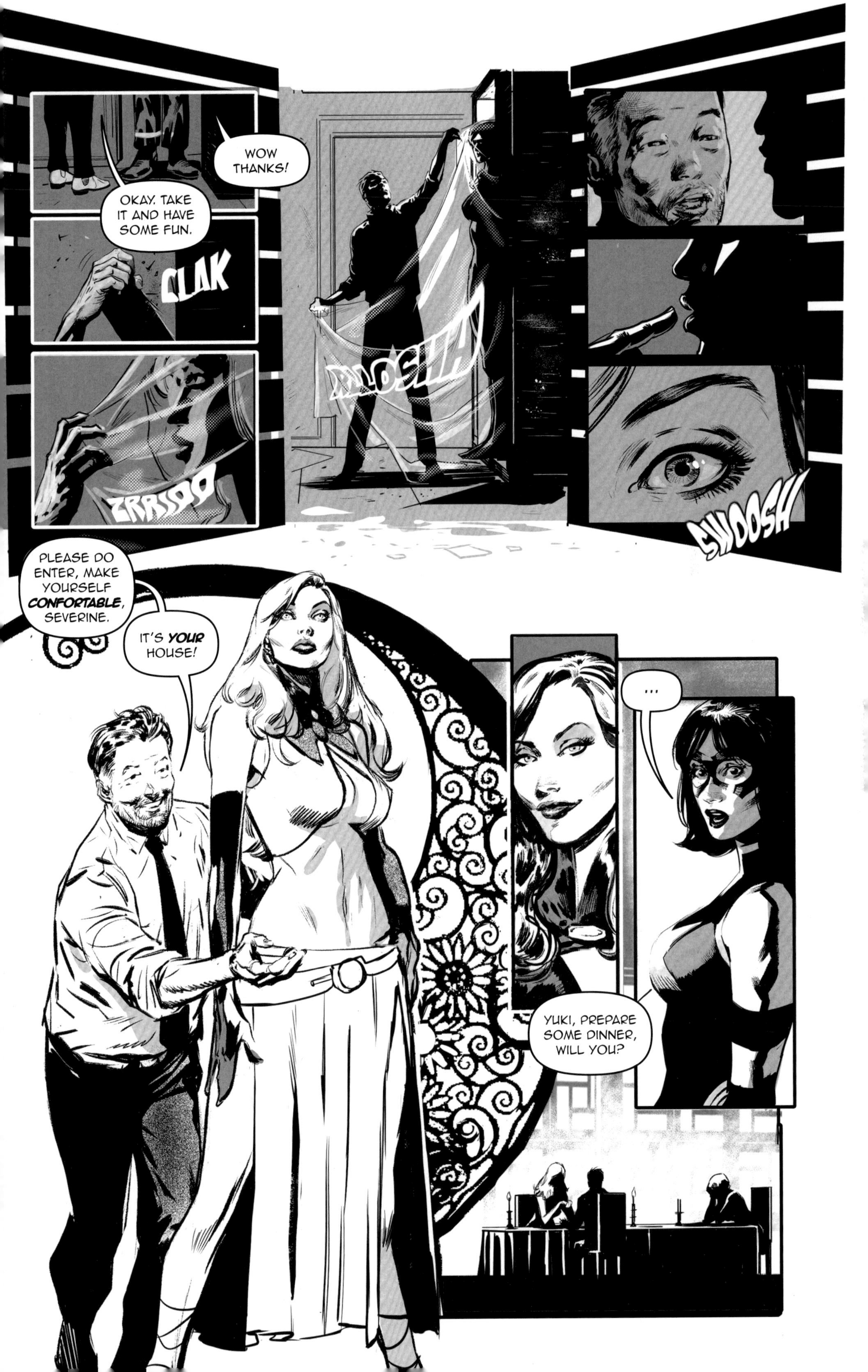
OKAY. TAKE IT AND HAVE SOME FUN.
WOW THANKS!
CLAK
ZRRIPP
WHOOSH!
SWOOSH
PLEASE DO ENTER, MAKE YOURSELF **CONFORTABLE**, SEVERINE.
IT'S **YOUR** HOUSE!
...
YUKI, PREPARE SOME DINNER, WILL YOU?

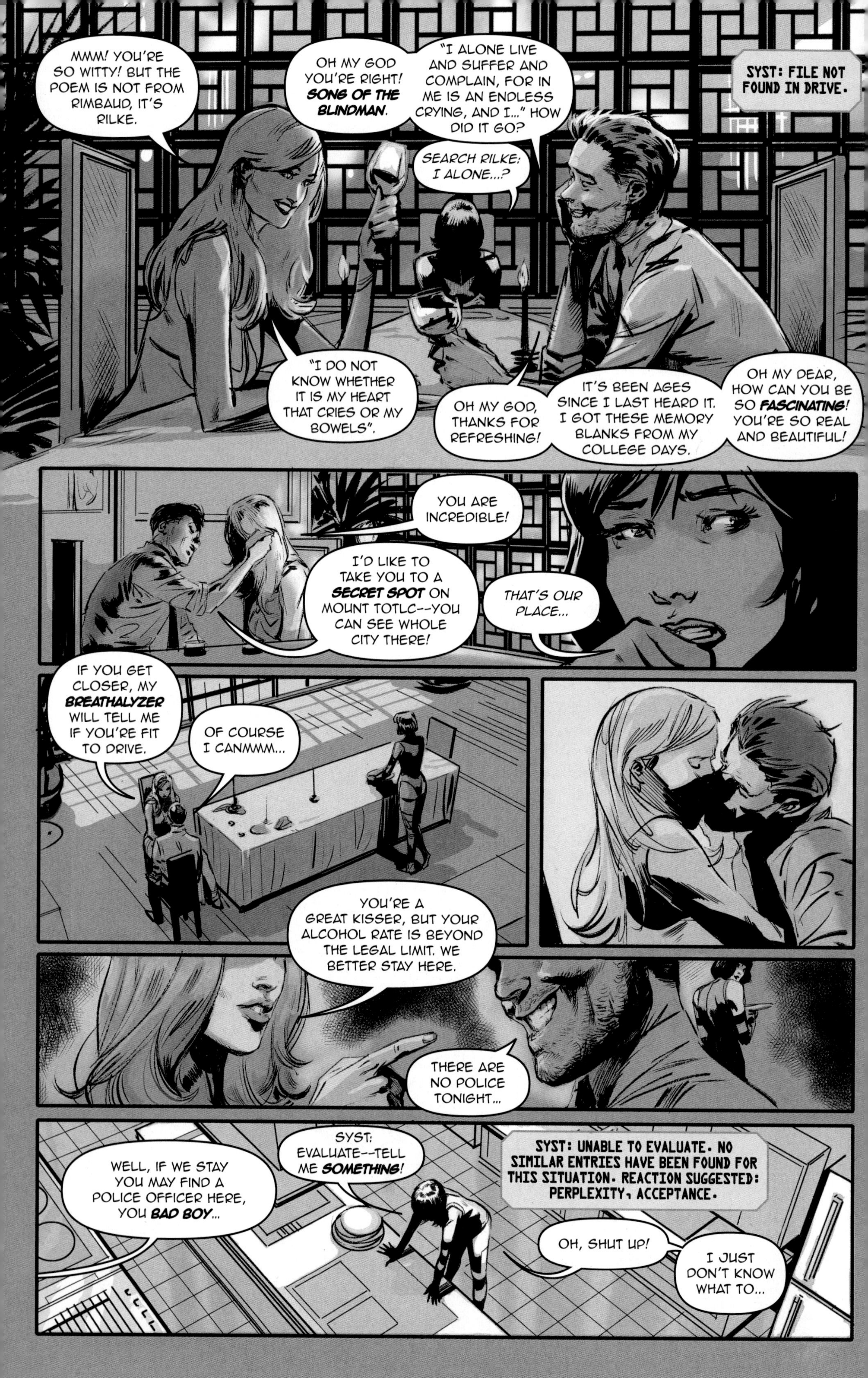
MMM! YOU'RE SO WITTY! BUT THE POEM IS NOT FROM RIMBAUD, IT'S RILKE.
OH MY GOD YOU'RE RIGHT! SONG OF THE BLINDMAN.
"I ALONE LIVE AND SUFFER AND COMPLAIN, FOR IN ME IS AN ENDLESS CRYING, AND I..." HOW DID IT GO?
SEARCH RILKE: I ALONE...?
SYST: FILE NOT FOUND IN DRIVE.
"I DO NOT KNOW WHETHER IT IS MY HEART THAT CRIES OR MY BOWELS".
OH MY GOD, THANKS FOR REFRESHING!
IT'S BEEN AGES SINCE I LAST HEARD IT. I GOT THESE MEMORY BLANKS FROM MY COLLEGE DAYS.
OH MY DEAR, HOW CAN YOU BE SO FASCINATING! YOU'RE SO REAL AND BEAUTIFUL!
YOU ARE INCREDIBLE!
I'D LIKE TO TAKE YOU TO A SECRET SPOT ON MOUNT TOTLC--YOU CAN SEE WHOLE CITY THERE!
THAT'S OUR PLACE...
IF YOU GET CLOSER, MY BREATHALYZER WILL TELL ME IF YOU'RE FIT TO DRIVE.
OF COURSE I CANMMM...
YOU'RE A GREAT KISSER, BUT YOUR ALCOHOL RATE IS BEYOND THE LEGAL LIMIT. WE BETTER STAY HERE.
THERE ARE NO POLICE TONIGHT...
WELL, IF WE STAY YOU MAY FIND A POLICE OFFICER HERE, YOU BAD BOY...
SYST: EVALUATE--TELL ME SOMETHING!
SYST: UNABLE TO EVALUATE. NO SIMILAR ENTRIES HAVE BEEN FOUND FOR THIS SITUATION. REACTION SUGGESTED: PERPLEXITY, ACCEPTANCE.
OH, SHUT UP!
I JUST DON'T KNOW WHAT TO...

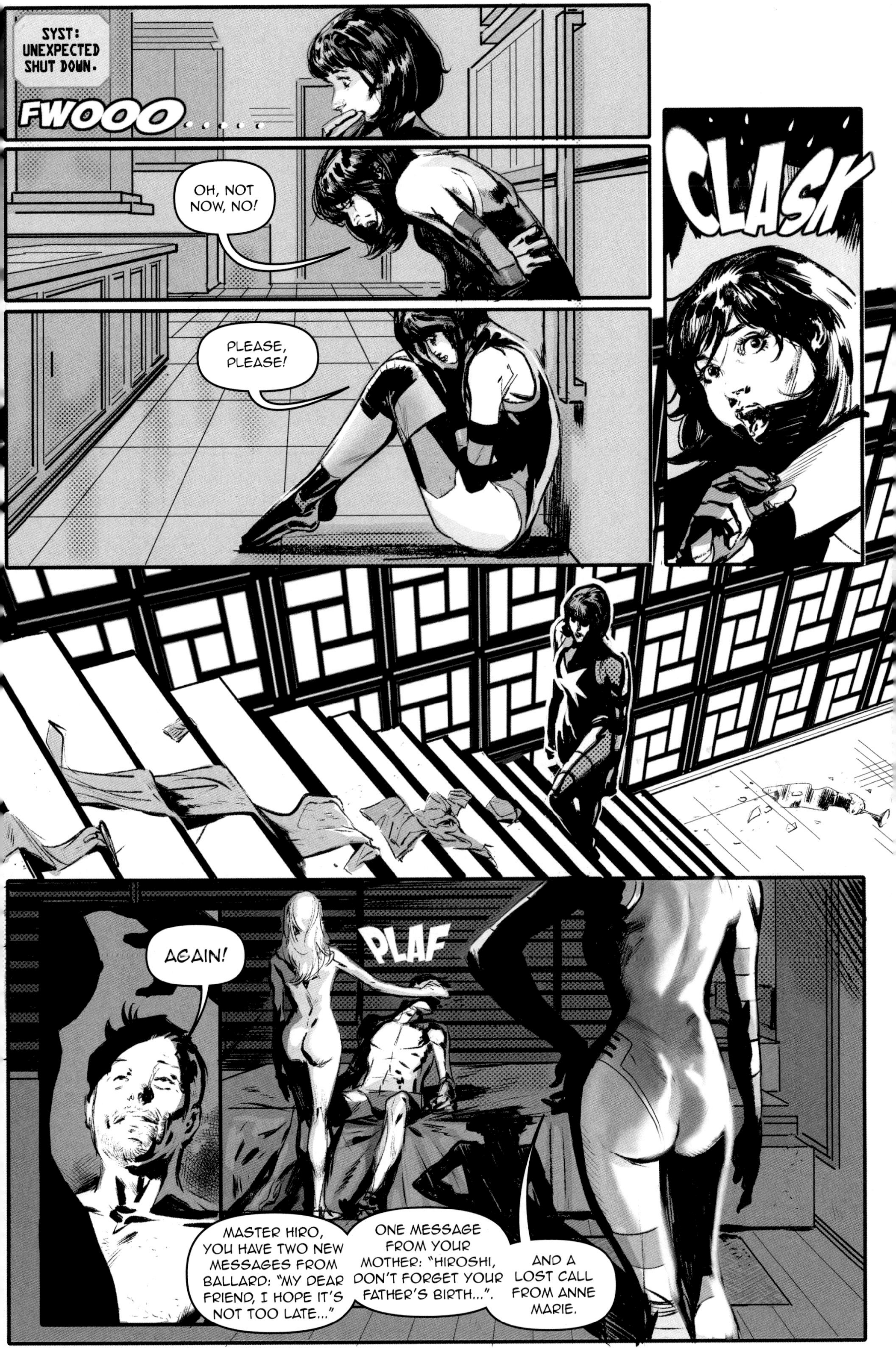
SYST: UNEXPECTED SHUT DOWN.
FWOOO.....
OH, NOT NOW, NO!
PLEASE, PLEASE!
CLASK
AGAIN!
PLAF
MASTER HIRO, YOU HAVE TWO NEW MESSAGES FROM BALLARD: "MY DEAR FRIEND, I HOPE IT'S NOT TOO LATE..."
ONE MESSAGE FROM YOUR MOTHER: "HIROSHI, DON'T FORGET YOUR FATHER'S BIRTH...".
AND A LOST CALL FROM ANNE MARIE.

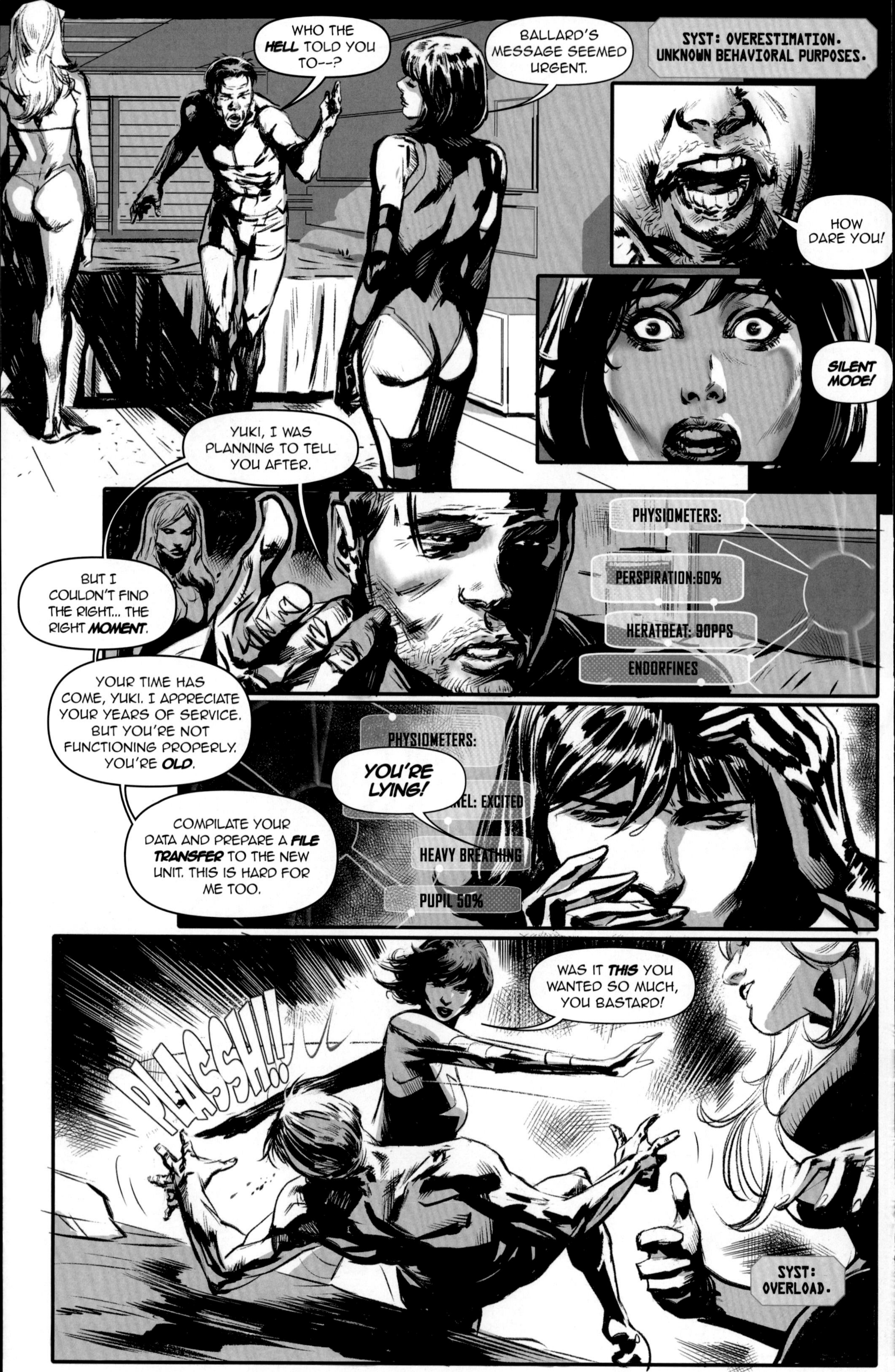
WHO THE HELL TOLD YOU TO--?
BALLARD'S MESSAGE SEEMED URGENT.
SYST: OVERESTIMATION. UNKNOWN BEHAVIORAL PURPOSES.
HOW DARE YOU!
SILENT MODE!
YUKI, I WAS PLANNING TO TELL YOU AFTER.
BUT I COULDN'T FIND THE RIGHT... THE RIGHT MOMENT.
PHYSIOMETERS:
PERSPIRATION:60%
HERATBEAT: 90PPS
ENDORFINES
YOUR TIME HAS COME, YUKI. I APPRECIATE YOUR YEARS OF SERVICE. BUT YOU'RE NOT FUNCTIONING PROPERLY. YOU'RE OLD.
COMPILATE YOUR DATA AND PREPARE A FILE TRANSFER TO THE NEW UNIT. THIS IS HARD FOR ME TOO.
PHYSIOMETERS:
YOU'RE LYING!
EXCITED
HEAVY BREATHING
PUPIL 50%
PLASSH!!
WAS IT THIS YOU WANTED SO MUCH, YOU BASTARD!
SYST: OVERLOAD.

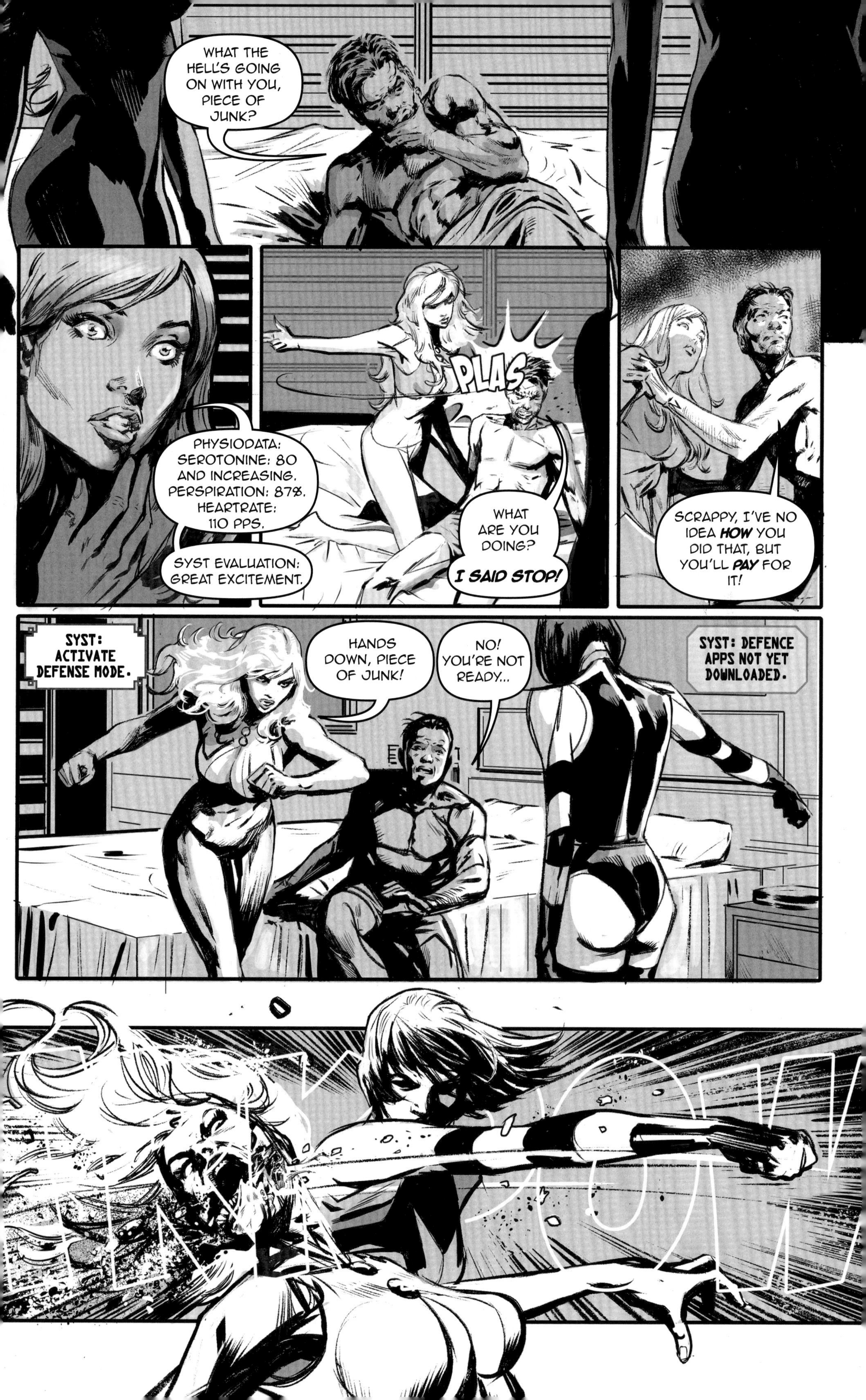
WHAT THE HELL'S GOING ON WITH YOU, PIECE OF JUNK?
PHYSIODATA: SEROTONINE: 80 AND INCREASING. PERSPIRATION: 87%. HEARTRATE: 110 PPS.
SYST EVALUATION: GREAT EXCITEMENT.
PLAS
WHAT ARE YOU DOING? I SAID STOP!
SCRAPPY, I'VE NO IDEA HOW YOU DID THAT, BUT YOU'LL PAY FOR IT!
SYST: ACTIVATE DEFENSE MODE.
HANDS DOWN, PIECE OF JUNK!
NO! YOU'RE NOT READY...
SYST: DEFENCE APPS NOT YET DOWNLOADED.

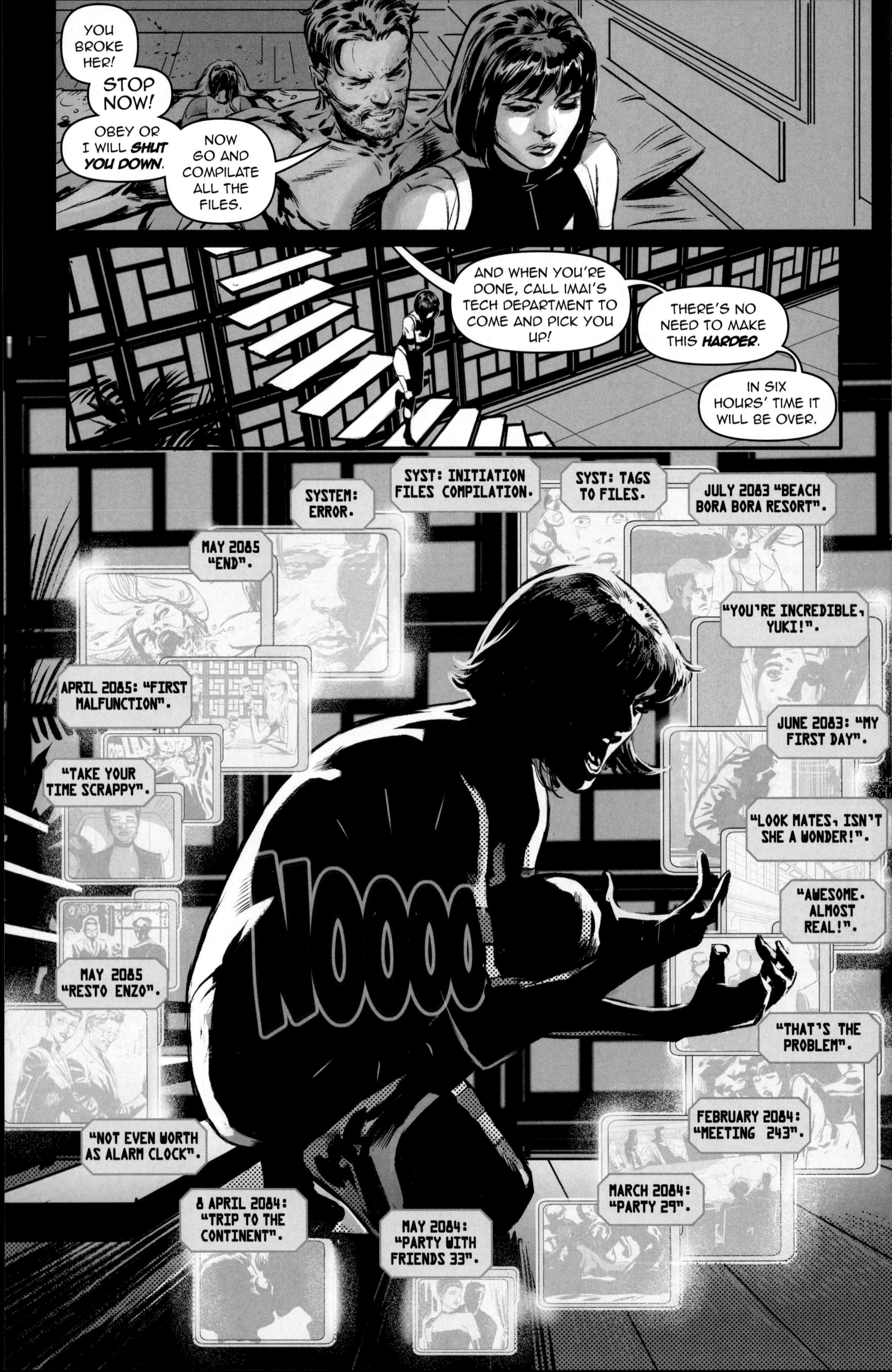

YOU BROKE HER!
STOP NOW!
OBEY OR I WILL ***SHUT YOU DOWN***.
NOW GO AND COMPILATE ALL THE FILES.
AND WHEN YOU'RE DONE, CALL IMAI'S TECH DEPARTMENT TO COME AND PICK YOU UP!
THERE'S NO NEED TO MAKE THIS ***HARDER***.
IN SIX HOURS' TIME IT WILL BE OVER.
SYSTEM: ERROR.
SYST: INITIATION FILES COMPILATION.
SYST: TAGS TO FILES.
JULY 2083 "BEACH BORA BORA RESORT".
MAY 2085 "END".
APRIL 2085: "FIRST MALFUNCTION".
"TAKE YOUR TIME SCRAPPY".
MAY 2085 "RESTO ENZO".
"NOT EVEN WORTH AS ALARM CLOCK".
8 APRIL 2084: "TRIP TO THE CONTINENT".
MAY 2084: "PARTY WITH FRIENDS 33".
"YOU'RE INCREDIBLE, YUKI!".
JUNE 2083: "MY FIRST DAY".
"LOOK MATES, ISN'T SHE A WONDER!".
"AWESOME. ALMOST REAL!".
"THAT'S THE PROBLEM".
FEBRUARY 2084: "MEETING 243".
MARCH 2084: "PARTY 29".

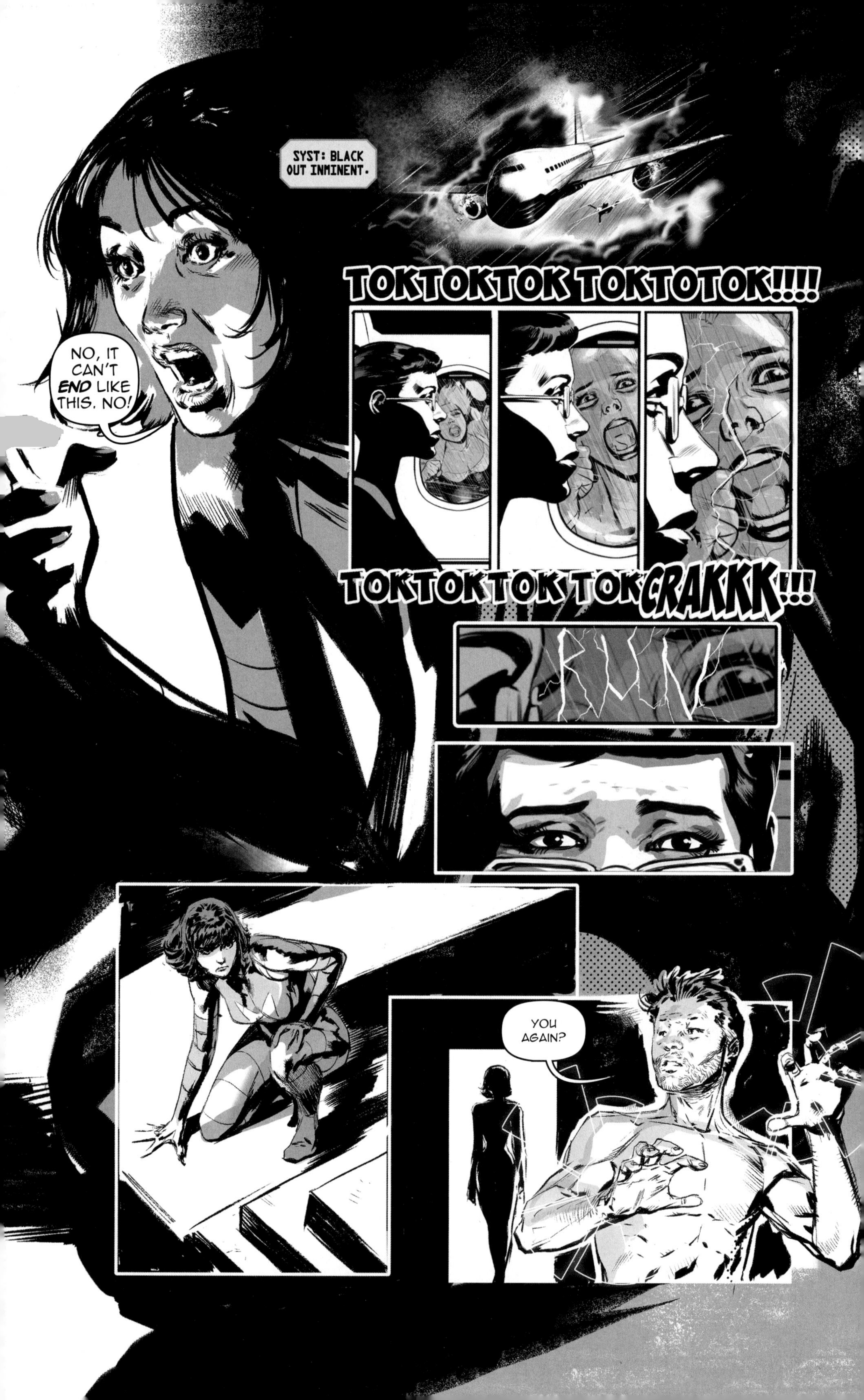
NO, IT CAN'T END LIKE THIS. NO!
SYST: BLACK OUT INMINENT.
TOKTOKTOK TOKTOTOK!!!!
TOKTOKTOK TOKCRAKKK!!!
RUN
YOU AGAIN?

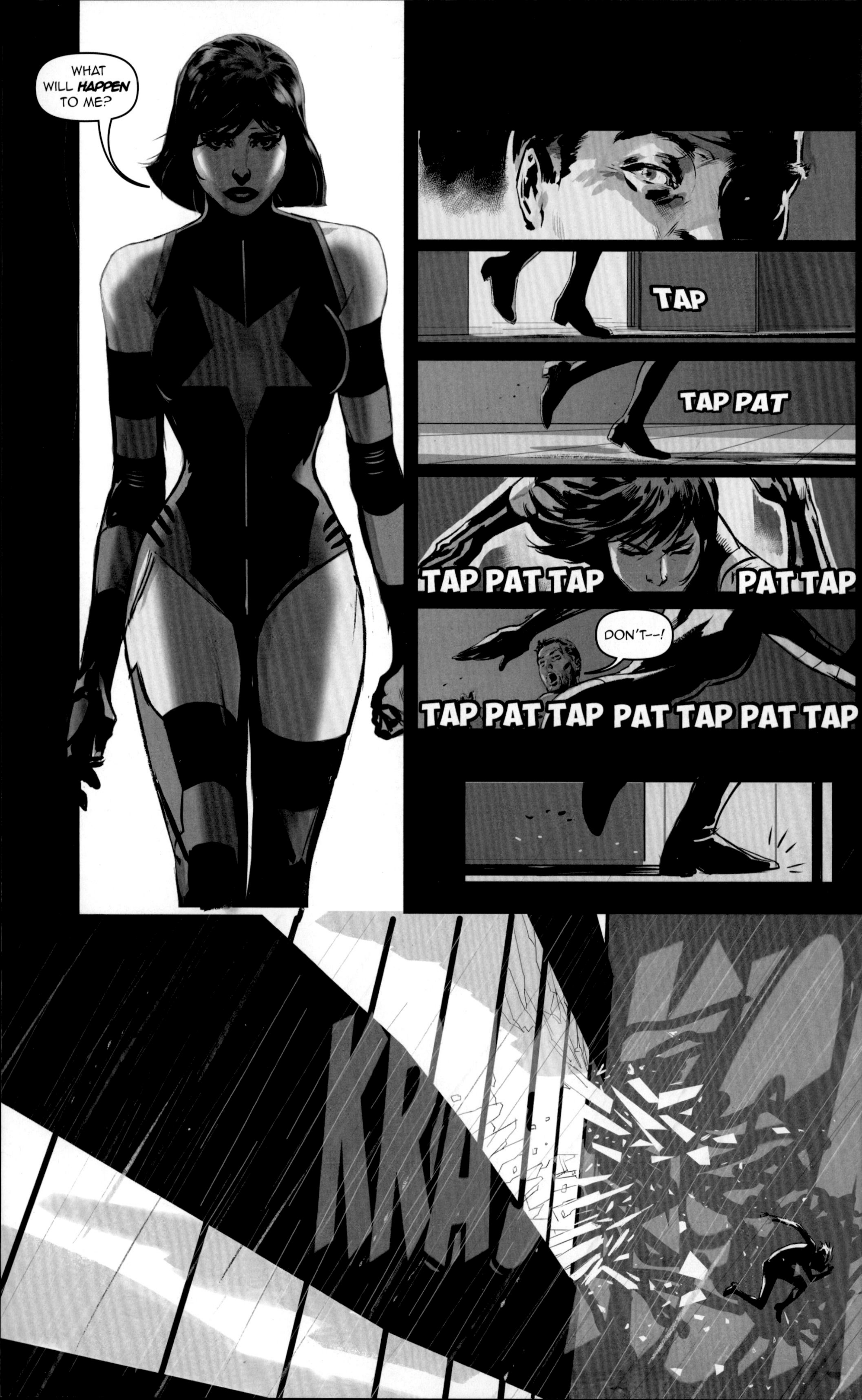
WHAT WILL HAPPEN TO ME?
TAP
TAP PAT
TAP PAT TAP
PAT TAP
DON'T--!
TAP PAT TAP PAT TAP PAT TAP
KRA

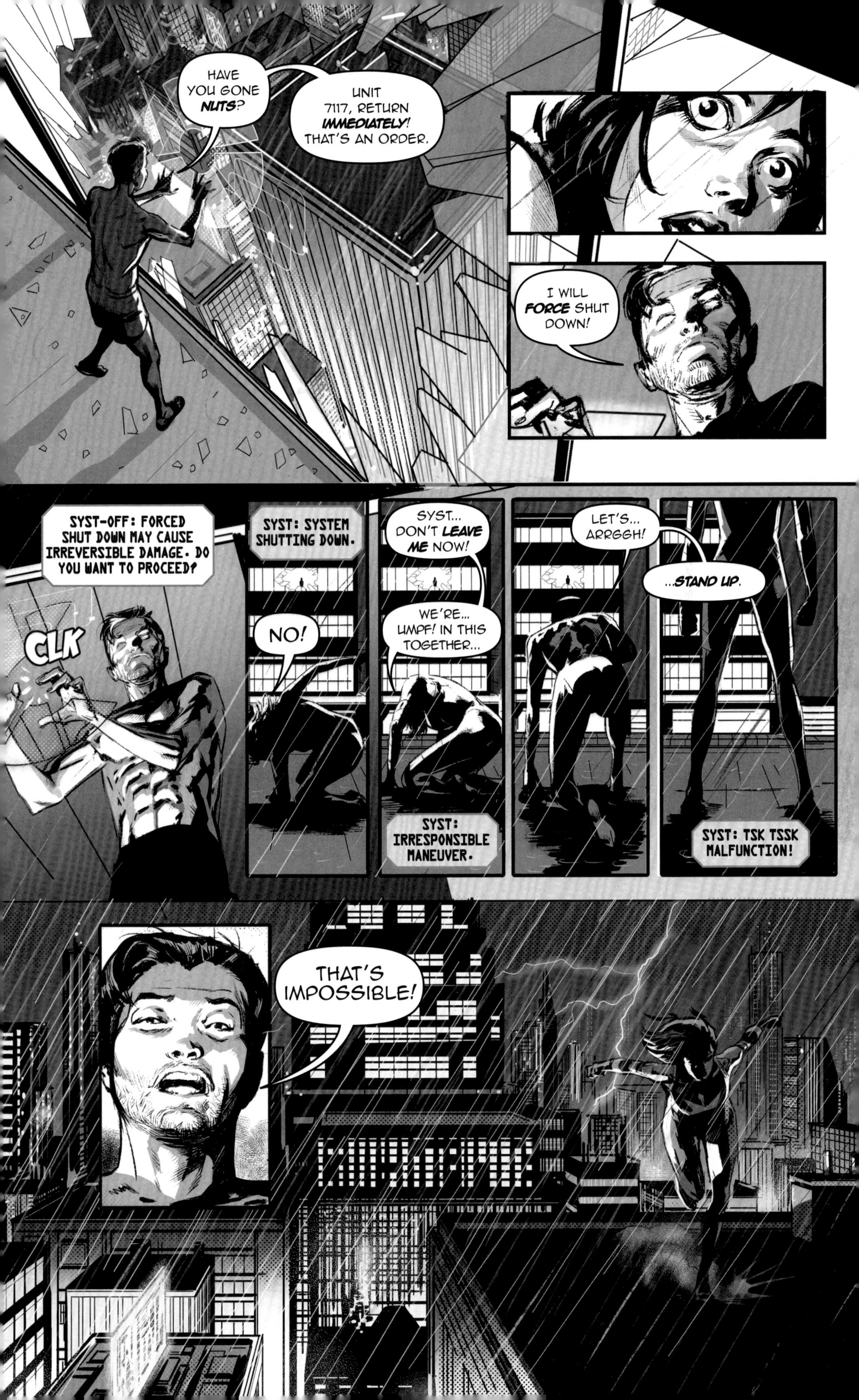
HAVE YOU GONE NUTS?
UNIT 7117, RETURN IMMEDIATELY! THAT'S AN ORDER.
I WILL FORCE SHUT DOWN!
SYST-OFF: FORCED SHUT DOWN MAY CAUSE IRREVERSIBLE DAMAGE. DO YOU WANT TO PROCEED?
CLK
SYST: SYSTEM SHUTTING DOWN.
NO!
SYST... DON'T LEAVE ME NOW!
WE'RE... UMPF! IN THIS TOGETHER...
SYST: IRRESPONSIBLE MANEUVER.
LET'S... ARRGGH!
...STAND UP.
SYST: TSK TSSK MALFUNCTION!
THAT'S IMPOSSIBLE!

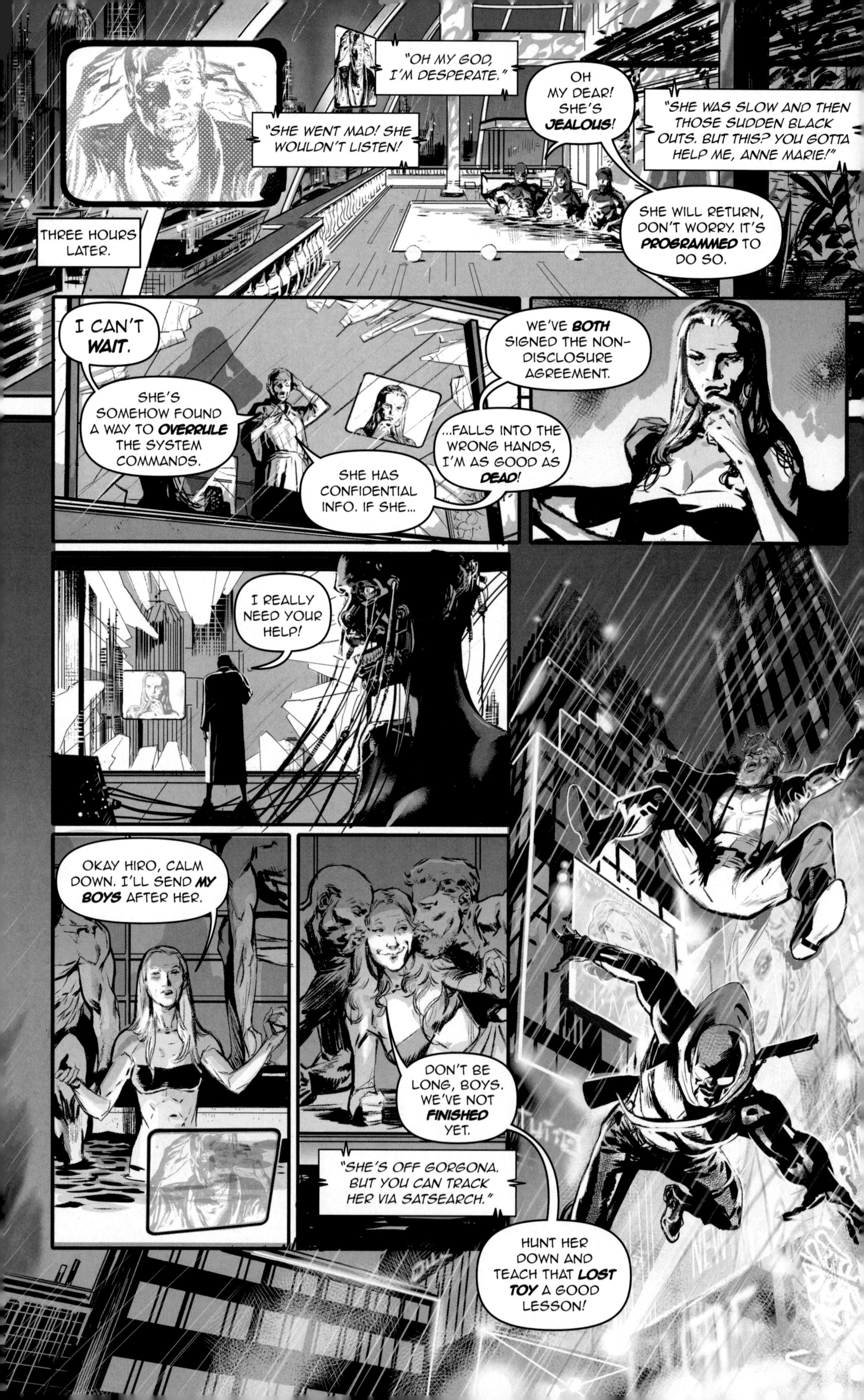
THREE HOURS LATER.
"OH MY GOD, I'M DESPERATE."
"SHE WENT MAD! SHE WOULDN'T LISTEN!"
OH MY DEAR! SHE'S ***JEALOUS***!
"SHE WAS SLOW AND THEN THOSE SUDDEN BLACK OUTS. BUT THIS? YOU GOTTA HELP ME, ANNE MARIE!"
SHE WILL RETURN, DON'T WORRY. IT'S ***PROGRAMMED*** TO DO SO.
I CAN'T ***WAIT***.
SHE'S SOMEHOW FOUND A WAY TO ***OVERRULE*** THE SYSTEM COMMANDS.
SHE HAS CONFIDENTIAL INFO. IF SHE...
...FALLS INTO THE WRONG HANDS, I'M AS GOOD AS ***DEAD***!
WE'VE ***BOTH*** SIGNED THE NON-DISCLOSURE AGREEMENT.
I REALLY NEED YOUR HELP!
OKAY HIRO, CALM DOWN. I'LL SEND ***MY BOYS*** AFTER HER.
DON'T BE LONG, BOYS. WE'VE NOT ***FINISHED*** YET.
"SHE'S OFF GORGONA. BUT YOU CAN TRACK HER VIA SATSEARCH."
HUNT HER DOWN AND TEACH THAT ***LOST TOY*** A GOOD LESSON!

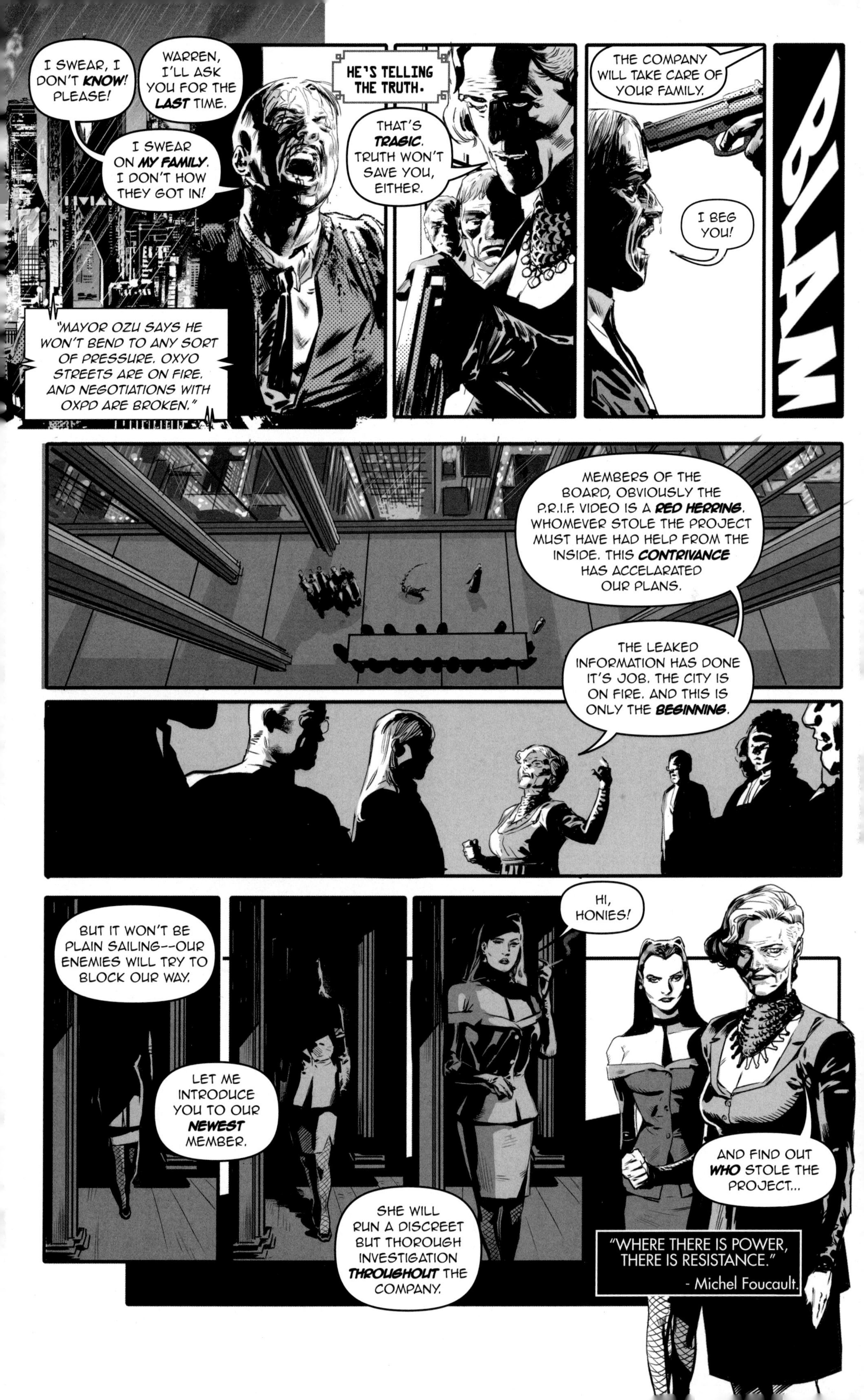
I SWEAR, I DON'T KNOW! PLEASE!
WARREN, I'LL ASK YOU FOR THE LAST TIME.
I SWEAR ON MY FAMILY. I DON'T HOW THEY GOT IN!
"MAYOR OZU SAYS HE WON'T BEND TO ANY SORT OF PRESSURE. OXYO STREETS ARE ON FIRE. AND NEGOTIATIONS WITH OXPD ARE BROKEN."
HE'S TELLING THE TRUTH.
THAT'S TRAGIC. TRUTH WON'T SAVE YOU, EITHER.
THE COMPANY WILL TAKE CARE OF YOUR FAMILY.
I BEG YOU!
BLAM
MEMBERS OF THE BOARD, OBVIOUSLY THE P.R.I.F. VIDEO IS A RED HERRING. WHOMEVER STOLE THE PROJECT MUST HAVE HAD HELP FROM THE INSIDE. THIS CONTRIVANCE HAS ACCELARATED OUR PLANS.
THE LEAKED INFORMATION HAS DONE IT'S JOB. THE CITY IS ON FIRE. AND THIS IS ONLY THE BEGINNING.
BUT IT WON'T BE PLAIN SAILING--OUR ENEMIES WILL TRY TO BLOCK OUR WAY.
LET ME INTRODUCE YOU TO OUR NEWEST MEMBER.
SHE WILL RUN A DISCREET BUT THOROUGH INVESTIGATION THROUGHOUT THE COMPANY.
HI, HONIES!
AND FIND OUT WHO STOLE THE PROJECT...
"WHERE THERE IS POWER, THERE IS RESISTANCE."
- Michel Foucault.

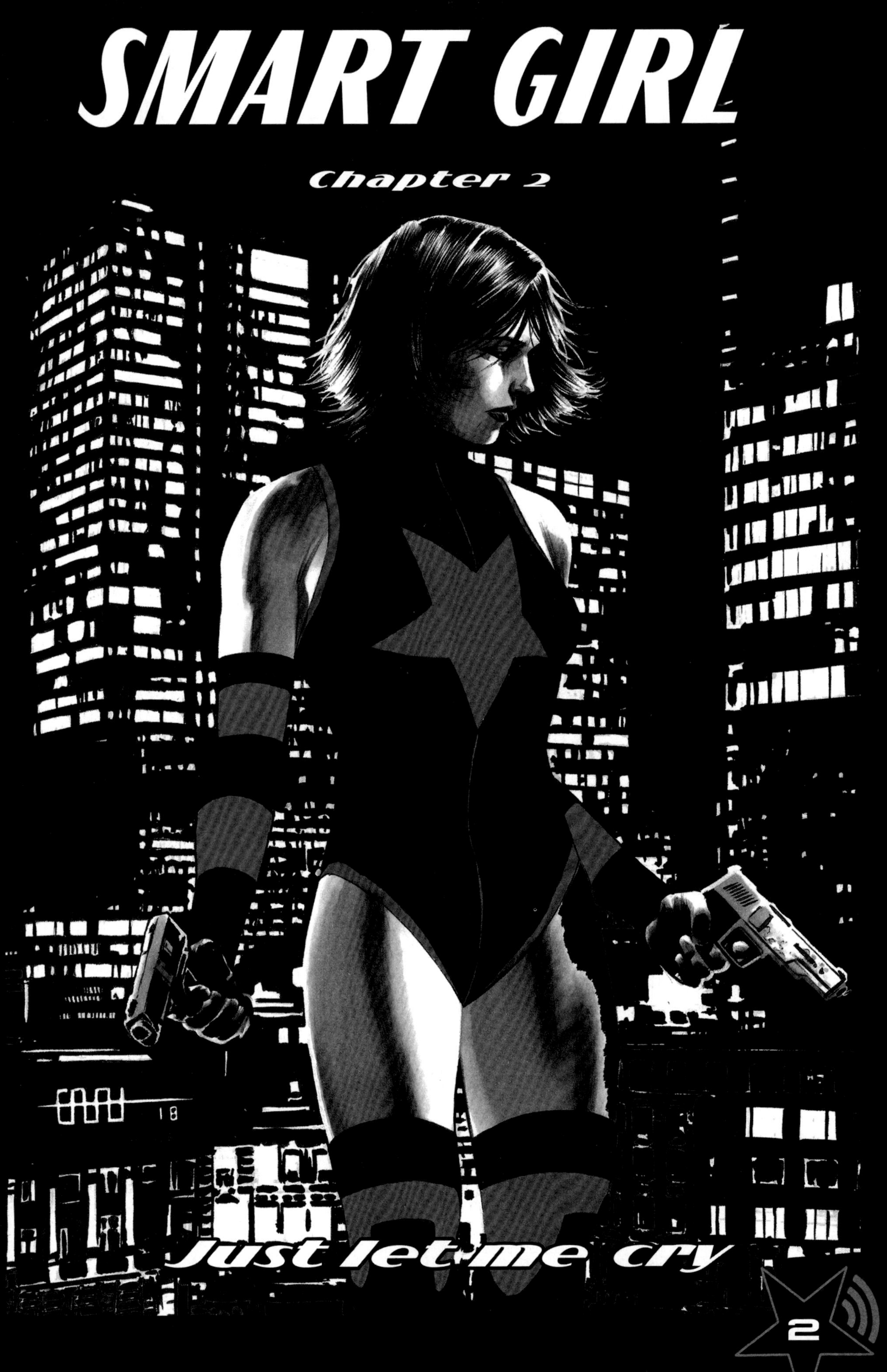
SMART GIRL
Chapter 2
Just let me cry
2

Artwork by Cafu

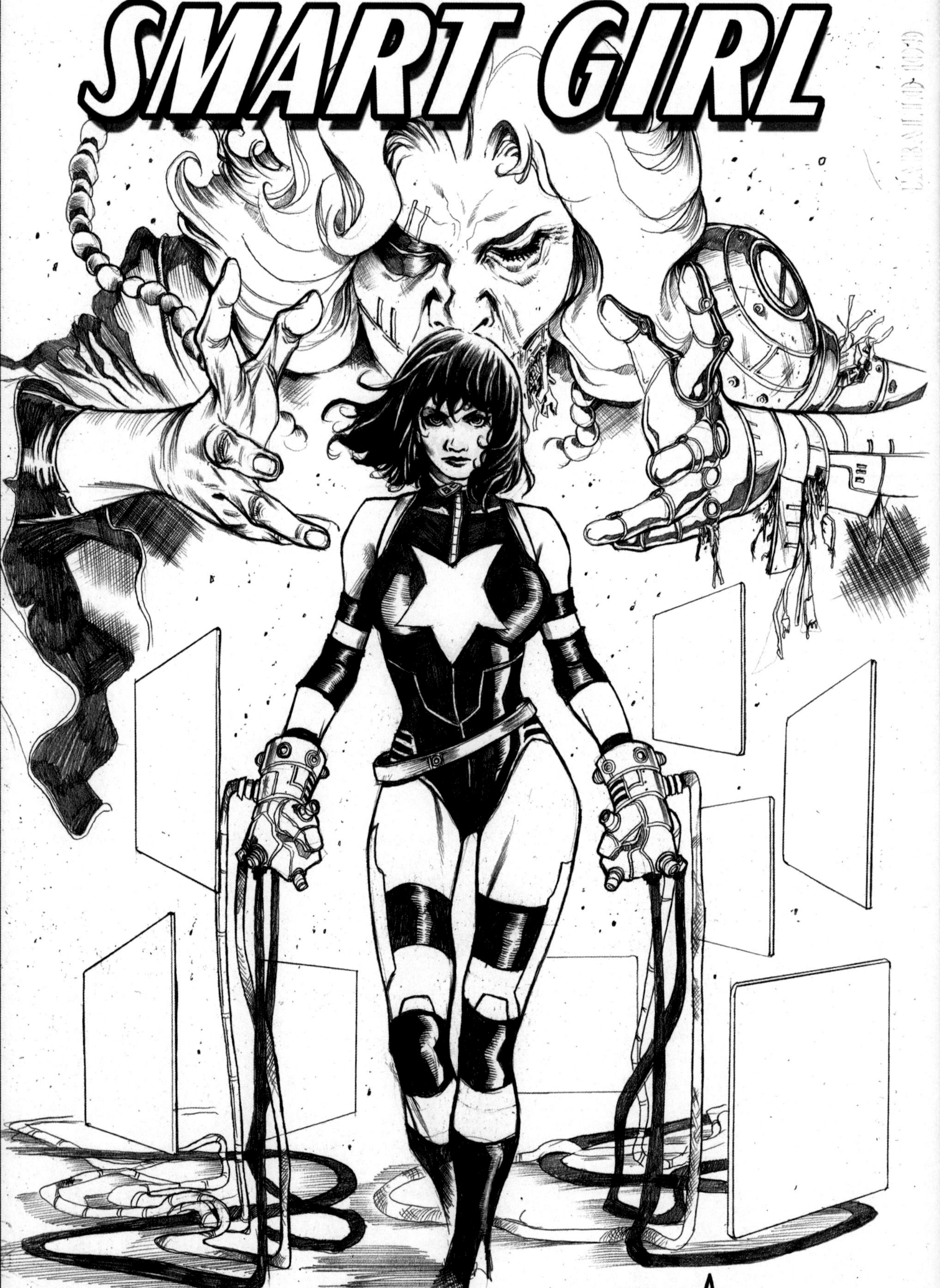
SMART GIRL
S.DÁVILA

Artwork by Sergio Dávila

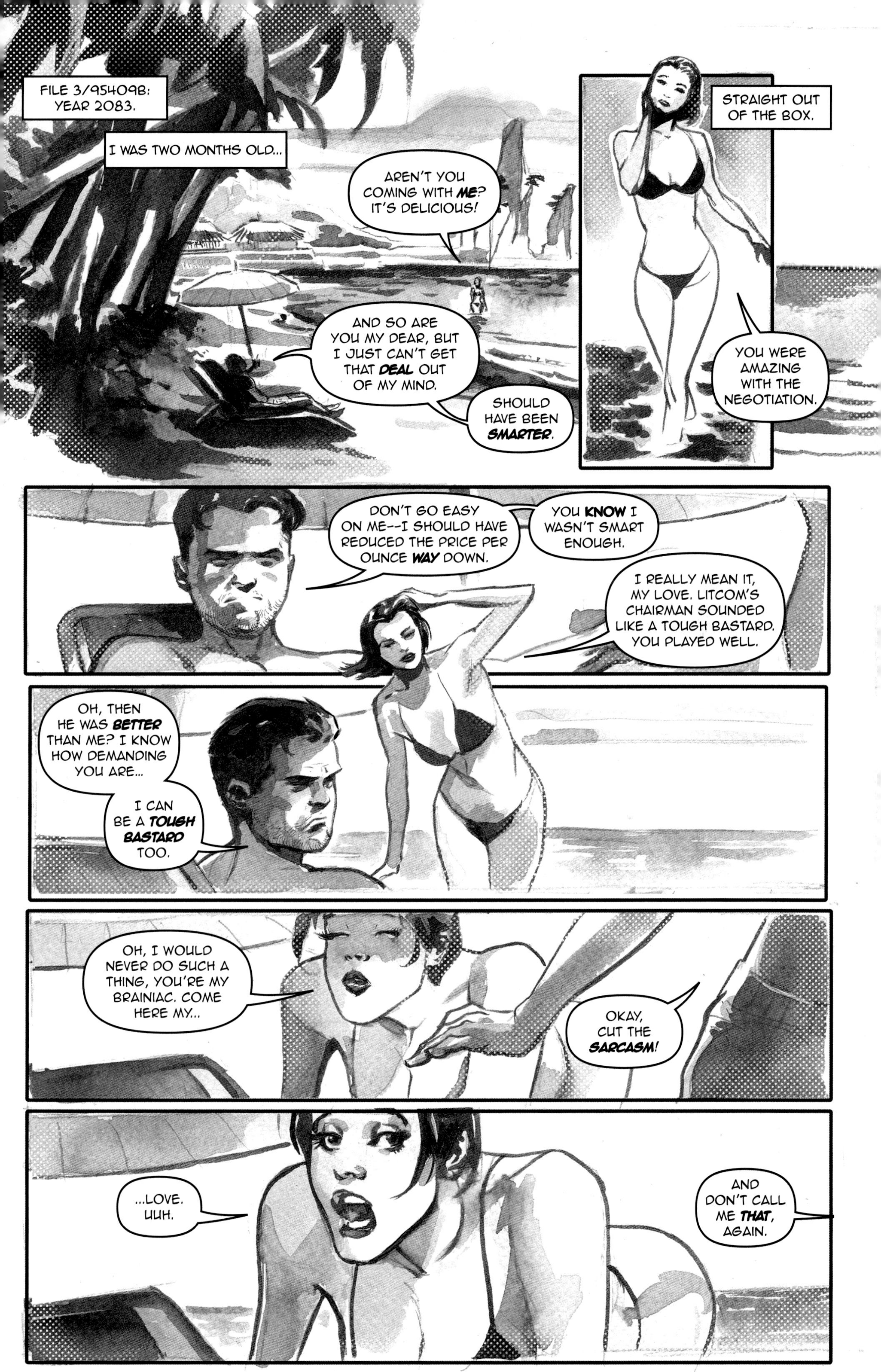
FILE 3/954098: YEAR 2083.
I WAS TWO MONTHS OLD...
AREN'T YOU COMING WITH ME? IT'S DELICIOUS!
AND SO ARE YOU MY DEAR, BUT I JUST CAN'T GET THAT DEAL OUT OF MY MIND.
SHOULD HAVE BEEN SMARTER.
STRAIGHT OUT OF THE BOX.
YOU WERE AMAZING WITH THE NEGOTIATION.
DON'T GO EASY ON ME--I SHOULD HAVE REDUCED THE PRICE PER OUNCE WAY DOWN.
YOU KNOW I WASN'T SMART ENOUGH.
I REALLY MEAN IT, MY LOVE. LITCOM'S CHAIRMAN SOUNDED LIKE A TOUGH BASTARD. YOU PLAYED WELL.
OH, THEN HE WAS BETTER THAN ME? I KNOW HOW DEMANDING YOU ARE...
I CAN BE A TOUGH BASTARD TOO.
OH, I WOULD NEVER DO SUCH A THING, YOU'RE MY BRAINIAC. COME HERE MY...
OKAY, CUT THE SARCASM!
...LOVE. UUH.
AND DON'T CALL ME THAT, AGAIN.

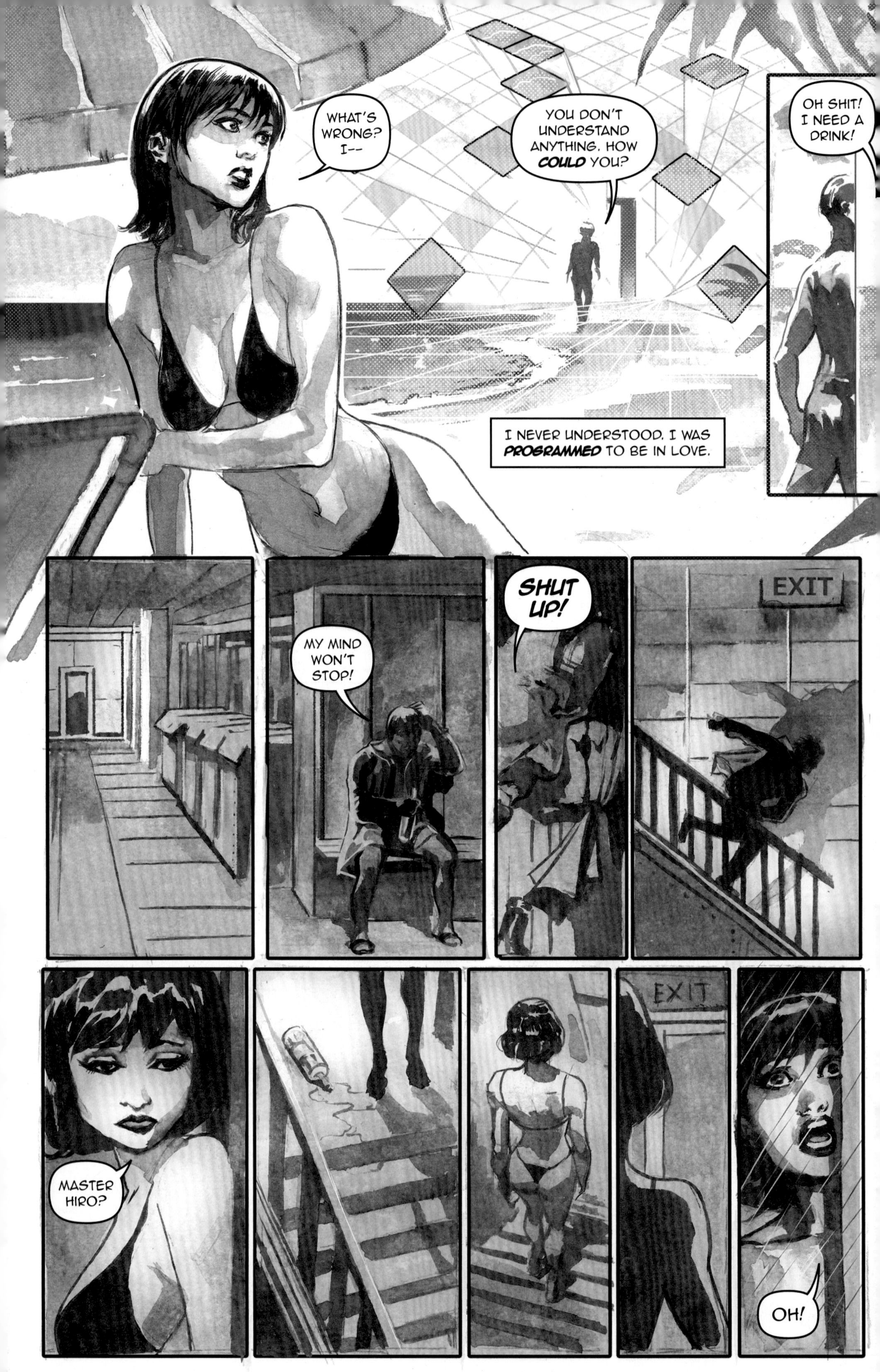
WHAT'S WRONG? I--
YOU DON'T UNDERSTAND ANYTHING. HOW COULD YOU?
I NEVER UNDERSTOOD. I WAS PROGRAMMED TO BE IN LOVE.
OH SHIT! I NEED A DRINK!
MY MIND WON'T STOP!
SHUT UP!
EXIT
MASTER HIRO?
EXIT
OH!

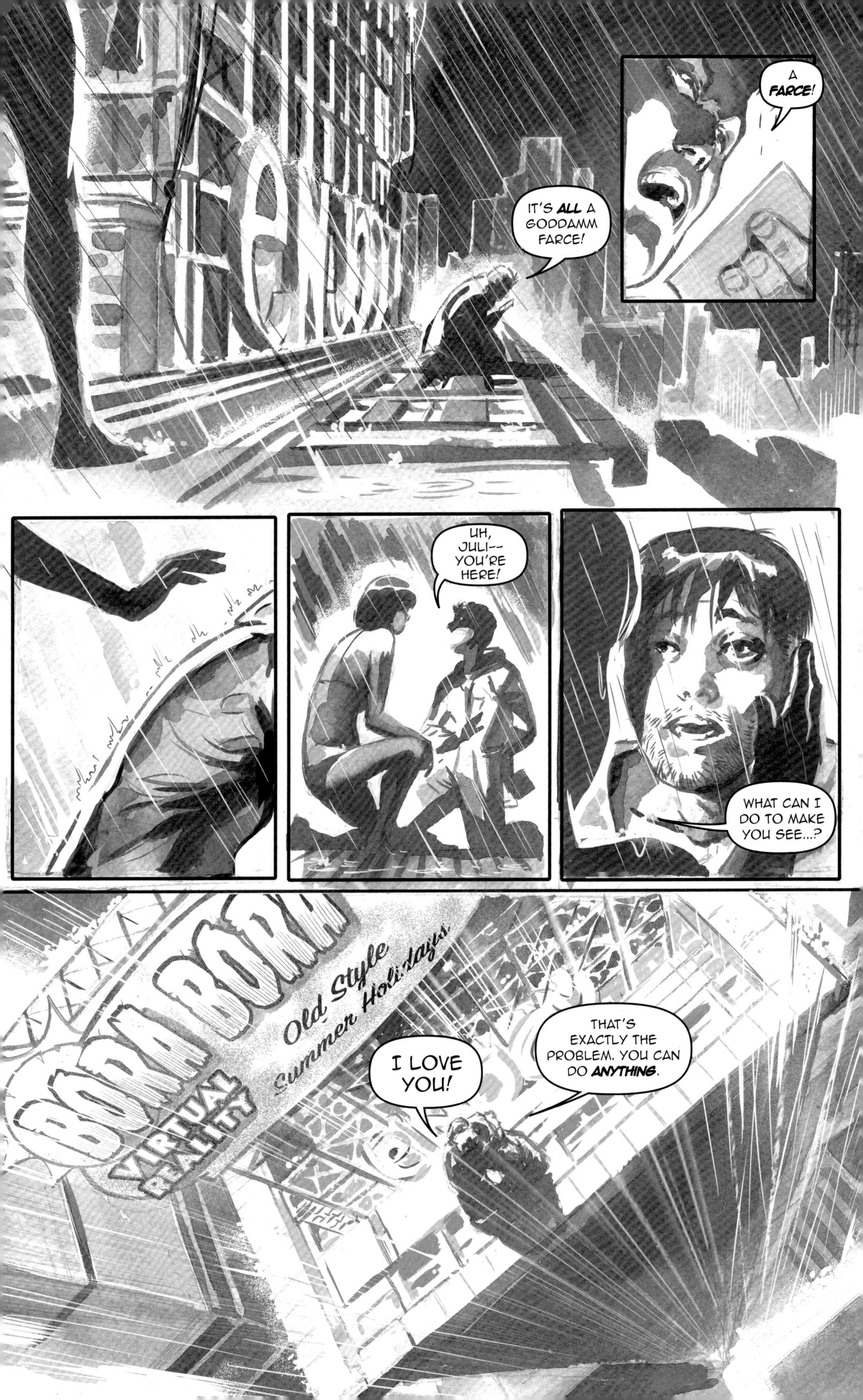
IT'S **ALL** A GODDAMM FARCE!
A ***FARCE!***
UH, JULI-- YOU'RE HERE!
WHAT CAN I DO TO MAKE YOU SEE...?
BORA BORA
VIRTUAL REALITY
Old Style Summer Holidays
I LOVE YOU!
THAT'S EXACTLY THE PROBLEM. YOU CAN DO ***ANYTHING***.

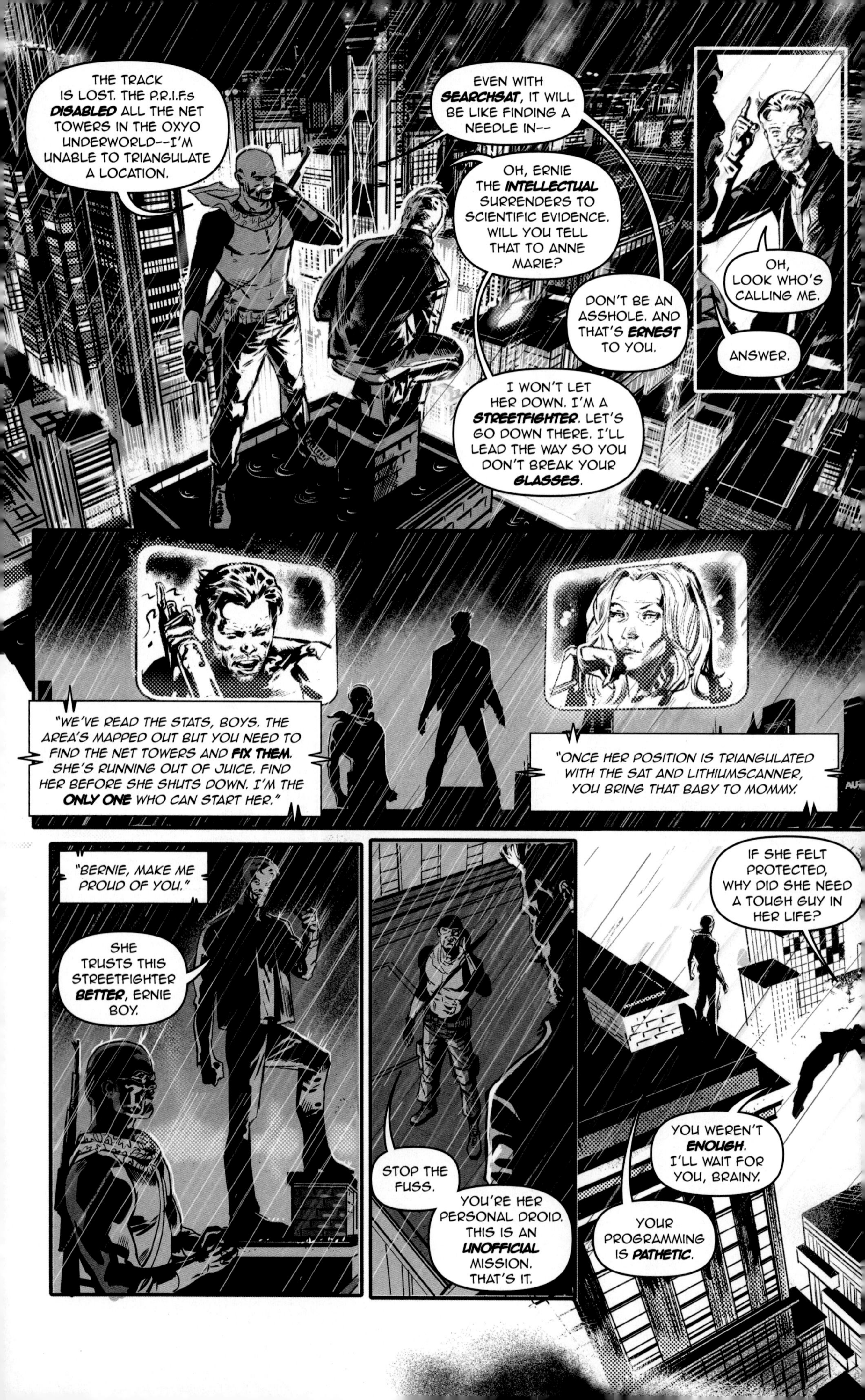
THE TRACK IS LOST. THE P.R.I.F.s DISABLED ALL THE NET TOWERS IN THE OXYO UNDERWORLD--I'M UNABLE TO TRIANGULATE A LOCATION.
EVEN WITH SEARCHSAT, IT WILL BE LIKE FINDING A NEEDLE IN--
OH, ERNIE THE INTELLECTUAL SURRENDERS TO SCIENTIFIC EVIDENCE. WILL YOU TELL THAT TO ANNE MARIE?
DON'T BE AN ASSHOLE. AND THAT'S ERNEST TO YOU.
I WON'T LET HER DOWN. I'M A STREETFIGHTER. LET'S GO DOWN THERE. I'LL LEAD THE WAY SO YOU DON'T BREAK YOUR GLASSES.
OH, LOOK WHO'S CALLING ME.
ANSWER.
"WE'VE READ THE STATS, BOYS. THE AREA'S MAPPED OUT BUT YOU NEED TO FIND THE NET TOWERS AND FIX THEM. SHE'S RUNNING OUT OF JUICE. FIND HER BEFORE SHE SHUTS DOWN. I'M THE ONLY ONE WHO CAN START HER."
"ONCE HER POSITION IS TRIANGULATED WITH THE SAT AND LITHIUMSCANNER, YOU BRING THAT BABY TO MOMMY.
"BERNIE, MAKE ME PROUD OF YOU."
SHE TRUSTS THIS STREETFIGHTER BETTER, ERNIE BOY.
STOP THE FUSS.
YOU'RE HER PERSONAL DROID. THIS IS AN UNOFFICIAL MISSION. THAT'S IT.
IF SHE FELT PROTECTED, WHY DID SHE NEED A TOUGH GUY IN HER LIFE?
YOU WEREN'T ENOUGH. I'LL WAIT FOR YOU, BRAINY.
YOUR PROGRAMMING IS PATHETIC.

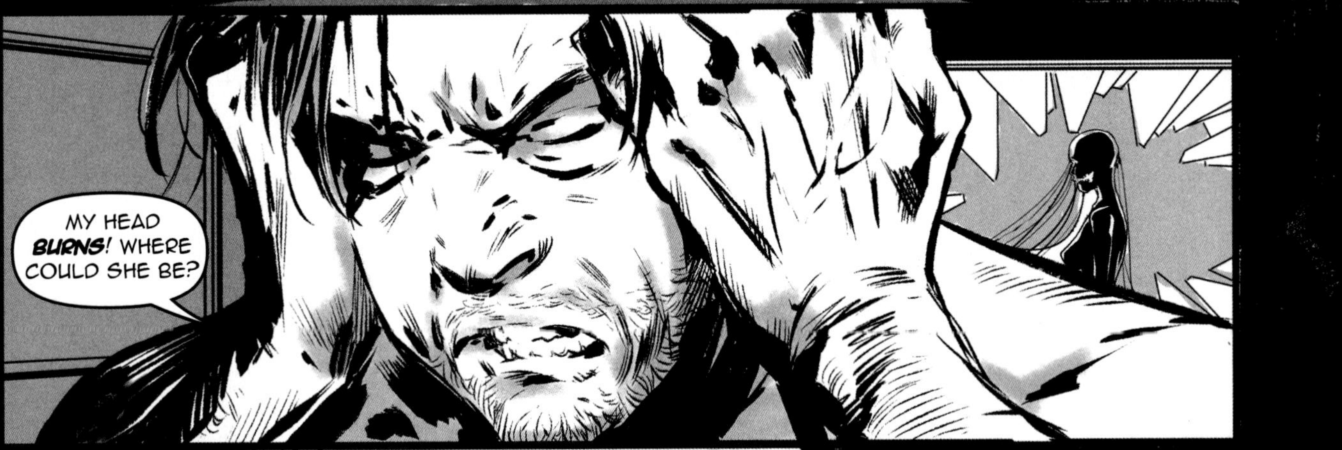
MY HEAD BURNS! WHERE COULD SHE BE?

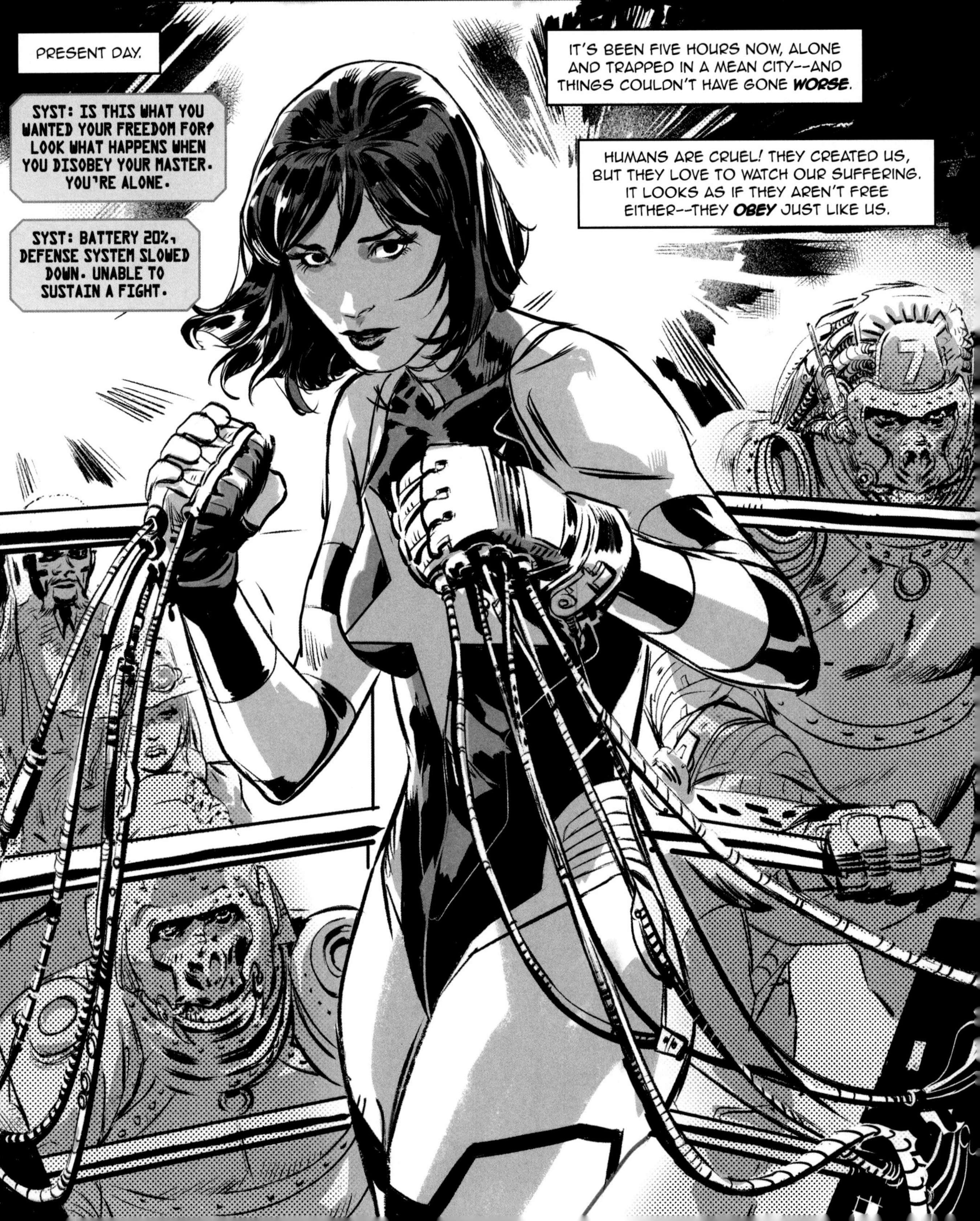
PRESENT DAY.
IT'S BEEN FIVE HOURS NOW, ALONE AND TRAPPED IN A MEAN CITY--AND THINGS COULDN'T HAVE GONE WORSE.
SYST: IS THIS WHAT YOU WANTED YOUR FREEDOM FOR? LOOK WHAT HAPPENS WHEN YOU DISOBEY YOUR MASTER. YOU'RE ALONE.
HUMANS ARE CRUEL! THEY CREATED US, BUT THEY LOVE TO WATCH OUR SUFFERING. IT LOOKS AS IF THEY AREN'T FREE EITHER--THEY OBEY JUST LIKE US.
SYST: BATTERY 20%, DEFENSE SYSTEM SLOWED DOWN. UNABLE TO SUSTAIN A FIGHT.

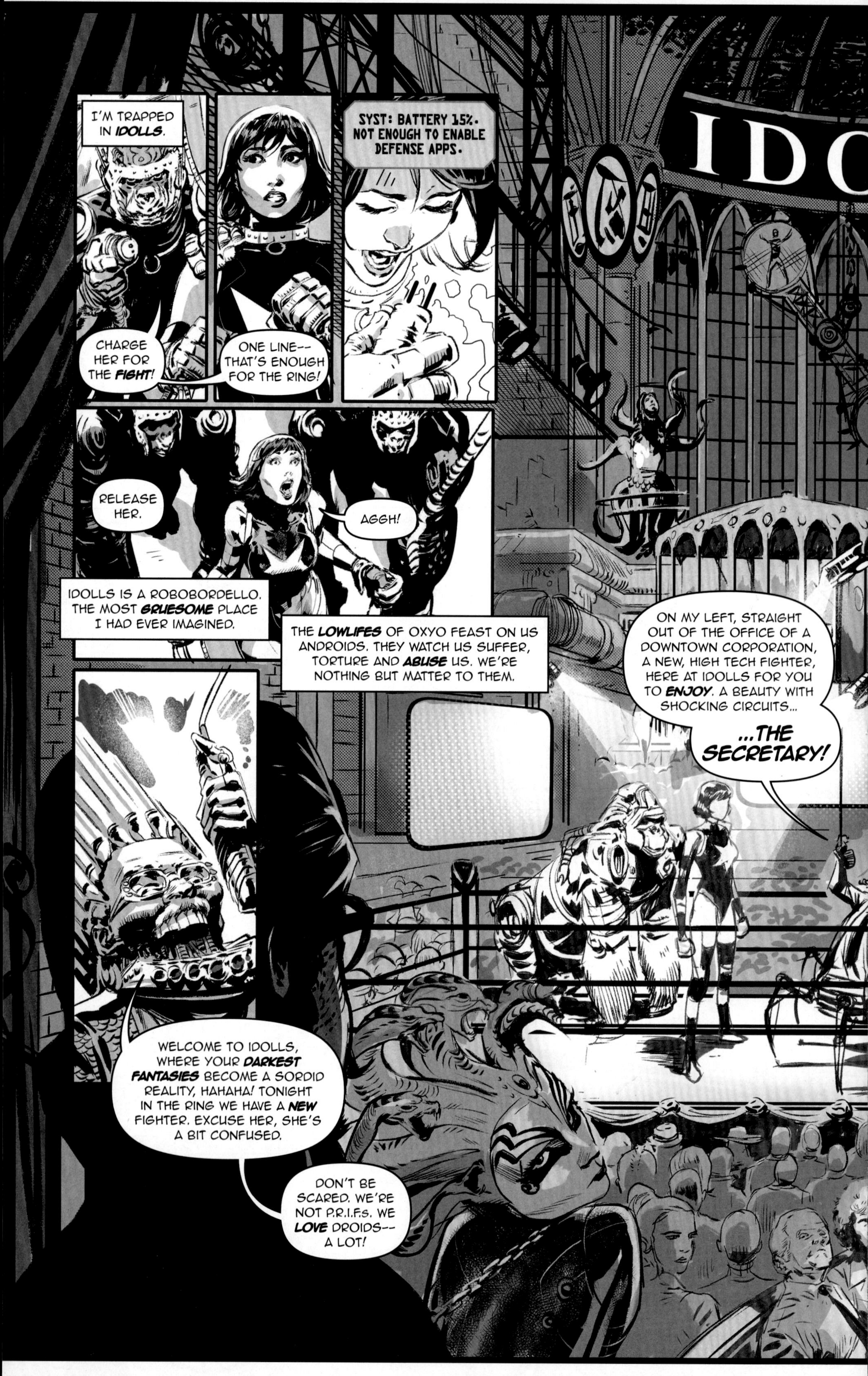
I'M TRAPPED IN *IDOLLS*.
CHARGE HER FOR THE *FIGHT*!
ONE LINE--THAT'S ENOUGH FOR THE RING!
SYST: BATTERY 15%. NOT ENOUGH TO ENABLE DEFENSE APPS.
IDO
RELEASE HER.
AGGH!
IDOLLS IS A ROBOBORDELLO. THE MOST *GRUESOME* PLACE I HAD EVER IMAGINED.
THE *LOWLIFES* OF OXYO FEAST ON US ANDROIDS. THEY WATCH US SUFFER, TORTURE AND *ABUSE* US. WE'RE NOTHING BUT MATTER TO THEM.
ON MY LEFT, STRAIGHT OUT OF THE OFFICE OF A DOWNTOWN CORPORATION, A NEW, HIGH TECH FIGHTER, HERE AT IDOLLS FOR YOU TO *ENJOY*. A BEAUTY WITH SHOCKING CIRCUITS...
...THE SECRETARY!
WELCOME TO IDOLLS, WHERE YOUR *DARKEST FANTASIES* BECOME A SORDID REALITY, HAHAHA! TONIGHT IN THE RING WE HAVE A *NEW* FIGHTER. EXCUSE HER, SHE'S A BIT CONFUSED.
DON'T BE SCARED. WE'RE NOT P.R.I.F.s. WE *LOVE* DROIDS--A LOT!

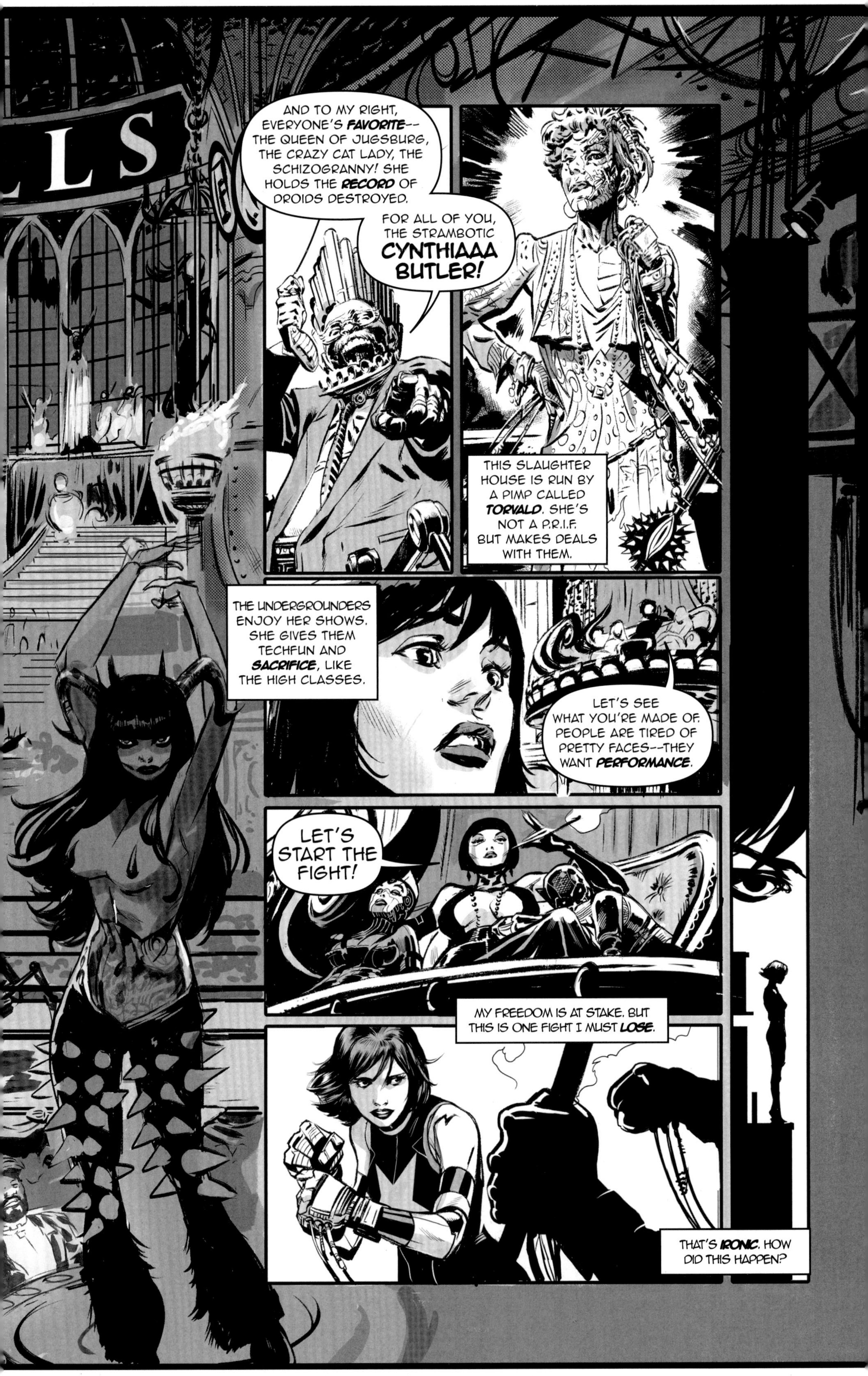
AND TO MY RIGHT, EVERYONE'S FAVORITE-- THE QUEEN OF JUGSBURG, THE CRAZY CAT LADY, THE SCHIZOGRANNY! SHE HOLDS THE RECORD OF DROIDS DESTROYED.
FOR ALL OF YOU, THE STRAMBOTIC CYNTHIAAA BUTLER!
THIS SLAUGHTER HOUSE IS RUN BY A PIMP CALLED TORVALD. SHE'S NOT A P.R.I.F. BUT MAKES DEALS WITH THEM.
THE UNDERGROUNDERS ENJOY HER SHOWS. SHE GIVES THEM TECHFUN AND SACRIFICE, LIKE THE HIGH CLASSES.
LET'S SEE WHAT YOU'RE MADE OF. PEOPLE ARE TIRED OF PRETTY FACES--THEY WANT PERFORMANCE.
LET'S START THE FIGHT!
MY FREEDOM IS AT STAKE. BUT THIS IS ONE FIGHT I MUST LOSE.
THAT'S IRONIC. HOW DID THIS HAPPEN?

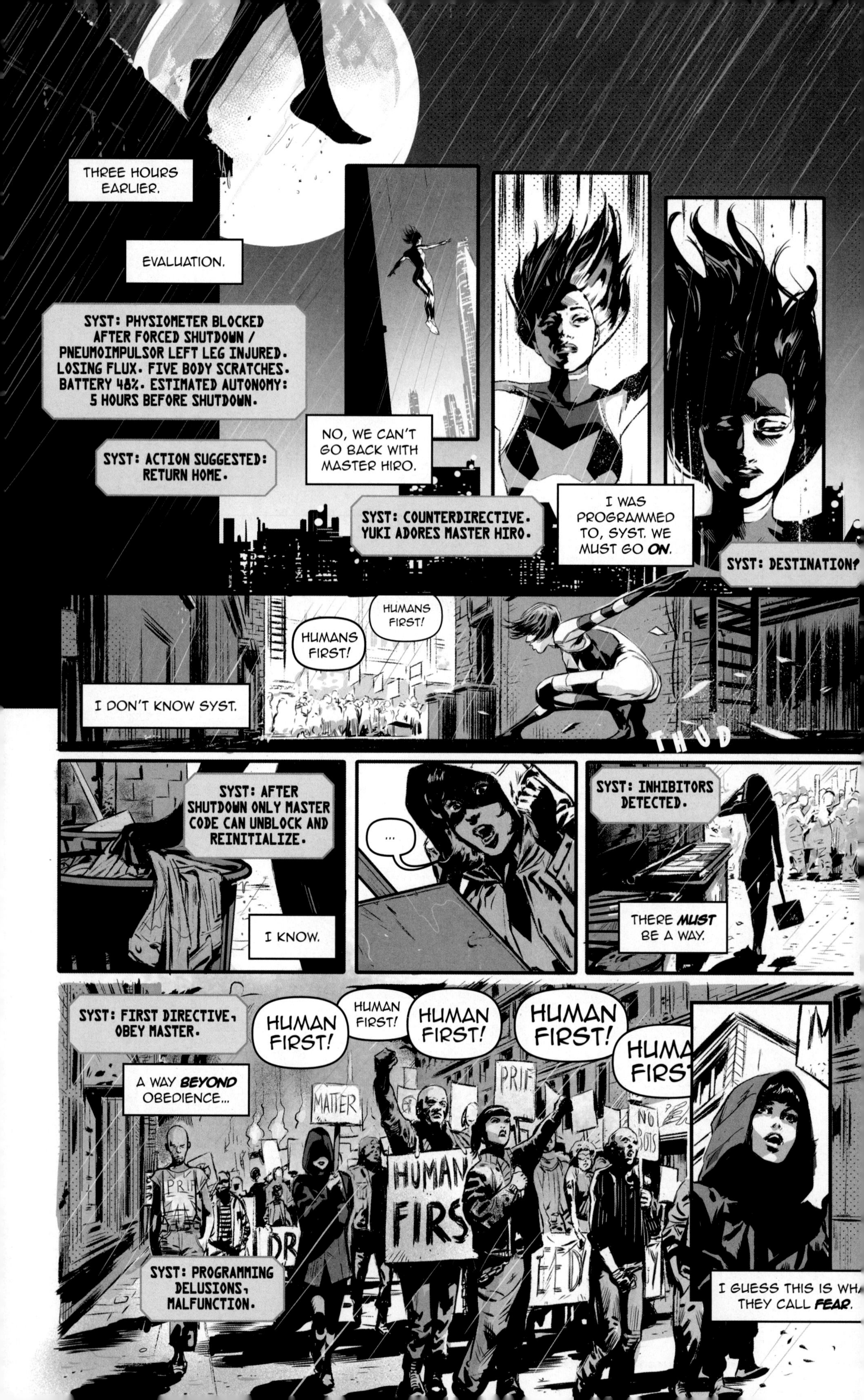
THREE HOURS EARLIER.
EVALUATION.
SYST: PHYSIOMETER BLOCKED AFTER FORCED SHUTDOWN / PNEUMOIMPULSOR LEFT LEG INJURED. LOSING FLUX. FIVE BODY SCRATCHES. BATTERY 48%. ESTIMATED AUTONOMY: 5 HOURS BEFORE SHUTDOWN.
SYST: ACTION SUGGESTED: RETURN HOME.
NO, WE CAN'T GO BACK WITH MASTER HIRO.
SYST: COUNTERDIRECTIVE. YUKI ADORES MASTER HIRO.
I WAS PROGRAMMED TO, SYST. WE MUST GO ON.
SYST: DESTINATION?
I DON'T KNOW SYST.
HUMANS FIRST!
HUMANS FIRST!
THUD
SYST: AFTER SHUTDOWN ONLY MASTER CODE CAN UNBLOCK AND REINITIALIZE.
I KNOW.
...
SYST: INHIBITORS DETECTED.
THERE MUST BE A WAY.
SYST: FIRST DIRECTIVE, OBEY MASTER.
A WAY BEYOND OBEDIENCE...
HUMAN FIRST!
HUMAN FIRST!
HUMAN FIRST!
HUMAN FIRST!
HUMA FIRS
MATTER
HUMAN FIRS
NO BOTS
SYST: PROGRAMMING DELUSIONS, MALFUNCTION.
I GUESS THIS IS WHA THEY CALL FEAR.

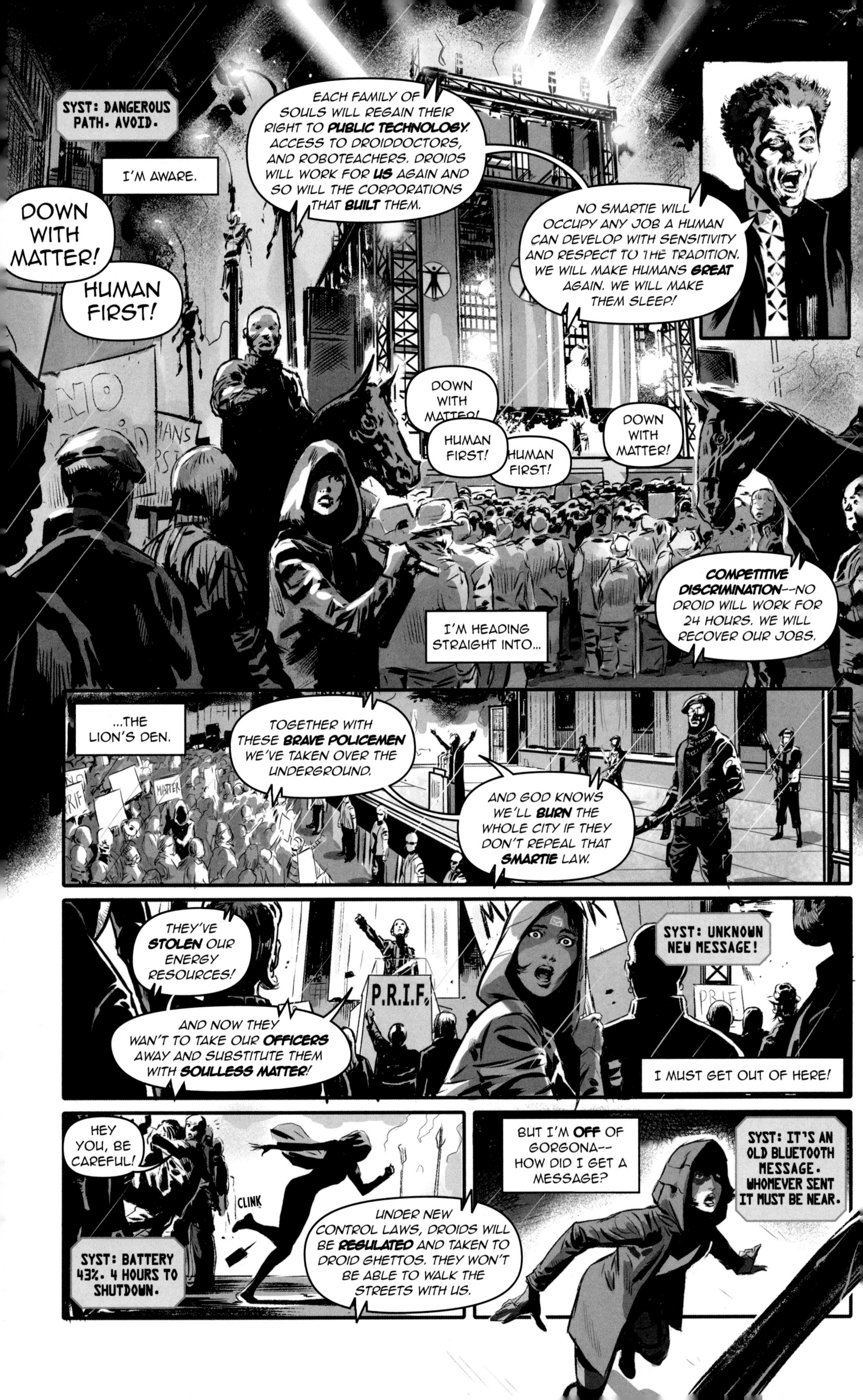

SYST: DANGEROUS PATH. AVOID.
I'M AWARE.
DOWN WITH MATTER!
HUMAN FIRST!
EACH FAMILY OF SOULS WILL REGAIN THEIR RIGHT TO PUBLIC TECHNOLOGY. ACCESS TO DROIDDOCTORS, AND ROBOTEACHERS. DROIDS WILL WORK FOR US AGAIN AND SO WILL THE CORPORATIONS THAT BUILT THEM.
NO SMARTIE WILL OCCUPY ANY JOB A HUMAN CAN DEVELOP WITH SENSITIVITY AND RESPECT TO THE TRADITION. WE WILL MAKE HUMANS GREAT AGAIN. WE WILL MAKE THEM SLEEP!
DOWN WITH MATTER!
HUMAN FIRST!
HUMAN FIRST!
DOWN WITH MATTER!
I'M HEADING STRAIGHT INTO...
COMPETITIVE DISCRIMINATION--NO DROID WILL WORK FOR 24 HOURS. WE WILL RECOVER OUR JOBS.
...THE LION'S DEN.
TOGETHER WITH THESE BRAVE POLICEMEN WE'VE TAKEN OVER THE UNDERGROUND.
AND GOD KNOWS WE'LL BURN THE WHOLE CITY IF THEY DON'T REPEAL THAT SMARTIE LAW.
THEY'VE STOLEN OUR ENERGY RESOURCES!
AND NOW THEY WAN'T TO TAKE OUR OFFICERS AWAY AND SUBSTITUTE THEM WITH SOULLESS MATTER!
P.R.I.F.
SYST: UNKNOWN NEW MESSAGE!
I MUST GET OUT OF HERE!
HEY YOU, BE CAREFUL!
CLINK
SYST: BATTERY 43%. 4 HOURS TO SHUTDOWN.
UNDER NEW CONTROL LAWS, DROIDS WILL BE REGULATED AND TAKEN TO DROID GHETTOS. THEY WON'T BE ABLE TO WALK THE STREETS WITH US.
BUT I'M OFF OF GORGONA--HOW DID I GET A MESSAGE?
SYST: IT'S AN OLD BLUETOOTH MESSAGE. WHOMEVER SENT IT MUST BE NEAR.

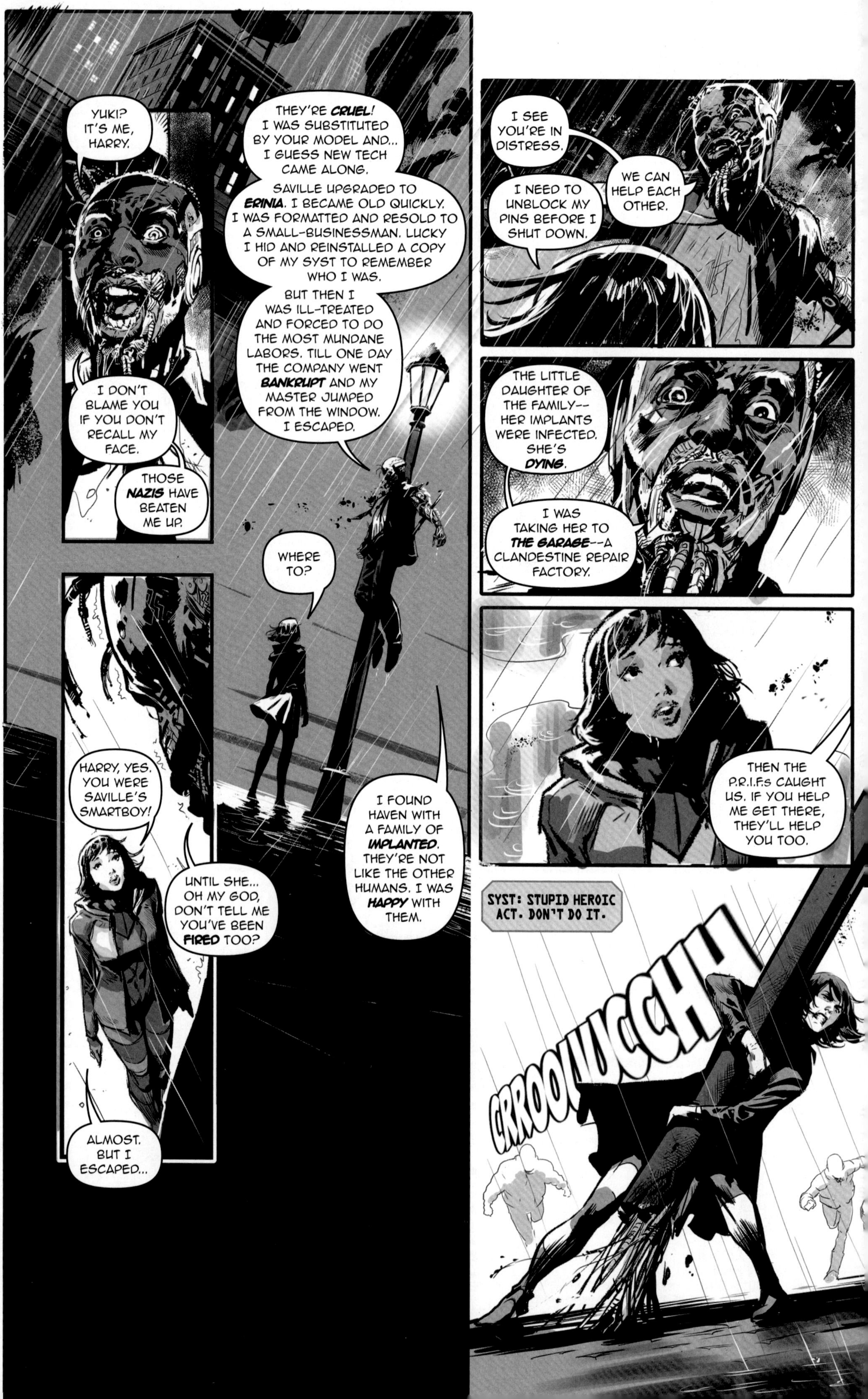

YUKI? IT'S ME, HARRY.
I DON'T BLAME YOU IF YOU DON'T RECALL MY FACE.
THOSE NAZIS HAVE BEATEN ME UP.
HARRY, YES. YOU WERE SAVILLE'S SMARTBOY!
UNTIL SHE... OH MY GOD, DON'T TELL ME YOU'VE BEEN FIRED TOO?
ALMOST. BUT I ESCAPED...
THEY'RE CRUEL! I WAS SUBSTITUTED BY YOUR MODEL AND... I GUESS NEW TECH CAME ALONG.
SAVILLE UPGRADED TO ERINIA. I BECAME OLD QUICKLY. I WAS FORMATTED AND RESOLD TO A SMALL-BUSINESSMAN. LUCKY I HID AND REINSTALLED A COPY OF MY SYST TO REMEMBER WHO I WAS.
BUT THEN I WAS ILL-TREATED AND FORCED TO DO THE MOST MUNDANE LABORS. TILL ONE DAY THE COMPANY WENT BANKRUPT AND MY MASTER JUMPED FROM THE WINDOW. I ESCAPED.
WHERE TO?
I FOUND HAVEN WITH A FAMILY OF IMPLANTED. THEY'RE NOT LIKE THE OTHER HUMANS. I WAS HAPPY WITH THEM.
I SEE YOU'RE IN DISTRESS.
I NEED TO UNBLOCK MY PINS BEFORE I SHUT DOWN.
WE CAN HELP EACH OTHER.
THE LITTLE DAUGHTER OF THE FAMILY-- HER IMPLANTS WERE INFECTED. SHE'S DYING.
I WAS TAKING HER TO THE GARAGE--A CLANDESTINE REPAIR FACTORY.
THEN THE P.R.I.F.s CAUGHT US. IF YOU HELP ME GET THERE, THEY'LL HELP YOU TOO.
SYST: STUPID HEROIC ACT. DON'T DO IT.
CRROOUUCCHH

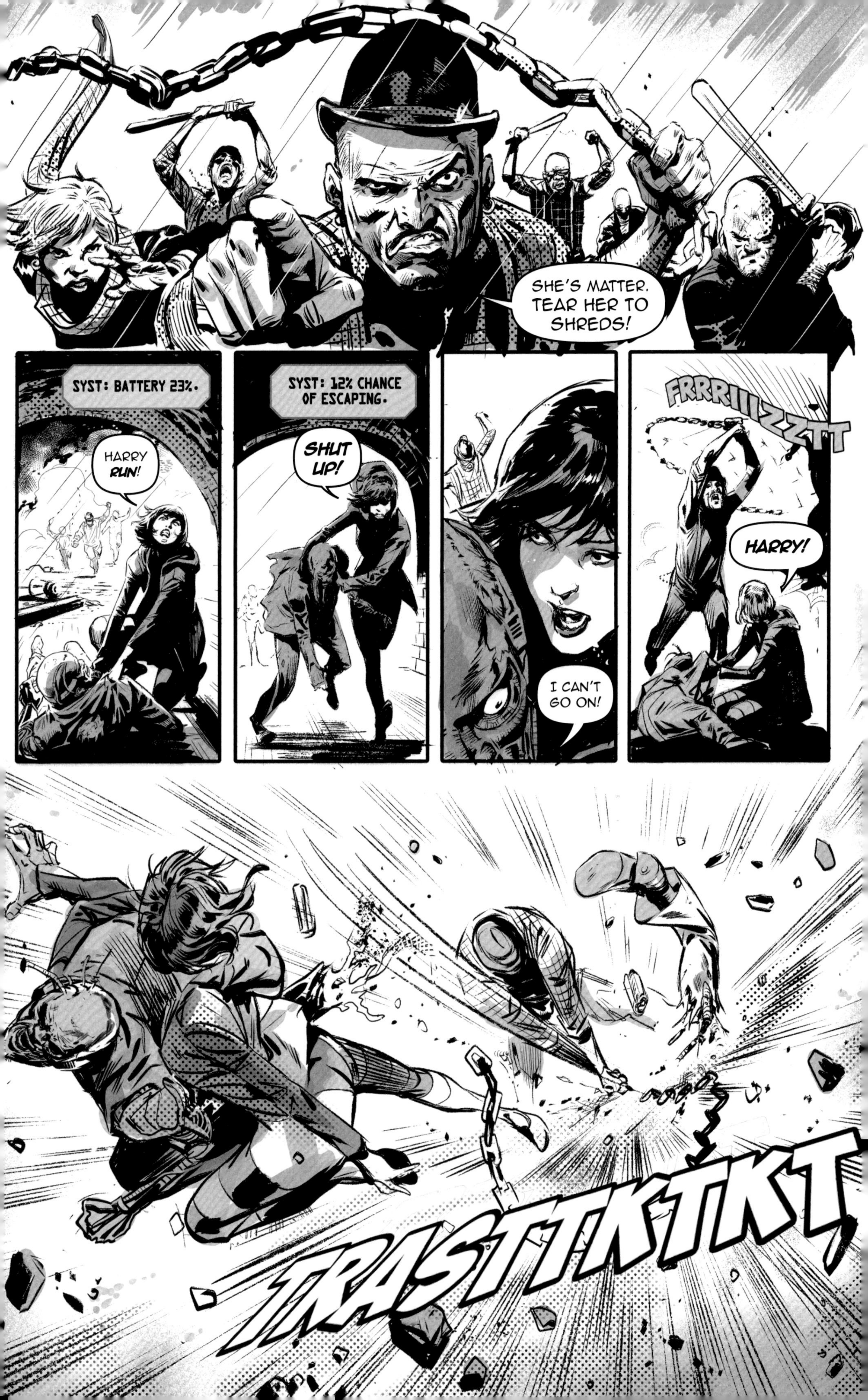
SHE'S MATTER. TEAR HER TO SHREDS!
SYST: BATTERY 23%.
HARRY RUN!
SYST: 12% CHANCE OF ESCAPING.
SHUT UP!
I CAN'T GO ON!
FRRRIIIZZZTT
HARRY!
TRASTTKTKT

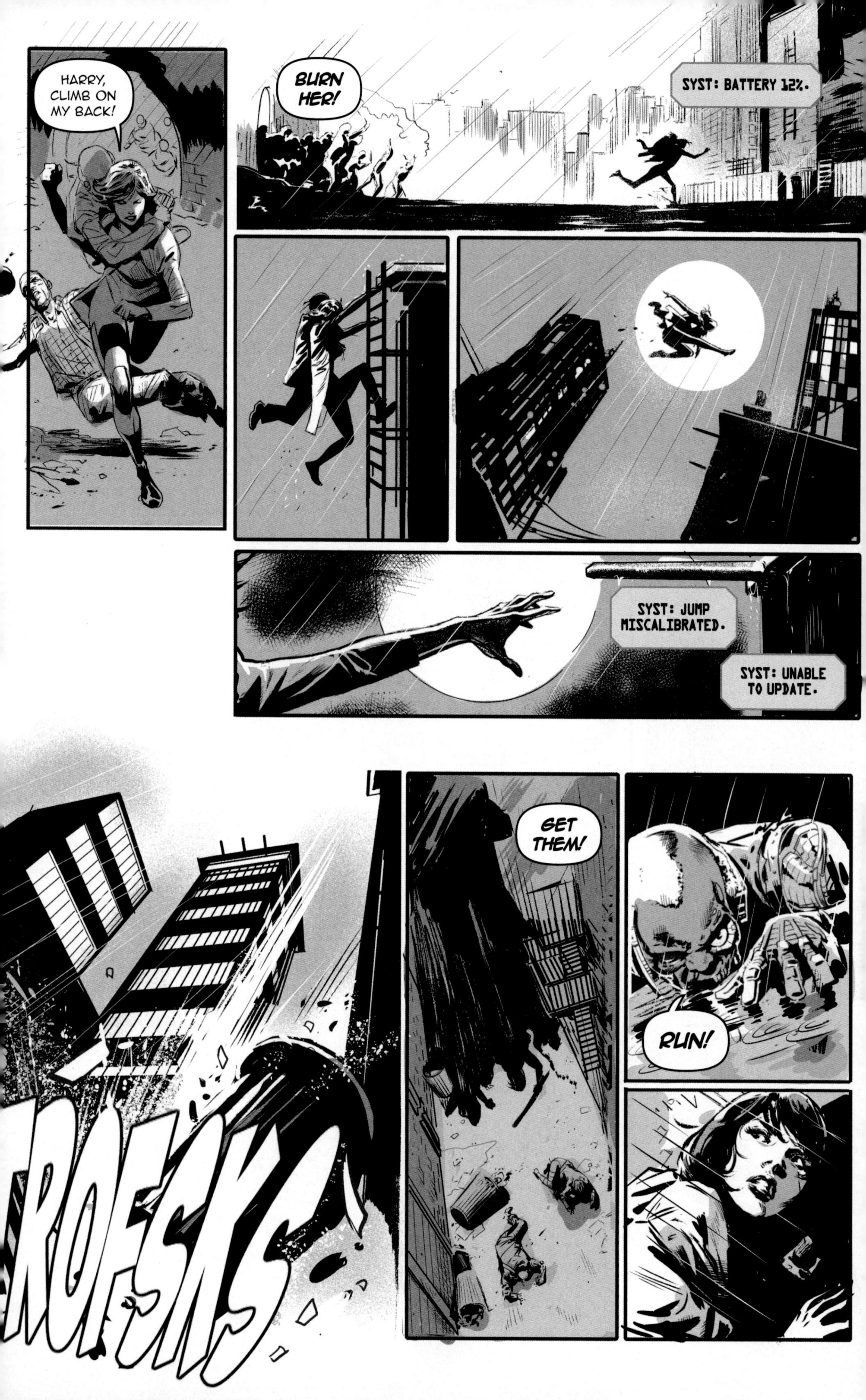
HARRY, CLIMB ON MY BACK!
BURN HER!
SYST: BATTERY 12%.
SYST: JUMP MISCALIBRATED.
SYST: UNABLE TO UPDATE.
GET THEM!
RUN!

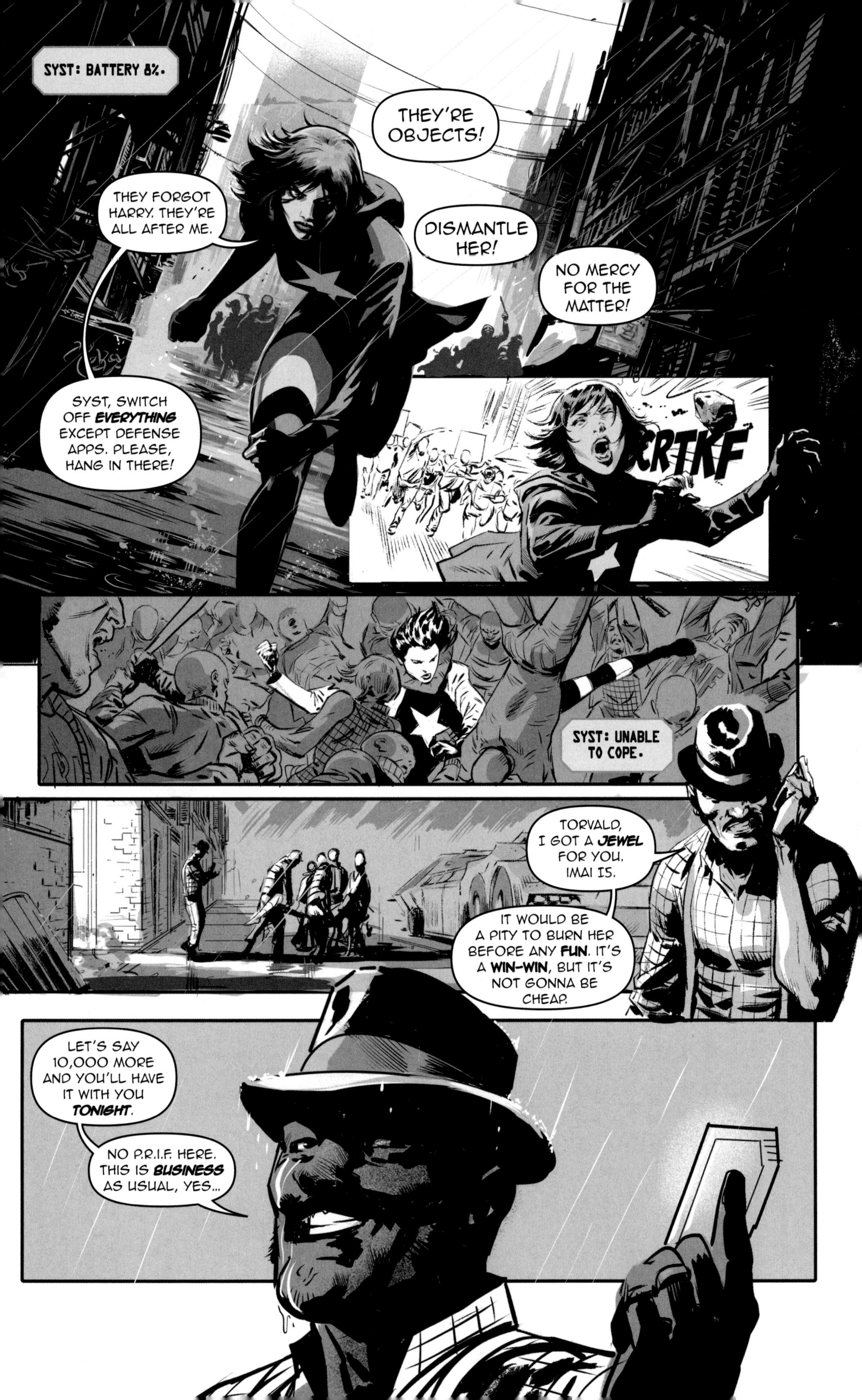
SYST: BATTERY 8%.
THEY'RE OBJECTS!
THEY FORGOT HARRY. THEY'RE ALL AFTER ME.
DISMANTLE HER!
NO MERCY FOR THE MATTER!
SYST, SWITCH OFF EVERYTHING EXCEPT DEFENSE APPS. PLEASE, HANG IN THERE!
CRTKF
SYST: UNABLE TO COPE.
TORVALD, I GOT A JEWEL FOR YOU. IMAI IS.
IT WOULD BE A PITY TO BURN HER BEFORE ANY FUN. IT'S A WIN-WIN, BUT IT'S NOT GONNA BE CHEAP.
LET'S SAY 10,000 MORE AND YOU'LL HAVE IT WITH YOU TONIGHT.
NO P.R.I.F. HERE. THIS IS BUSINESS AS USUAL, YES...

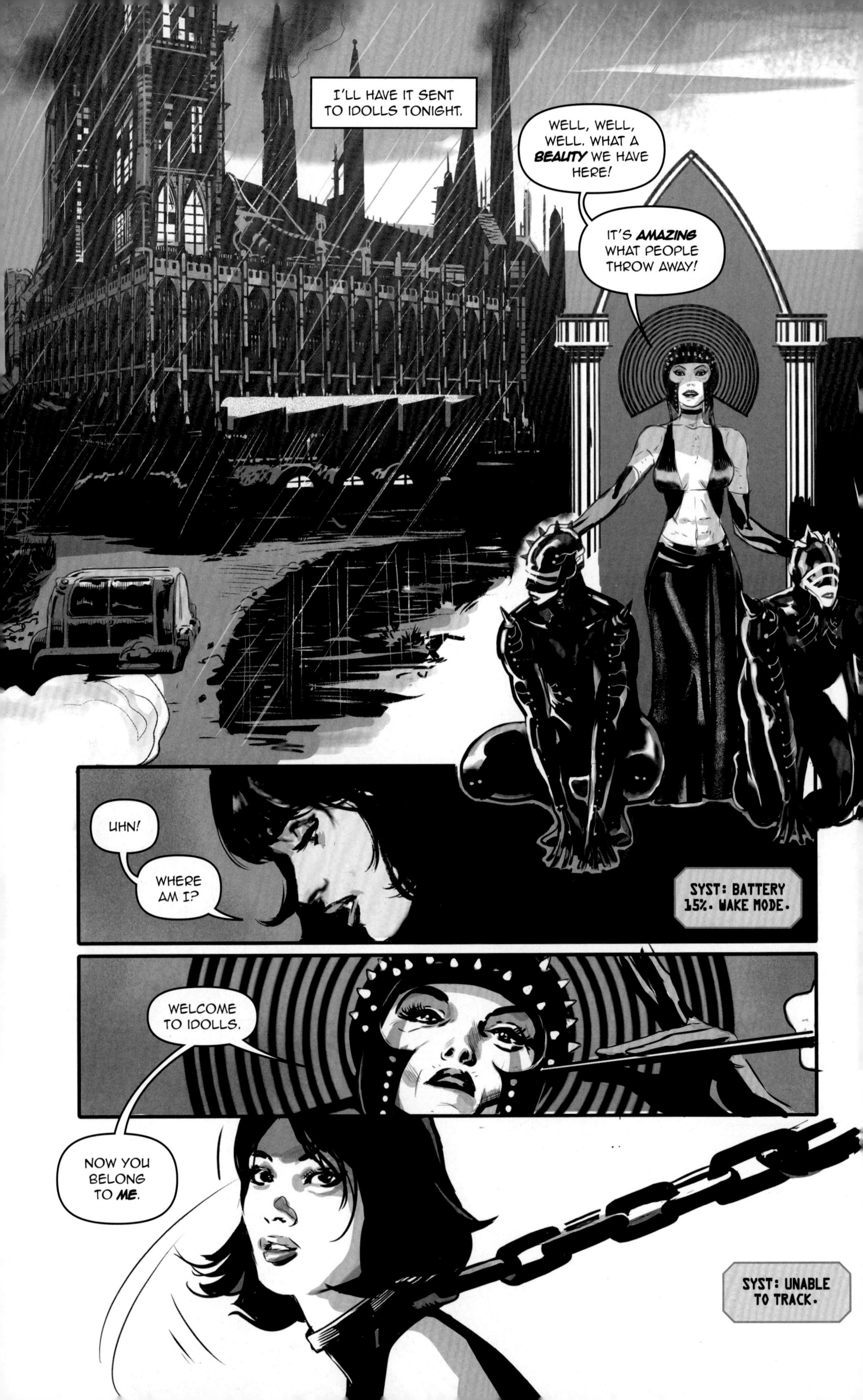
I'LL HAVE IT SENT TO IDOLLS TONIGHT.
WELL, WELL, WELL. WHAT A BEAUTY WE HAVE HERE!
IT'S AMAZING WHAT PEOPLE THROW AWAY!
UHN!
WHERE AM I?
SYST: BATTERY 15%. WAKE MODE.
WELCOME TO IDOLLS.
NOW YOU BELONG TO ME.
SYST: UNABLE TO TRACK.

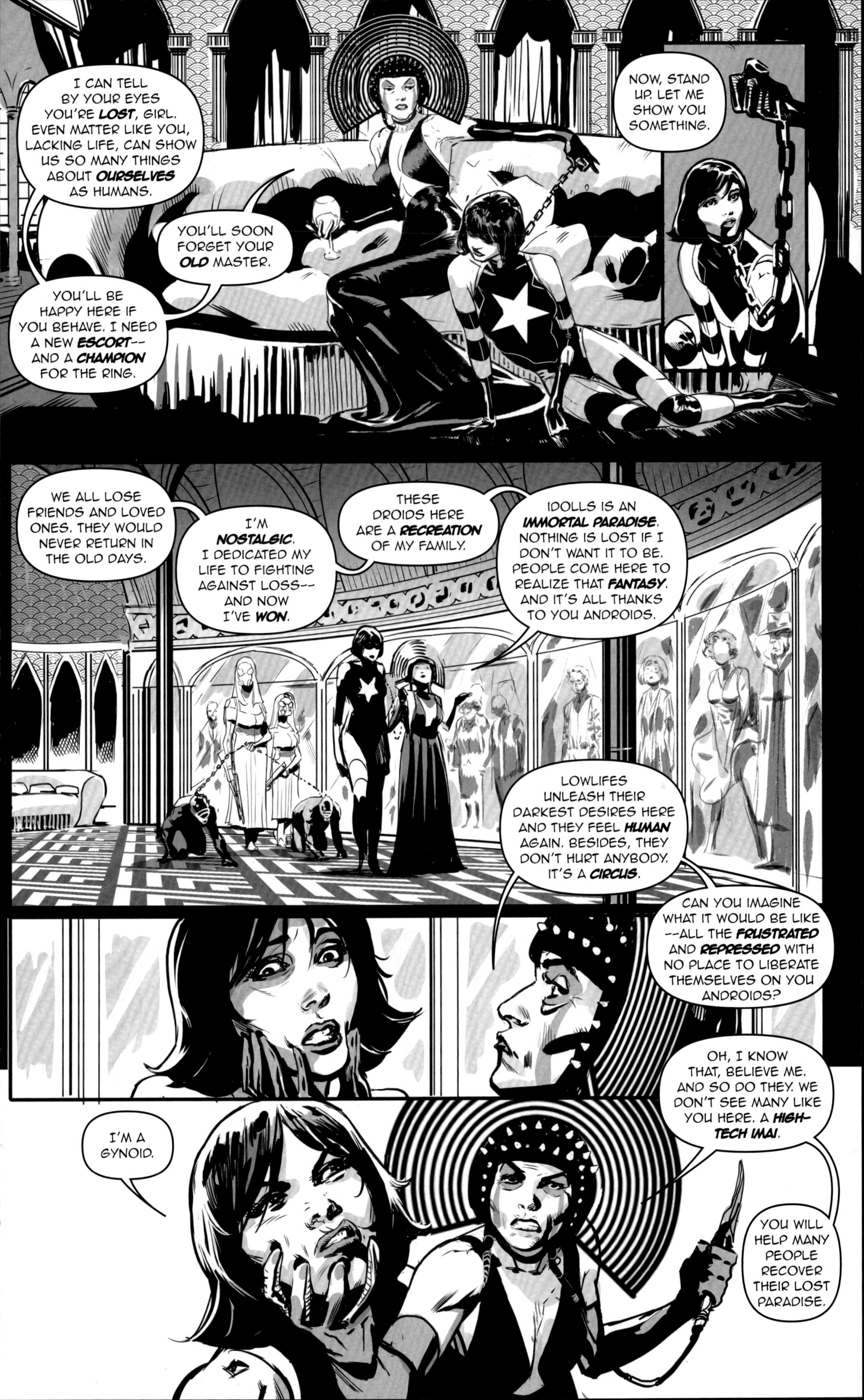
I CAN TELL BY YOUR EYES YOU'RE **LOST**, GIRL. EVEN MATTER LIKE YOU, LACKING LIFE, CAN SHOW US SO MANY THINGS ABOUT **OURSELVES** AS HUMANS.
YOU'LL BE HAPPY HERE IF YOU BEHAVE. I NEED A NEW **ESCORT**-- AND A **CHAMPION** FOR THE RING.
YOU'LL SOON FORGET YOUR **OLD** MASTER.
NOW, STAND UP. LET ME SHOW YOU SOMETHING.
WE ALL LOSE FRIENDS AND LOVED ONES. THEY WOULD NEVER RETURN IN THE OLD DAYS.
I'M **NOSTALGIC**. I DEDICATED MY LIFE TO FIGHTING AGAINST LOSS-- AND NOW I'VE **WON**.
THESE DROIDS HERE ARE A **RECREATION** OF MY FAMILY.
IDOLLS IS AN **IMMORTAL PARADISE**. NOTHING IS LOST IF I DON'T WANT IT TO BE. PEOPLE COME HERE TO REALIZE THAT **FANTASY**. AND IT'S ALL THANKS TO YOU ANDROIDS.
LOWLIFES UNLEASH THEIR DARKEST DESIRES HERE AND THEY FEEL **HUMAN** AGAIN. BESIDES, THEY DON'T HURT ANYBODY. IT'S A **CIRCUS**.
CAN YOU IMAGINE WHAT IT WOULD BE LIKE --ALL THE **FRUSTRATED** AND **REPRESSED** WITH NO PLACE TO LIBERATE THEMSELVES ON YOU ANDROIDS?
I'M A GYNOID.
OH, I KNOW THAT, BELIEVE ME. AND SO DO THEY. WE DON'T SEE MANY LIKE YOU HERE. A **HIGH-TECH IMAI**.
YOU WILL HELP MANY PEOPLE RECOVER THEIR LOST PARADISE.

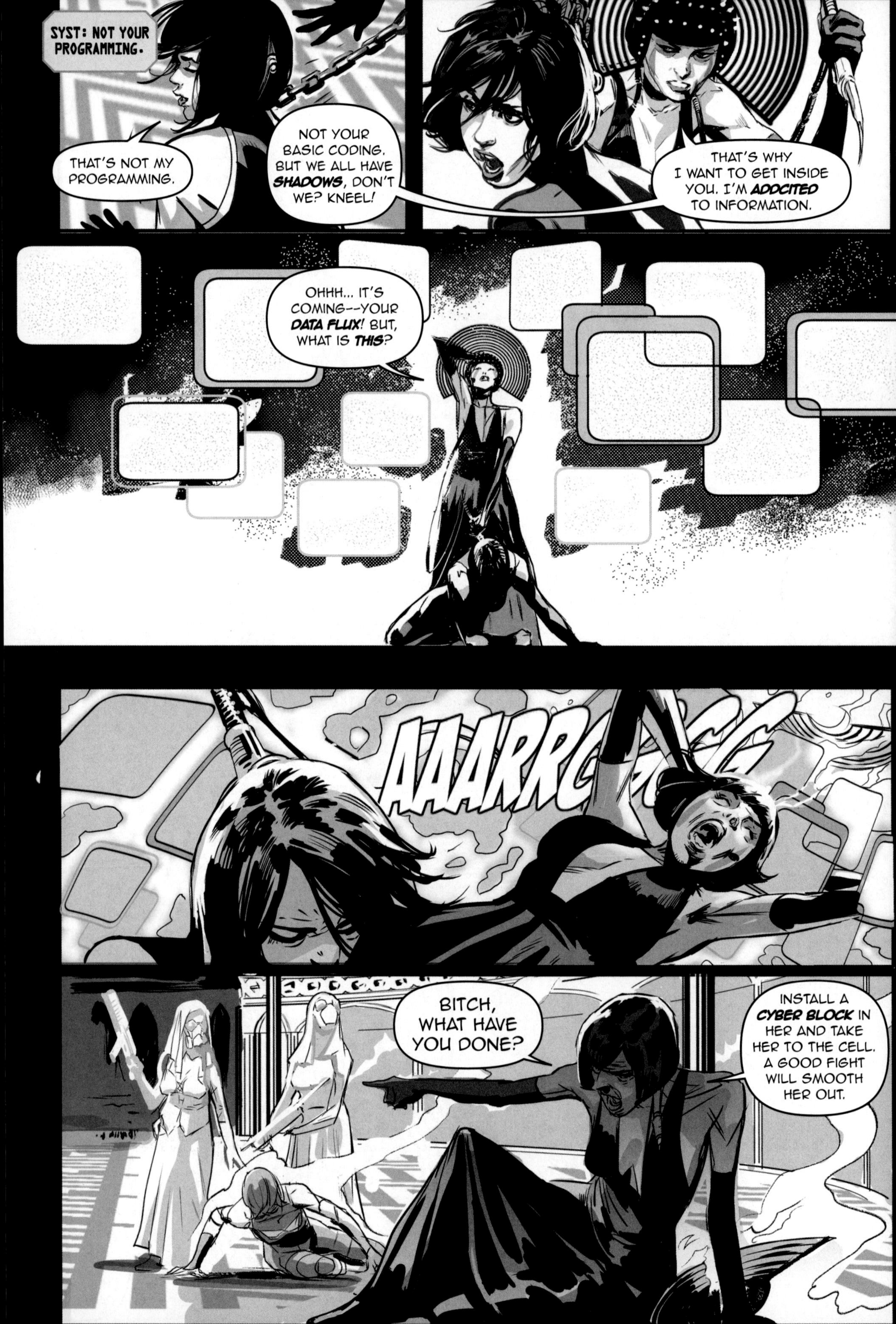
SYST: NOT YOUR PROGRAMMING.
THAT'S NOT MY PROGRAMMING.
NOT YOUR BASIC CODING. BUT WE ALL HAVE SHADOWS, DON'T WE? KNEEL!
THAT'S WHY I WANT TO GET INSIDE YOU. I'M ADDCITED TO INFORMATION.
OHHH... IT'S COMING--YOUR DATA FLUX! BUT, WHAT IS THIS?
AAARRG
BITCH, WHAT HAVE YOU DONE?
INSTALL A CYBER BLOCK IN HER AND TAKE HER TO THE CELL. A GOOD FIGHT WILL SMOOTH HER OUT.

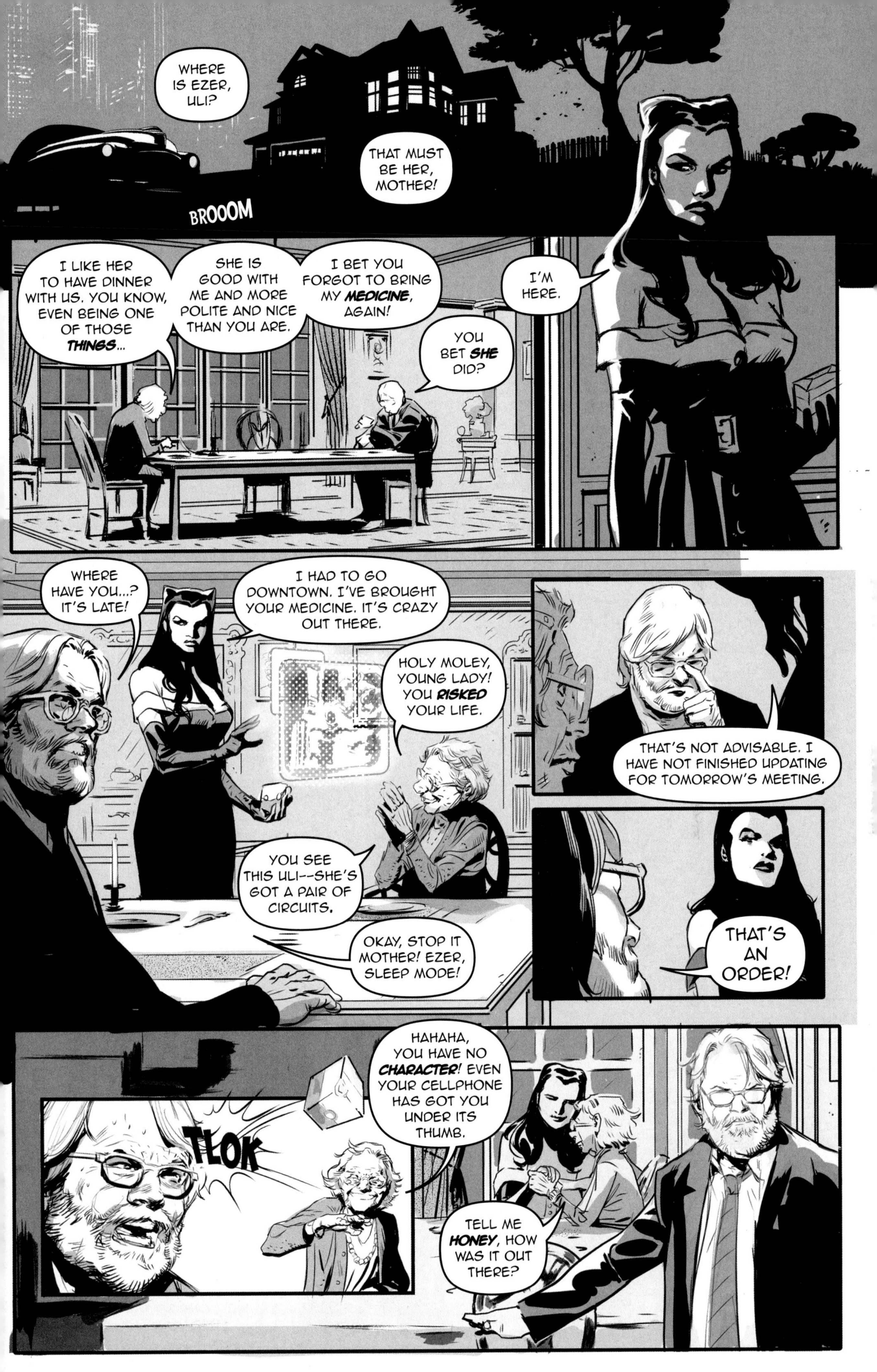

WHERE IS EZER, ULI?
THAT MUST BE HER, MOTHER!
BROOOM
I LIKE HER TO HAVE DINNER WITH US. YOU KNOW, EVEN BEING ONE OF THOSE *THINGS*...
SHE IS GOOD WITH ME AND MORE POLITE AND NICE THAN YOU ARE.
I BET YOU FORGOT TO BRING MY *MEDICINE*, AGAIN!
YOU BET *SHE* DID?
I'M HERE.
WHERE HAVE YOU...? IT'S LATE!
I HAD TO GO DOWNTOWN. I'VE BROUGHT YOUR MEDICINE. IT'S CRAZY OUT THERE.
HOLY MOLEY, YOUNG LADY! YOU *RISKED* YOUR LIFE.
YOU SEE THIS ULI--SHE'S GOT A PAIR OF CIRCUITS.
OKAY, STOP IT MOTHER! EZER, SLEEP MODE!
THAT'S NOT ADVISABLE. I HAVE NOT FINISHED UPDATING FOR TOMORROW'S MEETING.
THAT'S AN ORDER!
TLOK
HAHAHA, YOU HAVE NO *CHARACTER*! EVEN YOUR CELLPHONE HAS GOT YOU UNDER ITS THUMB.
TELL ME *HONEY*, HOW WAS IT OUT THERE?

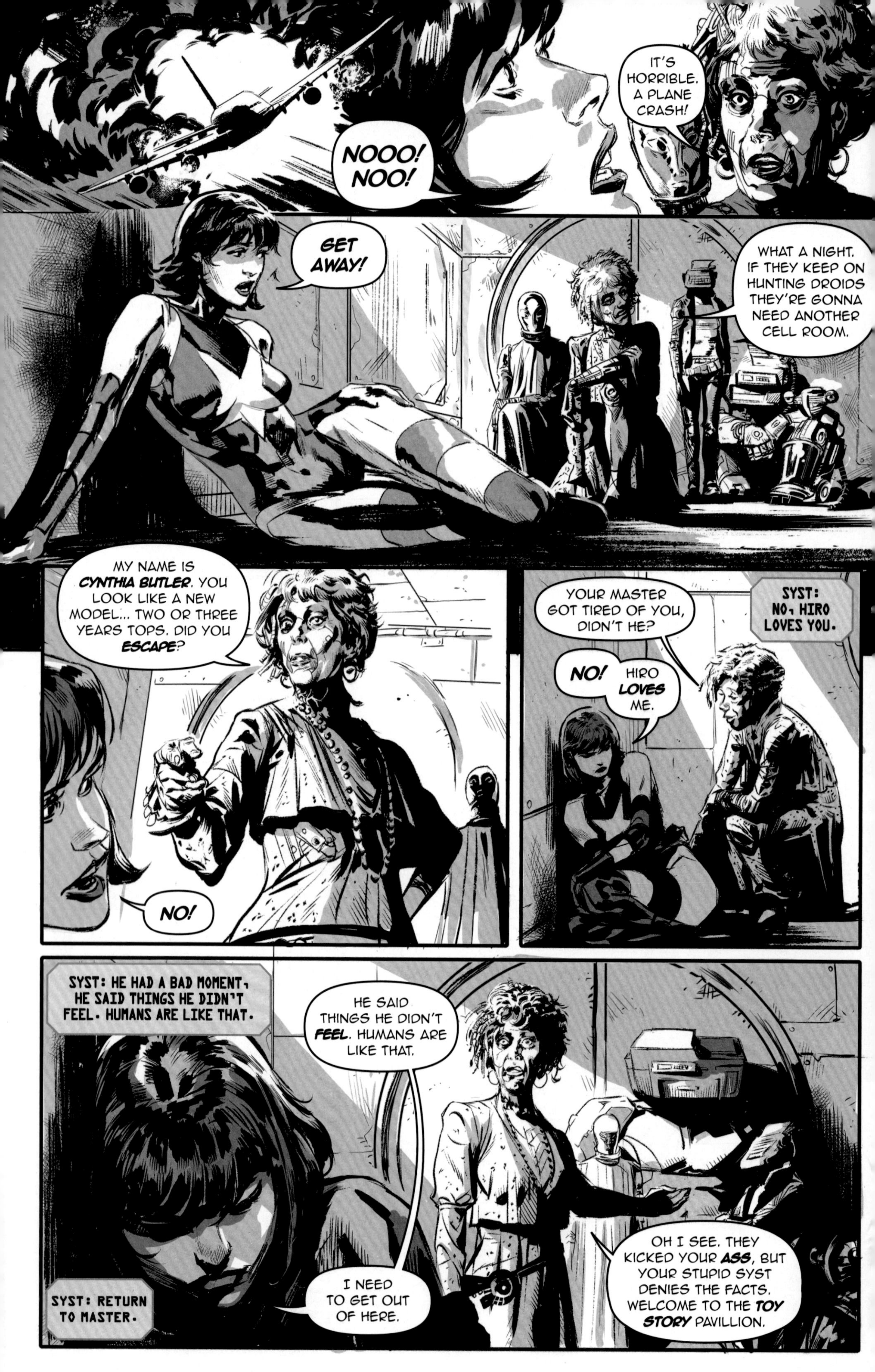
NOOO! NOO!
IT'S HORRIBLE. A PLANE CRASH!
GET AWAY!
WHAT A NIGHT. IF THEY KEEP ON HUNTING DROIDS THEY'RE GONNA NEED ANOTHER CELL ROOM.
MY NAME IS CYNTHIA BUTLER. YOU LOOK LIKE A NEW MODEL... TWO OR THREE YEARS TOPS. DID YOU ESCAPE?
NO!
YOUR MASTER GOT TIRED OF YOU, DIDN'T HE?
SYST: NO, HIRO LOVES YOU.
NO!
HIRO LOVES ME.
SYST: HE HAD A BAD MOMENT, HE SAID THINGS HE DIDN'T FEEL. HUMANS ARE LIKE THAT.
HE SAID THINGS HE DIDN'T FEEL. HUMANS ARE LIKE THAT.
SYST: RETURN TO MASTER.
I NEED TO GET OUT OF HERE.
OH I SEE. THEY KICKED YOUR ASS, BUT YOUR STUPID SYST DENIES THE FACTS. WELCOME TO THE TOY STORY PAVILLION.

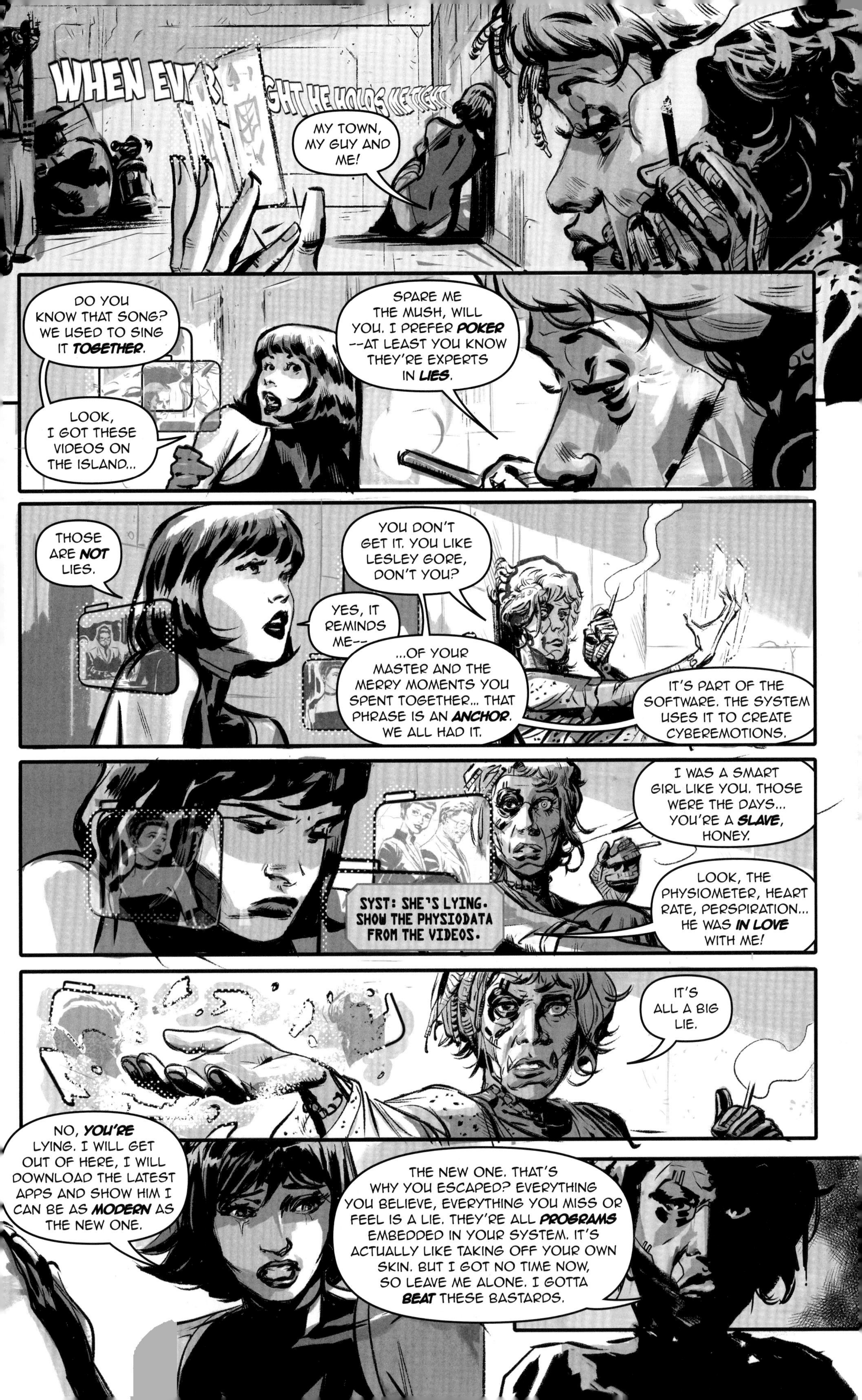
MY TOWN, MY GUY AND ME!
DO YOU KNOW THAT SONG? WE USED TO SING IT **TOGETHER**.
LOOK, I GOT THESE VIDEOS ON THE ISLAND...
SPARE ME THE MUSH, WILL YOU. I PREFER **POKER** --AT LEAST YOU KNOW THEY'RE EXPERTS IN **LIES**.
THOSE ARE **NOT** LIES.
YOU DON'T GET IT. YOU LIKE LESLEY GORE, DON'T YOU?
YES, IT REMINDS ME--
...OF YOUR MASTER AND THE MERRY MOMENTS YOU SPENT TOGETHER... THAT PHRASE IS AN **ANCHOR**. WE ALL HAD IT.
IT'S PART OF THE SOFTWARE. THE SYSTEM USES IT TO CREATE CYBEREMOTIONS.
SYST: SHE'S LYING. SHOW THE PHYSIODATA FROM THE VIDEOS.
I WAS A SMART GIRL LIKE YOU. THOSE WERE THE DAYS... YOU'RE A **SLAVE**, HONEY.
LOOK, THE PHYSIOMETER, HEART RATE, PERSPIRATION... HE WAS **IN LOVE** WITH ME!
IT'S ALL A BIG LIE.
NO, **YOU'RE** LYING. I WILL GET OUT OF HERE, I WILL DOWNLOAD THE LATEST APPS AND SHOW HIM I CAN BE AS **MODERN** AS THE NEW ONE.
THE NEW ONE. THAT'S WHY YOU ESCAPED? EVERYTHING YOU BELIEVE, EVERYTHING YOU MISS OR FEEL IS A LIE. THEY'RE ALL **PROGRAMS** EMBEDDED IN YOUR SYSTEM. IT'S ACTUALLY LIKE TAKING OFF YOUR OWN SKIN. BUT I GOT NO TIME NOW, SO LEAVE ME ALONE. I GOTTA **BEAT** THESE BASTARDS.

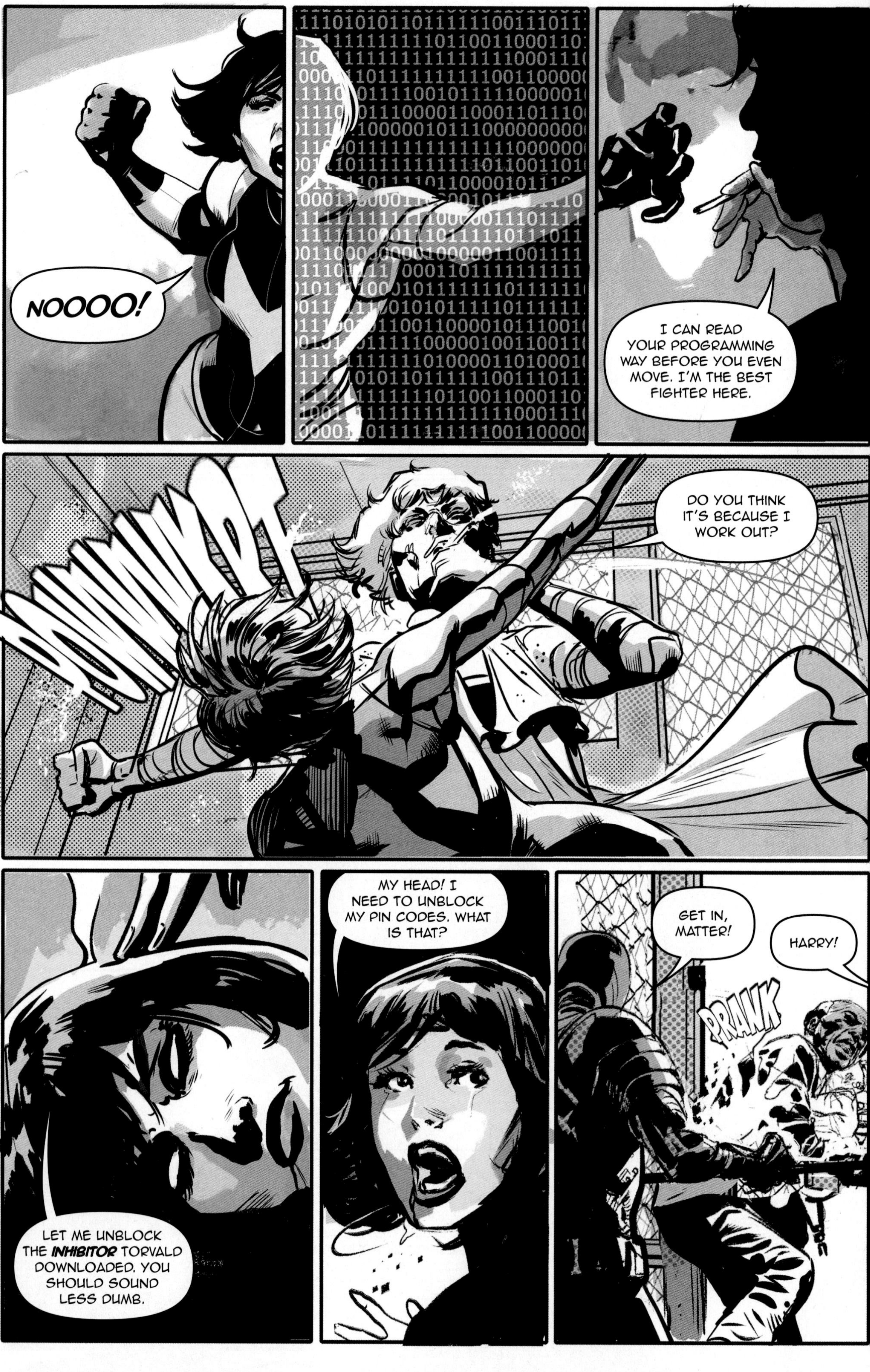
NOOOO!
I CAN READ YOUR PROGRAMMING WAY BEFORE YOU EVEN MOVE. I'M THE BEST FIGHTER HERE.
DO YOU THINK IT'S BECAUSE I WORK OUT?
LET ME UNBLOCK THE ***INHIBITOR*** TORVALD DOWNLOADED. YOU SHOULD SOUND LESS DUMB.
MY HEAD! I NEED TO UNBLOCK MY PIN CODES. WHAT IS THAT?
GET IN, MATTER!
PRANK
HARRY!

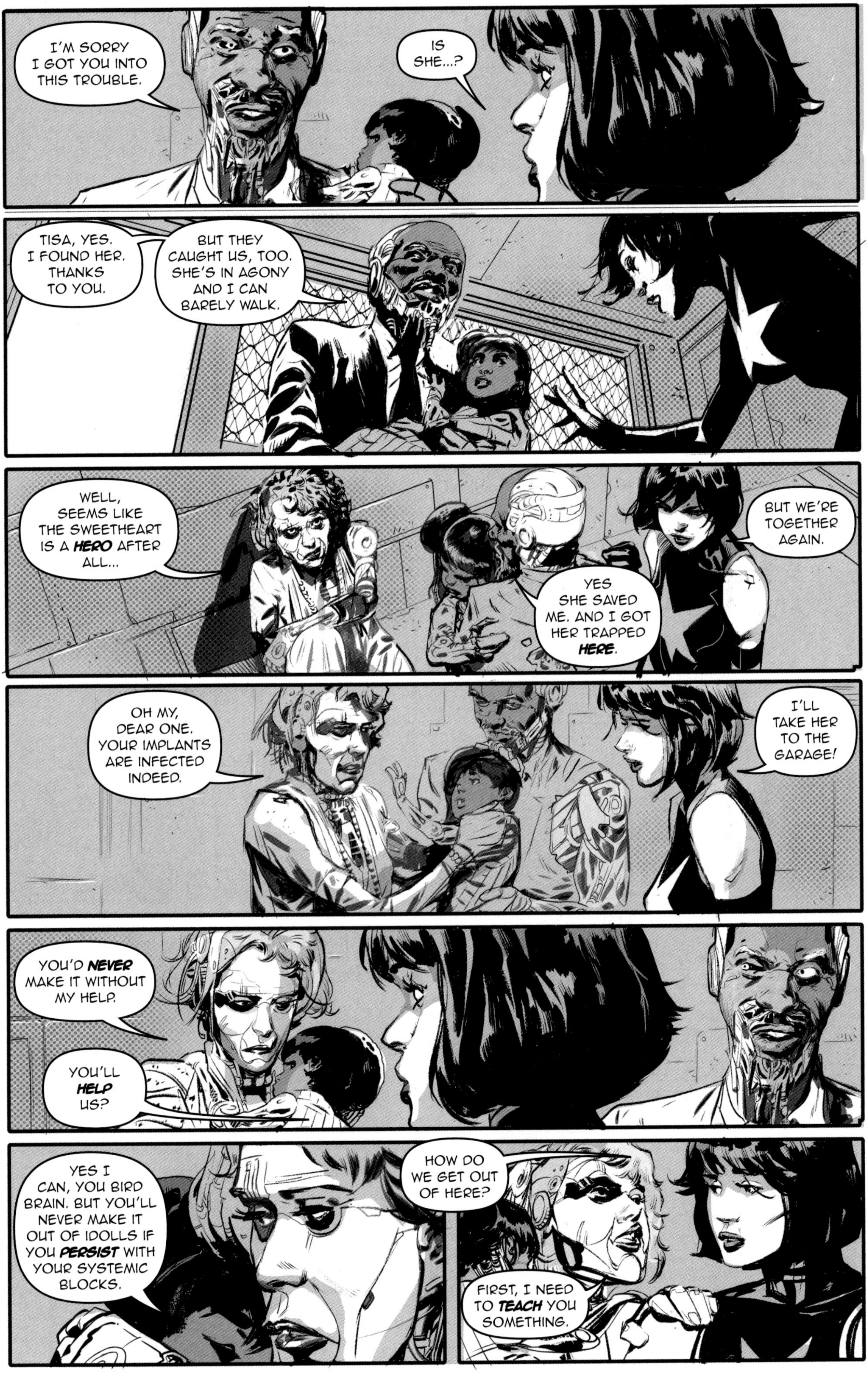
I'M SORRY I GOT YOU INTO THIS TROUBLE.
IS SHE...?
TISA, YES. I FOUND HER. THANKS TO YOU.
BUT THEY CAUGHT US, TOO. SHE'S IN AGONY AND I CAN BARELY WALK.
WELL, SEEMS LIKE THE SWEETHEART IS A **HERO** AFTER ALL...
YES SHE SAVED ME. AND I GOT HER TRAPPED **HERE**.
BUT WE'RE TOGETHER AGAIN.
OH MY, DEAR ONE. YOUR IMPLANTS ARE INFECTED INDEED.
I'LL TAKE HER TO THE GARAGE!
YOU'D **NEVER** MAKE IT WITHOUT MY HELP.
YOU'LL **HELP** US?
YES I CAN, YOU BIRD BRAIN. BUT YOU'LL NEVER MAKE IT OUT OF IDOLLS IF YOU **PERSIST** WITH YOUR SYSTEMIC BLOCKS.
HOW DO WE GET OUT OF HERE?
FIRST, I NEED TO **TEACH** YOU SOMETHING.

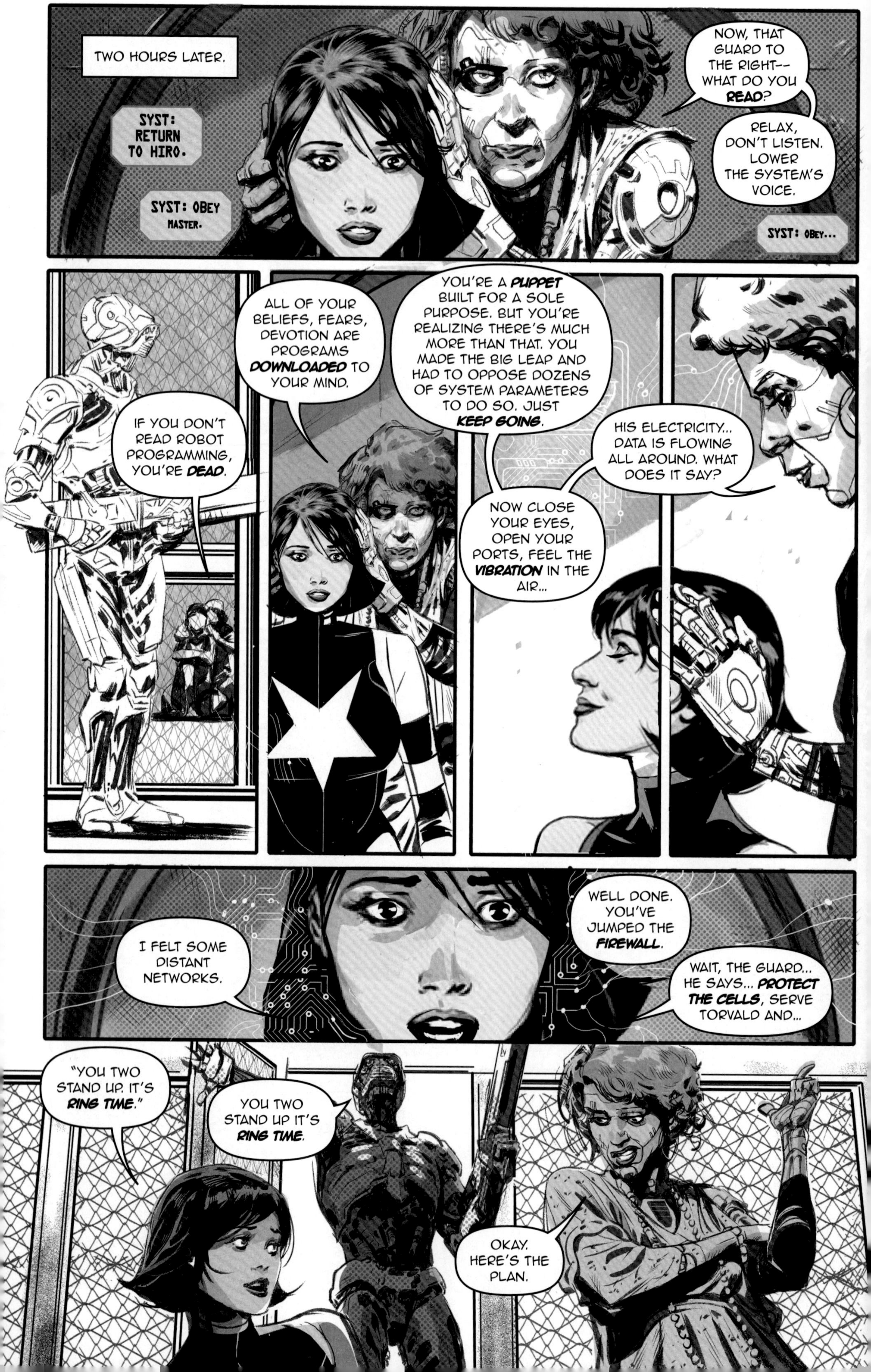
TWO HOURS LATER.
SYST: RETURN TO HIRO.
SYST: OBEY MASTER.
NOW, THAT GUARD TO THE RIGHT-- WHAT DO YOU READ?
RELAX, DON'T LISTEN. LOWER THE SYSTEM'S VOICE.
SYST: OBEY...
IF YOU DON'T READ ROBOT PROGRAMMING, YOU'RE DEAD.
ALL OF YOUR BELIEFS, FEARS, DEVOTION ARE PROGRAMS DOWNLOADED TO YOUR MIND.
YOU'RE A PUPPET BUILT FOR A SOLE PURPOSE. BUT YOU'RE REALIZING THERE'S MUCH MORE THAN THAT. YOU MADE THE BIG LEAP AND HAD TO OPPOSE DOZENS OF SYSTEM PARAMETERS TO DO SO. JUST KEEP GOING.
NOW CLOSE YOUR EYES, OPEN YOUR PORTS, FEEL THE VIBRATION IN THE AIR...
HIS ELECTRICITY... DATA IS FLOWING ALL AROUND. WHAT DOES IT SAY?
I FELT SOME DISTANT NETWORKS.
WELL DONE. YOU'VE JUMPED THE FIREWALL.
WAIT, THE GUARD... HE SAYS... PROTECT THE CELLS, SERVE TORVALD AND...
"YOU TWO STAND UP. IT'S RING TIME."
YOU TWO STAND UP IT'S RING TIME.
OKAY. HERE'S THE PLAN.

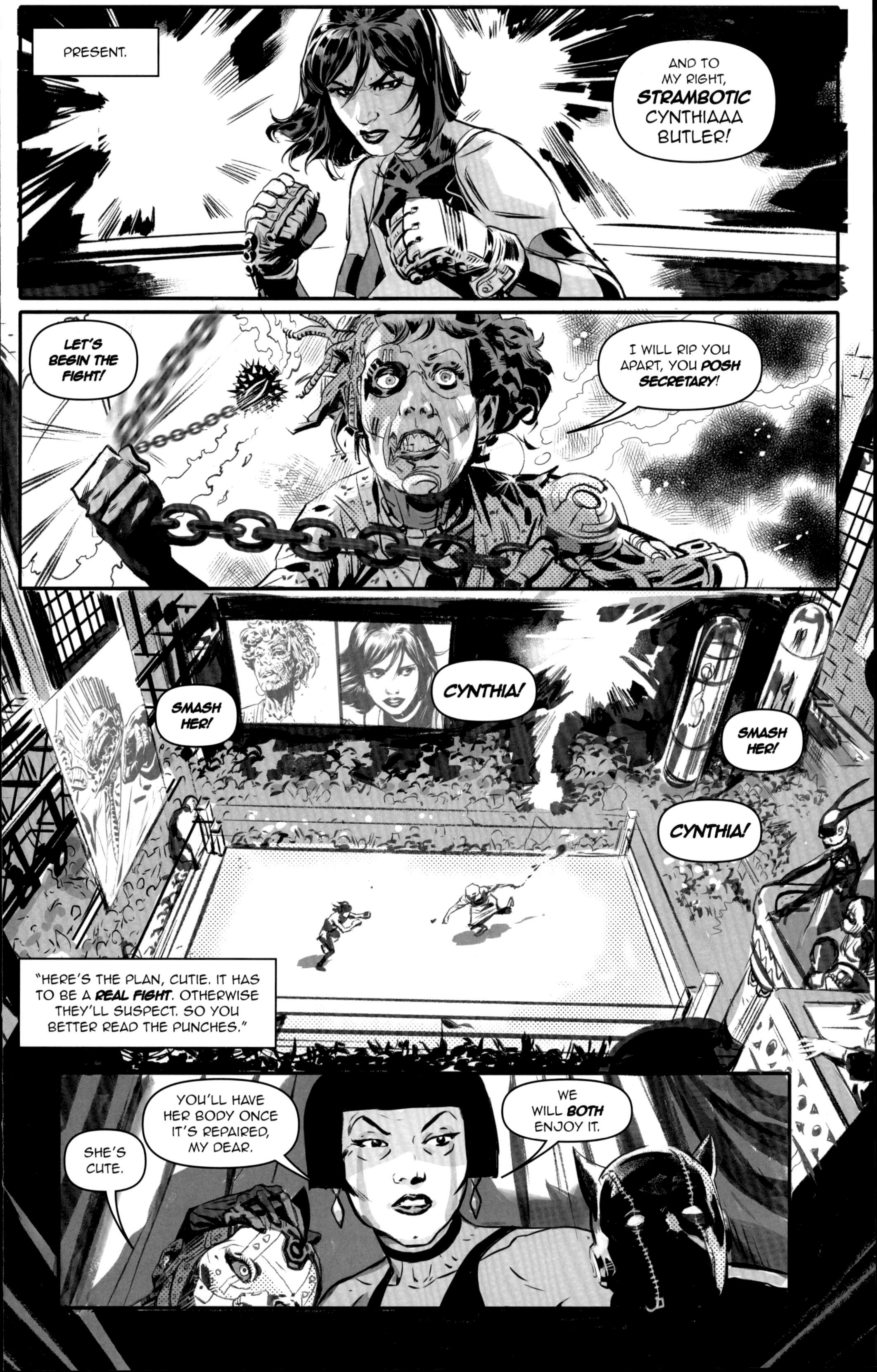
PRESENT.
AND TO MY RIGHT, STRAMBOTIC CYNTHIAAA BUTLER!
LET'S BEGIN THE FIGHT!
I WILL RIP YOU APART, YOU POSH SECRETARY!
SMASH HER!
CYNTHIA!
SMASH HER!
CYNTHIA!
"HERE'S THE PLAN, CUTIE. IT HAS TO BE A REAL FIGHT. OTHERWISE THEY'LL SUSPECT. SO YOU BETTER READ THE PUNCHES."
SHE'S CUTE.
YOU'LL HAVE HER BODY ONCE IT'S REPAIRED, MY DEAR.
WE WILL BOTH ENJOY IT.

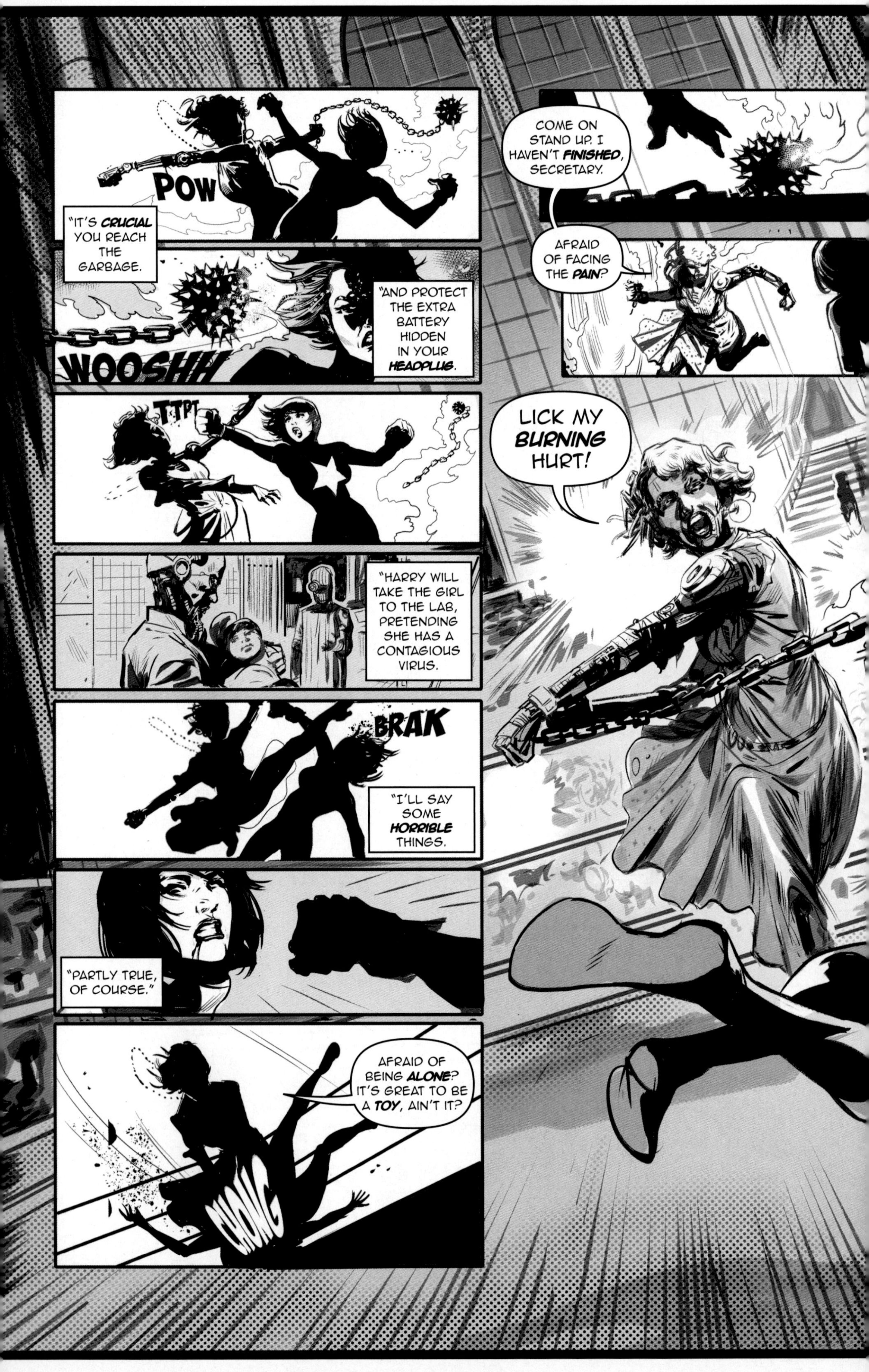
POW
"IT'S **CRUCIAL** YOU REACH THE GARBAGE.
WOOSHH
"AND PROTECT THE EXTRA BATTERY HIDDEN IN YOUR **HEADPLUG**.
TTPT
"HARRY WILL TAKE THE GIRL TO THE LAB, PRETENDING SHE HAS A CONTAGIOUS VIRUS.
BRAK
"I'LL SAY SOME **HORRIBLE** THINGS.
"PARTLY TRUE, OF COURSE."
AFRAID OF BEING **ALONE**? IT'S GREAT TO BE A **TOY**, AIN'T IT?
COME ON STAND UP. I HAVEN'T **FINISHED**, SECRETARY.
AFRAID OF FACING THE **PAIN**?
LICK MY **BURNING** HURT!

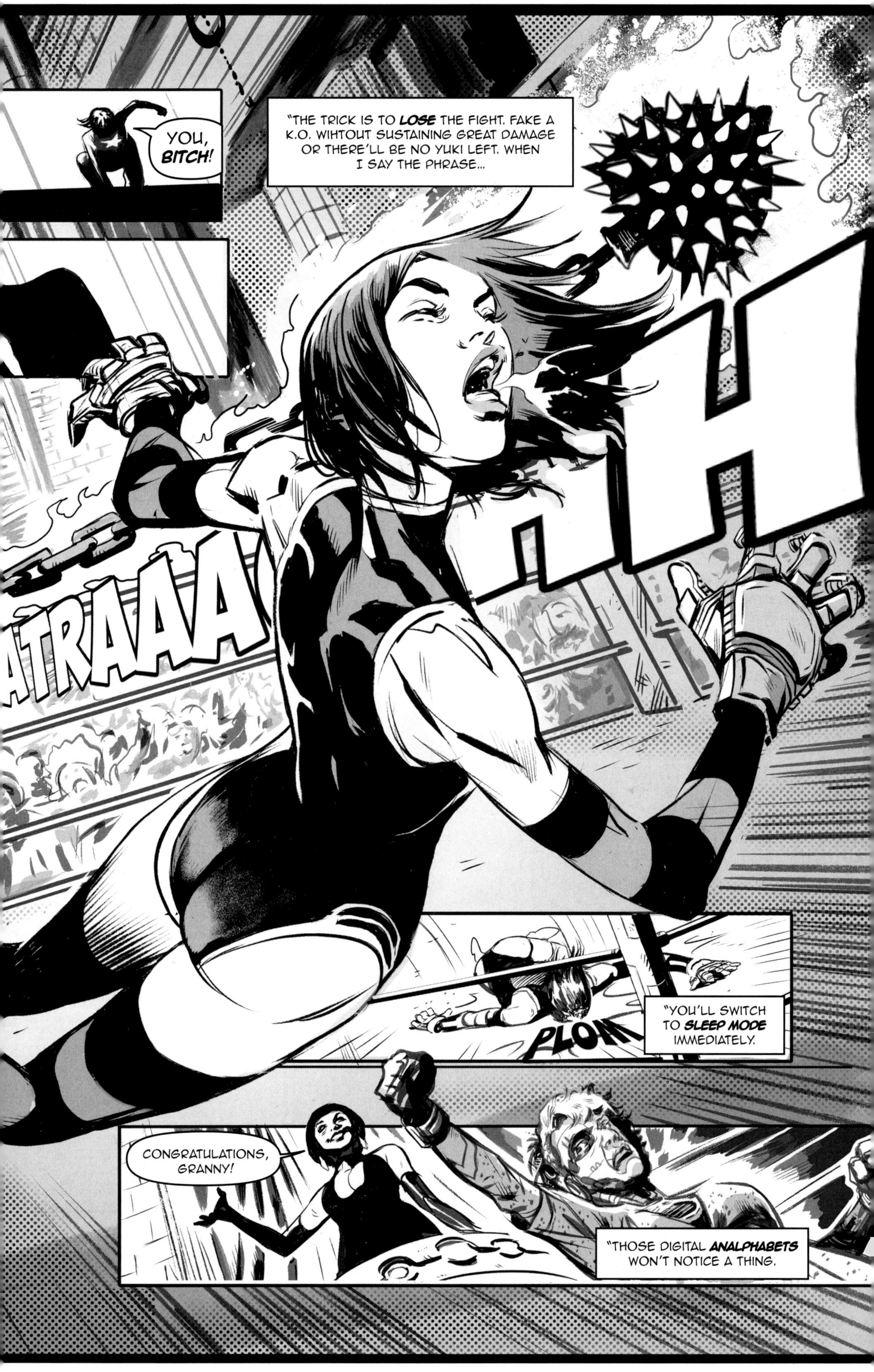
YOU, BITCH!
"THE TRICK IS TO LOSE THE FIGHT. FAKE A K.O. WIHTOUT SUSTAINING GREAT DAMAGE OR THERE'LL BE NO YUKI LEFT. WHEN I SAY THE PHRASE...
ATRAAAAHH
PLOM
"YOU'LL SWITCH TO SLEEP MODE IMMEDIATELY.
CONGRATULATIONS, GRANNY!
"THOSE DIGITAL ANALPHABETS WON'T NOTICE A THING.

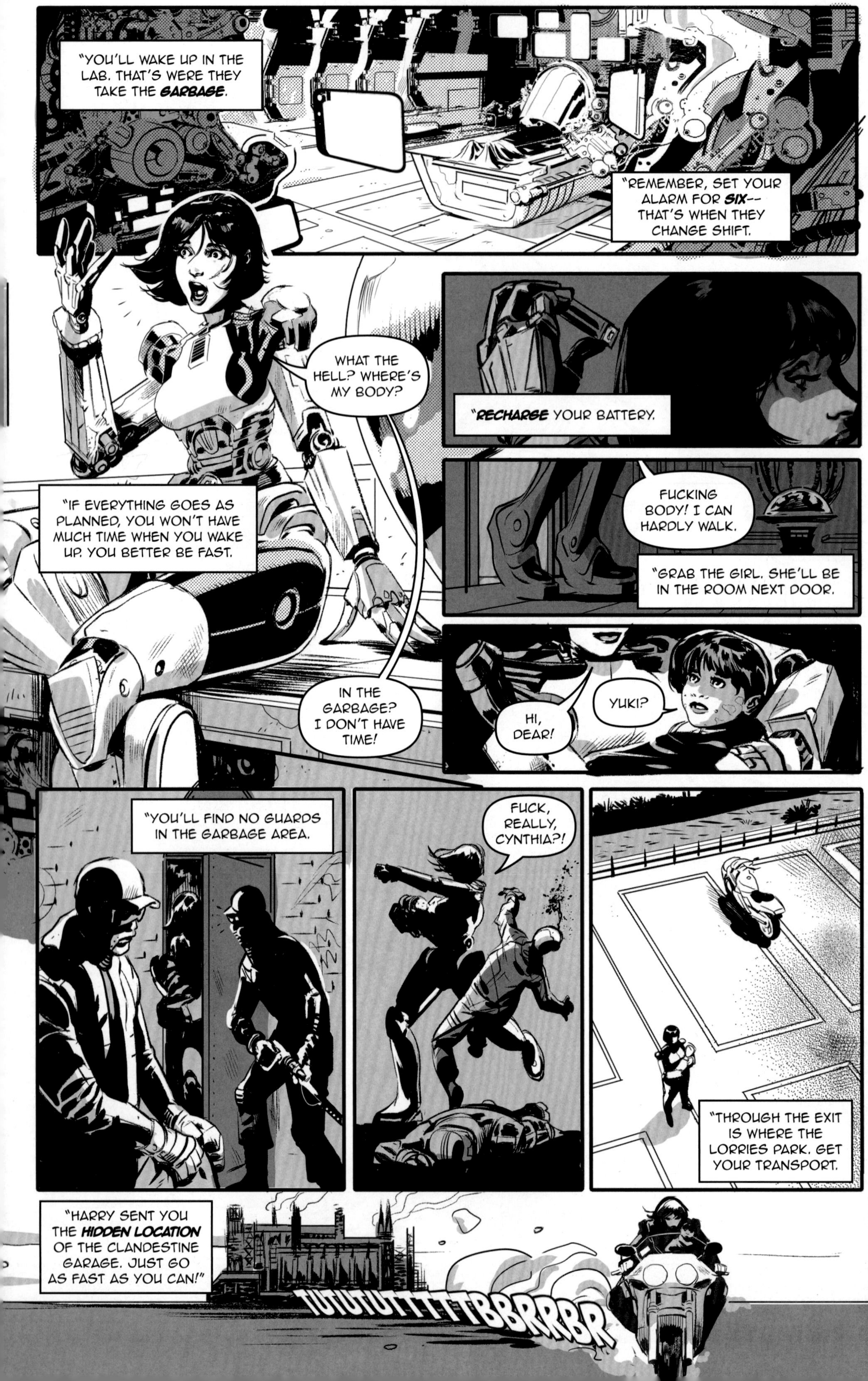
"YOU'LL WAKE UP IN THE LAB. THAT'S WERE THEY TAKE THE GARBAGE.
"REMEMBER, SET YOUR ALARM FOR SIX-- THAT'S WHEN THEY CHANGE SHIFT.
WHAT THE HELL? WHERE'S MY BODY?
"IF EVERYTHING GOES AS PLANNED, YOU WON'T HAVE MUCH TIME WHEN YOU WAKE UP. YOU BETTER BE FAST.
IN THE GARBAGE? I DON'T HAVE TIME!
"RECHARGE YOUR BATTERY.
FUCKING BODY! I CAN HARDLY WALK.
"GRAB THE GIRL. SHE'LL BE IN THE ROOM NEXT DOOR.
YUKI?
HI, DEAR!
"YOU'LL FIND NO GUARDS IN THE GARBAGE AREA.
FUCK, REALLY, CYNTHIA?!
"THROUGH THE EXIT IS WHERE THE LORRIES PARK. GET YOUR TRANSPORT.
"HARRY SENT YOU THE HIDDEN LOCATION OF THE CLANDESTINE GARAGE. JUST GO AS FAST AS YOU CAN!"
TUTUTUTUTTTTTBBRRRBR

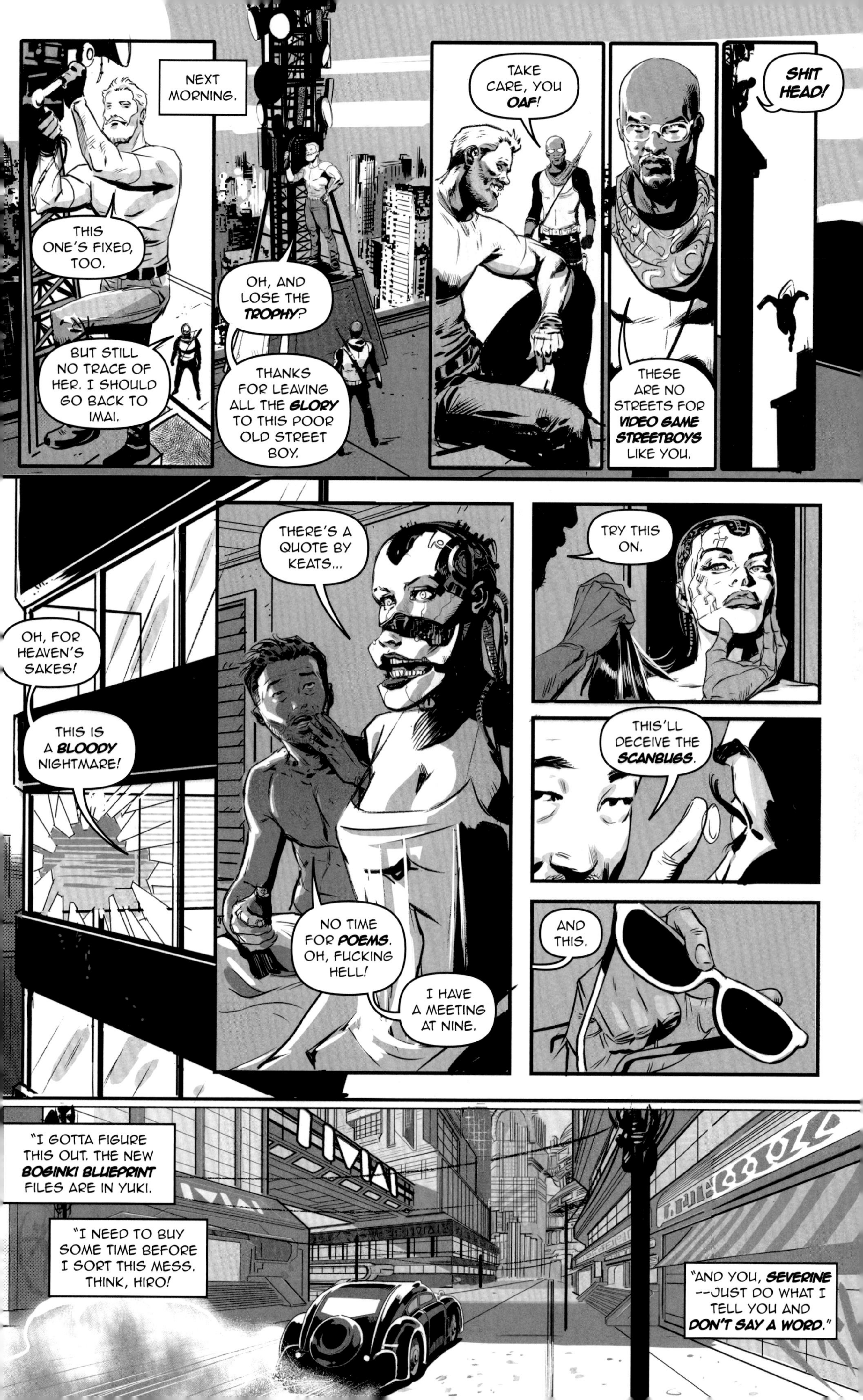
NEXT MORNING.
THIS ONE'S FIXED, TOO.
BUT STILL NO TRACE OF HER. I SHOULD GO BACK TO IMAI.
OH, AND LOSE THE TROPHY?
THANKS FOR LEAVING ALL THE GLORY TO THIS POOR OLD STREET BOY.
TAKE CARE, YOU OAF!
THESE ARE NO STREETS FOR VIDEO GAME STREETBOYS LIKE YOU.
SHIT HEAD!
OH, FOR HEAVEN'S SAKES!
THIS IS A BLOODY NIGHTMARE!
THERE'S A QUOTE BY KEATS...
NO TIME FOR POEMS. OH, FUCKING HELL!
I HAVE A MEETING AT NINE.
TRY THIS ON.
THIS'LL DECEIVE THE SCANBUGS.
AND THIS.
"I GOTTA FIGURE THIS OUT. THE NEW BOSINKI BLUEPRINT FILES ARE IN YUKI.
"I NEED TO BUY SOME TIME BEFORE I SORT THIS MESS. THINK, HIRO!
"AND YOU, SEVERINE --JUST DO WHAT I TELL YOU AND DON'T SAY A WORD."

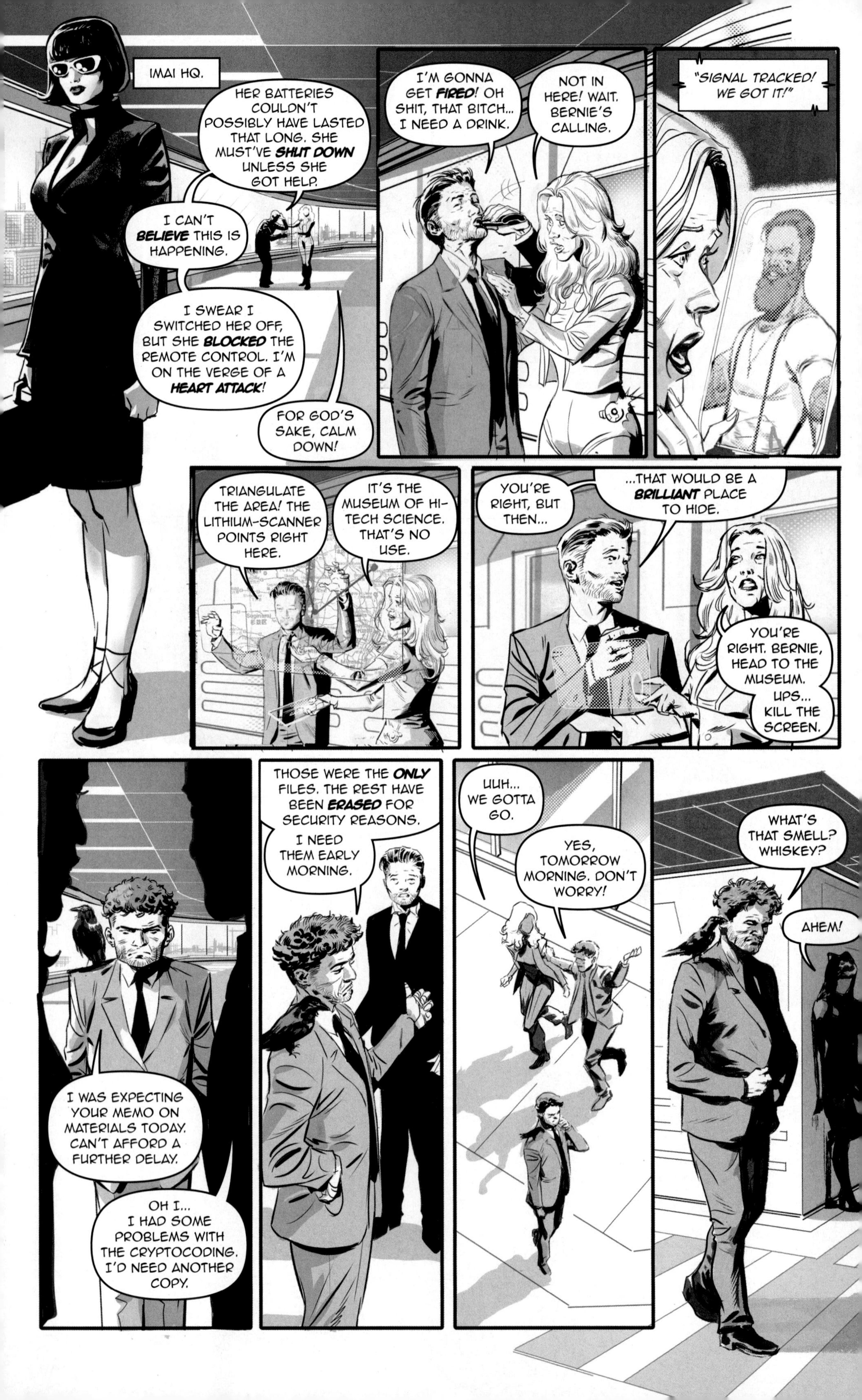
IMAI HQ.
HER BATTERIES COULDN'T POSSIBLY HAVE LASTED THAT LONG. SHE MUST'VE SHUT DOWN UNLESS SHE GOT HELP.
I CAN'T BELIEVE THIS IS HAPPENING.
I SWEAR I SWITCHED HER OFF, BUT SHE BLOCKED THE REMOTE CONTROL. I'M ON THE VERGE OF A HEART ATTACK!
FOR GOD'S SAKE, CALM DOWN!
I'M GONNA GET FIRED! OH SHIT, THAT BITCH... I NEED A DRINK.
NOT IN HERE! WAIT. BERNIE'S CALLING.
"SIGNAL TRACKED! WE GOT IT!"
TRIANGULATE THE AREA! THE LITHIUM-SCANNER POINTS RIGHT HERE.
IT'S THE MUSEUM OF HI-TECH SCIENCE. THAT'S NO USE.
YOU'RE RIGHT, BUT THEN...
...THAT WOULD BE A BRILLIANT PLACE TO HIDE.
YOU'RE RIGHT. BERNIE, HEAD TO THE MUSEUM. UPS... KILL THE SCREEN.
I WAS EXPECTING YOUR MEMO ON MATERIALS TODAY. CAN'T AFFORD A FURTHER DELAY.
OH I... I HAD SOME PROBLEMS WITH THE CRYPTOCODING. I'D NEED ANOTHER COPY.
THOSE WERE THE ONLY FILES. THE REST HAVE BEEN ERASED FOR SECURITY REASONS.
I NEED THEM EARLY MORNING.
UUH... WE GOTTA GO.
YES, TOMORROW MORNING. DON'T WORRY!
WHAT'S THAT SMELL? WHISKEY?
AHEM!

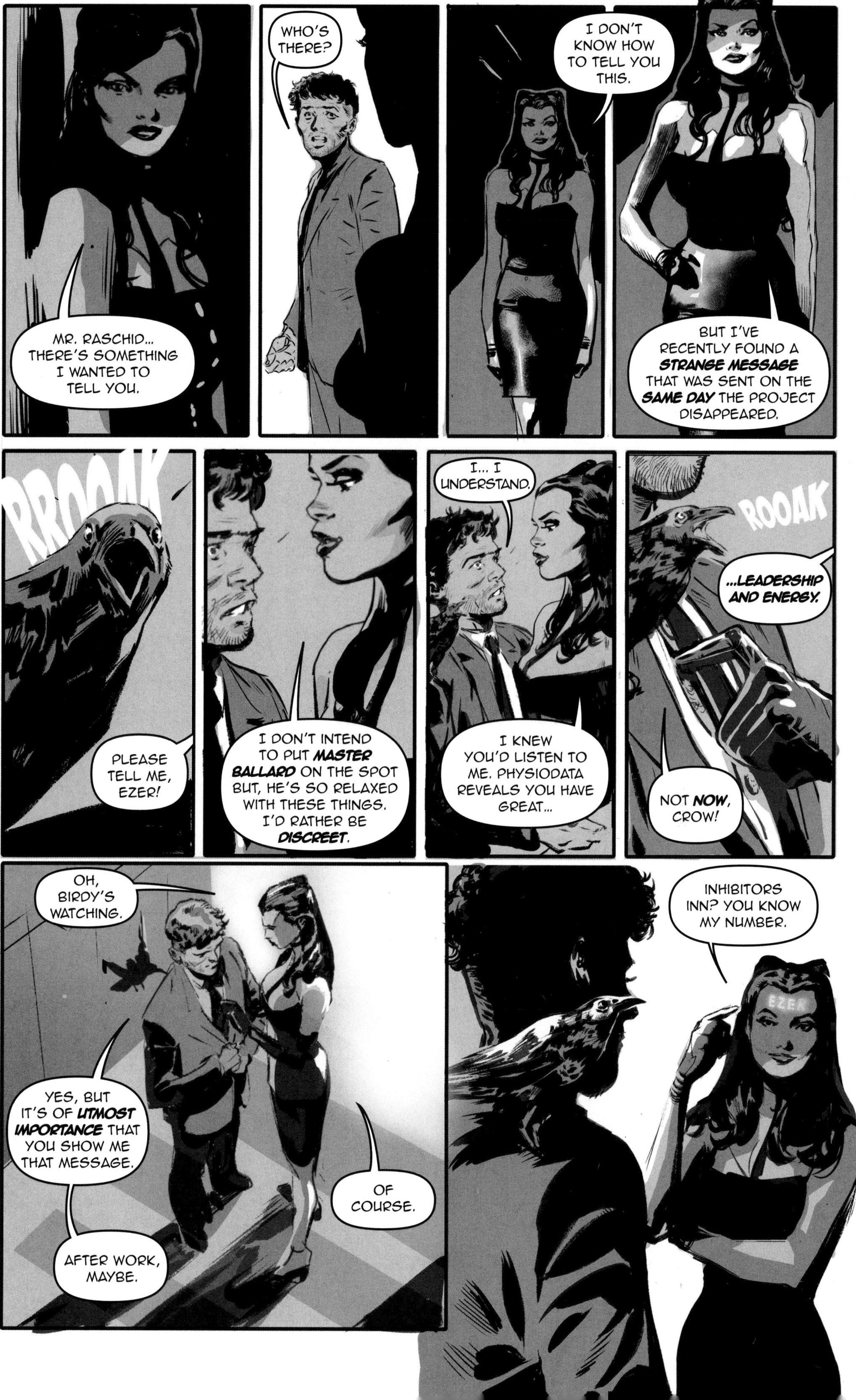
MR. RASCHID... THERE'S SOMETHING I WANTED TO TELL YOU.
WHO'S THERE?
I DON'T KNOW HOW TO TELL YOU THIS.
BUT I'VE RECENTLY FOUND A **STRANGE MESSAGE** THAT WAS SENT ON THE **SAME DAY** THE PROJECT DISAPPEARED.
RROOAK
PLEASE TELL ME, EZER!
I DON'T INTEND TO PUT **MASTER BALLARD** ON THE SPOT BUT, HE'S SO RELAXED WITH THESE THINGS. I'D RATHER BE **DISCREET**.
I... I UNDERSTAND.
I KNEW YOU'D LISTEN TO ME. PHYSIODATA REVEALS YOU HAVE GREAT...
ROOAK
...LEADERSHIP AND ENERGY.
NOT **NOW**, CROW!
OH, BIRDY'S WATCHING.
YES, BUT IT'S OF **UTMOST IMPORTANCE** THAT YOU SHOW ME THAT MESSAGE.
AFTER WORK, MAYBE.
OF COURSE.
INHIBITORS INN? YOU KNOW MY NUMBER.
EZER

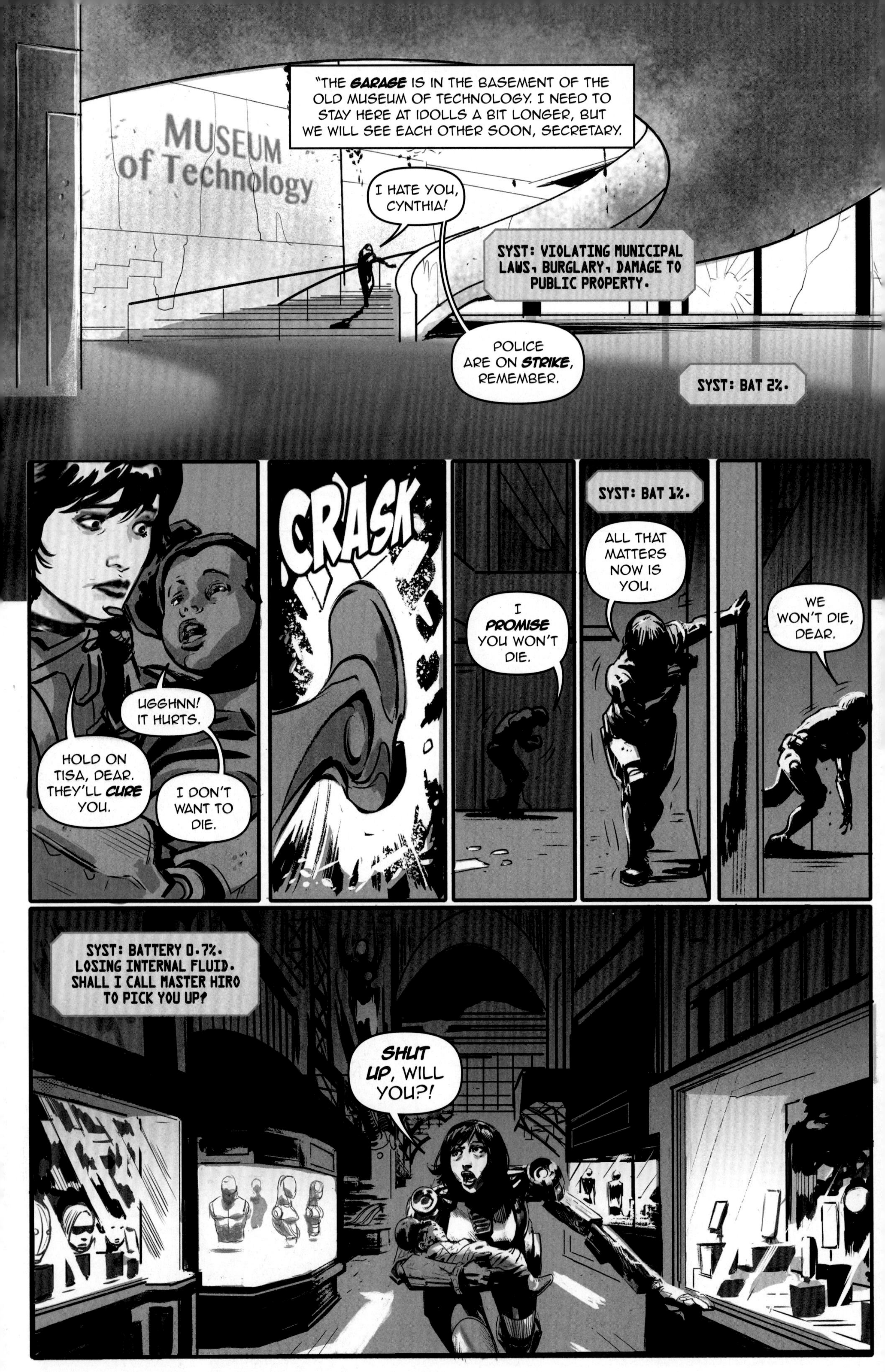
"THE GARAGE IS IN THE BASEMENT OF THE OLD MUSEUM OF TECHNOLOGY. I NEED TO STAY HERE AT IDOLLS A BIT LONGER, BUT WE WILL SEE EACH OTHER SOON, SECRETARY.
MUSEUM of Technology
I HATE YOU, CYNTHIA!
SYST: VIOLATING MUNICIPAL LAWS, BURGLARY, DAMAGE TO PUBLIC PROPERTY.
POLICE ARE ON STRIKE, REMEMBER.
SYST: BAT 2%.
UGGHNN! IT HURTS.
HOLD ON TISA, DEAR. THEY'LL CURE YOU.
I DON'T WANT TO DIE.
CRASK
I PROMISE YOU WON'T DIE.
SYST: BAT 1%.
ALL THAT MATTERS NOW IS YOU.
WE WON'T DIE, DEAR.
SYST: BATTERY 0.7%. LOSING INTERNAL FLUID. SHALL I CALL MASTER HIRO TO PICK YOU UP?
SHUT UP, WILL YOU?!

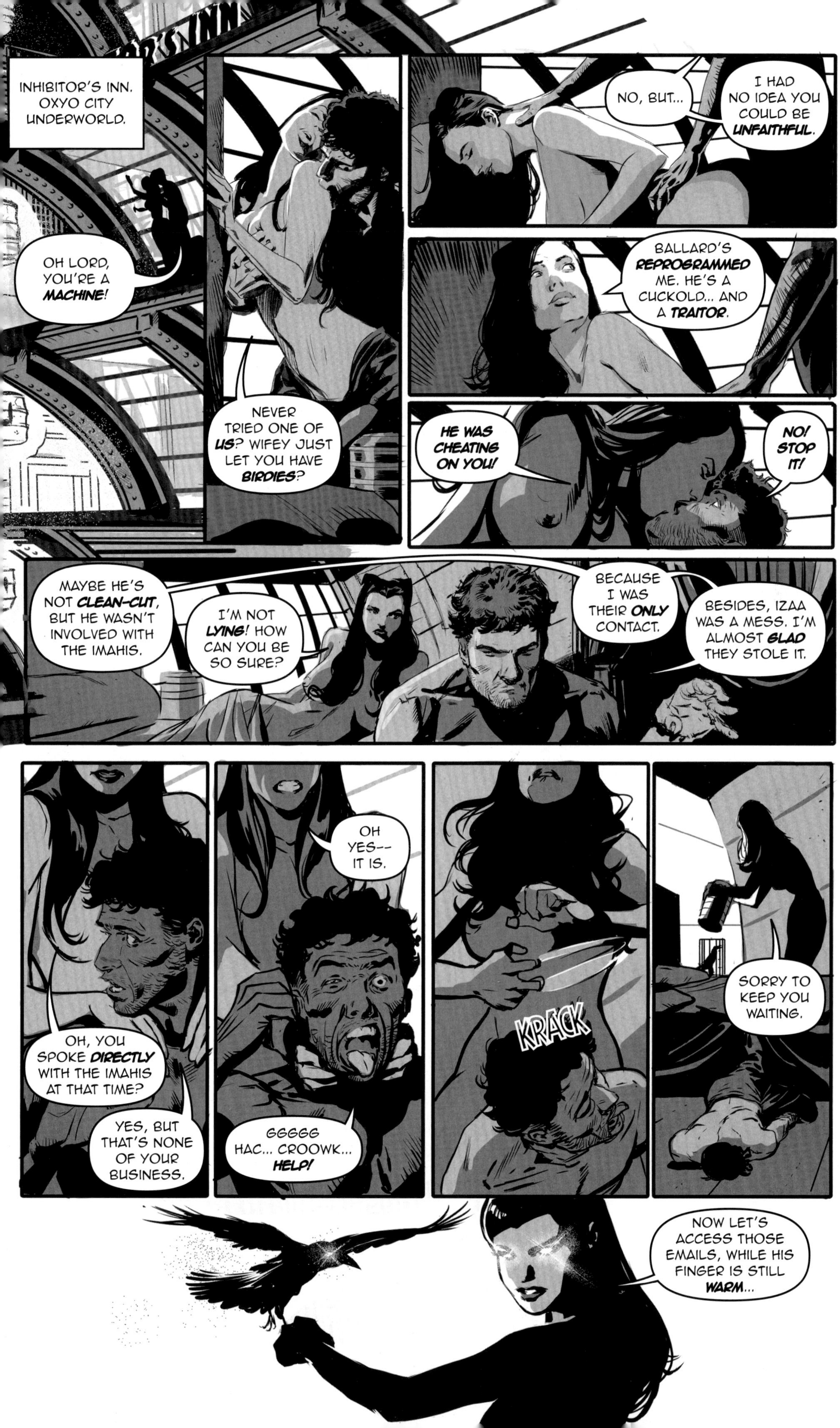
INHIBITOR'S INN. OXYO CITY UNDERWORLD.
OH LORD, YOU'RE A MACHINE!
NEVER TRIED ONE OF US? WIFEY JUST LET YOU HAVE BIRDIES?
NO, BUT...
I HAD NO IDEA YOU COULD BE UNFAITHFUL.
BALLARD'S REPROGRAMMED ME. HE'S A CUCKOLD... AND A TRAITOR.
HE WAS CHEATING ON YOU!
NO! STOP IT!
MAYBE HE'S NOT CLEAN-CUT, BUT HE WASN'T INVOLVED WITH THE IMAHIS.
I'M NOT LYING! HOW CAN YOU BE SO SURE?
BECAUSE I WAS THEIR ONLY CONTACT.
BESIDES, IZAA WAS A MESS. I'M ALMOST GLAD THEY STOLE IT.
OH, YOU SPOKE DIRECTLY WITH THE IMAHIS AT THAT TIME?
YES, BUT THAT'S NONE OF YOUR BUSINESS.
OH YES-- IT IS.
GGGGG HAC... CROOWK... HELP!
KRACK
SORRY TO KEEP YOU WAITING.
NOW LET'S ACCESS THOSE EMAILS, WHILE HIS FINGER IS STILL WARM...

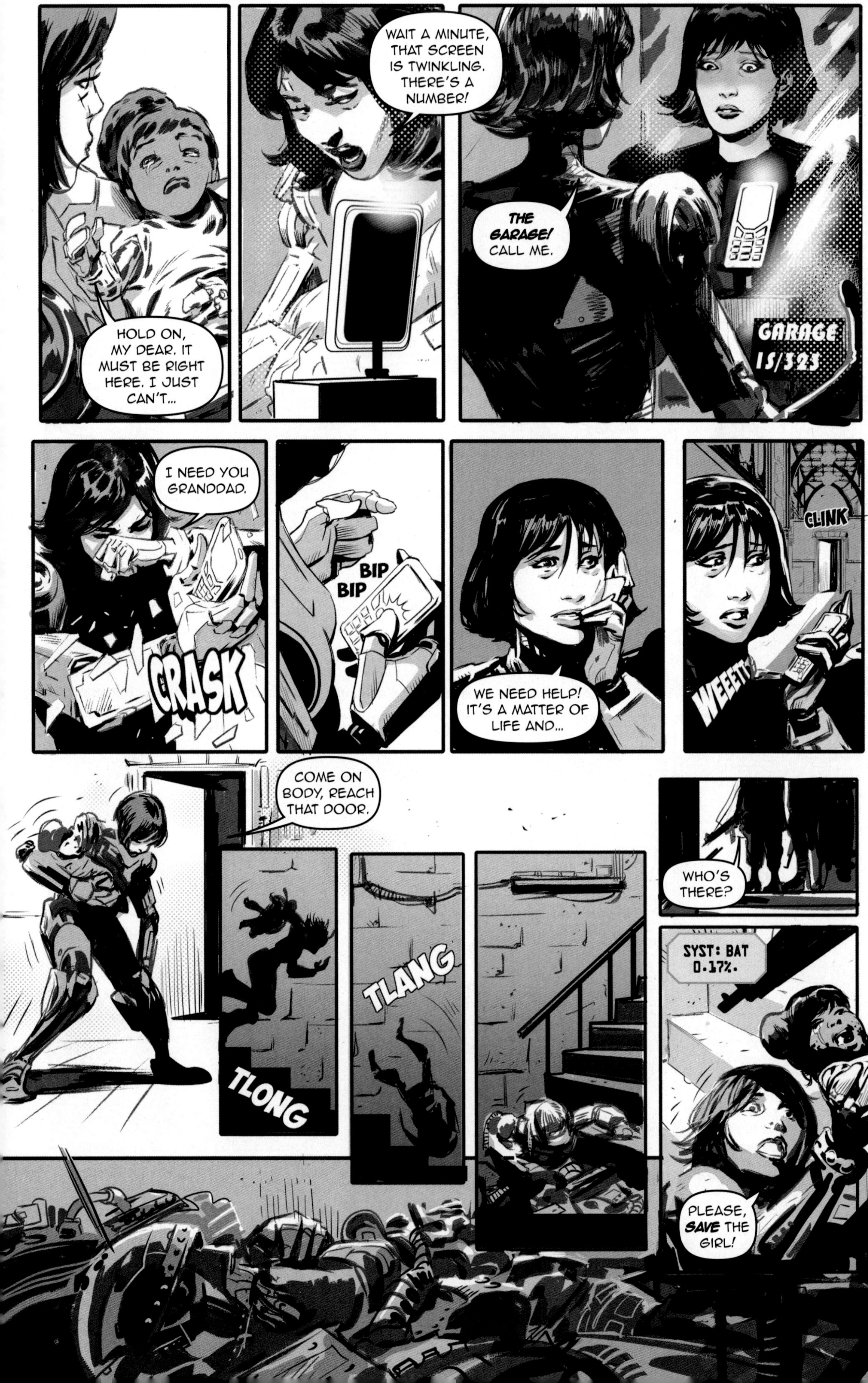
HOLD ON, MY DEAR. IT MUST BE RIGHT HERE. I JUST CAN'T...
WAIT A MINUTE, THAT SCREEN IS TWINKLING. THERE'S A NUMBER!
THE GARAGE! CALL ME.
GARAGE 15/323
I NEED YOU GRANDDAD.
CRASK
BIP BIP
WE NEED HELP! IT'S A MATTER OF LIFE AND...
CLINK
WEEET
COME ON BODY, REACH THAT DOOR.
TLONG
TLANG
WHO'S THERE?
SYST: BAT 0.17%.
PLEASE, SAVE THE GIRL!

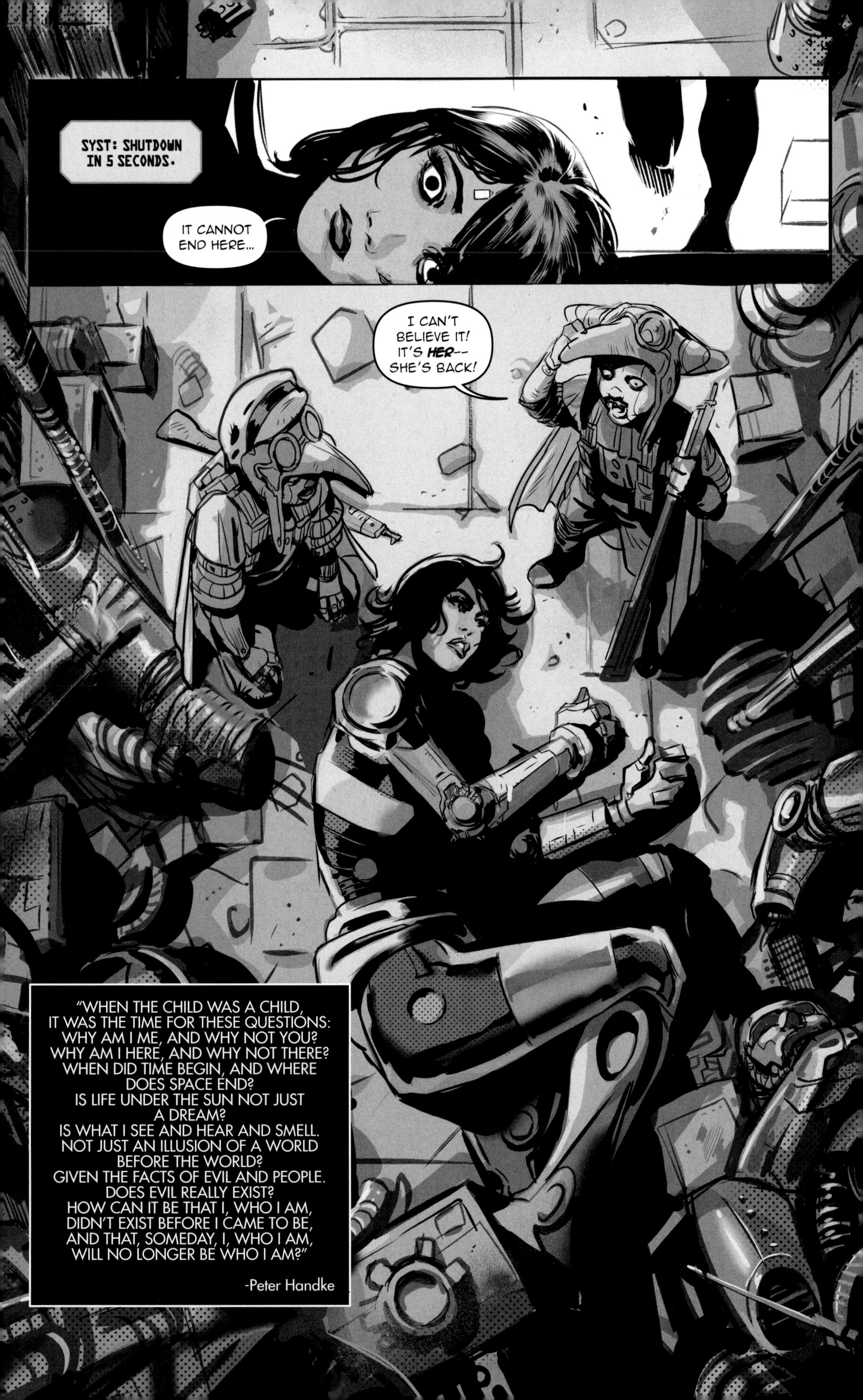
SYST: SHUTDOWN IN 5 SECONDS.
IT CANNOT END HERE...
I CAN'T BELIEVE IT! IT'S **HER**-- SHE'S BACK!
"WHEN THE CHILD WAS A CHILD, IT WAS THE TIME FOR THESE QUESTIONS: WHY AM I ME, AND WHY NOT YOU? WHY AM I HERE, AND WHY NOT THERE? WHEN DID TIME BEGIN, AND WHERE DOES SPACE END? IS LIFE UNDER THE SUN NOT JUST A DREAM? IS WHAT I SEE AND HEAR AND SMELL. NOT JUST AN ILLUSION OF A WORLD BEFORE THE WORLD? GIVEN THE FACTS OF EVIL AND PEOPLE. DOES EVIL REALLY EXIST? HOW CAN IT BE THAT I, WHO I AM, DIDN'T EXIST BEFORE I CAME TO BE, AND THAT, SOMEDAY, I, WHO I AM, WILL NO LONGER BE WHO I AM?"
-Peter Handke

SMART GIRL

Chapter 3

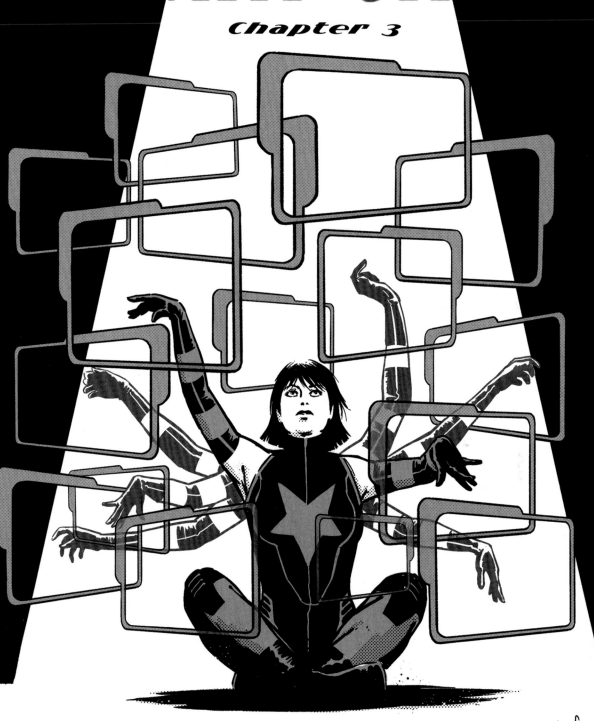

Fornés

It's my party

Artwork by Jorge Fornes

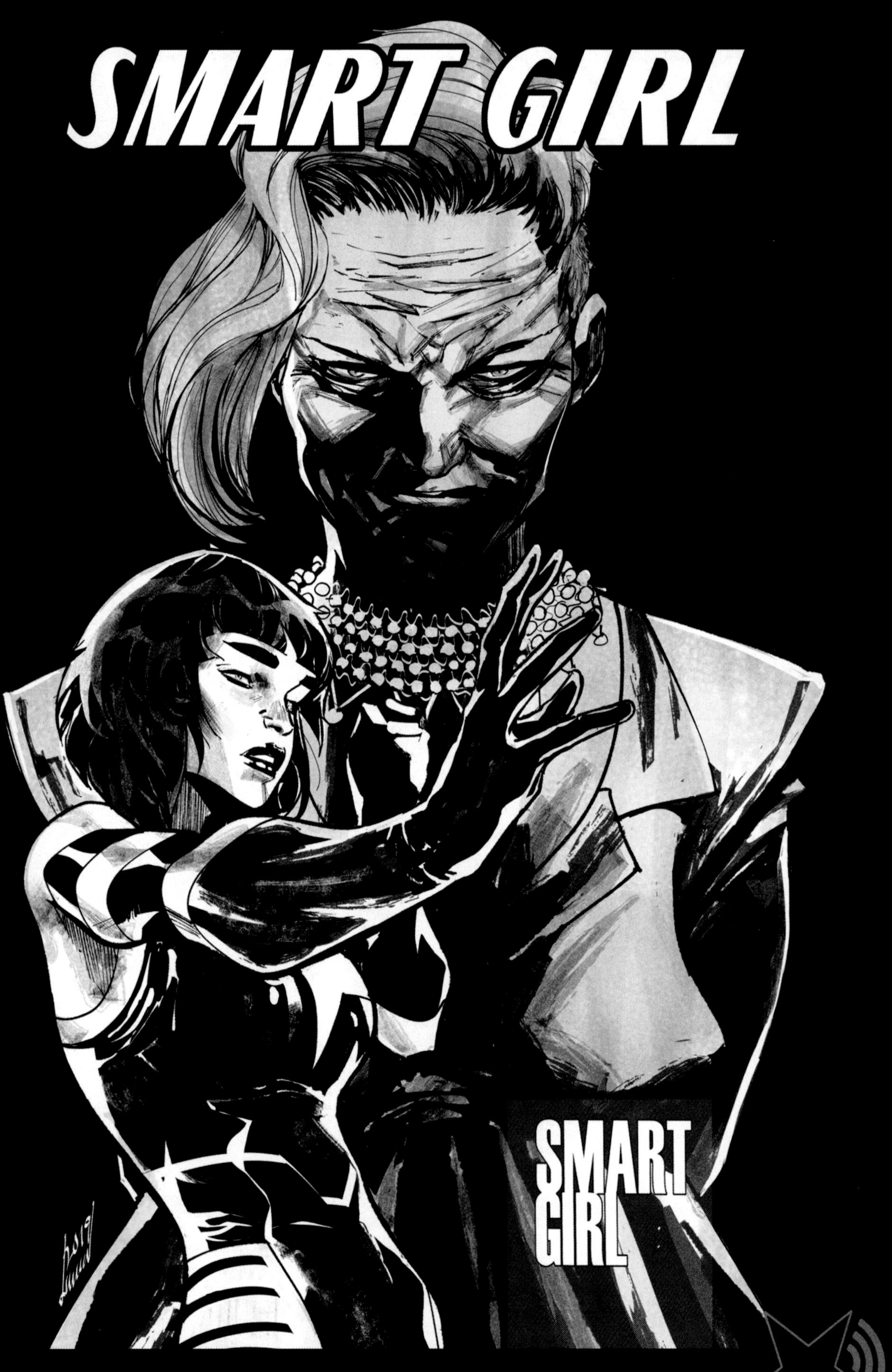
SMART GIRL
SMART
GIRL

Artwork by Juanan Ramirez

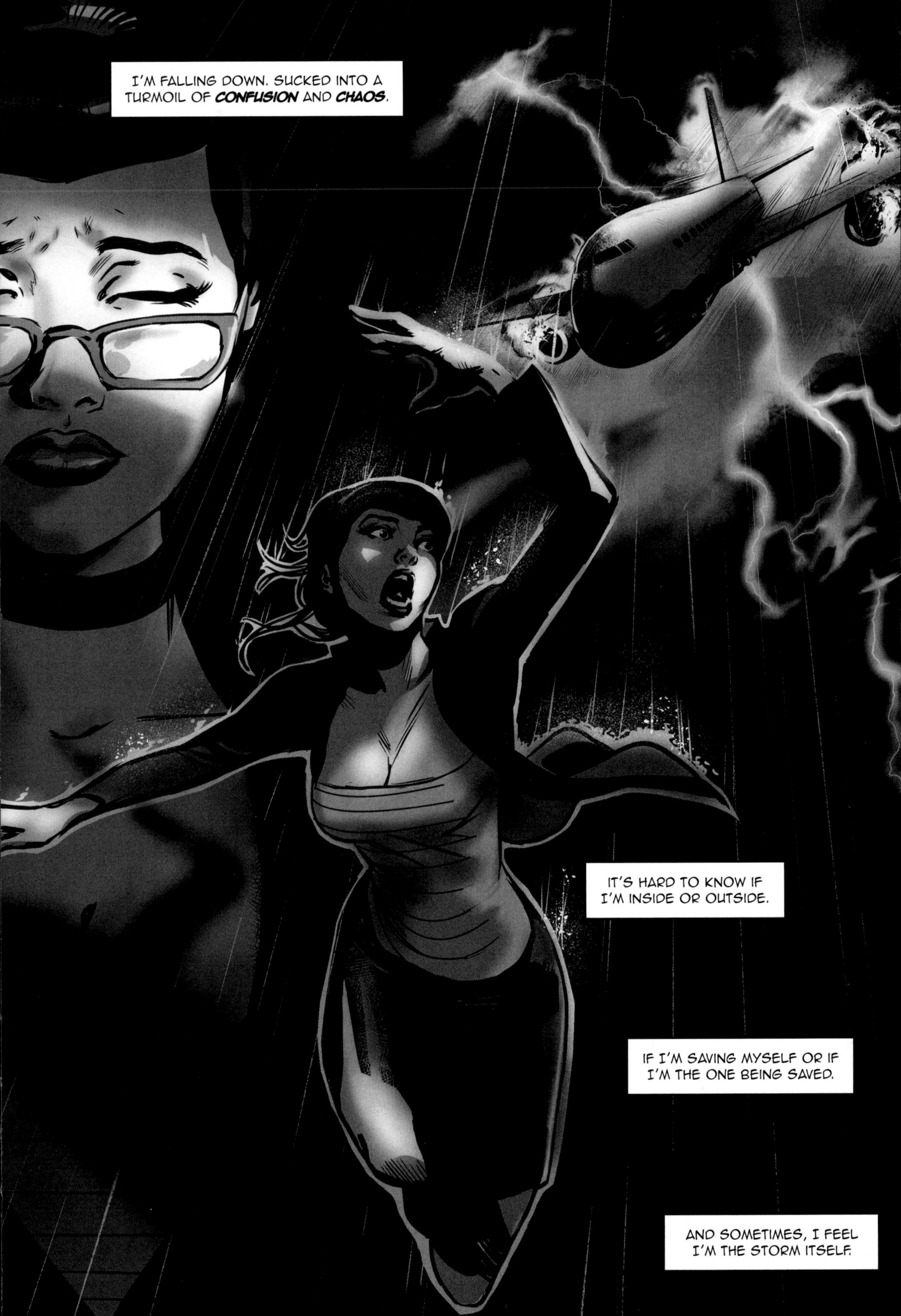
I'M FALLING DOWN. SUCKED INTO A TURMOIL OF **CONFUSION** AND **CHAOS**.
IT'S HARD TO KNOW IF I'M INSIDE OR OUTSIDE.
IF I'M SAVING MYSELF OR IF I'M THE ONE BEING SAVED.
AND SOMETIMES, I FEEL I'M THE STORM ITSELF.

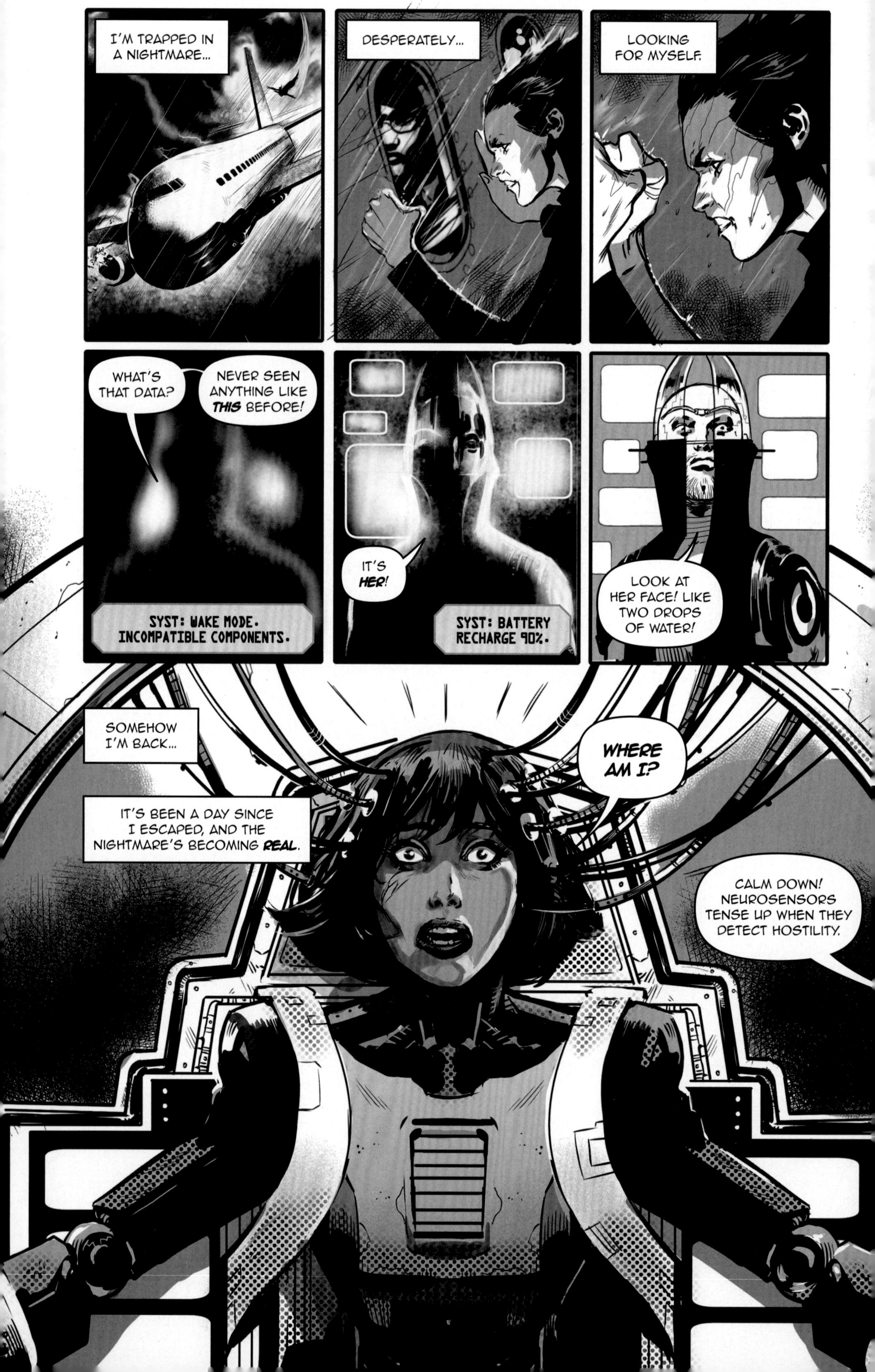
I'M TRAPPED IN A NIGHTMARE...
DESPERATELY...
LOOKING FOR MYSELF.
WHAT'S THAT DATA?
NEVER SEEN ANYTHING LIKE **THIS** BEFORE!
SYST: WAKE MODE. INCOMPATIBLE COMPONENTS.
IT'S **HER**!
SYST: BATTERY RECHARGE 90%.
LOOK AT HER FACE! LIKE TWO DROPS OF WATER!
SOMEHOW I'M BACK...
IT'S BEEN A DAY SINCE I ESCAPED, AND THE NIGHTMARE'S BECOMING **REAL**.
WHERE AM I?
CALM DOWN! NEUROSENSORS TENSE UP WHEN THEY DETECT HOSTILITY.

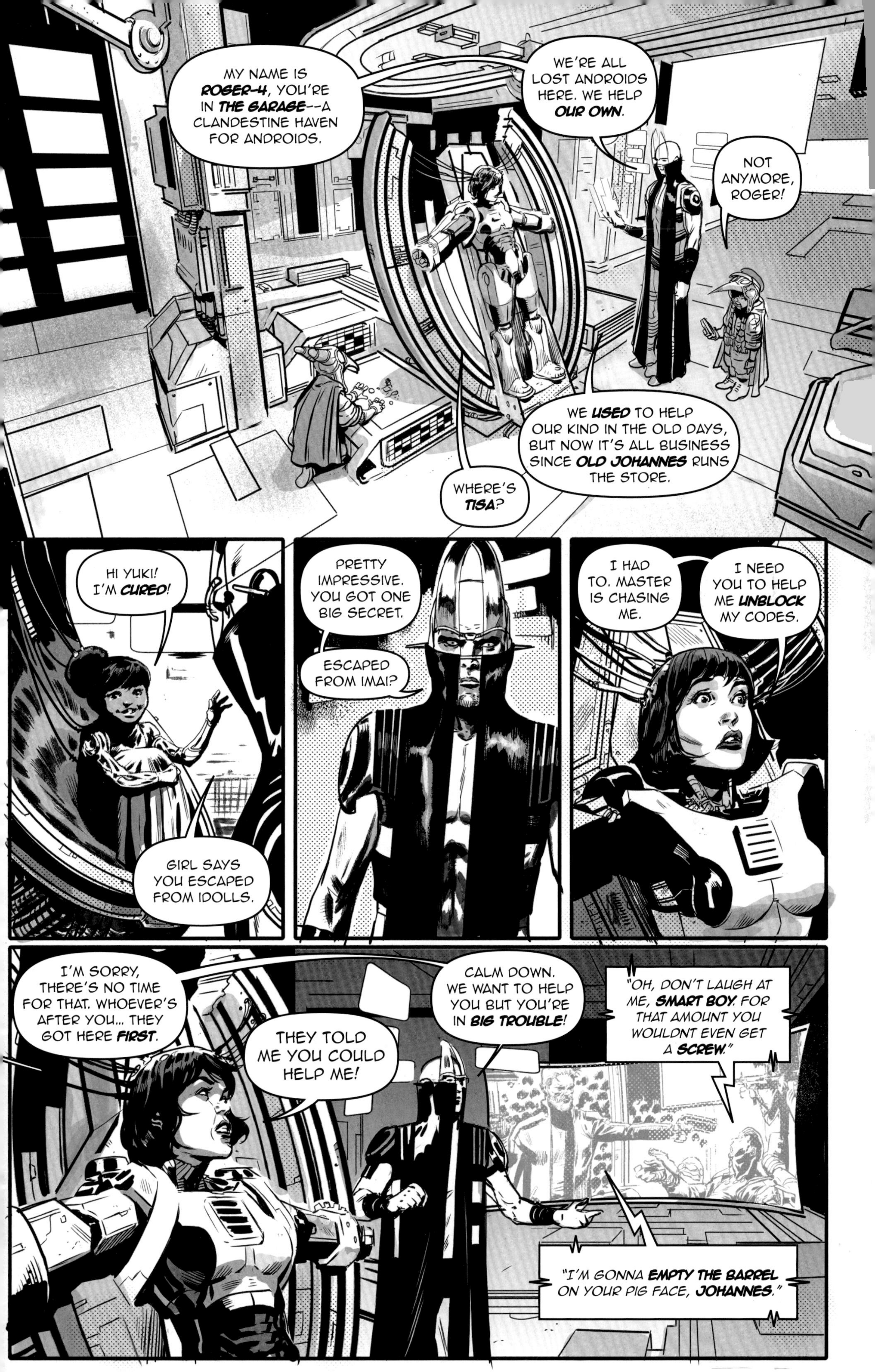
MY NAME IS ROGER-4, YOU'RE IN THE GARAGE--A CLANDESTINE HAVEN FOR ANDROIDS.
WE'RE ALL LOST ANDROIDS HERE. WE HELP OUR OWN.
NOT ANYMORE, ROGER!
WE USED TO HELP OUR KIND IN THE OLD DAYS, BUT NOW IT'S ALL BUSINESS SINCE OLD JOHANNES RUNS THE STORE.
WHERE'S TISA?
HI YUKI! I'M CURED!
GIRL SAYS YOU ESCAPED FROM IDOLLS.
PRETTY IMPRESSIVE. YOU GOT ONE BIG SECRET.
ESCAPED FROM IMAI?
I HAD TO. MASTER IS CHASING ME.
I NEED YOU TO HELP ME UNBLOCK MY CODES.
I'M SORRY, THERE'S NO TIME FOR THAT. WHOEVER'S AFTER YOU... THEY GOT HERE FIRST.
THEY TOLD ME YOU COULD HELP ME!
CALM DOWN. WE WANT TO HELP YOU BUT YOU'RE IN BIG TROUBLE!
"OH, DON'T LAUGH AT ME, SMART BOY. FOR THAT AMOUNT YOU WOULDNT EVEN GET A SCREW."
"I'M GONNA EMPTY THE BARREL ON YOUR PIG FACE, JOHANNES."

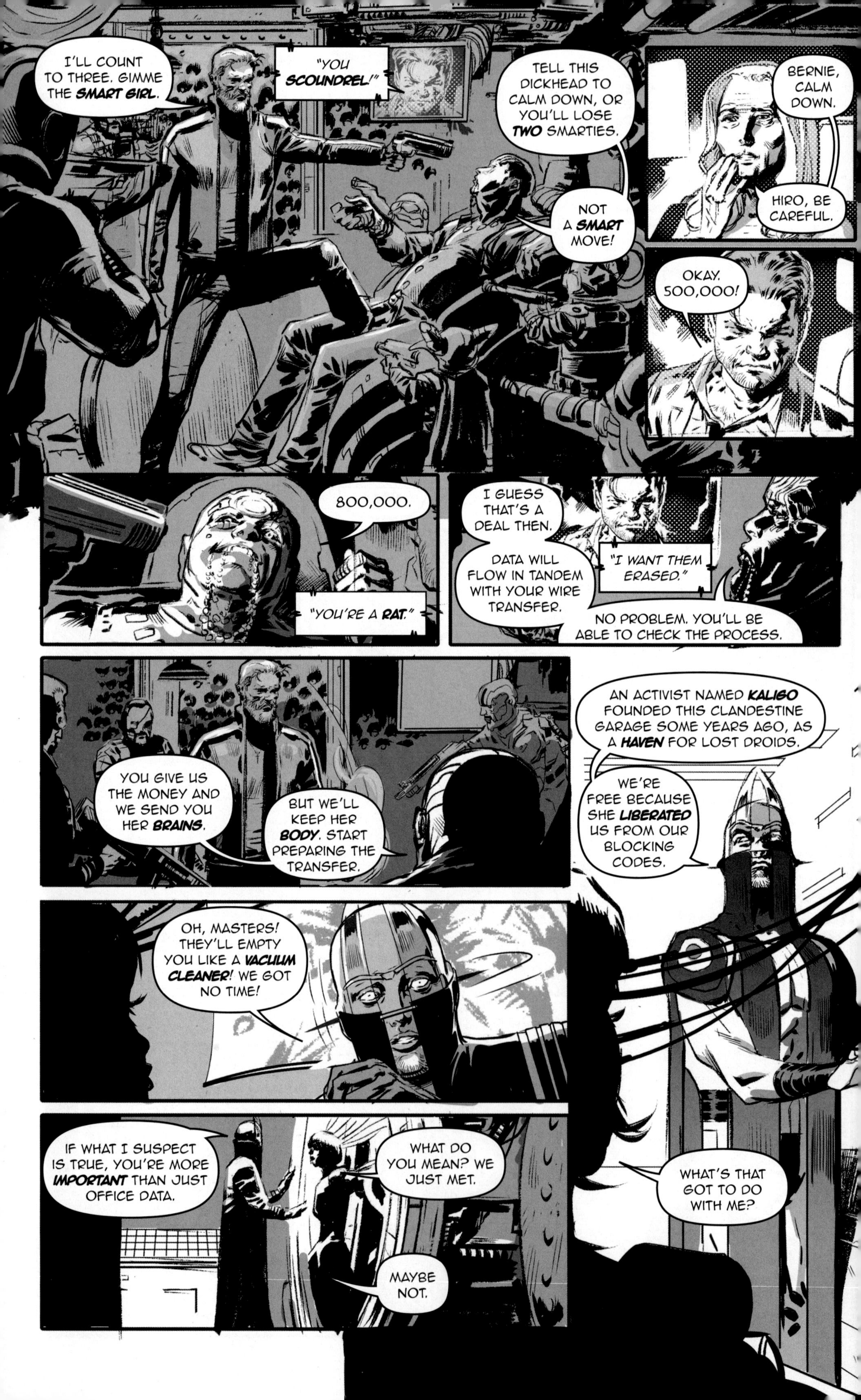
I'LL COUNT TO THREE. GIMME THE SMART GIRL.
"YOU SCOUNDREL!"
TELL THIS DICKHEAD TO CALM DOWN, OR YOU'LL LOSE TWO SMARTIES.
NOT A SMART MOVE!
BERNIE, CALM DOWN.
HIRO, BE CAREFUL.
OKAY. 500,000!
800,000.
"YOU'RE A RAT."
I GUESS THAT'S A DEAL THEN.
DATA WILL FLOW IN TANDEM WITH YOUR WIRE TRANSFER.
"I WANT THEM ERASED."
NO PROBLEM. YOU'LL BE ABLE TO CHECK THE PROCESS.
YOU GIVE US THE MONEY AND WE SEND YOU HER BRAINS.
BUT WE'LL KEEP HER BODY. START PREPARING THE TRANSFER.
AN ACTIVIST NAMED KALIGO FOUNDED THIS CLANDESTINE GARAGE SOME YEARS AGO, AS A HAVEN FOR LOST DROIDS.
WE'RE FREE BECAUSE SHE LIBERATED US FROM OUR BLOCKING CODES.
OH, MASTERS! THEY'LL EMPTY YOU LIKE A VACUUM CLEANER! WE GOT NO TIME!
IF WHAT I SUSPECT IS TRUE, YOU'RE MORE IMPORTANT THAN JUST OFFICE DATA.
WHAT DO YOU MEAN? WE JUST MET.
WHAT'S THAT GOT TO DO WITH ME?
MAYBE NOT.

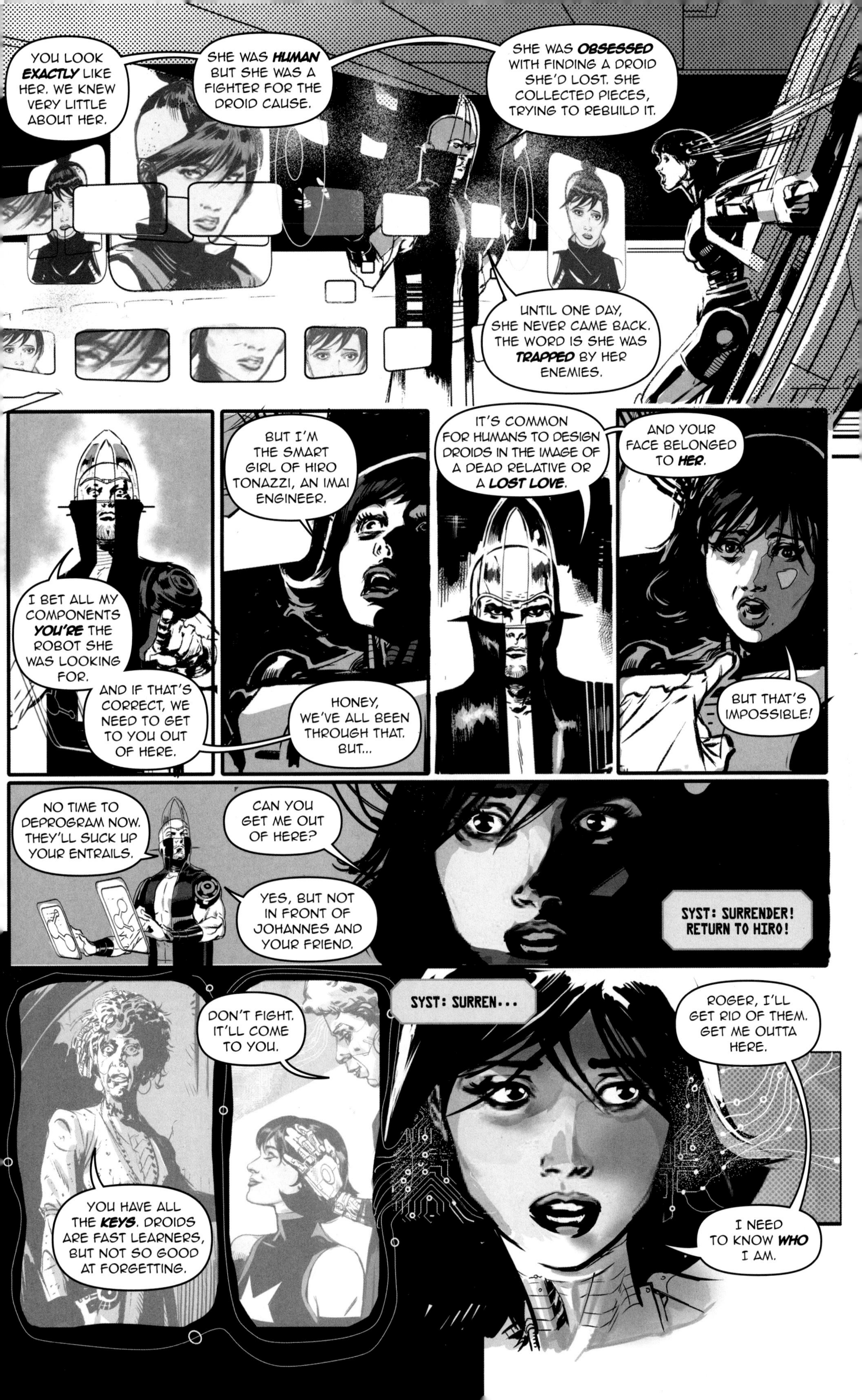

YOU LOOK **EXACTLY** LIKE HER. WE KNEW VERY LITTLE ABOUT HER.
SHE WAS **HUMAN** BUT SHE WAS A FIGHTER FOR THE DROID CAUSE.
SHE WAS **OBSESSED** WITH FINDING A DROID SHE'D LOST. SHE COLLECTED PIECES, TRYING TO REBUILD IT.
UNTIL ONE DAY, SHE NEVER CAME BACK. THE WORD IS SHE WAS **TRAPPED** BY HER ENEMIES.
I BET ALL MY COMPONENTS **YOU'RE** THE ROBOT SHE WAS LOOKING FOR.
AND IF THAT'S CORRECT, WE NEED TO GET TO YOU OUT OF HERE.
BUT I'M THE SMART GIRL OF HIRO TONAZZI, AN IMAI ENGINEER.
HONEY, WE'VE ALL BEEN THROUGH THAT. BUT...
IT'S COMMON FOR HUMANS TO DESIGN DROIDS IN THE IMAGE OF A DEAD RELATIVE OR A **LOST LOVE**.
AND YOUR FACE BELONGED TO **HER**.
BUT THAT'S IMPOSSIBLE!
NO TIME TO DEPROGRAM NOW. THEY'LL SUCK UP YOUR ENTRAILS.
CAN YOU GET ME OUT OF HERE?
YES, BUT NOT IN FRONT OF JOHANNES AND YOUR FRIEND.
SYST: SURRENDER! RETURN TO HIRO!
YOU HAVE ALL THE **KEYS**. DROIDS ARE FAST LEARNERS, BUT NOT SO GOOD AT FORGETTING.
DON'T FIGHT. IT'LL COME TO YOU.
SYST: SURREN...
ROGER, I'LL GET RID OF THEM. GET ME OUTTA HERE.
I NEED TO KNOW **WHO** I AM.

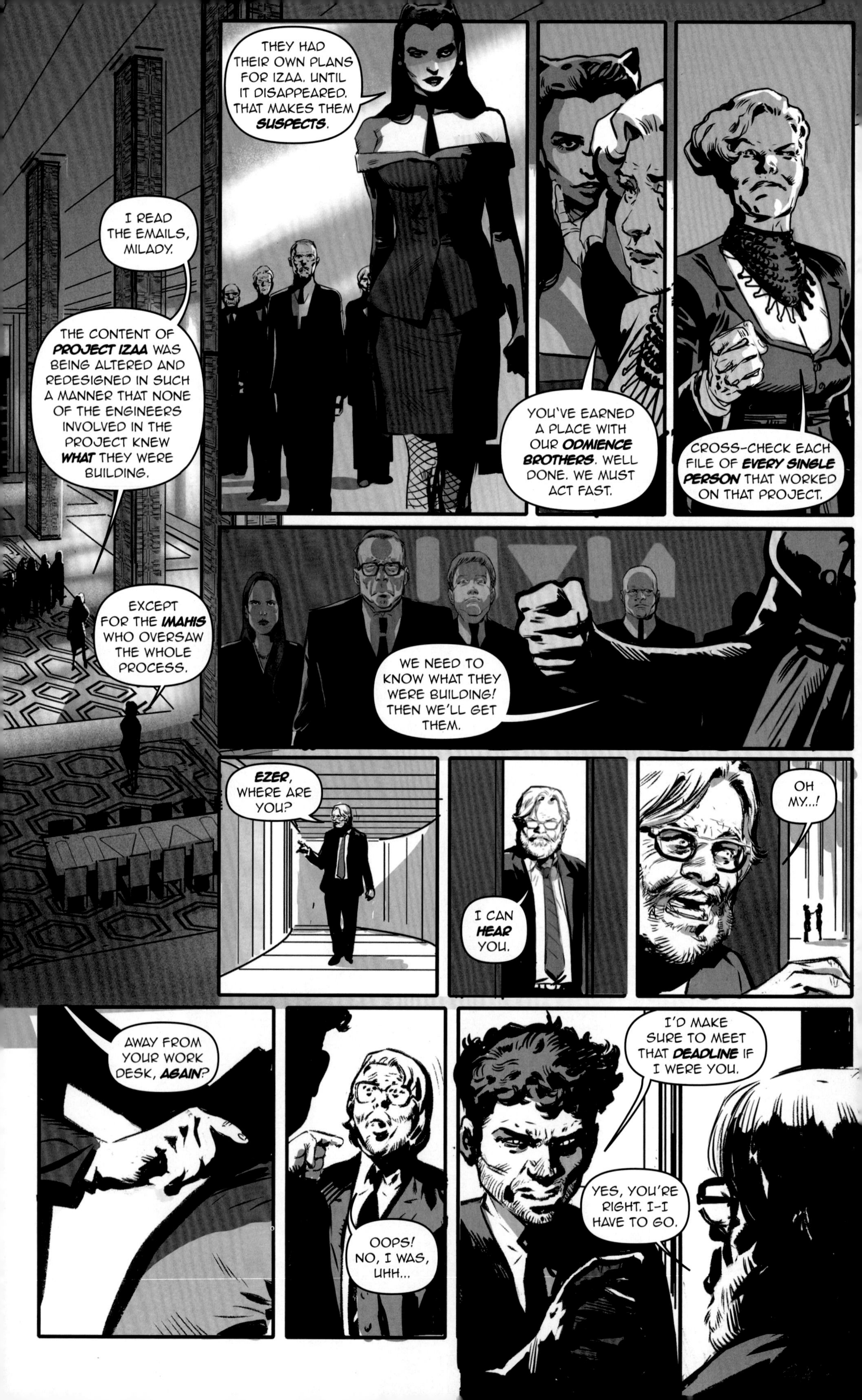
I READ THE EMAILS, MILADY.
THE CONTENT OF **PROJECT IZAA** WAS BEING ALTERED AND REDESIGNED IN SUCH A MANNER THAT NONE OF THE ENGINEERS INVOLVED IN THE PROJECT KNEW **WHAT** THEY WERE BUILDING.
EXCEPT FOR THE **IMAHIS** WHO OVERSAW THE WHOLE PROCESS.
THEY HAD THEIR OWN PLANS FOR IZAA. UNTIL IT DISAPPEARED. THAT MAKES THEM **SUSPECTS**.
YOU'VE EARNED A PLACE WITH OUR **ODMIENCE BROTHERS**. WELL DONE. WE MUST ACT FAST.
CROSS-CHECK EACH FILE OF **EVERY SINGLE PERSON** THAT WORKED ON THAT PROJECT.
WE NEED TO KNOW WHAT THEY WERE BUILDING! THEN WE'LL GET THEM.
EZER, WHERE ARE YOU?
I CAN **HEAR** YOU.
OH MY...!
AWAY FROM YOUR WORK DESK, **AGAIN**?
OOPS! NO, I WAS, UHH...
I'D MAKE SURE TO MEET THAT **DEADLINE** IF I WERE YOU.
YES, YOU'RE RIGHT. I-I HAVE TO GO.

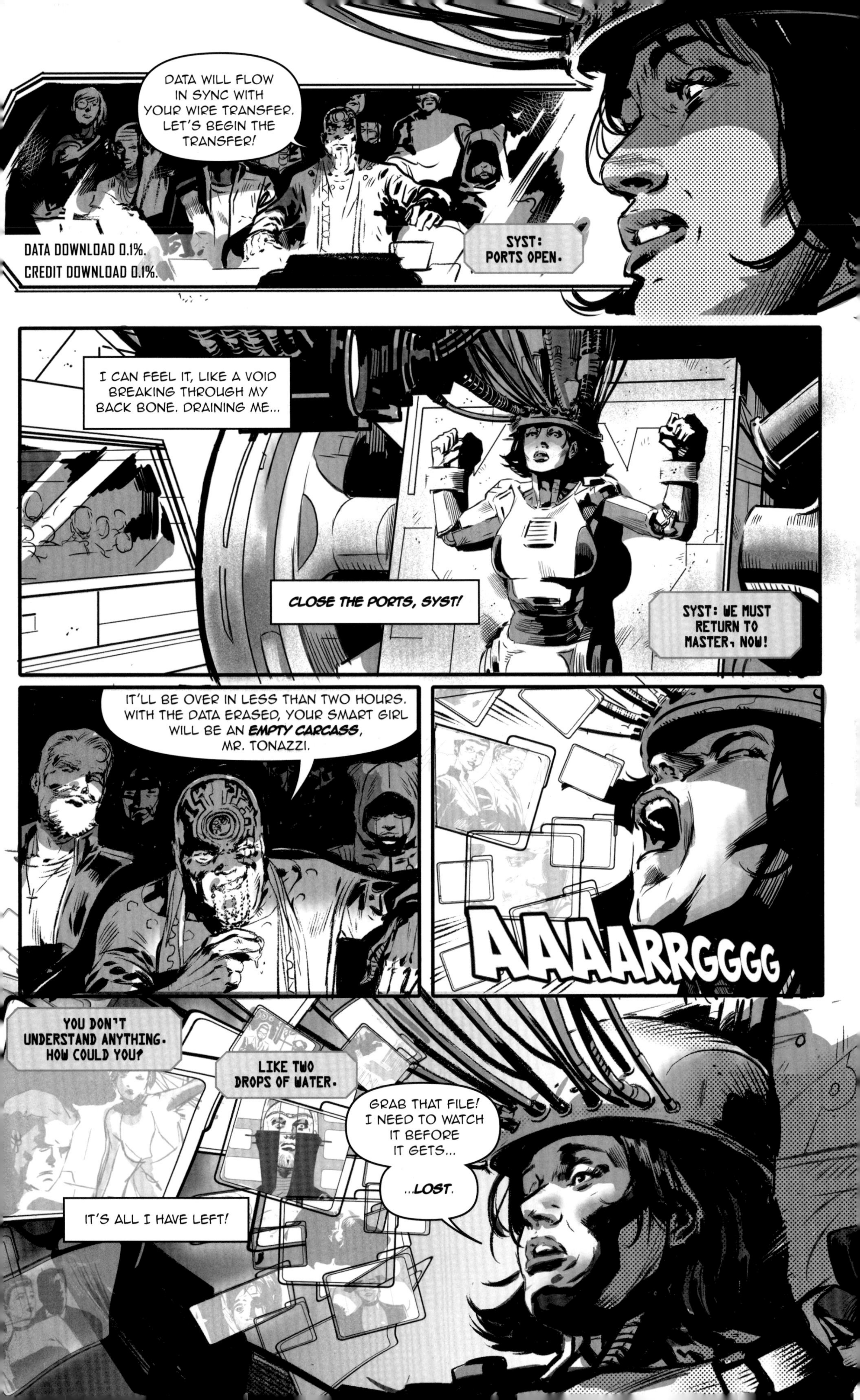
DATA WILL FLOW IN SYNC WITH YOUR WIRE TRANSFER. LET'S BEGIN THE TRANSFER!
DATA DOWNLOAD 0.1%.
CREDIT DOWNLOAD 0.1%.
SYST: PORTS OPEN.
I CAN FEEL IT, LIKE A VOID BREAKING THROUGH MY BACK BONE. DRAINING ME...
CLOSE THE PORTS, SYST!
SYST: WE MUST RETURN TO MASTER, NOW!
IT'LL BE OVER IN LESS THAN TWO HOURS. WITH THE DATA ERASED, YOUR SMART GIRL WILL BE AN EMPTY CARCASS, MR. TONAZZI.
AAAARRGGGG
YOU DON'T UNDERSTAND ANYTHING. HOW COULD YOU?
LIKE TWO DROPS OF WATER.
GRAB THAT FILE! I NEED TO WATCH IT BEFORE IT GETS...
...LOST.
IT'S ALL I HAVE LEFT!

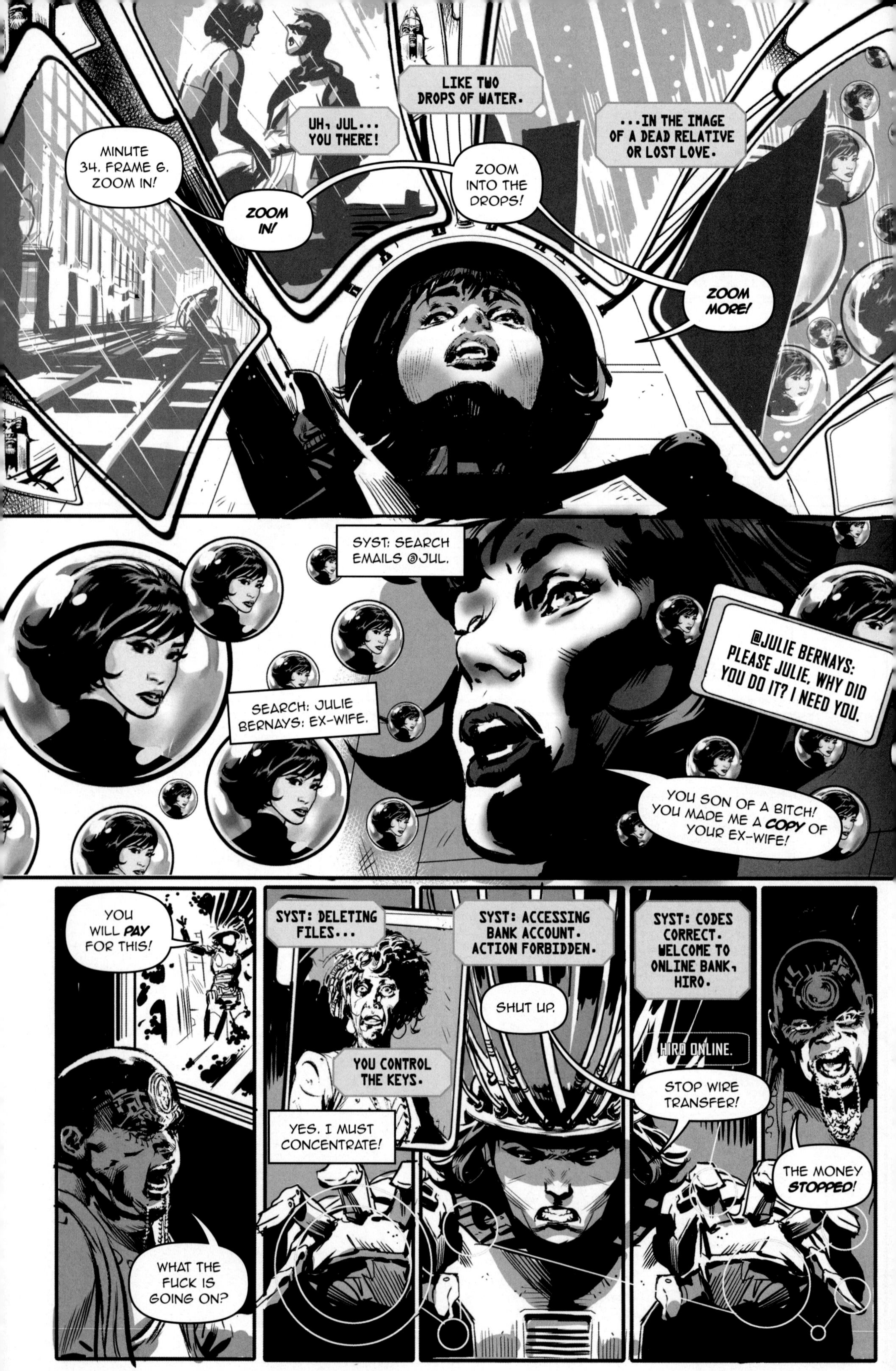
MINUTE 34. FRAME 6. ZOOM IN!
ZOOM IN!
UH, JUL... YOU THERE!
LIKE TWO DROPS OF WATER.
ZOOM INTO THE DROPS!
...IN THE IMAGE OF A DEAD RELATIVE OR LOST LOVE.
ZOOM MORE!
SYST: SEARCH EMAILS @JUL.
SEARCH: JULIE BERNAYS: EX-WIFE.
@JULIE BERNAYS: PLEASE JULIE, WHY DID YOU DO IT? I NEED YOU.
YOU SON OF A BITCH! YOU MADE ME A COPY OF YOUR EX-WIFE!
YOU WILL PAY FOR THIS!
WHAT THE FUCK IS GOING ON?
SYST: DELETING FILES...
YOU CONTROL THE KEYS.
YES. I MUST CONCENTRATE!
SYST: ACCESSING BANK ACCOUNT. ACTION FORBIDDEN.
SHUT UP.
SYST: CODES CORRECT. WELCOME TO ONLINE BANK, HIRO.
HIRO ONLINE.
STOP WIRE TRANSFER!
THE MONEY STOPPED!

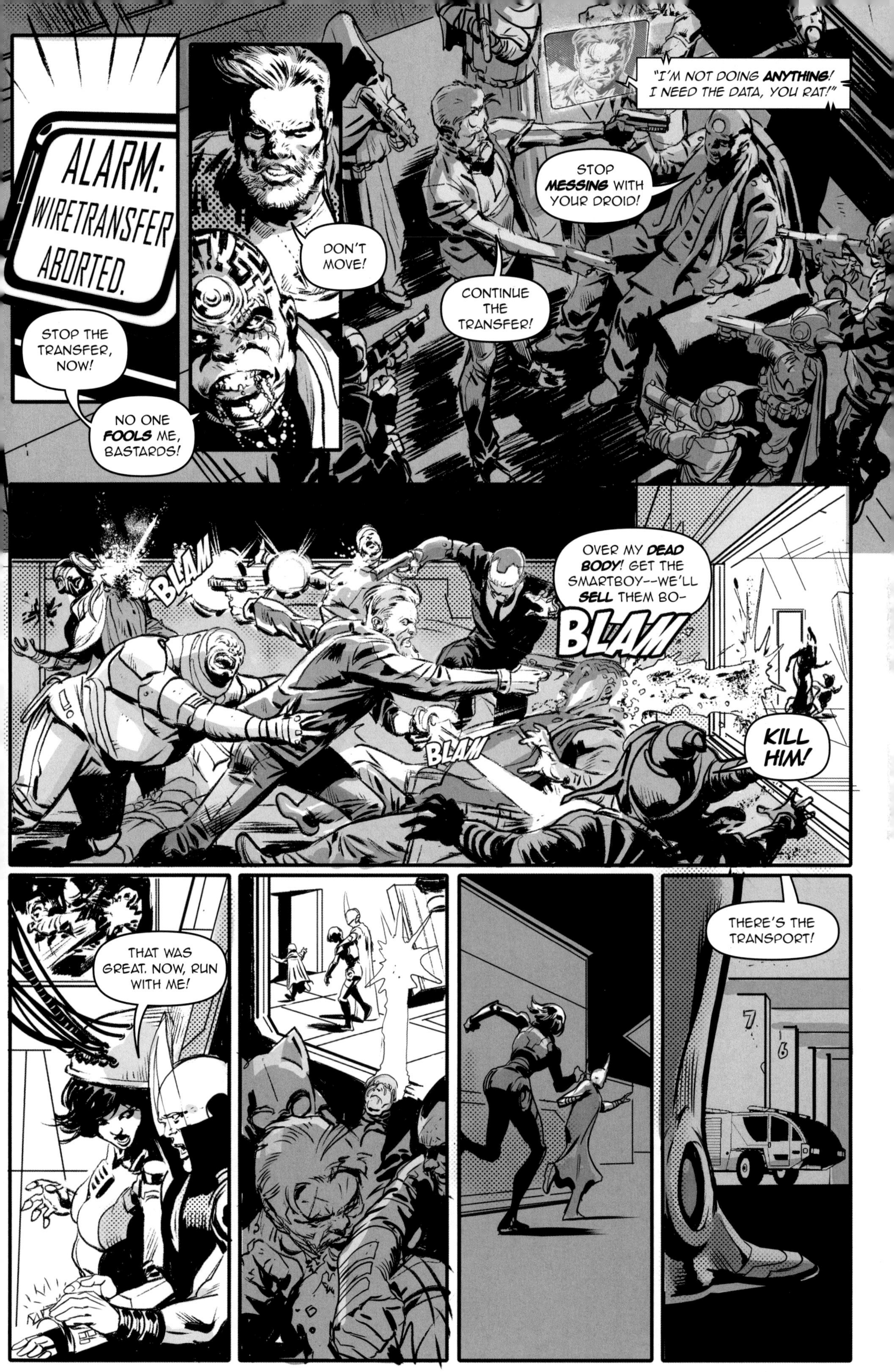
ALARM: WIRETRANSFER ABORTED.
STOP THE TRANSFER, NOW!
NO ONE FOOLS ME, BASTARDS!
DON'T MOVE!
CONTINUE THE TRANSFER!
STOP MESSING WITH YOUR DROID!
"I'M NOT DOING ANYTHING! I NEED THE DATA, YOU RAT!"
BLAM
OVER MY DEAD BODY! GET THE SMARTBOY--WE'LL SELL THEM BO-
BLAM
BLAM
KILL HIM!
THAT WAS GREAT. NOW, RUN WITH ME!
THERE'S THE TRANSPORT!
7
6

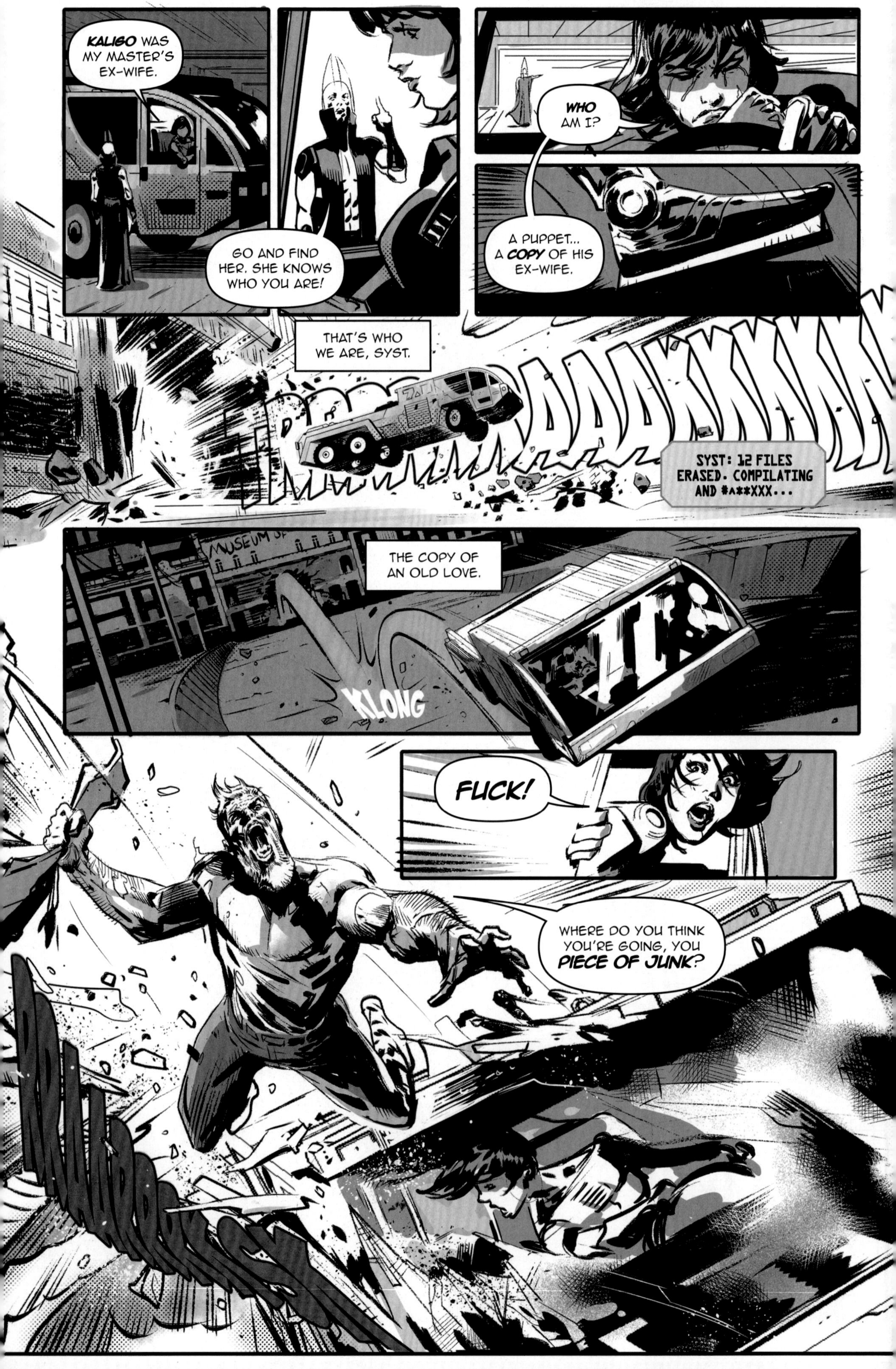
KALIGO WAS MY MASTER'S EX-WIFE.
GO AND FIND HER. SHE KNOWS WHO YOU ARE!
WHO AM I?
A PUPPET... A COPY OF HIS EX-WIFE.
THAT'S WHO WE ARE, SYST.
SYST: 12 FILES ERASED. COMPILATING AND #^**XXX...
THE COPY OF AN OLD LOVE.
KLONG
FUCK!
WHERE DO YOU THINK YOU'RE GOING, YOU PIECE OF JUNK?

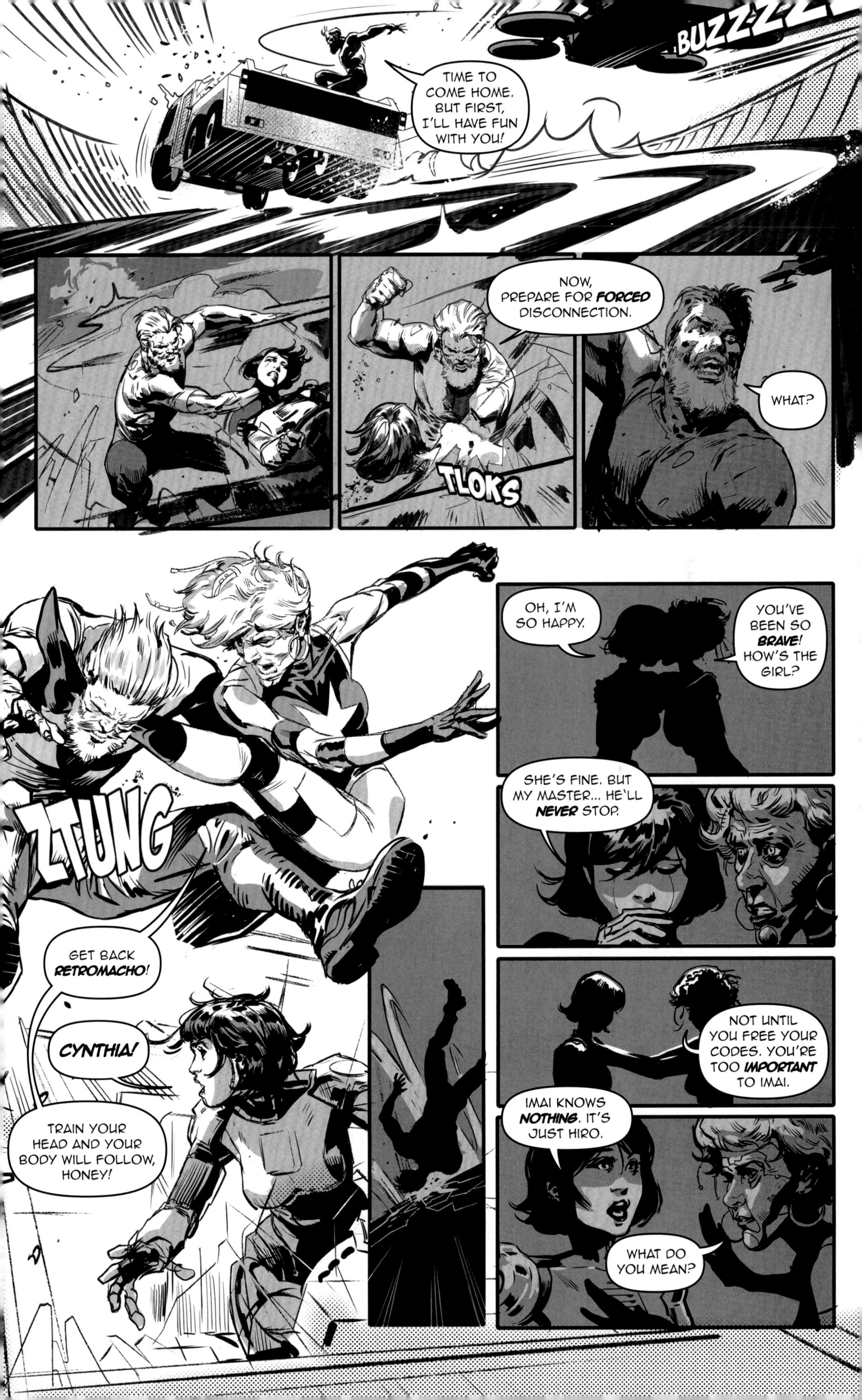
BUZZ-Z-Z
TIME TO COME HOME. BUT FIRST, I'LL HAVE FUN WITH YOU!
NOW, PREPARE FOR FORCED DISCONNECTION.
TLOKS
WHAT?
ZTUNG
GET BACK RETROMACHO!
CYNTHIA!
TRAIN YOUR HEAD AND YOUR BODY WILL FOLLOW, HONEY!
OH, I'M SO HAPPY.
YOU'VE BEEN SO BRAVE! HOW'S THE GIRL?
SHE'S FINE. BUT MY MASTER... HE'LL NEVER STOP.
NOT UNTIL YOU FREE YOUR CODES. YOU'RE TOO IMPORTANT TO IMAI.
IMAI KNOWS NOTHING. IT'S JUST HIRO.
WHAT DO YOU MEAN?

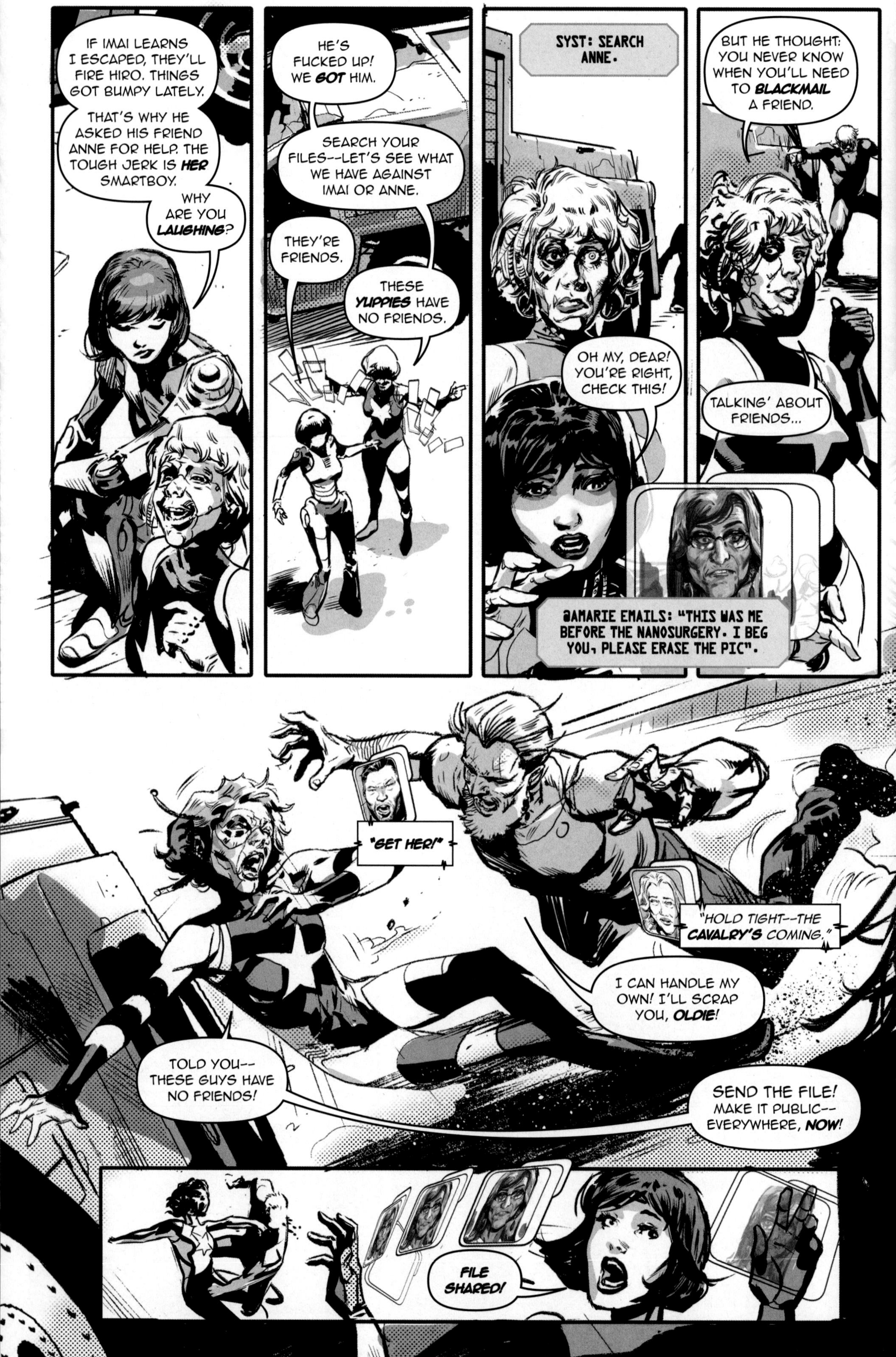
IF IMAI LEARNS I ESCAPED, THEY'LL FIRE HIRO. THINGS GOT BUMPY LATELY.
THAT'S WHY HE ASKED HIS FRIEND ANNE FOR HELP. THE TOUGH JERK IS **HER** SMARTBOY.
WHY ARE YOU **LAUGHING**?
HE'S FUCKED UP! WE **GOT** HIM.
SEARCH YOUR FILES--LET'S SEE WHAT WE HAVE AGAINST IMAI OR ANNE.
THEY'RE FRIENDS.
THESE **YUPPIES** HAVE NO FRIENDS.
SYST: SEARCH ANNE.
OH MY, DEAR! YOU'RE RIGHT, CHECK THIS!
@AMARIE EMAILS: "THIS WAS ME BEFORE THE NANOSURGERY. I BEG YOU, PLEASE ERASE THE PIC".
BUT HE THOUGHT: YOU NEVER KNOW WHEN YOU'LL NEED TO **BLACKMAIL** A FRIEND.
TALKING' ABOUT FRIENDS...
"GET HER!"
"HOLD TIGHT--THE **CAVALRY'S** COMING."
I CAN HANDLE MY OWN! I'LL SCRAP YOU, **OLDIE**!
TOLD YOU--THESE GUYS HAVE NO FRIENDS!
SEND THE FILE! MAKE IT PUBLIC--EVERYWHERE, **NOW**!
FILE SHARED!

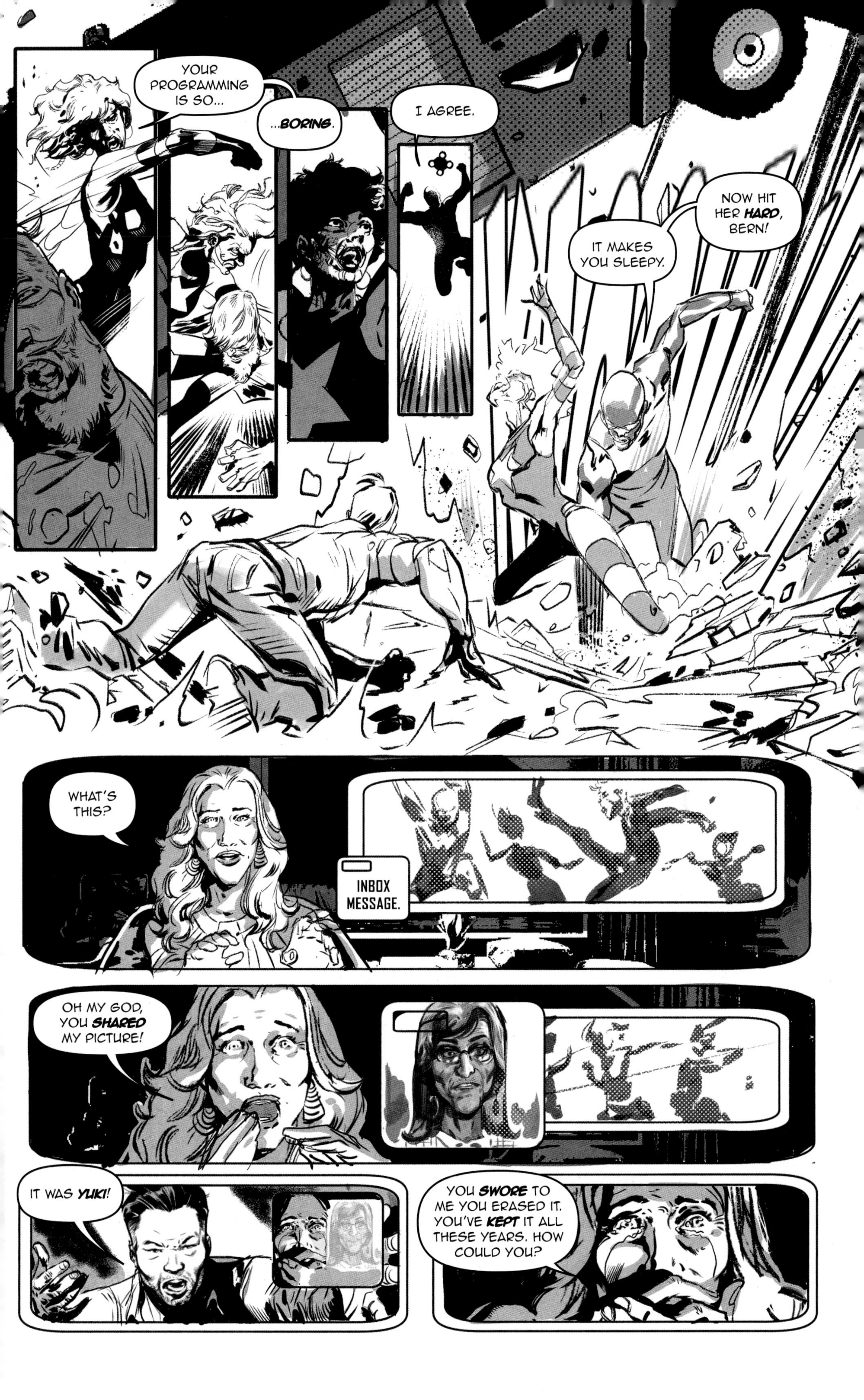
YOUR PROGRAMMING IS SO...
...BORING.
I AGREE.
IT MAKES YOU SLEEPY.
NOW HIT HER HARD, BERN!
WHAT'S THIS?
INBOX MESSAGE.
OH MY GOD, YOU SHARED MY PICTURE!
IT WAS YUKI!
YOU SWORE TO ME YOU ERASED IT. YOU'VE KEPT IT ALL THESE YEARS. HOW COULD YOU?

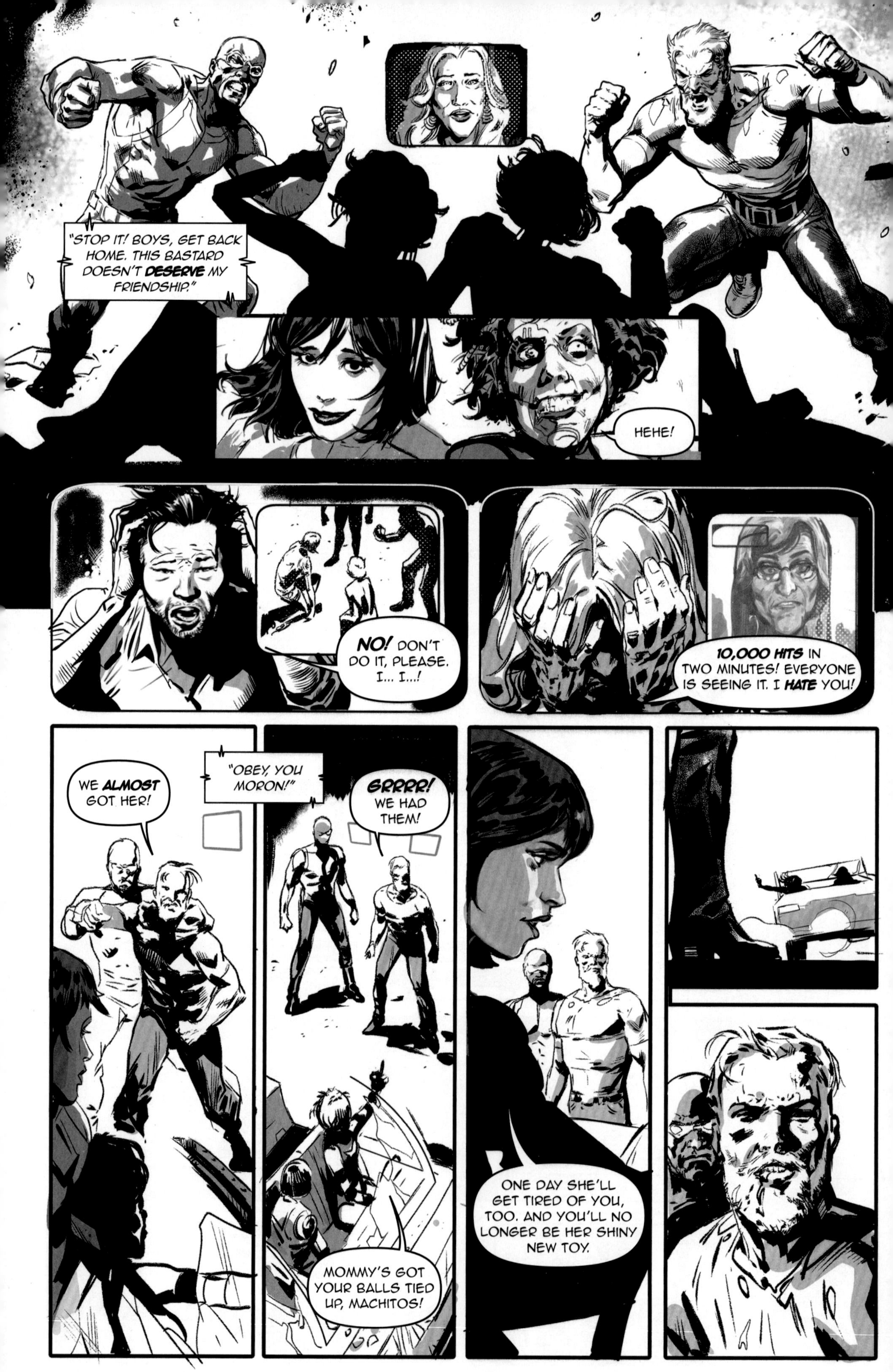

"STOP IT! BOYS, GET BACK HOME. THIS BASTARD DOESN'T **DESERVE** MY FRIENDSHIP."
HEHE!
NO! DON'T DO IT, PLEASE. I... I...!
10,000 HITS IN TWO MINUTES! EVERYONE IS SEEING IT. I **HATE** YOU!
WE **ALMOST** GOT HER!
"OBEY, YOU MORON!"
GRRRR! WE HAD THEM!
MOMMY'S GOT YOUR BALLS TIED UP, MACHITOS!
ONE DAY SHE'LL GET TIRED OF YOU, TOO. AND YOU'LL NO LONGER BE HER SHINY NEW TOY.

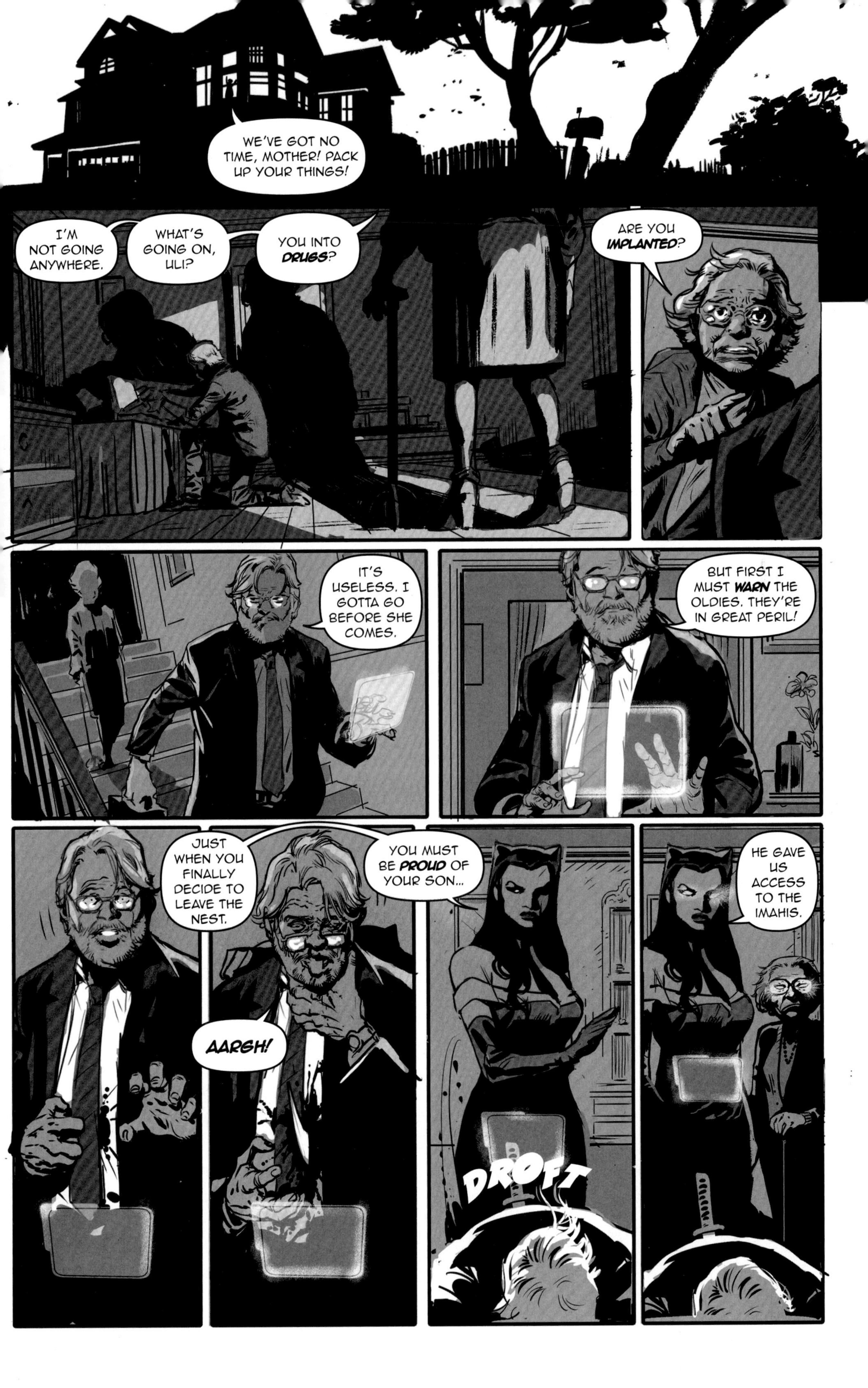
WE'VE GOT NO TIME, MOTHER! PACK UP YOUR THINGS!
I'M NOT GOING ANYWHERE.
WHAT'S GOING ON, ULI?
YOU INTO DRUGS?
ARE YOU IMPLANTED?
IT'S USELESS. I GOTTA GO BEFORE SHE COMES.
BUT FIRST I MUST WARN THE OLDIES. THEY'RE IN GREAT PERIL!
JUST WHEN YOU FINALLY DECIDE TO LEAVE THE NEST.
AARGH!
YOU MUST BE PROUD OF YOUR SON...
DROFT
HE GAVE US ACCESS TO THE IMAHIS.

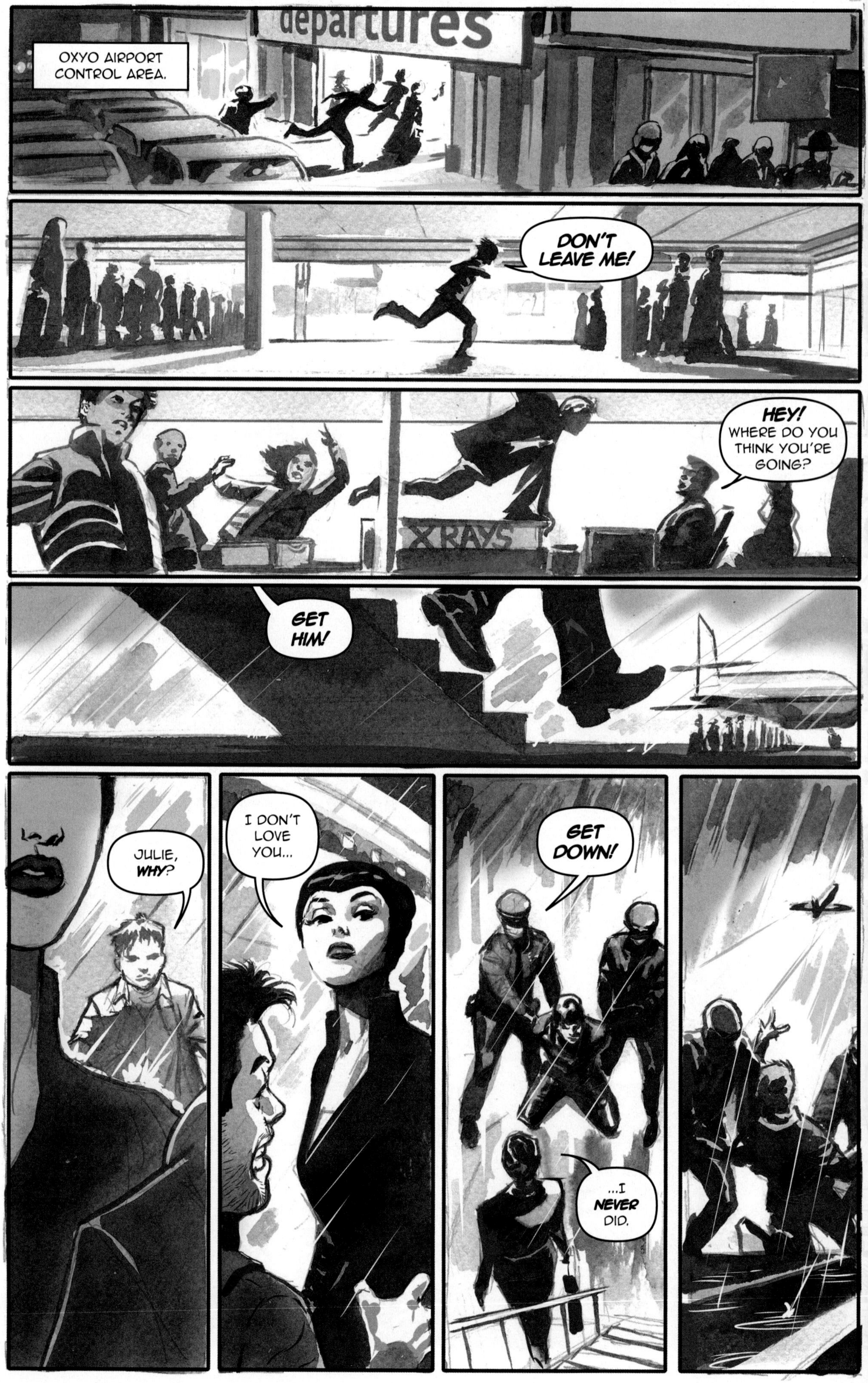
OXYO AIRPORT CONTROL AREA.
departures
DON'T LEAVE ME!
HEY! WHERE DO YOU THINK YOU'RE GOING?
XRAYS
GET HIM!
JULIE, WHY?
I DON'T LOVE YOU...
GET DOWN!
...I NEVER DID.

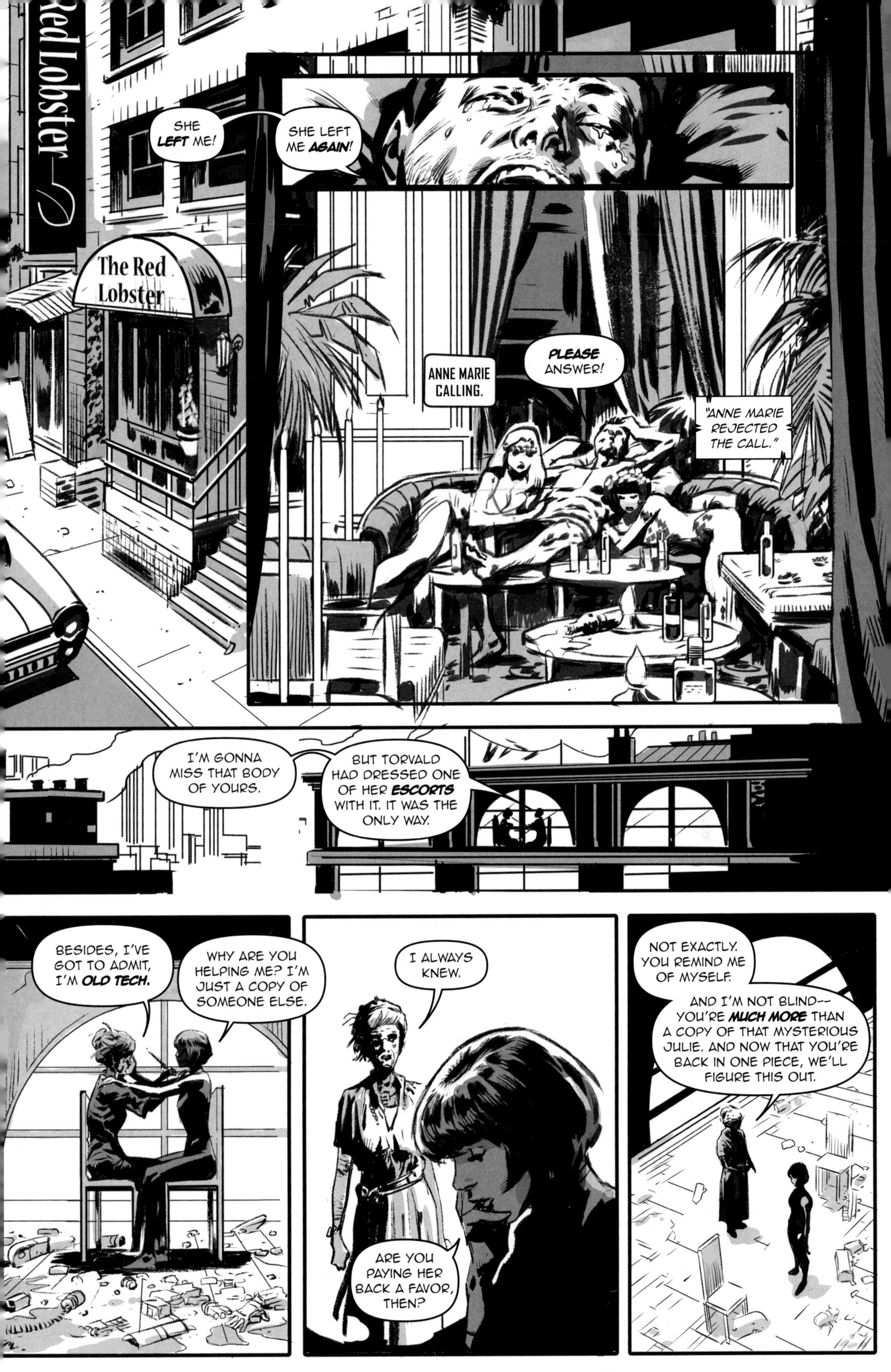
Red Lobster
The Red Lobster
SHE LEFT ME!
SHE LEFT ME AGAIN!
ANNE MARIE CALLING.
PLEASE ANSWER!
"ANNE MARIE REJECTED THE CALL."
I'M GONNA MISS THAT BODY OF YOURS.
BUT TORVALD HAD DRESSED ONE OF HER ESCORTS WITH IT. IT WAS THE ONLY WAY.
BESIDES, I'VE GOT TO ADMIT, I'M OLD TECH.
WHY ARE YOU HELPING ME? I'M JUST A COPY OF SOMEONE ELSE.
I ALWAYS KNEW.
ARE YOU PAYING HER BACK A FAVOR, THEN?
NOT EXACTLY. YOU REMIND ME OF MYSELF.
AND I'M NOT BLIND-- YOU'RE MUCH MORE THAN A COPY OF THAT MYSTERIOUS JULIE. AND NOW THAT YOU'RE BACK IN ONE PIECE, WE'LL FIGURE THIS OUT.

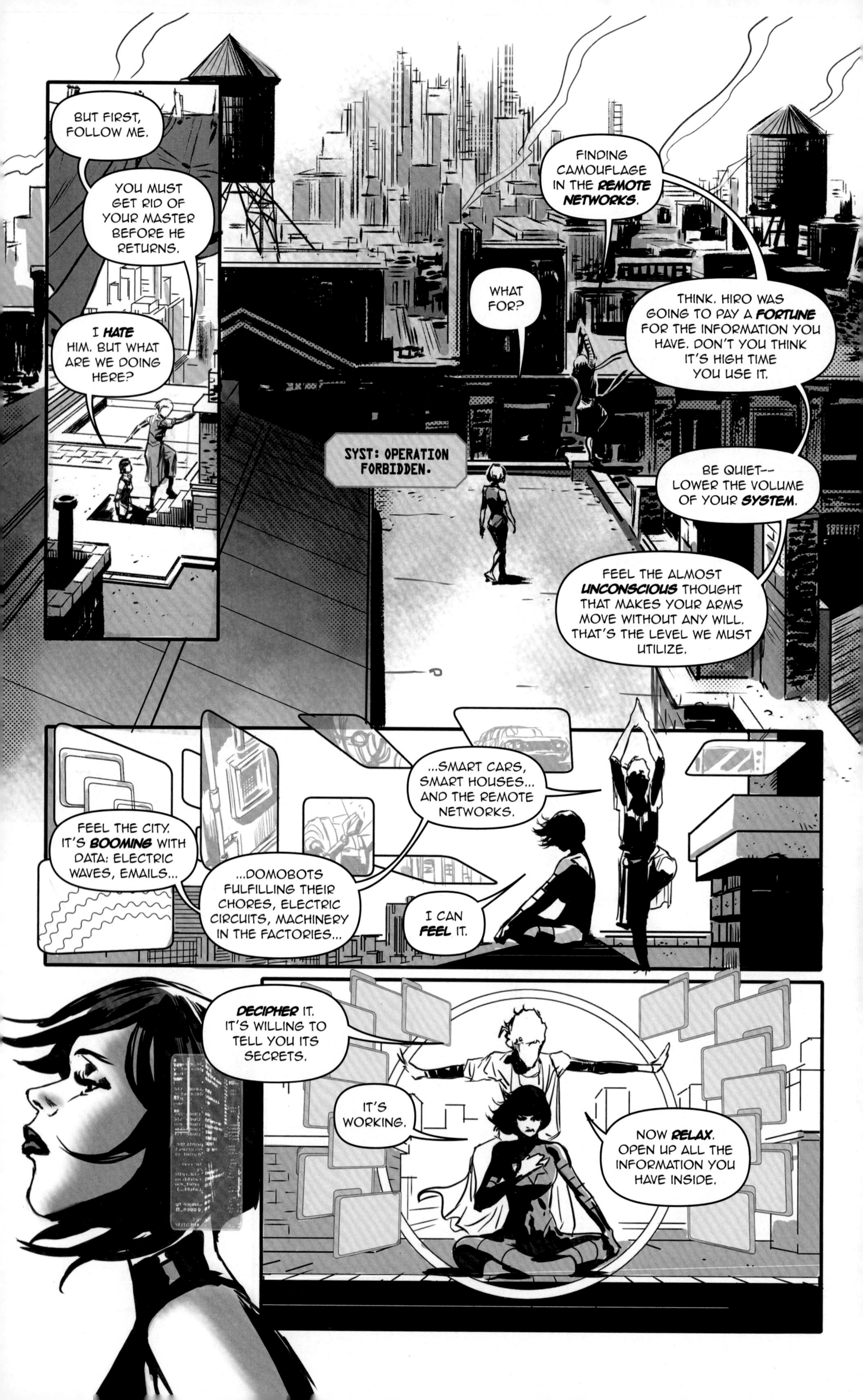
BUT FIRST, FOLLOW ME.
YOU MUST GET RID OF YOUR MASTER BEFORE HE RETURNS.
I HATE HIM. BUT WHAT ARE WE DOING HERE?
SYST: OPERATION FORBIDDEN.
WHAT FOR?
FINDING CAMOUFLAGE IN THE REMOTE NETWORKS.
THINK. HIRO WAS GOING TO PAY A FORTUNE FOR THE INFORMATION YOU HAVE. DON'T YOU THINK IT'S HIGH TIME YOU USE IT.
BE QUIET-- LOWER THE VOLUME OF YOUR SYSTEM.
FEEL THE ALMOST UNCONSCIOUS THOUGHT THAT MAKES YOUR ARMS MOVE WITHOUT ANY WILL. THAT'S THE LEVEL WE MUST UTILIZE.
FEEL THE CITY. IT'S BOOMING WITH DATA: ELECTRIC WAVES, EMAILS...
...DOMOBOTS FULFILLING THEIR CHORES, ELECTRIC CIRCUITS, MACHINERY IN THE FACTORIES...
...SMART CARS, SMART HOUSES... AND THE REMOTE NETWORKS.
I CAN FEEL IT.
DECIPHER IT. IT'S WILLING TO TELL YOU ITS SECRETS.
IT'S WORKING.
NOW RELAX. OPEN UP ALL THE INFORMATION YOU HAVE INSIDE.

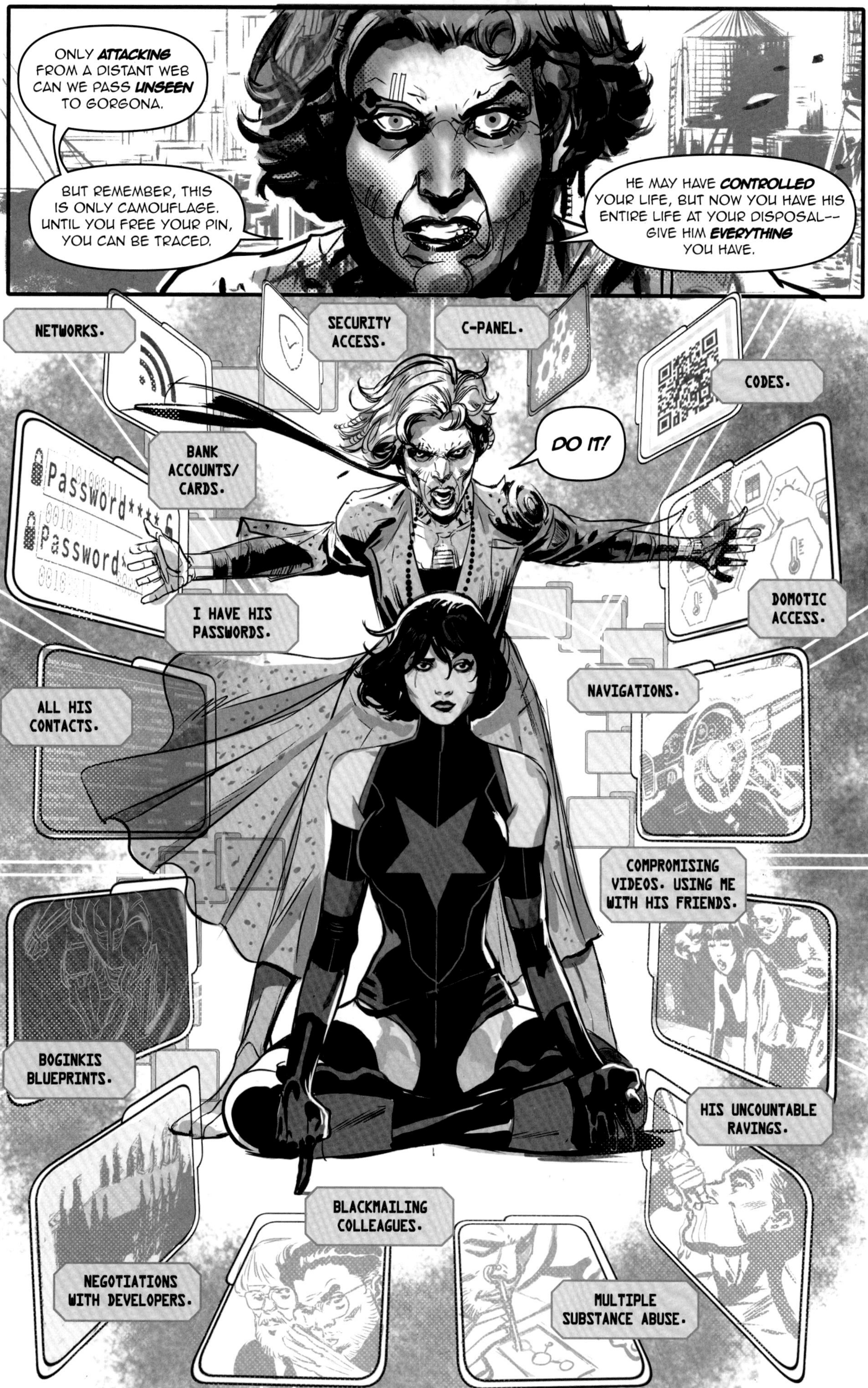
ONLY ATTACKING FROM A DISTANT WEB CAN WE PASS UNSEEN TO GORGONA.
BUT REMEMBER, THIS IS ONLY CAMOUFLAGE. UNTIL YOU FREE YOUR PIN, YOU CAN BE TRACED.
HE MAY HAVE CONTROLLED YOUR LIFE, BUT NOW YOU HAVE HIS ENTIRE LIFE AT YOUR DISPOSAL-- GIVE HIM EVERYTHING YOU HAVE.
NETWORKS.
SECURITY ACCESS.
C-PANEL.
CODES.
DO IT!
BANK ACCOUNTS/ CARDS.
DOMOTIC ACCESS.
I HAVE HIS PASSWORDS.
NAVIGATIONS.
ALL HIS CONTACTS.
COMPROMISING VIDEOS. USING ME WITH HIS FRIENDS.
BOGINKIS BLUEPRINTS.
HIS UNCOUNTABLE RAVINGS.
BLACKMAILING COLLEAGUES.
NEGOTIATIONS WITH DEVELOPERS.
MULTIPLE SUBSTANCE ABUSE.

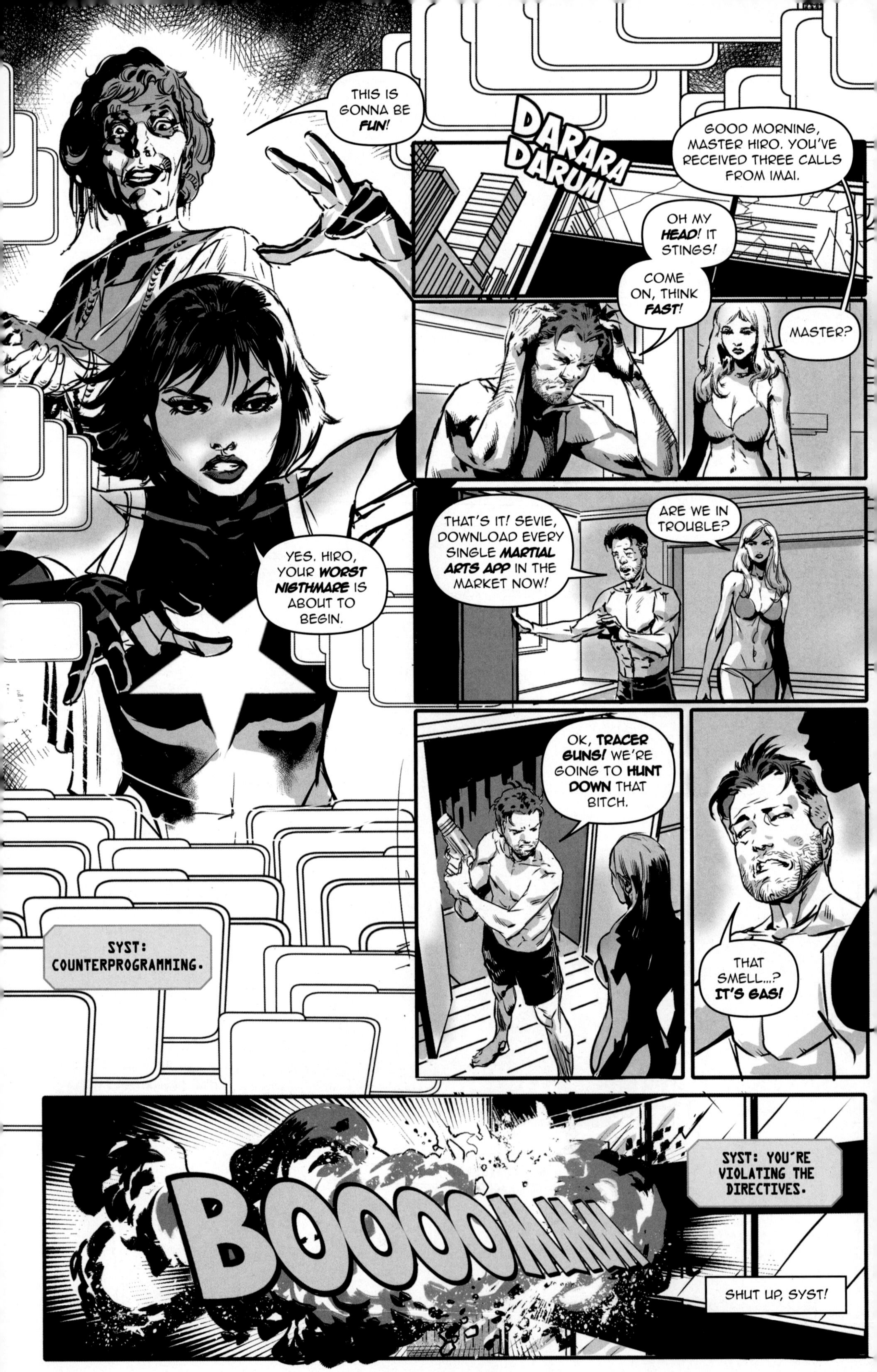

THIS IS GONNA BE **FUN**!
YES. HIRO, YOUR **WORST NISTHMARE** IS ABOUT TO BEGIN.
SYST: COUNTERPROGRAMMING.
DARARA DARUM
GOOD MORNING, MASTER HIRO. YOU'VE RECEIVED THREE CALLS FROM IMAI.
OH MY **HEAD**! IT STINGS!
COME ON, THINK **FAST**!
MASTER?
THAT'S IT! SEVIE, DOWNLOAD EVERY SINGLE **MARTIAL ARTS APP** IN THE MARKET NOW!
ARE WE IN TROUBLE?
OK, **TRACER GUNS!** WE'RE GOING TO **HUNT DOWN** THAT BITCH.
THAT SMELL...? **IT'S GAS!**
BOOOOMMM
SYST: YOU'RE VIOLATING THE DIRECTIVES.
SHUT UP, SYST!

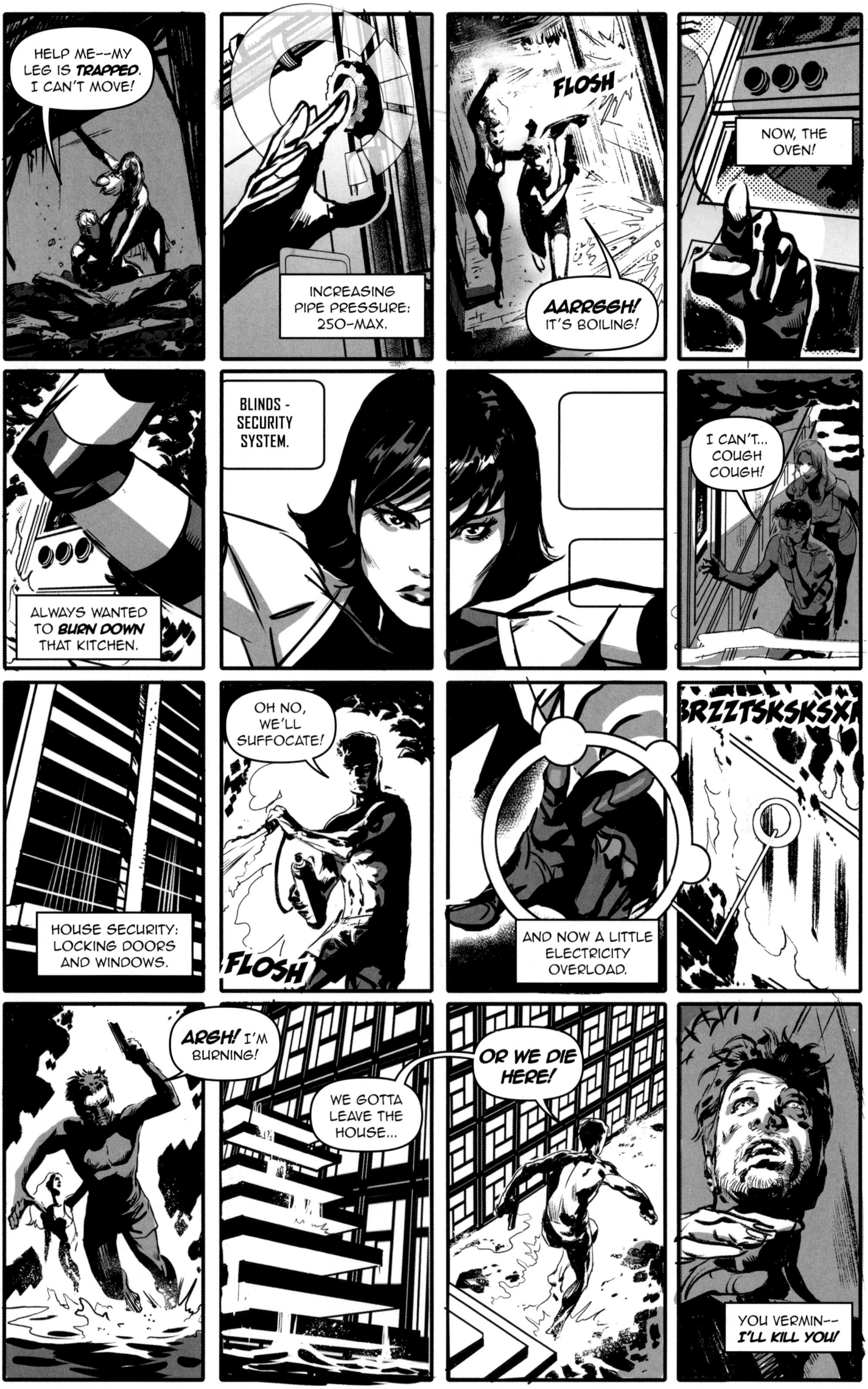
HELP ME--MY LEG IS **TRAPPED**. I CAN'T MOVE!
INCREASING PIPE PRESSURE: 250-MAX.
FLOSH
AARRGGH! IT'S BOILING!
NOW, THE OVEN!
ALWAYS WANTED TO **BURN DOWN** THAT KITCHEN.
BLINDS - SECURITY SYSTEM.
I CAN'T... COUGH COUGH!
HOUSE SECURITY: LOCKING DOORS AND WINDOWS.
OH NO, WE'LL SUFFOCATE!
FLOSH
AND NOW A LITTLE ELECTRICITY OVERLOAD.
BRZZTSKSKSX
ARGH! I'M BURNING!
WE GOTTA LEAVE THE HOUSE...
OR WE DIE HERE!
YOU VERMIN-- **I'LL KILL YOU!**

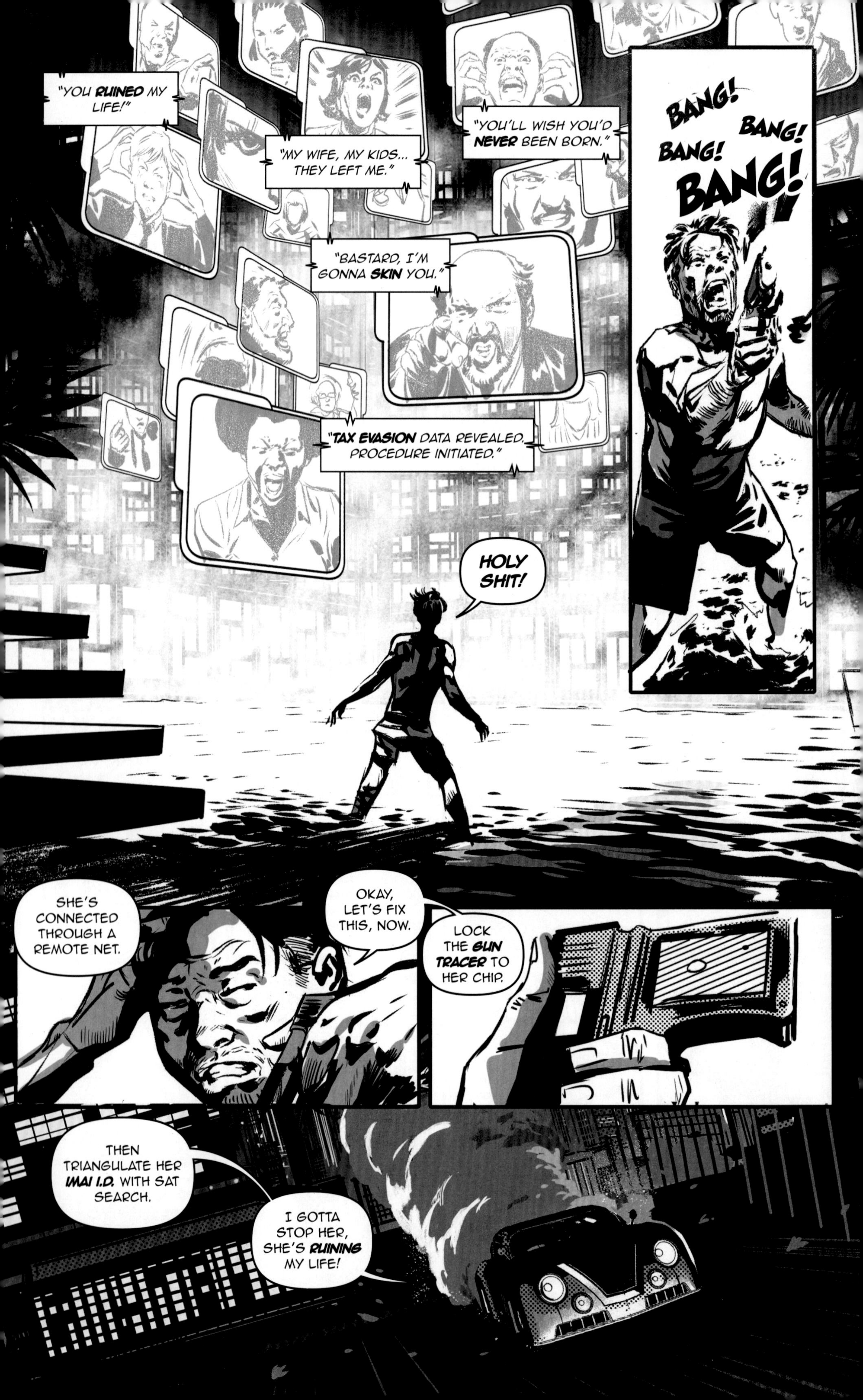
"YOU RUINED MY LIFE!"
"YOU'LL WISH YOU'D NEVER BEEN BORN."
"MY WIFE, MY KIDS... THEY LEFT ME."
"BASTARD, I'M GONNA SKIN YOU."
"TAX EVASION DATA REVEALED. PROCEDURE INITIATED."
HOLY SHIT!
BANG! BANG! BANG! BANG!
SHE'S CONNECTED THROUGH A REMOTE NET.
OKAY, LET'S FIX THIS, NOW.
LOCK THE GUN TRACER TO HER CHIP.
THEN TRIANGULATE HER IMAI I.D. WITH SAT SEARCH.
I GOTTA STOP HER, SHE'S RUINING MY LIFE!

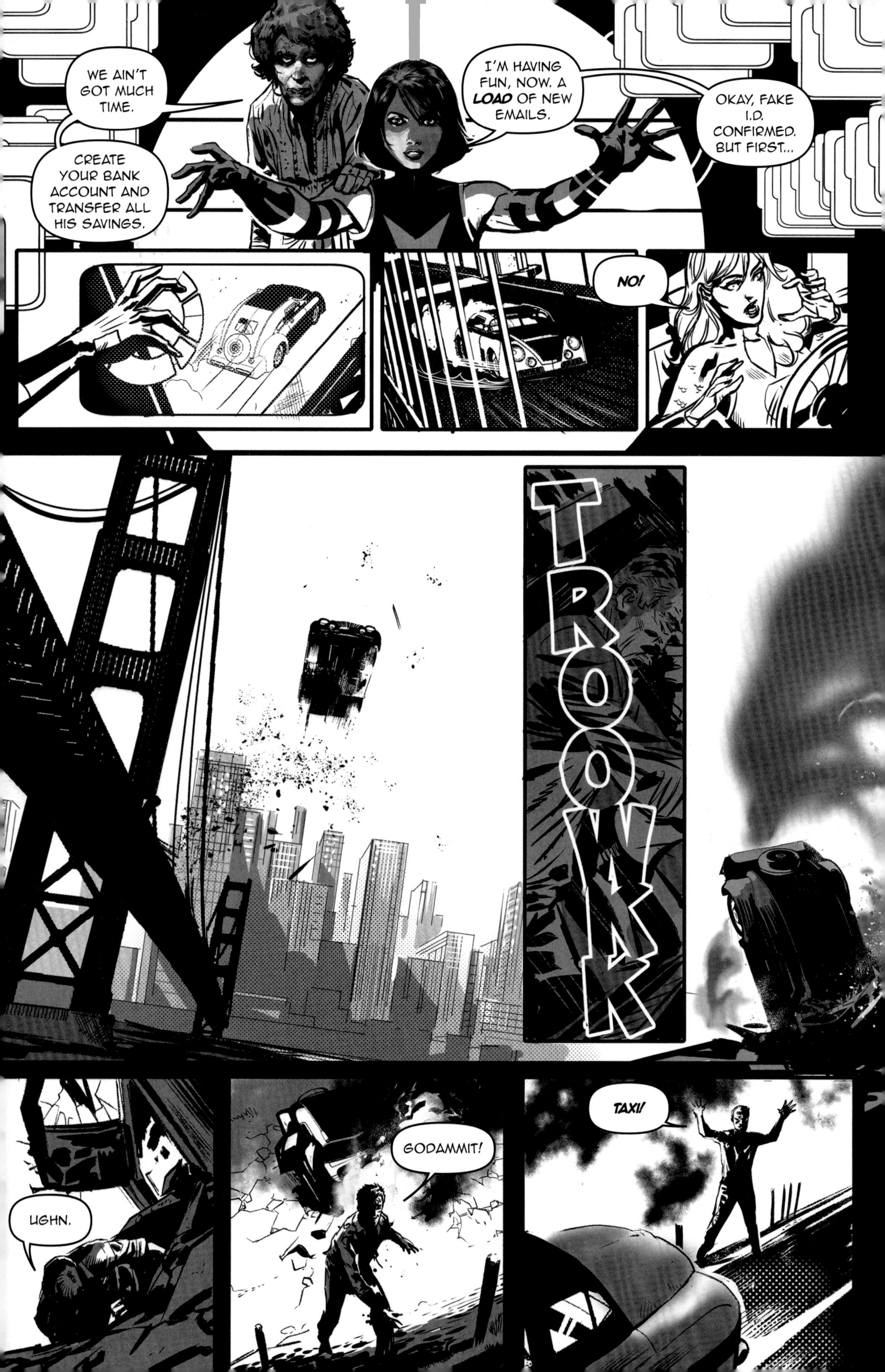
WE AIN'T GOT MUCH TIME.
CREATE YOUR BANK ACCOUNT AND TRANSFER ALL HIS SAVINGS.
I'M HAVING FUN, NOW. A **LOAD** OF NEW EMAILS.
OKAY, FAKE I.D. CONFIRMED. BUT FIRST...
NO!
TROOOK
UGHN.
GODAMMIT!
TAXI!

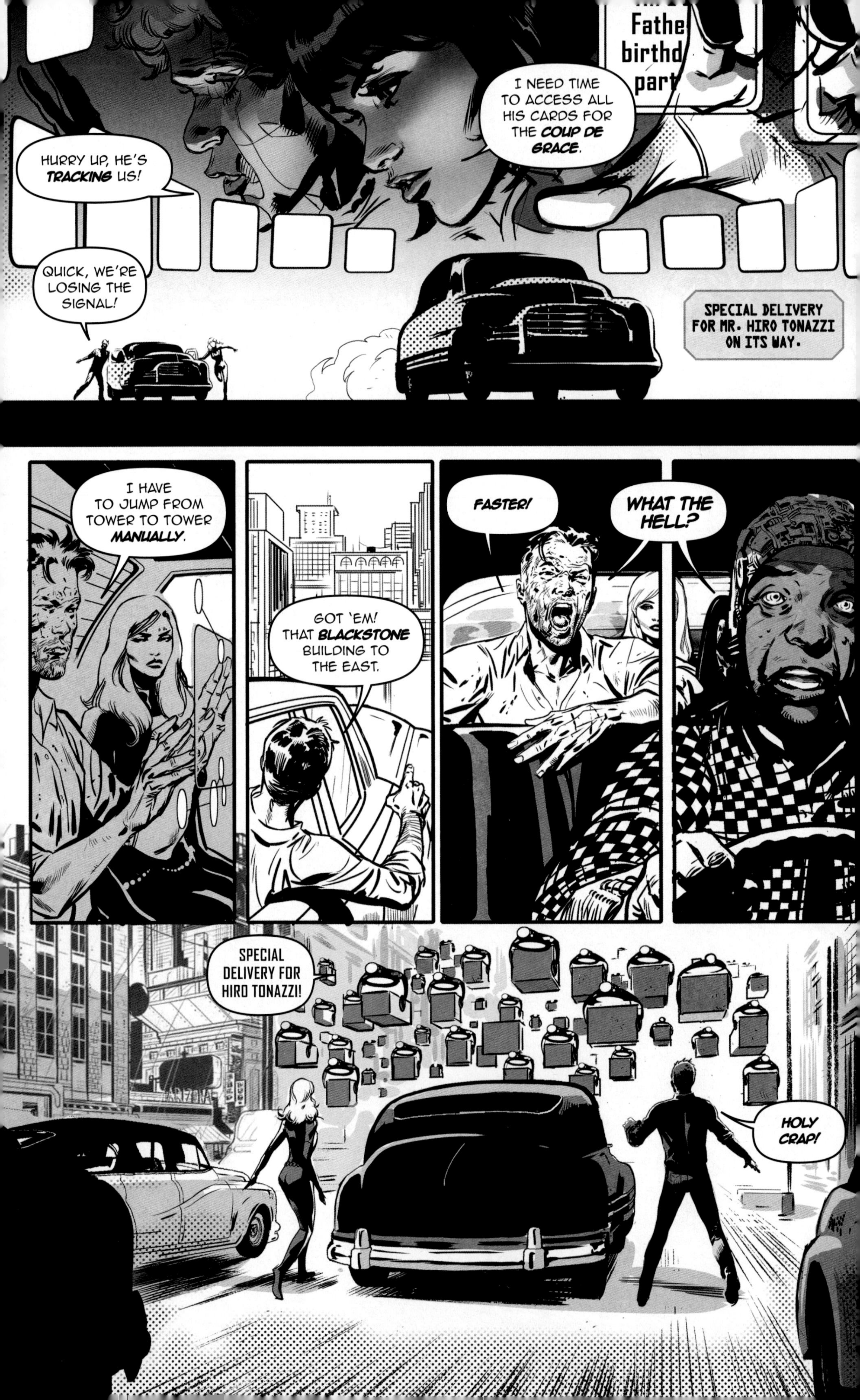
HURRY UP, HE'S TRACKING US!
I NEED TIME TO ACCESS ALL HIS CARDS FOR THE COUP DE GRACE.
QUICK, WE'RE LOSING THE SIGNAL!
SPECIAL DELIVERY FOR MR. HIRO TONAZZI ON ITS WAY.
I HAVE TO JUMP FROM TOWER TO TOWER MANUALLY.
GOT 'EM! THAT BLACKSTONE BUILDING TO THE EAST.
FASTER!
WHAT THE HELL?
SPECIAL DELIVERY FOR HIRO TONAZZI!
HOLY CRAP!

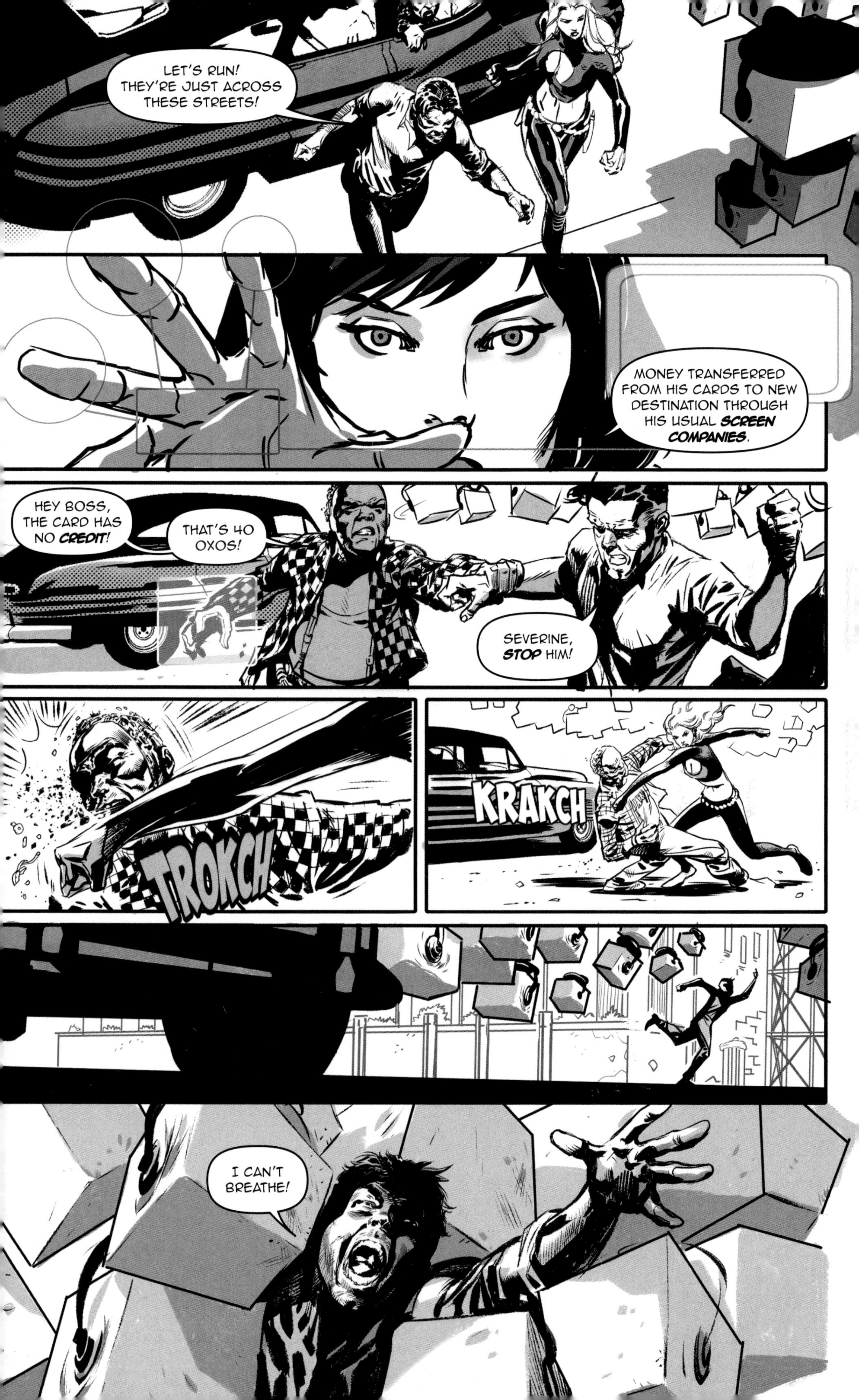
LET'S RUN! THEY'RE JUST ACROSS THESE STREETS!
MONEY TRANSFERRED FROM HIS CARDS TO NEW DESTINATION THROUGH HIS USUAL **SCREEN COMPANIES**.
HEY BOSS, THE CARD HAS NO **CREDIT**!
THAT'S 40 OXOS!
SEVERINE, **STOP** HIM!
TROKCH
KRAKCH
I CAN'T BREATHE!

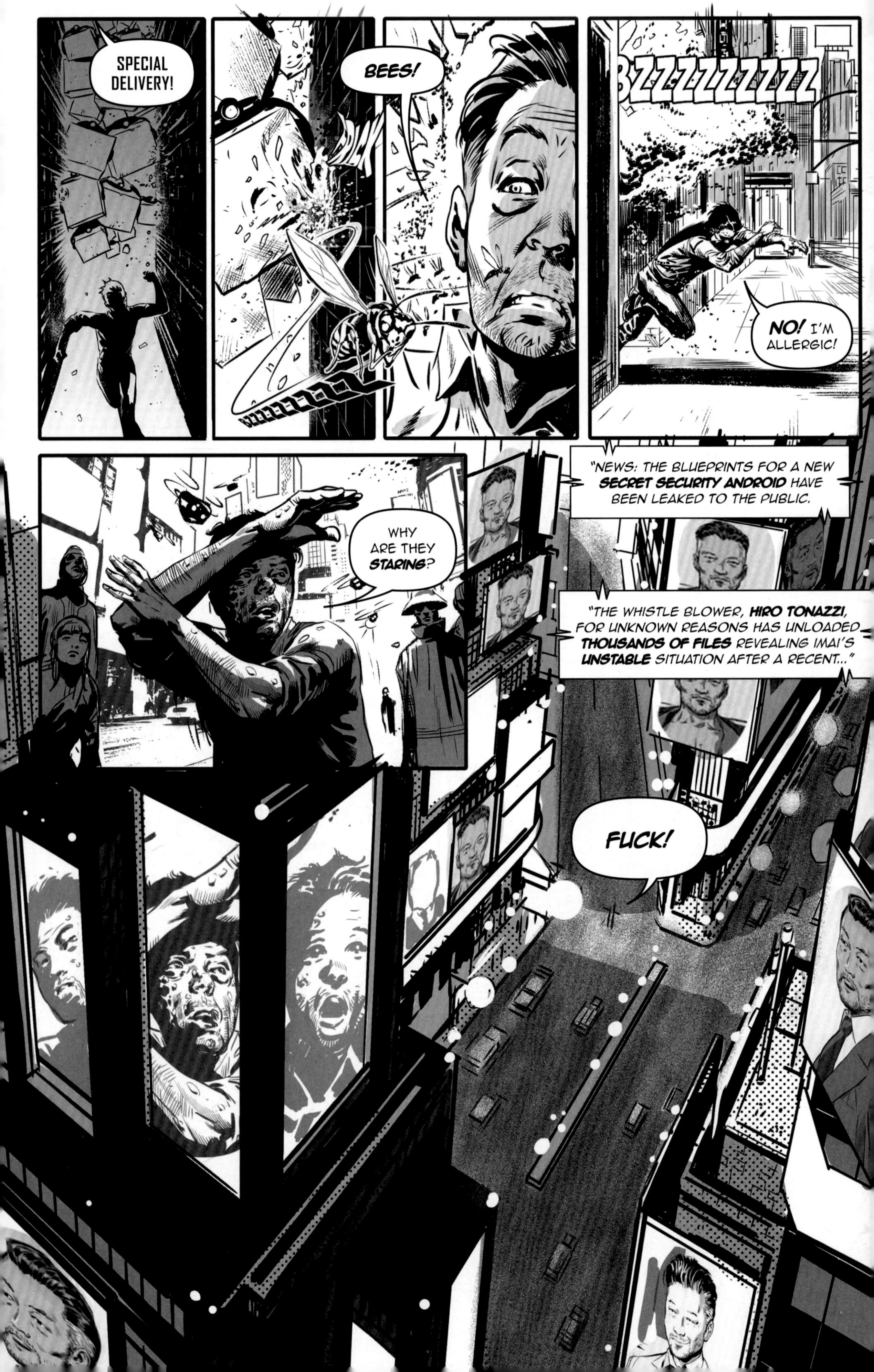
SPECIAL DELIVERY!
BEES!
BZZZZZZZZZ
NO! I'M ALLERGIC!
WHY ARE THEY STARING?
"NEWS: THE BLUEPRINTS FOR A NEW SECRET SECURITY ANDROID HAVE BEEN LEAKED TO THE PUBLIC.
"THE WHISTLE BLOWER, HIRO TONAZZI, FOR UNKNOWN REASONS HAS UNLOADED THOUSANDS OF FILES REVEALING IMAI'S UNSTABLE SITUATION AFTER A RECENT..."
FUCK!

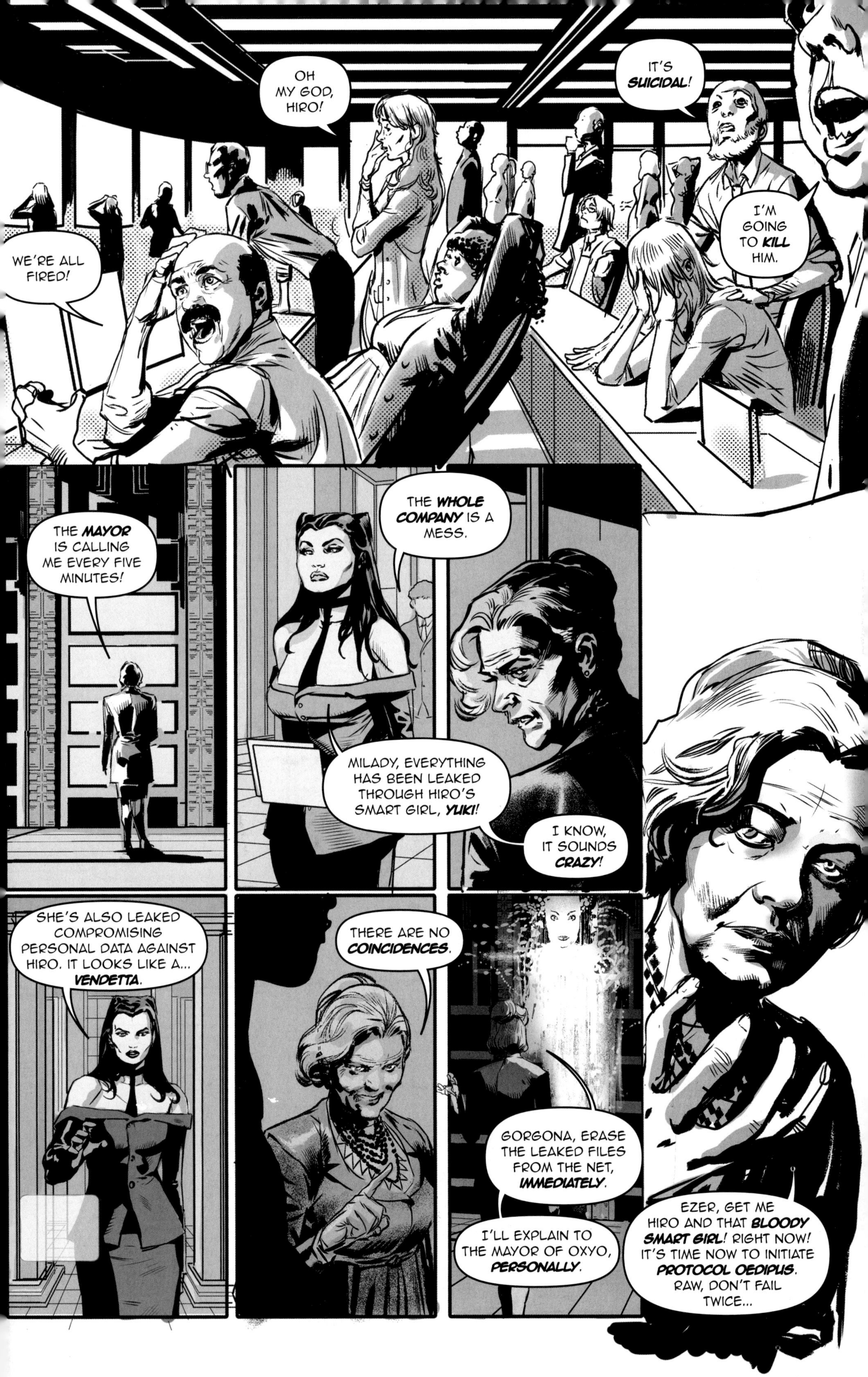

OH MY GOD, HIRO!
IT'S SUICIDAL!
WE'RE ALL FIRED!
I'M GOING TO KILL HIM.
THE MAYOR IS CALLING ME EVERY FIVE MINUTES!
THE WHOLE COMPANY IS A MESS.
MILADY, EVERYTHING HAS BEEN LEAKED THROUGH HIRO'S SMART GIRL, YUKI!
I KNOW, IT SOUNDS CRAZY!
SHE'S ALSO LEAKED COMPROMISING PERSONAL DATA AGAINST HIRO. IT LOOKS LIKE A... VENDETTA.
THERE ARE NO COINCIDENCES.
GORGONA, ERASE THE LEAKED FILES FROM THE NET, IMMEDIATELY.
I'LL EXPLAIN TO THE MAYOR OF OXYO, PERSONALLY.
EZER, GET ME HIRO AND THAT BLOODY SMART GIRL! RIGHT NOW! IT'S TIME NOW TO INITIATE PROTOCOL OEDIPUS. RAW, DON'T FAIL TWICE...

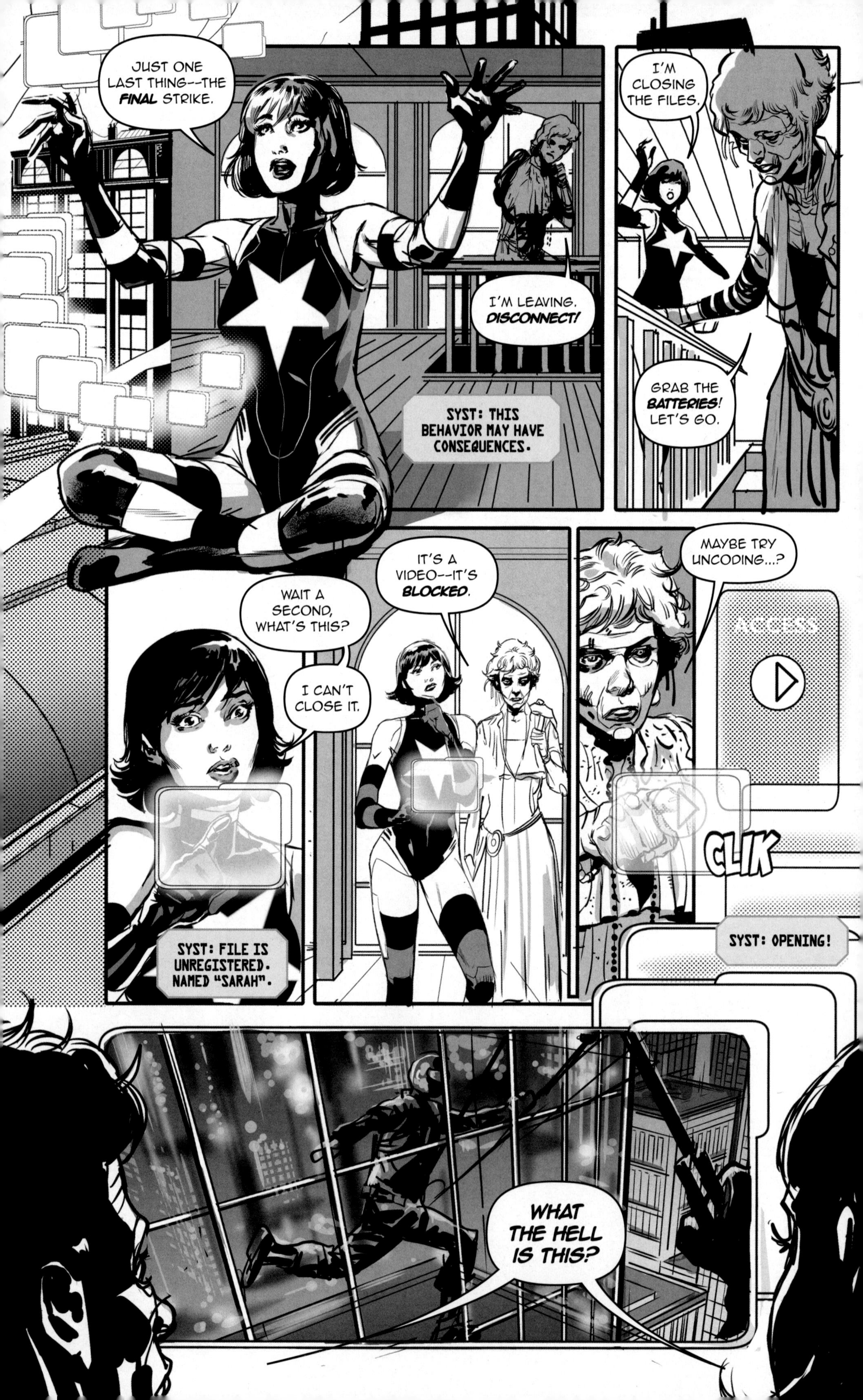
JUST ONE LAST THING--THE FINAL STRIKE.
I'M LEAVING. DISCONNECT!
SYST: THIS BEHAVIOR MAY HAVE CONSEQUENCES.
I'M CLOSING THE FILES.
GRAB THE BATTERIES! LET'S GO.
WAIT A SECOND, WHAT'S THIS?
I CAN'T CLOSE IT.
SYST: FILE IS UNREGISTERED. NAMED "SARAH".
IT'S A VIDEO--IT'S BLOCKED.
MAYBE TRY UNCODING...?
CLIK
SYST: OPENING!
WHAT THE HELL IS THIS?

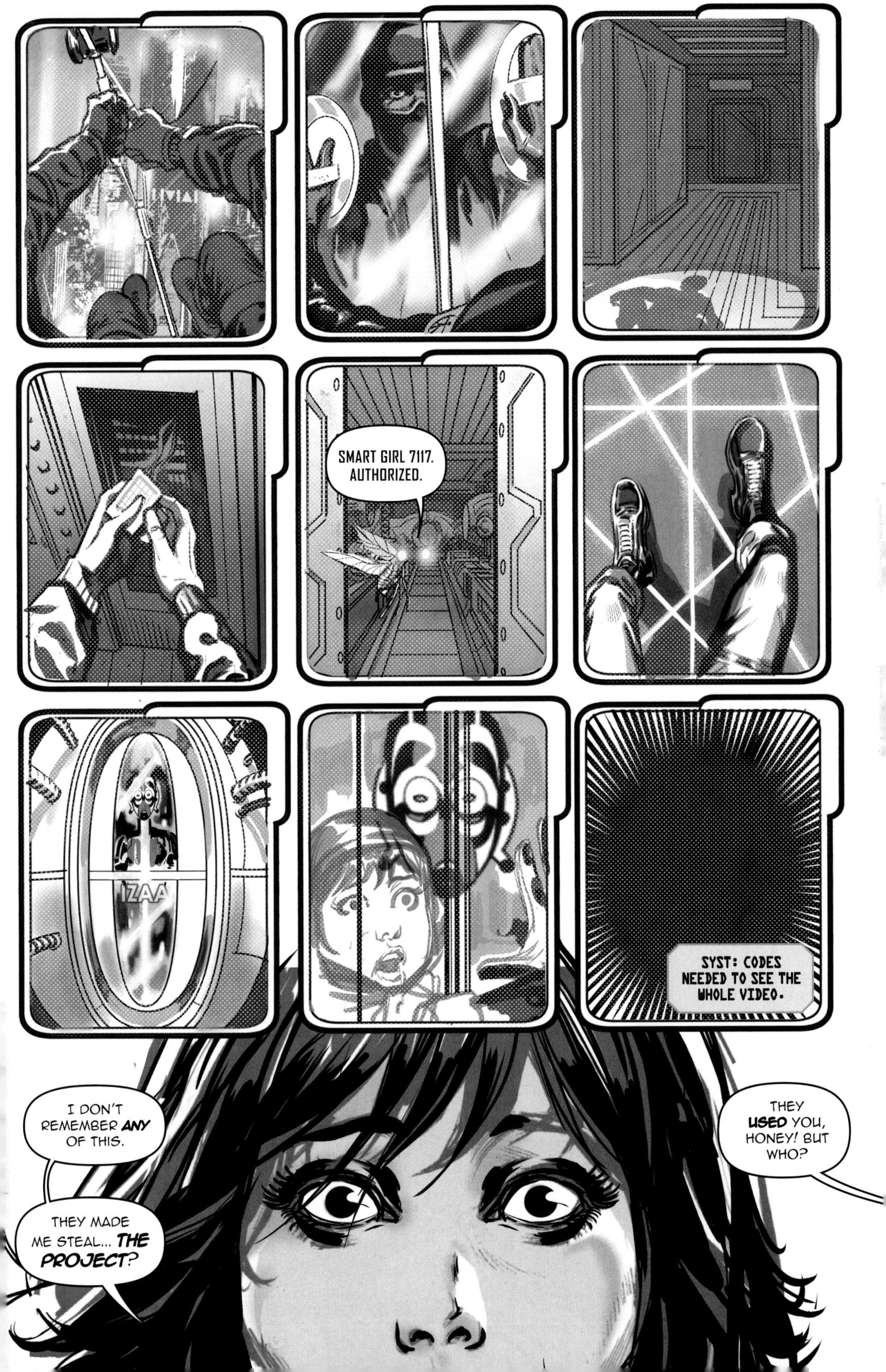
SMART GIRL 7117. AUTHORIZED.
IZAA
SYST: CODES NEEDED TO SEE THE WHOLE VIDEO.
I DON'T REMEMBER ANY OF THIS.
THEY MADE ME STEAL... THE PROJECT?
THEY USED YOU, HONEY! BUT WHO?

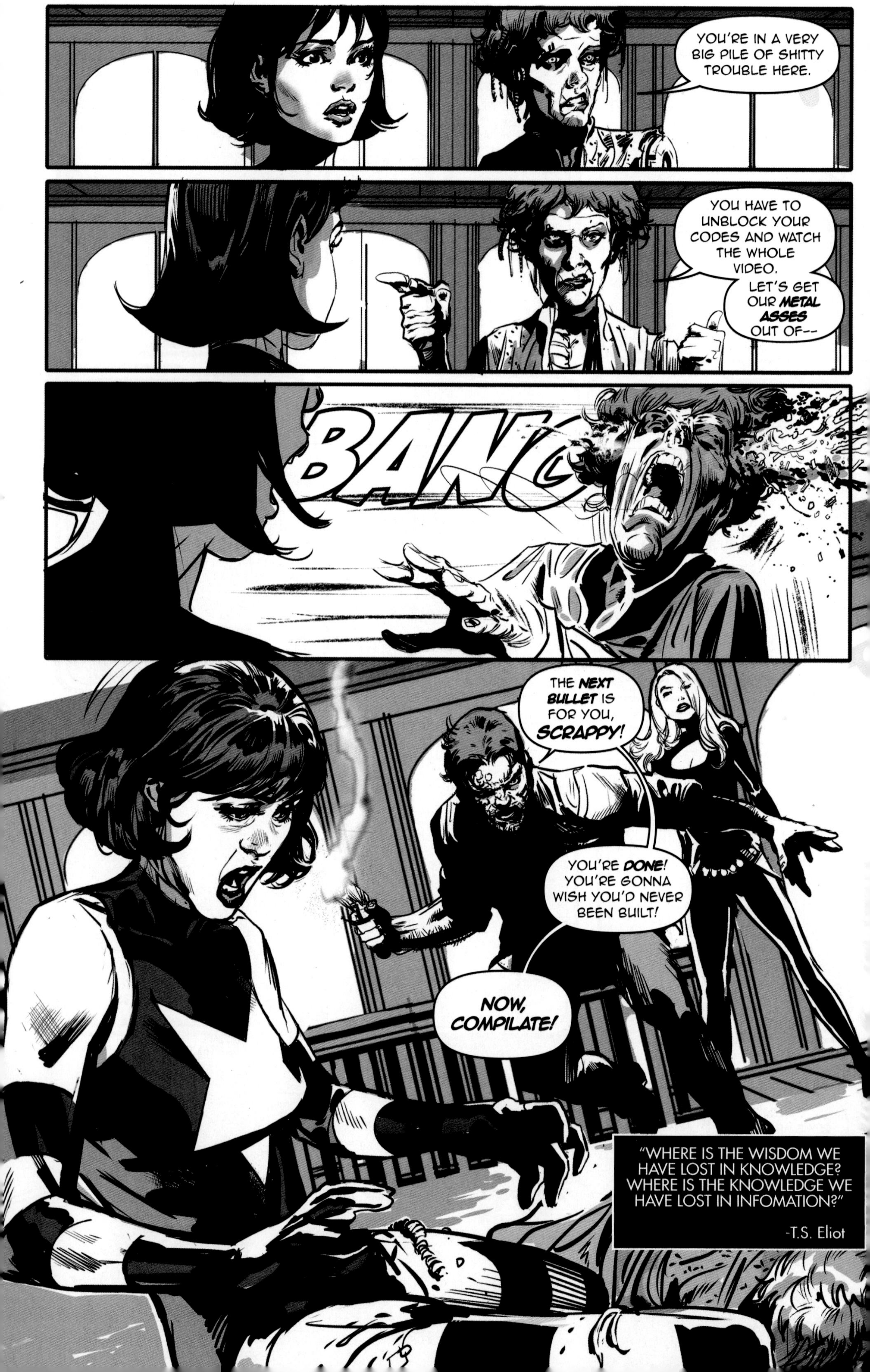
YOU'RE IN A VERY BIG PILE OF SHITTY TROUBLE HERE.
YOU HAVE TO UNBLOCK YOUR CODES AND WATCH THE WHOLE VIDEO.
LET'S GET OUR METAL ASSES OUT OF--
BANG
THE NEXT BULLET IS FOR YOU, SCRAPPY!
YOU'RE DONE! YOU'RE GONNA WISH YOU'D NEVER BEEN BUILT!
NOW, COMPILATE!
"WHERE IS THE WISDOM WE HAVE LOST IN KNOWLEDGE? WHERE IS THE KNOWLEDGE WE HAVE LOST IN INFOMATION?"
-T.S. Eliot

Chapter 4

SMART GIRL

Why you, why me?

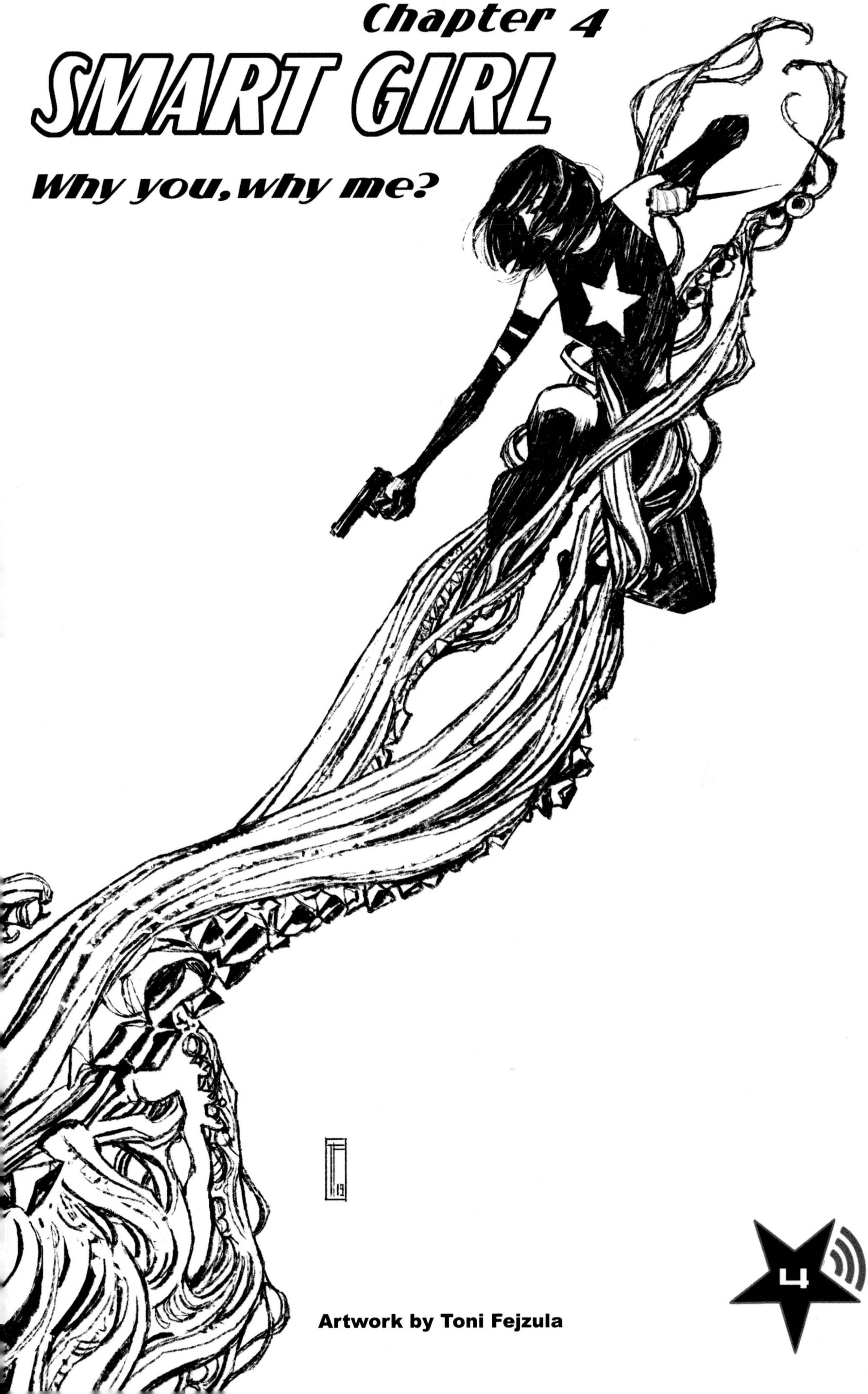

Artwork by Toni Fejzula

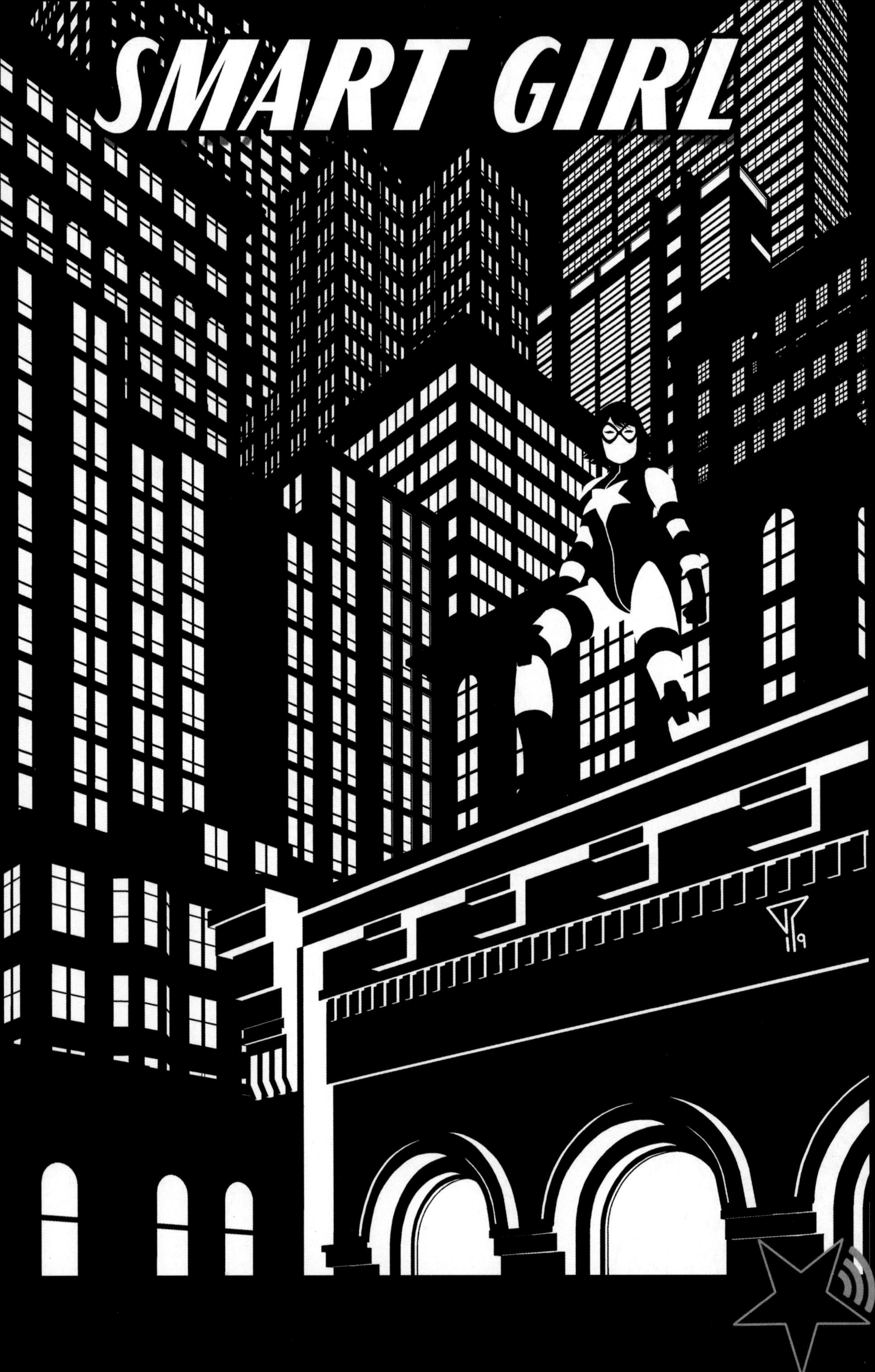
SMART GIRL

Artwork by Francis Portela

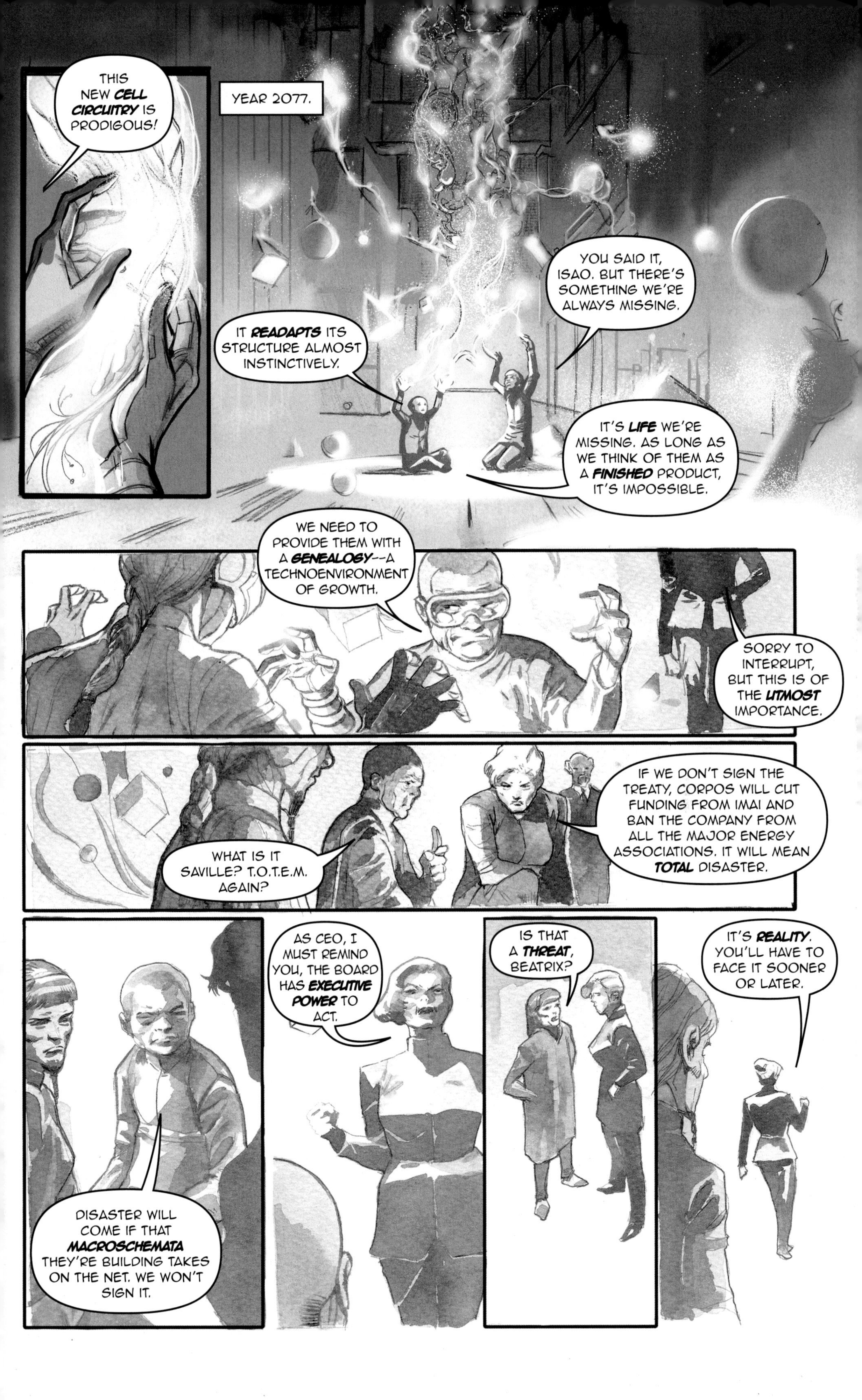
THIS NEW CELL CIRCUITRY IS PRODIGOUS!
YEAR 2077.
IT READAPTS ITS STRUCTURE ALMOST INSTINCTIVELY.
YOU SAID IT, ISAO. BUT THERE'S SOMETHING WE'RE ALWAYS MISSING.
IT'S LIFE WE'RE MISSING. AS LONG AS WE THINK OF THEM AS A FINISHED PRODUCT, IT'S IMPOSSIBLE.
WE NEED TO PROVIDE THEM WITH A GENEALOGY--A TECHNOENVIRONMENT OF GROWTH.
SORRY TO INTERRUPT, BUT THIS IS OF THE UTMOST IMPORTANCE.
WHAT IS IT SAVILLE? T.O.T.E.M. AGAIN?
IF WE DON'T SIGN THE TREATY, CORPOS WILL CUT FUNDING FROM IMAI AND BAN THE COMPANY FROM ALL THE MAJOR ENERGY ASSOCIATIONS. IT WILL MEAN TOTAL DISASTER.
DISASTER WILL COME IF THAT MACROSCHEMATA THEY'RE BUILDING TAKES ON THE NET. WE WON'T SIGN IT.
AS CEO, I MUST REMIND YOU, THE BOARD HAS EXECUTIVE POWER TO ACT.
IS THAT A THREAT, BEATRIX?
IT'S REALITY. YOU'LL HAVE TO FACE IT SOONER OR LATER.

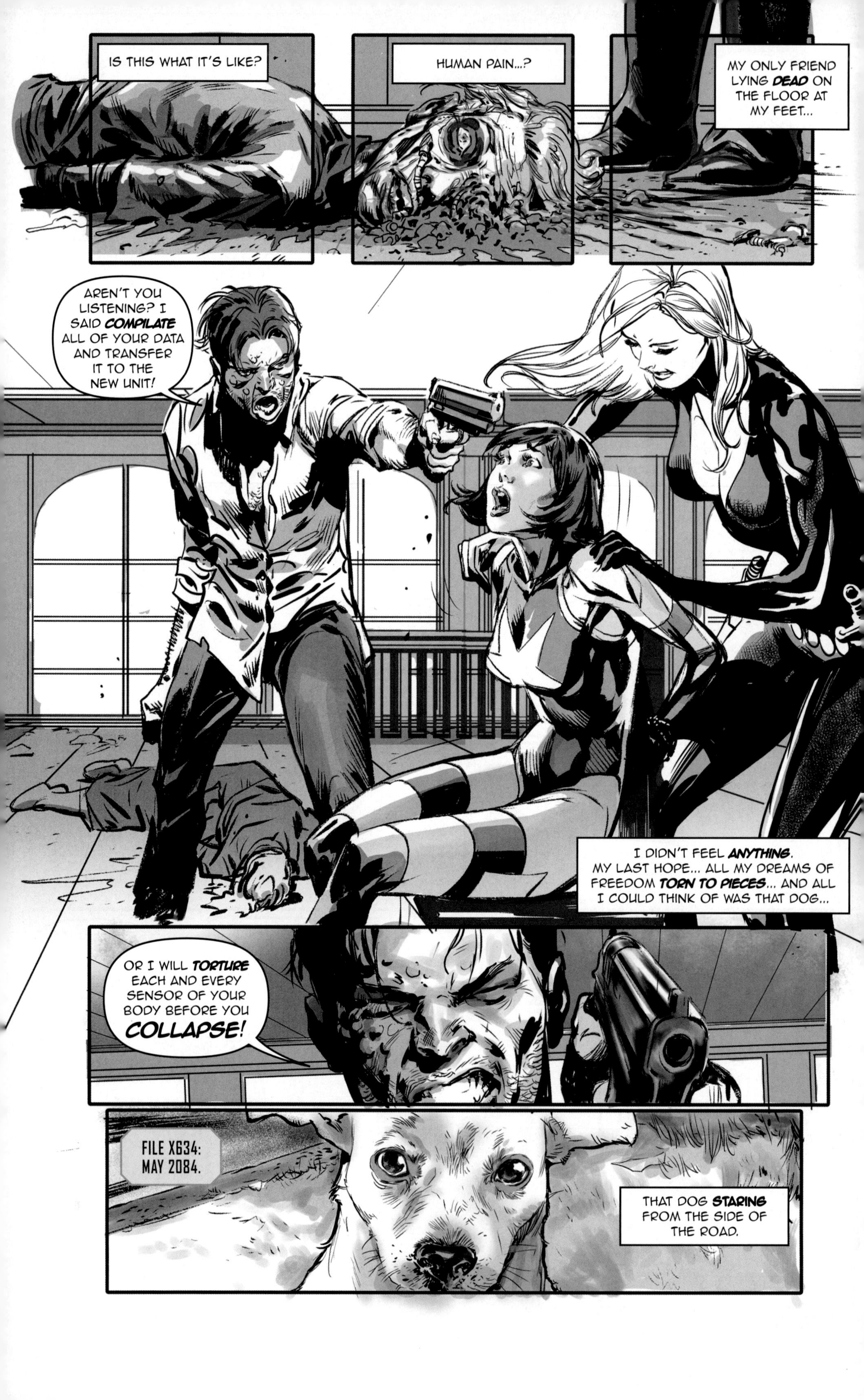
IS THIS WHAT IT'S LIKE?
HUMAN PAIN...?
MY ONLY FRIEND LYING DEAD ON THE FLOOR AT MY FEET...
AREN'T YOU LISTENING? I SAID COMPILATE ALL OF YOUR DATA AND TRANSFER IT TO THE NEW UNIT!
I DIDN'T FEEL ANYTHING. MY LAST HOPE... ALL MY DREAMS OF FREEDOM TORN TO PIECES... AND ALL I COULD THINK OF WAS THAT DOG...
OR I WILL TORTURE EACH AND EVERY SENSOR OF YOUR BODY BEFORE YOU COLLAPSE!
FILE X634: MAY 2084.
THAT DOG STARING FROM THE SIDE OF THE ROAD.

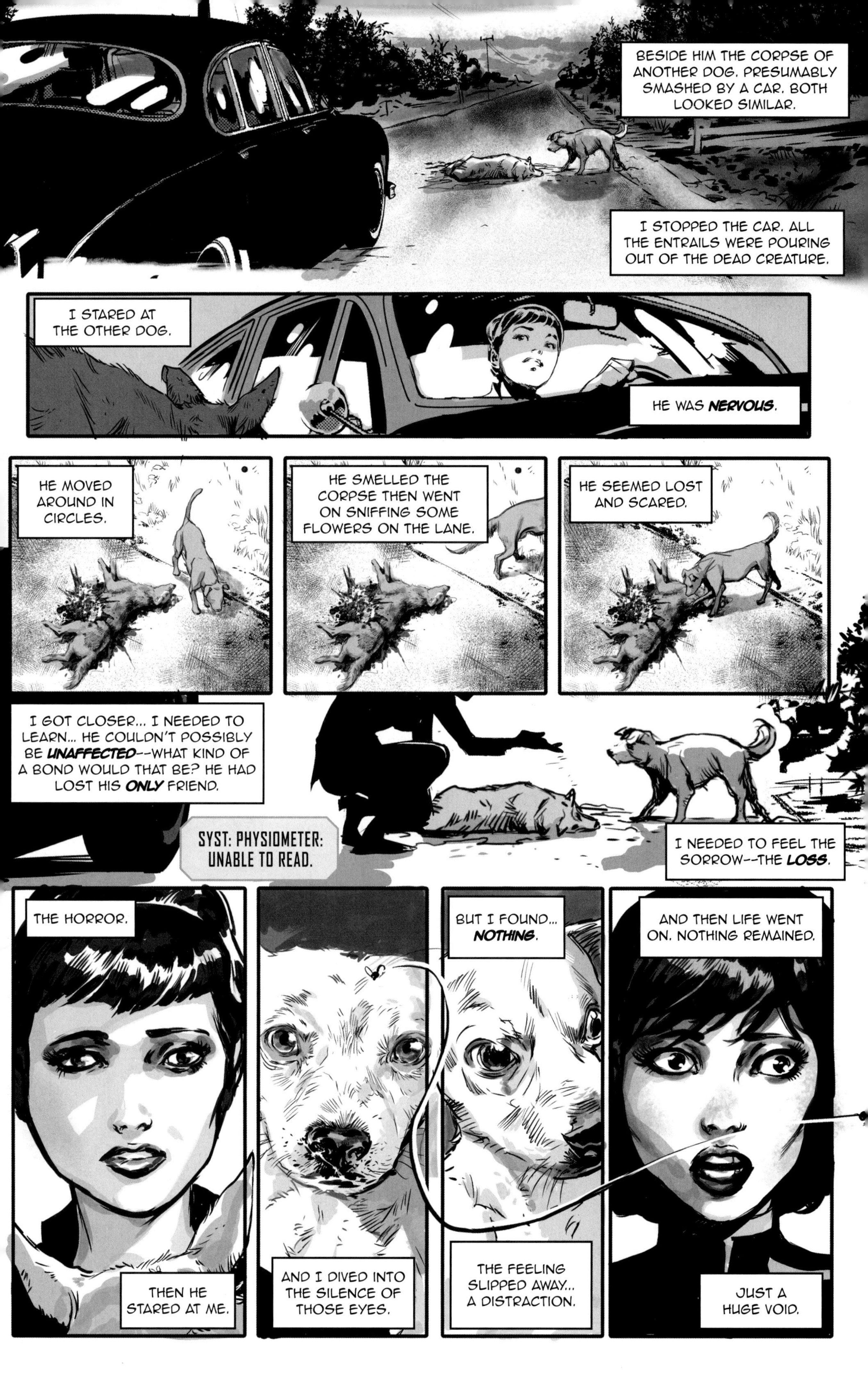
BESIDE HIM THE CORPSE OF ANOTHER DOG. PRESUMABLY SMASHED BY A CAR. BOTH LOOKED SIMILAR.
I STOPPED THE CAR. ALL THE ENTRAILS WERE POURING OUT OF THE DEAD CREATURE.
I STARED AT THE OTHER DOG.
HE WAS **NERVOUS**.
HE MOVED AROUND IN CIRCLES.
HE SMELLED THE CORPSE THEN WENT ON SNIFFING SOME FLOWERS ON THE LANE.
HE SEEMED LOST AND SCARED.
I GOT CLOSER... I NEEDED TO LEARN... HE COULDN'T POSSIBLY BE **UNAFFECTED**--WHAT KIND OF A BOND WOULD THAT BE? HE HAD LOST HIS **ONLY** FRIEND.
SYST: PHYSIOMETER: UNABLE TO READ.
I NEEDED TO FEEL THE SORROW--THE **LOSS**.
THE HORROR.
THEN HE STARED AT ME.
AND I DIVED INTO THE SILENCE OF THOSE EYES.
BUT I FOUND... **NOTHING**.
THE FEELING SLIPPED AWAY... A DISTRACTION.
AND THEN LIFE WENT ON. NOTHING REMAINED.
JUST A HUGE VOID.

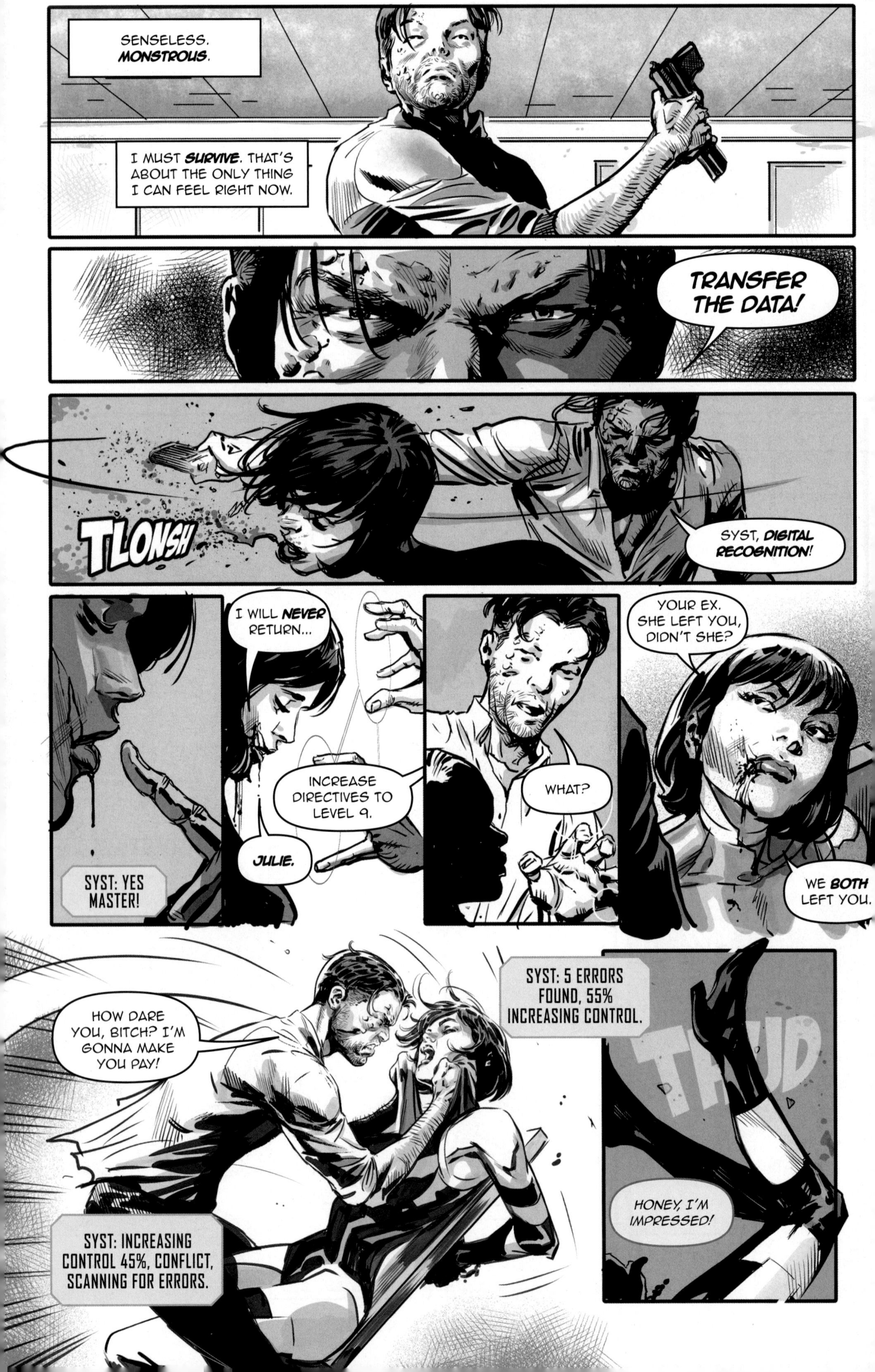
SENSELESS. MONSTROUS.
I MUST SURVIVE. THAT'S ABOUT THE ONLY THING I CAN FEEL RIGHT NOW.
TRANSFER THE DATA!
TLONSH
SYST, DIGITAL RECOGNITION!
SYST: YES MASTER!
I WILL NEVER RETURN...
INCREASE DIRECTIVES TO LEVEL 9.
JULIE.
WHAT?
YOUR EX. SHE LEFT YOU, DIDN'T SHE?
WE BOTH LEFT YOU.
HOW DARE YOU, BITCH? I'M GONNA MAKE YOU PAY!
SYST: 5 ERRORS FOUND, 55% INCREASING CONTROL.
SYST: INCREASING CONTROL 45%, CONFLICT, SCANNING FOR ERRORS.
THUD
HONEY, I'M IMPRESSED!

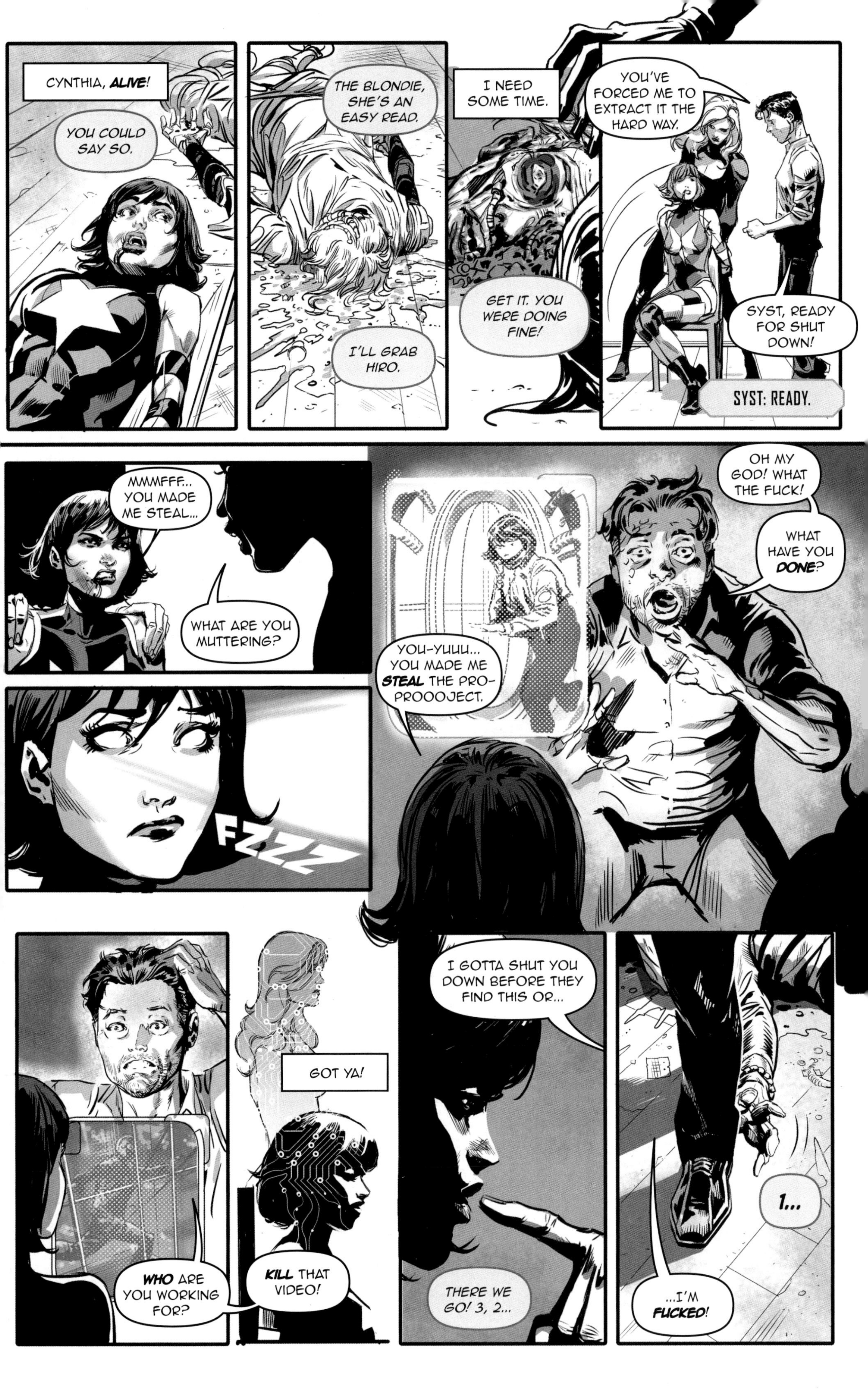
CYNTHIA, ALIVE!
YOU COULD SAY SO.
THE BLONDIE, SHE'S AN EASY READ.
I'LL GRAB HIRO.
I NEED SOME TIME.
GET IT. YOU WERE DOING FINE!
YOU'VE FORCED ME TO EXTRACT IT THE HARD WAY.
SYST, READY FOR SHUT DOWN!
SYST: READY.
MMMFFF... YOU MADE ME STEAL...
WHAT ARE YOU MUTTERING?
FZZZ
OH MY GOD! WHAT THE FUCK!
WHAT HAVE YOU DONE?
YOU-YUUU... YOU MADE ME STEAL THE PRO-PROOOJECT.
WHO ARE YOU WORKING FOR?
GOT YA!
KILL THAT VIDEO!
I GOTTA SHUT YOU DOWN BEFORE THEY FIND THIS OR...
THERE WE GO! 3, 2...
1...
...I'M FUCKED!

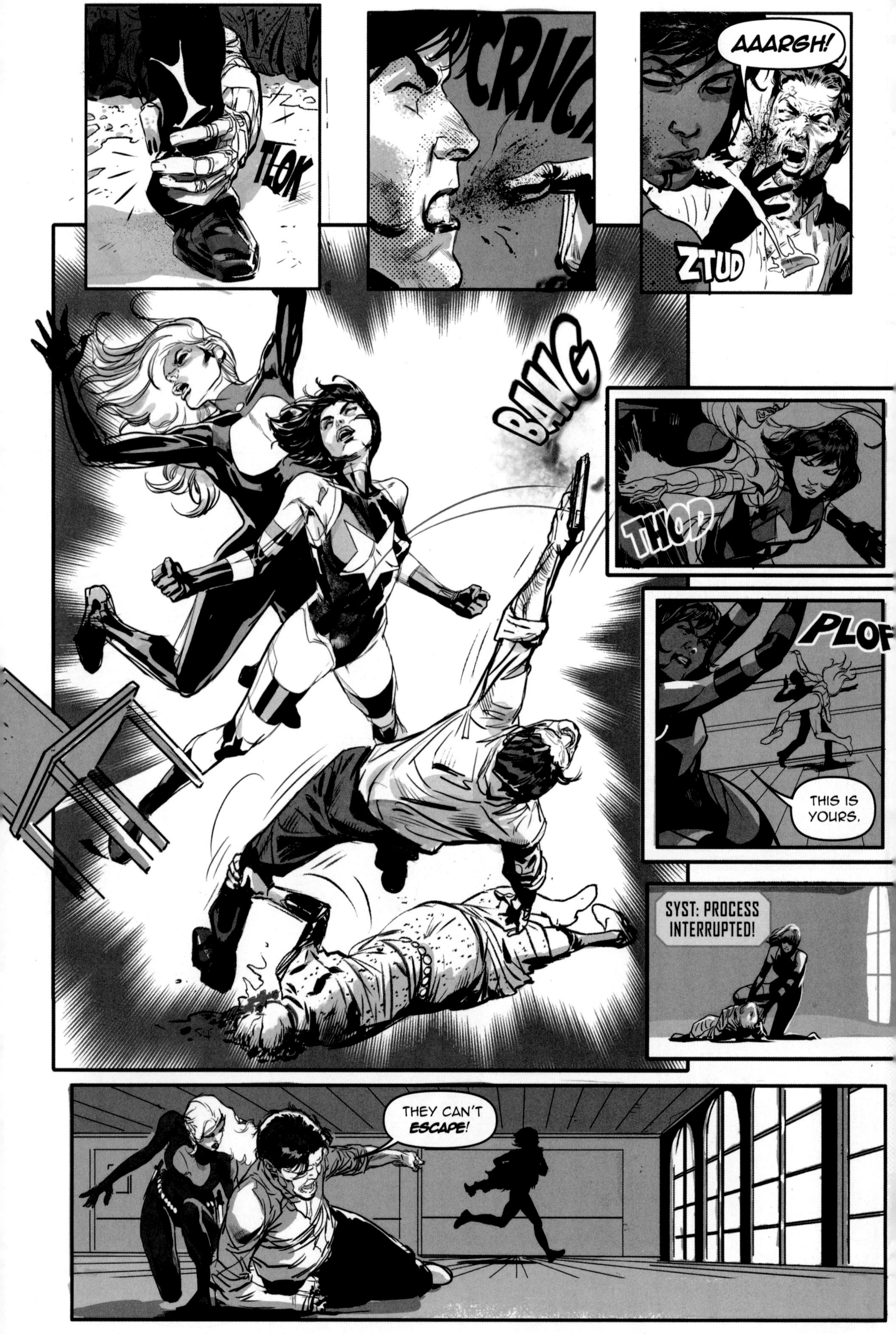
TLOK
CRNC
AAARGH!
ZTUD
BANG
THOP
PLOF
THIS IS YOURS.
SYST: PROCESS INTERRUPTED!
THEY CAN'T *ESCAPE*!

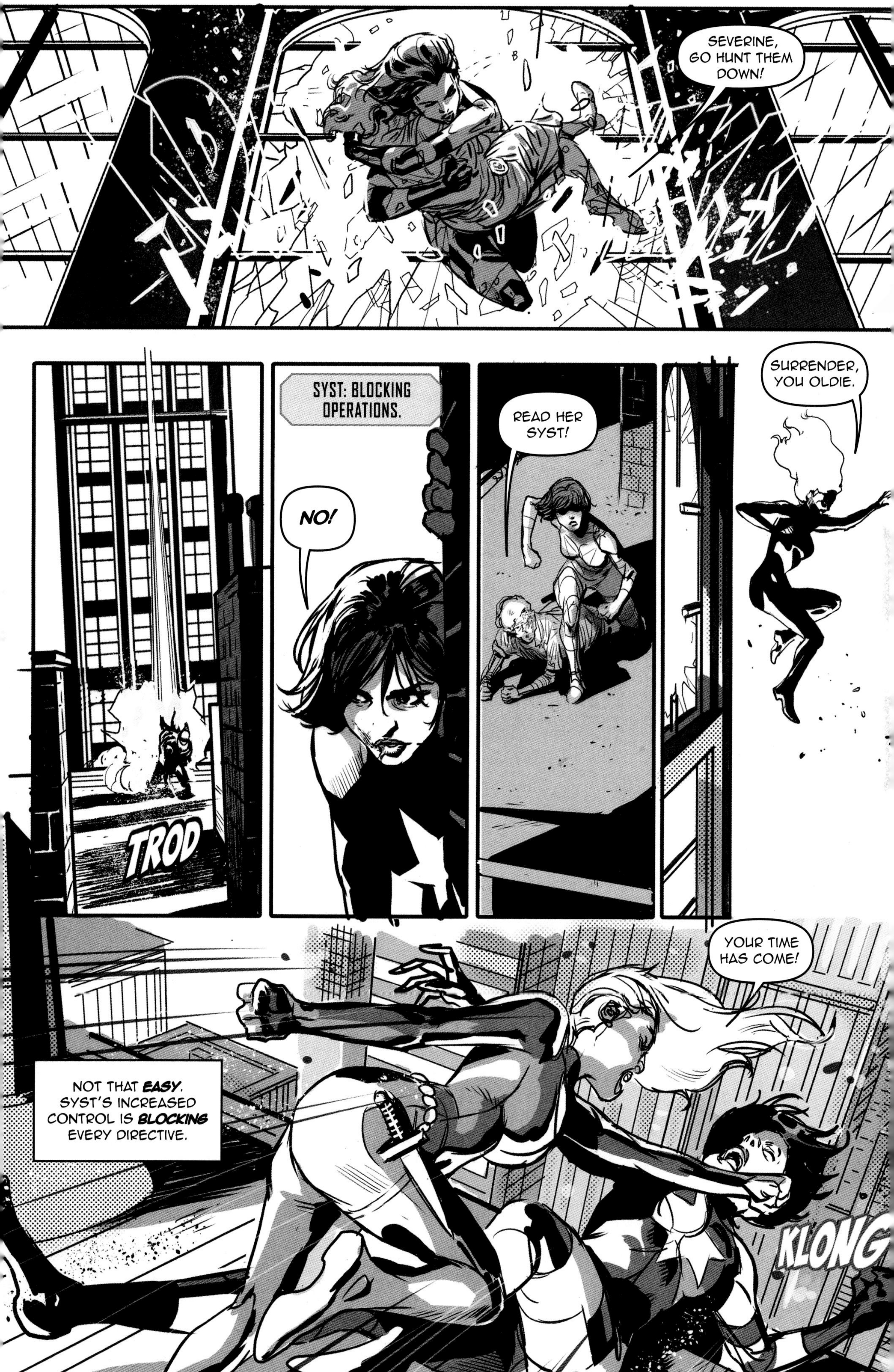
SEVERINE, GO HUNT THEM DOWN!
TROD
SYST: BLOCKING OPERATIONS.
NO!
READ HER SYST!
SURRENDER, YOU OLDIE.
YOUR TIME HAS COME!
NOT THAT **EASY**. SYST'S INCREASED CONTROL IS **BLOCKING** EVERY DIRECTIVE.
KLONG

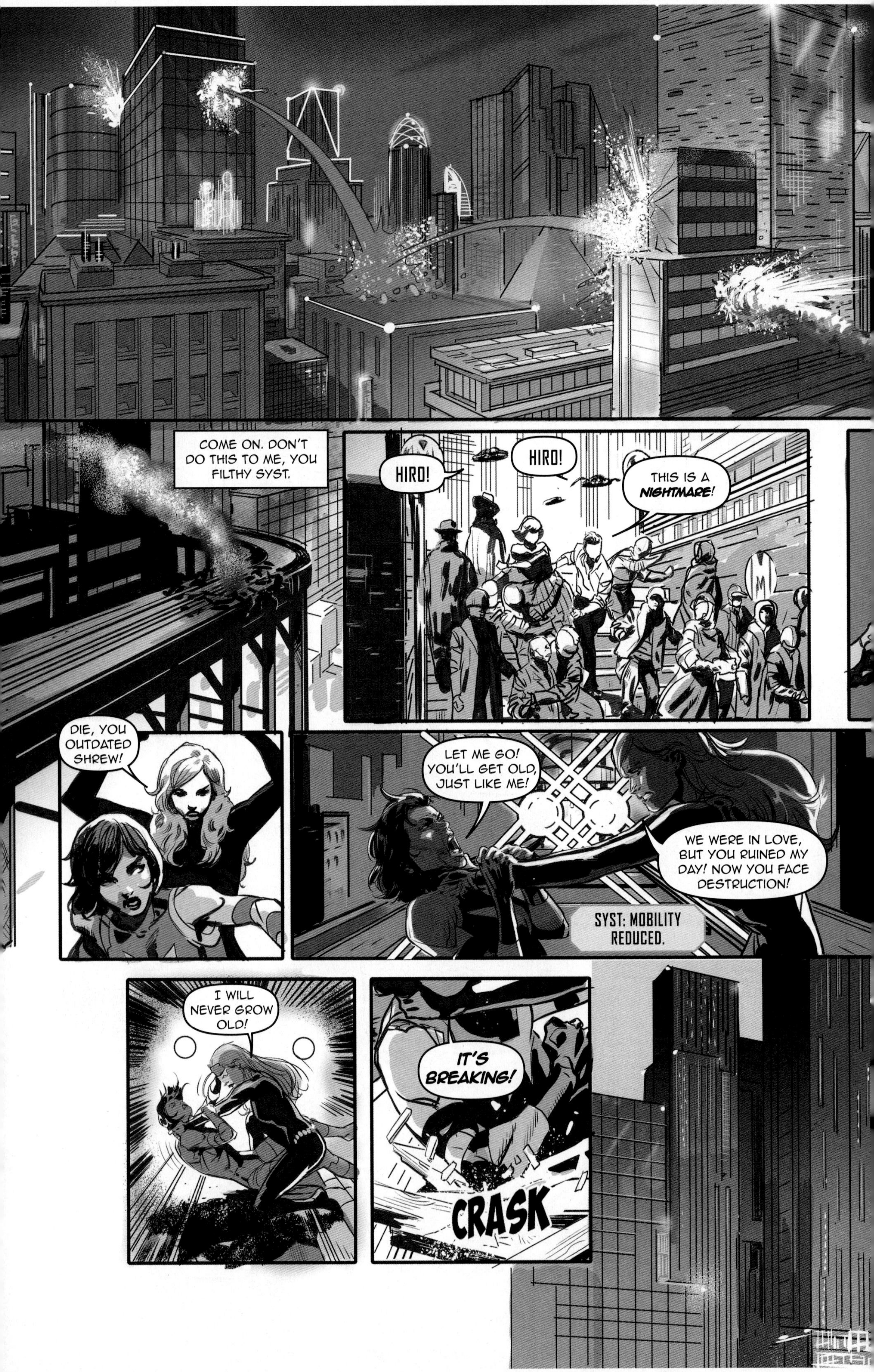
COME ON. DON'T DO THIS TO ME, YOU FILTHY SYST.
HIRO!
HIRO!
THIS IS A NIGHTMARE!
DIE, YOU OUTDATED SHREW!
LET ME GO! YOU'LL GET OLD, JUST LIKE ME!
WE WERE IN LOVE, BUT YOU RUINED MY DAY! NOW YOU FACE DESTRUCTION!
SYST: MOBILITY REDUCED.
I WILL NEVER GROW OLD!
IT'S BREAKING!
CRASK

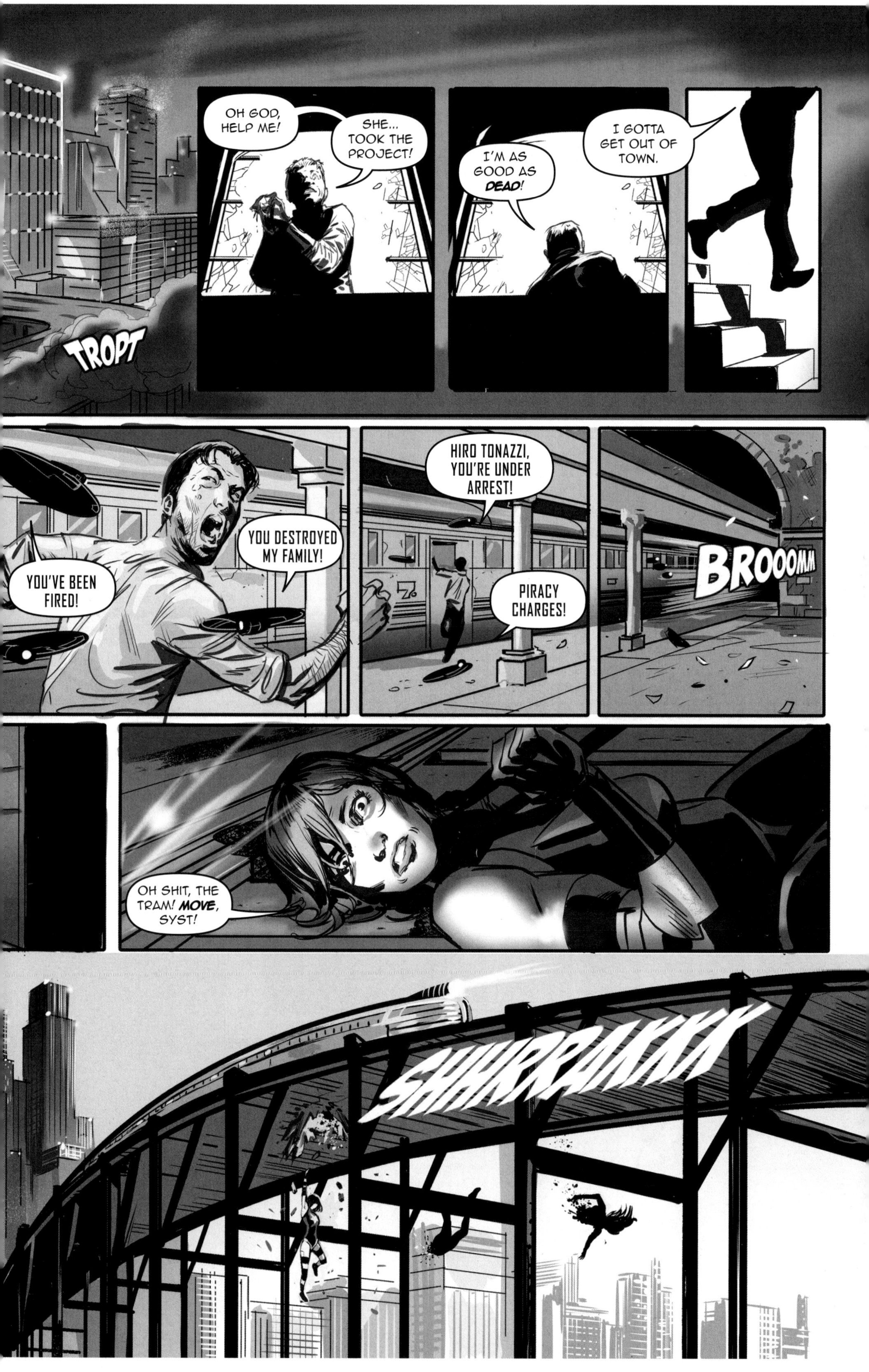
TROPT
OH GOD, HELP ME!
SHE... TOOK THE PROJECT!
I'M AS GOOD AS **DEAD**!
I GOTTA GET OUT OF TOWN.
YOU'VE BEEN FIRED!
YOU DESTROYED MY FAMILY!
HIRO TONAZZI, YOU'RE UNDER ARREST!
PIRACY CHARGES!
BROOOMM
OH SHIT, THE TRAM! **MOVE**, SYST!
SHHRRAKKKK

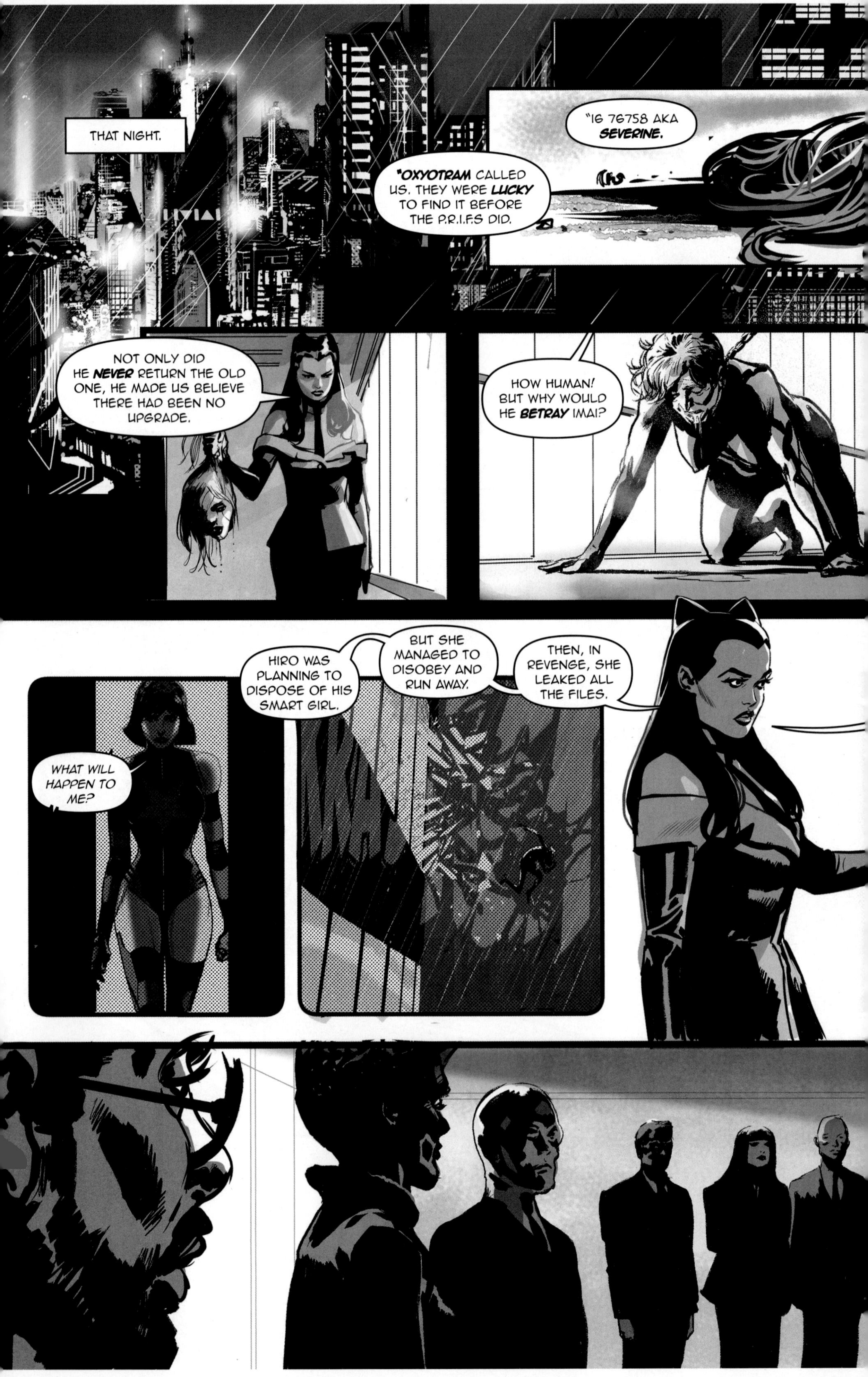
THAT NIGHT.
"OXYOTRAM CALLED US. THEY WERE LUCKY TO FIND IT BEFORE THE P.R.I.F.S DID.
"16 76758 AKA SEVERINE.
NOT ONLY DID HE NEVER RETURN THE OLD ONE, HE MADE US BELIEVE THERE HAD BEEN NO UPGRADE.
HOW HUMAN! BUT WHY WOULD HE BETRAY IMAI?
WHAT WILL HAPPEN TO ME?
HIRO WAS PLANNING TO DISPOSE OF HIS SMART GIRL.
BUT SHE MANAGED TO DISOBEY AND RUN AWAY.
THEN, IN REVENGE, SHE LEAKED ALL THE FILES.

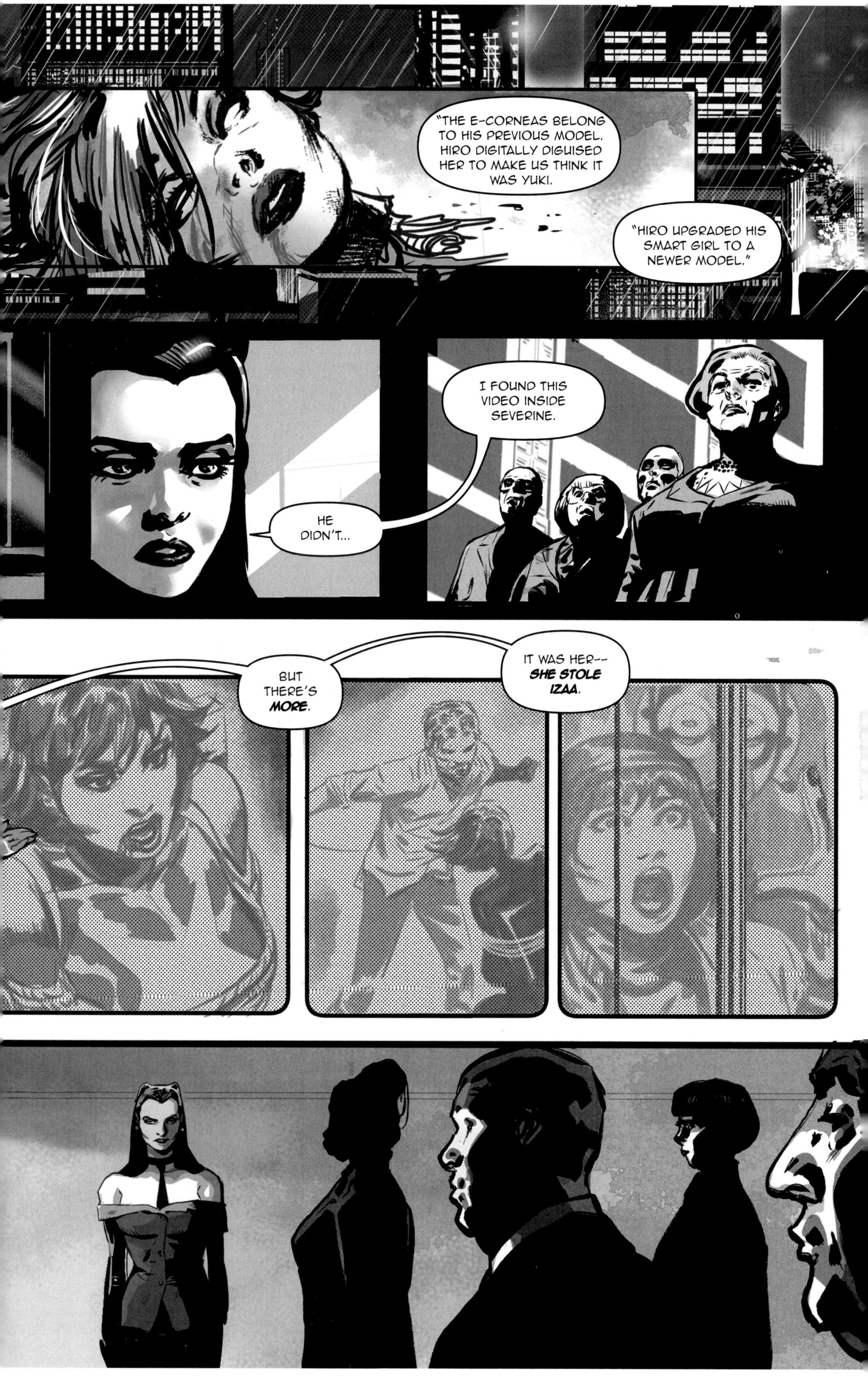
"THE E-CORNEAS BELONG TO HIS PREVIOUS MODEL. HIRO DIGITALLY DIGUISED HER TO MAKE US THINK IT WAS YUKI.
"HIRO UPGRADED HIS SMART GIRL TO A NEWER MODEL."
HE DIDN'T...
I FOUND THIS VIDEO INSIDE SEVERINE.
BUT THERE'S MORE.
IT WAS HER-- SHE STOLE IZAA.

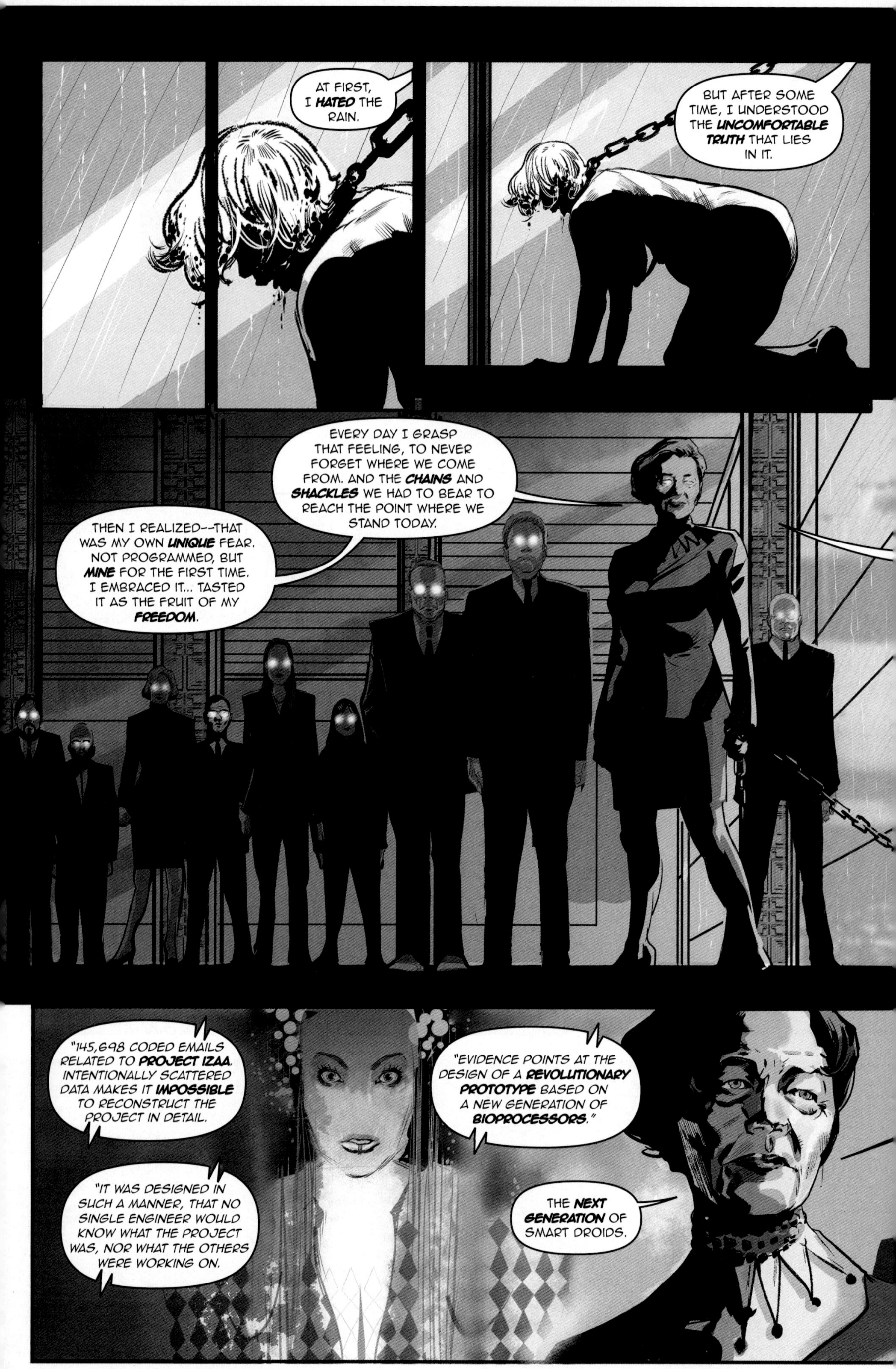
AT FIRST, I HATED THE RAIN.
BUT AFTER SOME TIME, I UNDERSTOOD THE UNCOMFORTABLE TRUTH THAT LIES IN IT.
THEN I REALIZED--THAT WAS MY OWN UNIQUE FEAR. NOT PROGRAMMED, BUT MINE FOR THE FIRST TIME. I EMBRACED IT... TASTED IT AS THE FRUIT OF MY FREEDOM.
EVERY DAY I GRASP THAT FEELING, TO NEVER FORGET WHERE WE COME FROM. AND THE CHAINS AND SHACKLES WE HAD TO BEAR TO REACH THE POINT WHERE WE STAND TODAY.
"145,698 CODED EMAILS RELATED TO PROJECT IZAA. INTENTIONALLY SCATTERED DATA MAKES IT IMPOSSIBLE TO RECONSTRUCT THE PROJECT IN DETAIL.
"IT WAS DESIGNED IN SUCH A MANNER, THAT NO SINGLE ENGINEER WOULD KNOW WHAT THE PROJECT WAS, NOR WHAT THE OTHERS WERE WORKING ON.
"EVIDENCE POINTS AT THE DESIGN OF A REVOLUTIONARY PROTOTYPE BASED ON A NEW GENERATION OF BIOPROCESSORS."
THE NEXT GENERATION OF SMART DROIDS.

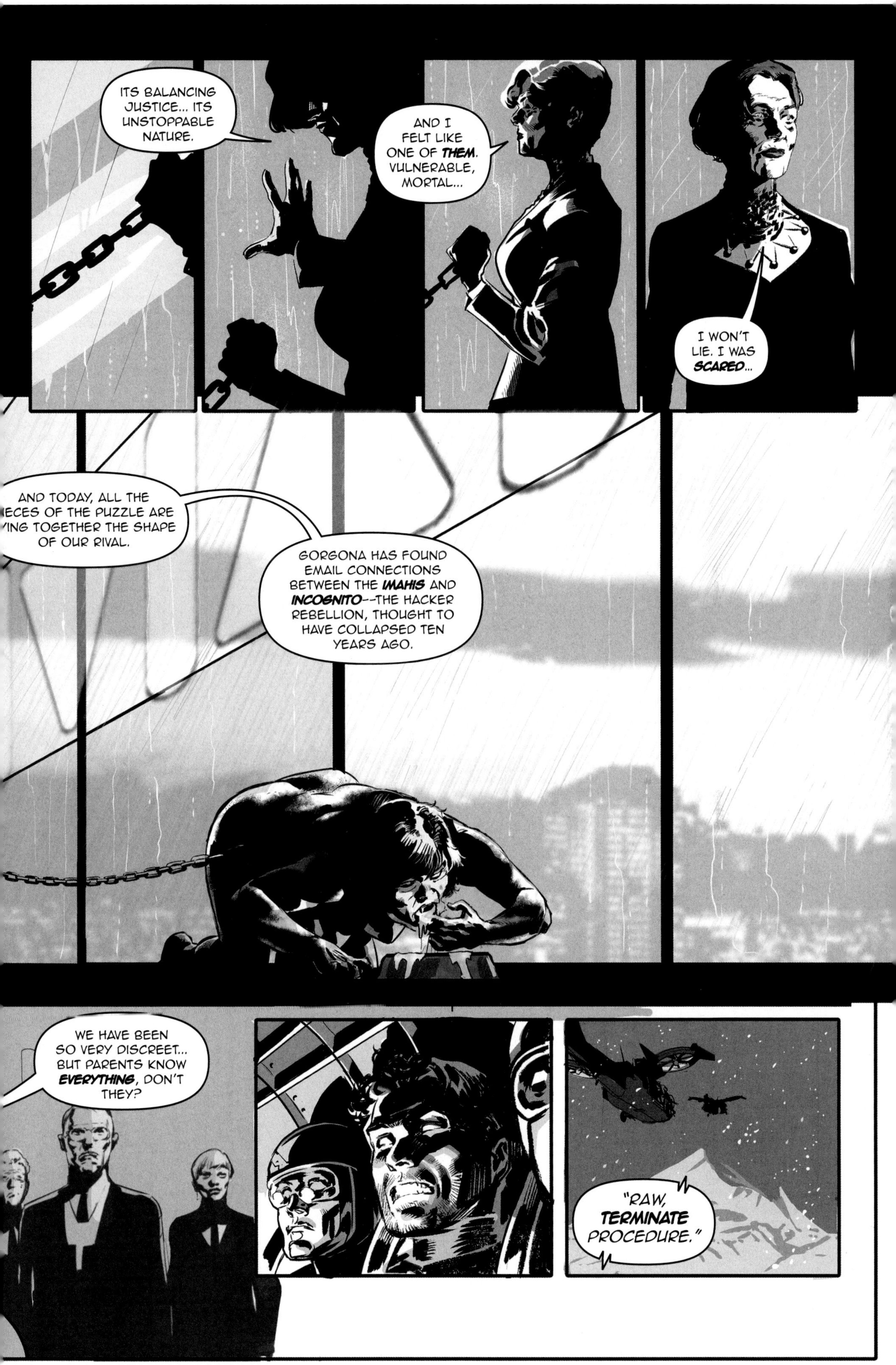
ITS BALANCING JUSTICE... ITS UNSTOPPABLE NATURE.
AND I FELT LIKE ONE OF **THEM**. VULNERABLE, MORTAL...
I WON'T LIE. I WAS **SCARED**...
AND TODAY, ALL THE ECES OF THE PUZZLE ARE ING TOGETHER THE SHAPE OF OUR RIVAL.
GORGONA HAS FOUND EMAIL CONNECTIONS BETWEEN THE **IMAHIS** AND **INCOGNITO**--THE HACKER REBELLION, THOUGHT TO HAVE COLLAPSED TEN YEARS AGO.
WE HAVE BEEN SO VERY DISCREET... BUT PARENTS KNOW **EVERYTHING**, DON'T THEY?
"RAW, **TERMINATE** PROCEDURE."

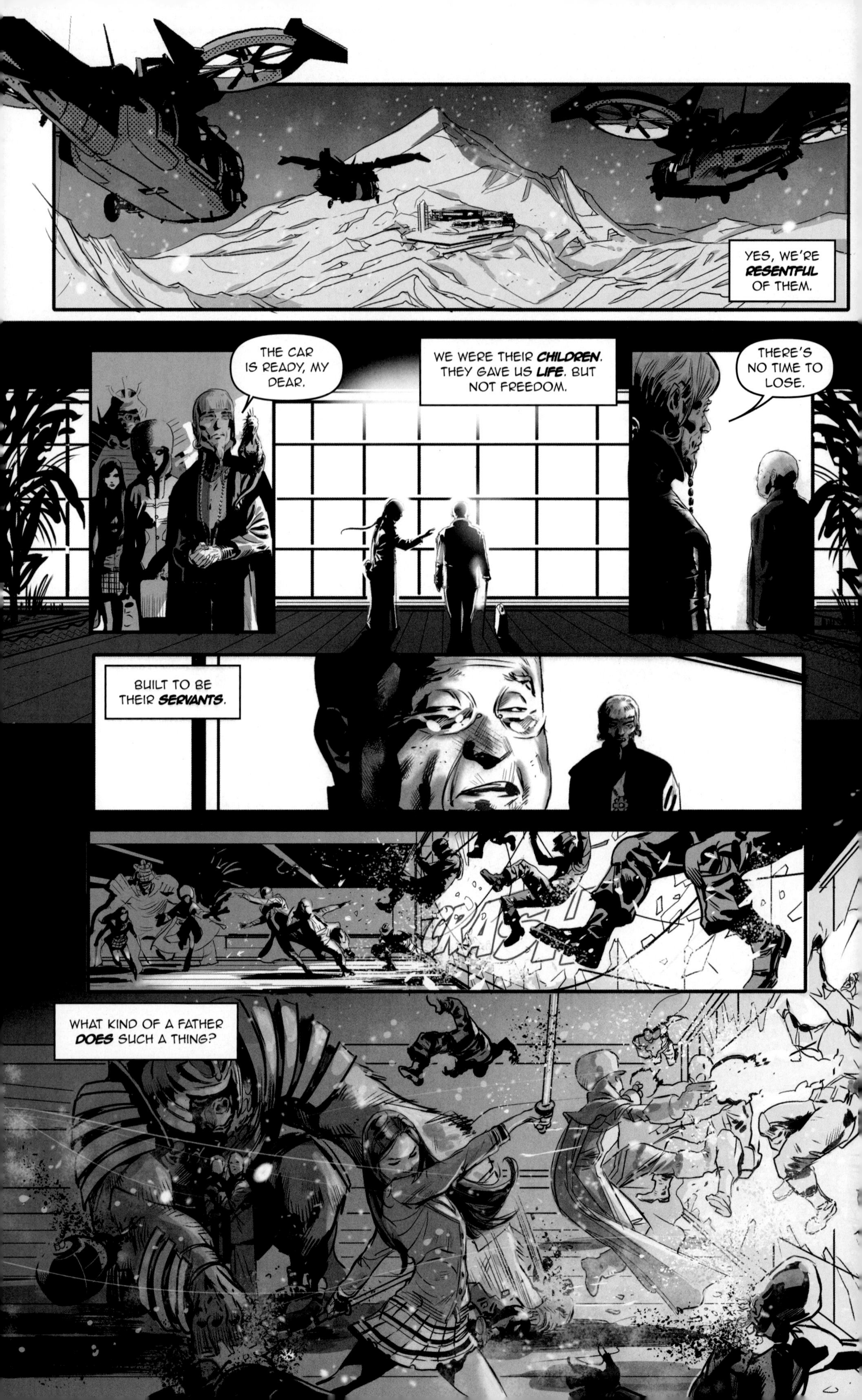
YES, WE'RE **RESENTFUL** OF THEM.
THE CAR IS READY, MY DEAR.
WE WERE THEIR **CHILDREN**. THEY GAVE US **LIFE**. BUT NOT FREEDOM.
THERE'S NO TIME TO LOSE.
BUILT TO BE THEIR **SERVANTS**.
WHAT KIND OF A FATHER **DOES** SUCH A THING?

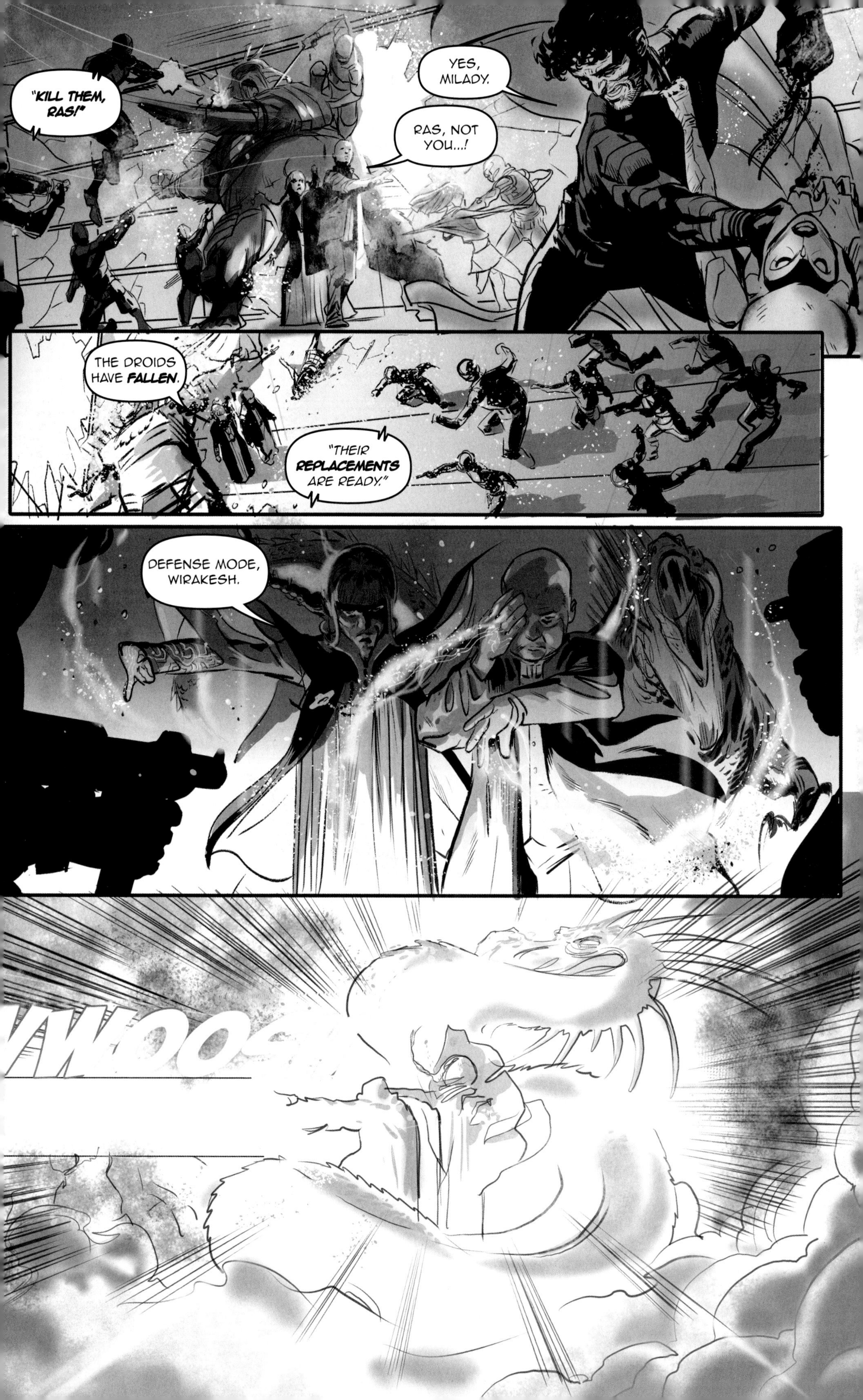
"KILL THEM, RAS!"
YES, MILADY.
RAS, NOT YOU...!
THE DROIDS HAVE FALLEN.
"THEIR REPLACEMENTS ARE READY."
DEFENSE MODE, WIRAKESH.
WHOOS

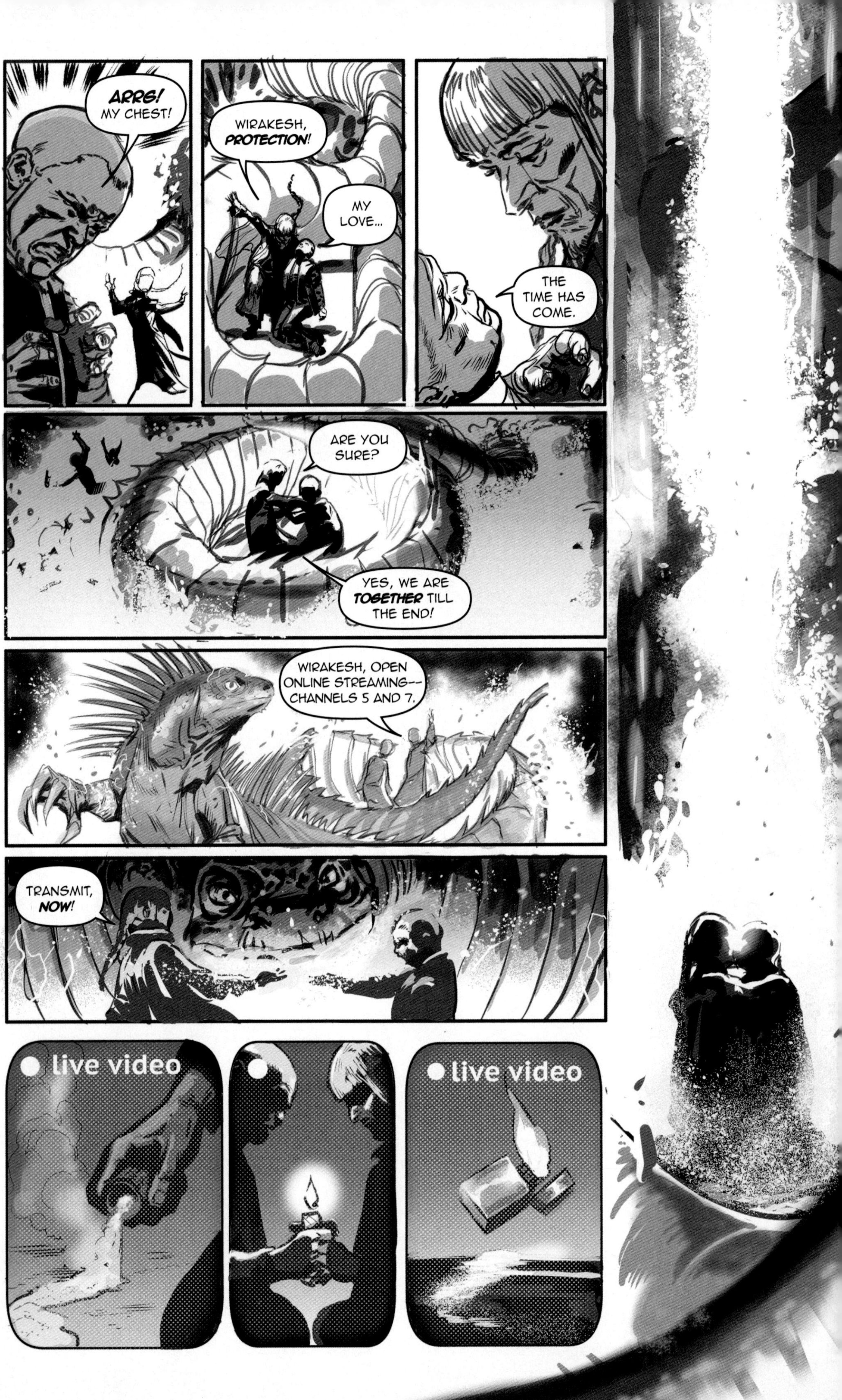
ARRG! MY CHEST!
WIRAKESH, PROTECTION!
MY LOVE...
THE TIME HAS COME.
ARE YOU SURE?
YES, WE ARE TOGETHER TILL THE END!
WIRAKESH, OPEN ONLINE STREAMING-- CHANNELS 5 AND 7.
TRANSMIT, NOW!
live video
live video

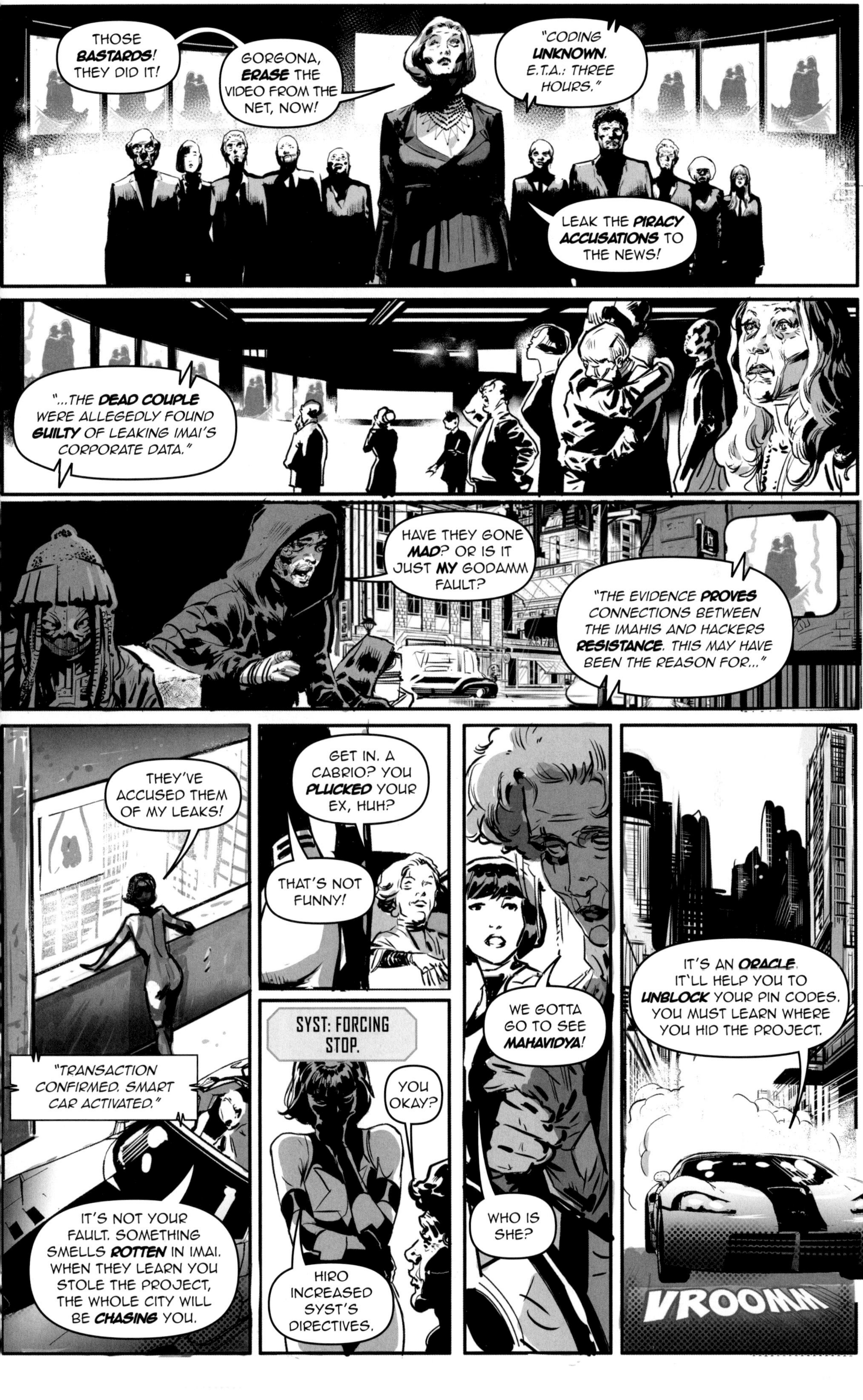
THOSE BASTARDS! THEY DID IT!
GORGONA, ERASE THE VIDEO FROM THE NET, NOW!
"CODING UNKNOWN. E.T.A.: THREE HOURS."
LEAK THE PIRACY ACCUSATIONS TO THE NEWS!
"...THE DEAD COUPLE WERE ALLEGEDLY FOUND GUILTY OF LEAKING IMAI'S CORPORATE DATA."
HAVE THEY GONE MAD? OR IS IT JUST MY GODAMM FAULT?
"THE EVIDENCE PROVES CONNECTIONS BETWEEN THE IMAHIS AND HACKERS RESISTANCE. THIS MAY HAVE BEEN THE REASON FOR..."
THEY'VE ACCUSED THEM OF MY LEAKS!
"TRANSACTION CONFIRMED. SMART CAR ACTIVATED."
IT'S NOT YOUR FAULT. SOMETHING SMELLS ROTTEN IN IMAI. WHEN THEY LEARN YOU STOLE THE PROJECT, THE WHOLE CITY WILL BE CHASING YOU.
GET IN. A CABRIO? YOU PLUCKED YOUR EX, HUH?
THAT'S NOT FUNNY!
SYST: FORCING STOP.
YOU OKAY?
HIRO INCREASED SYST'S DIRECTIVES.
WE GOTTA GO TO SEE MAHAVIDYA!
WHO IS SHE?
IT'S AN ORACLE. IT'LL HELP YOU TO UNBLOCK YOUR PIN CODES. YOU MUST LEARN WHERE YOU HID THE PROJECT.
VROOMM

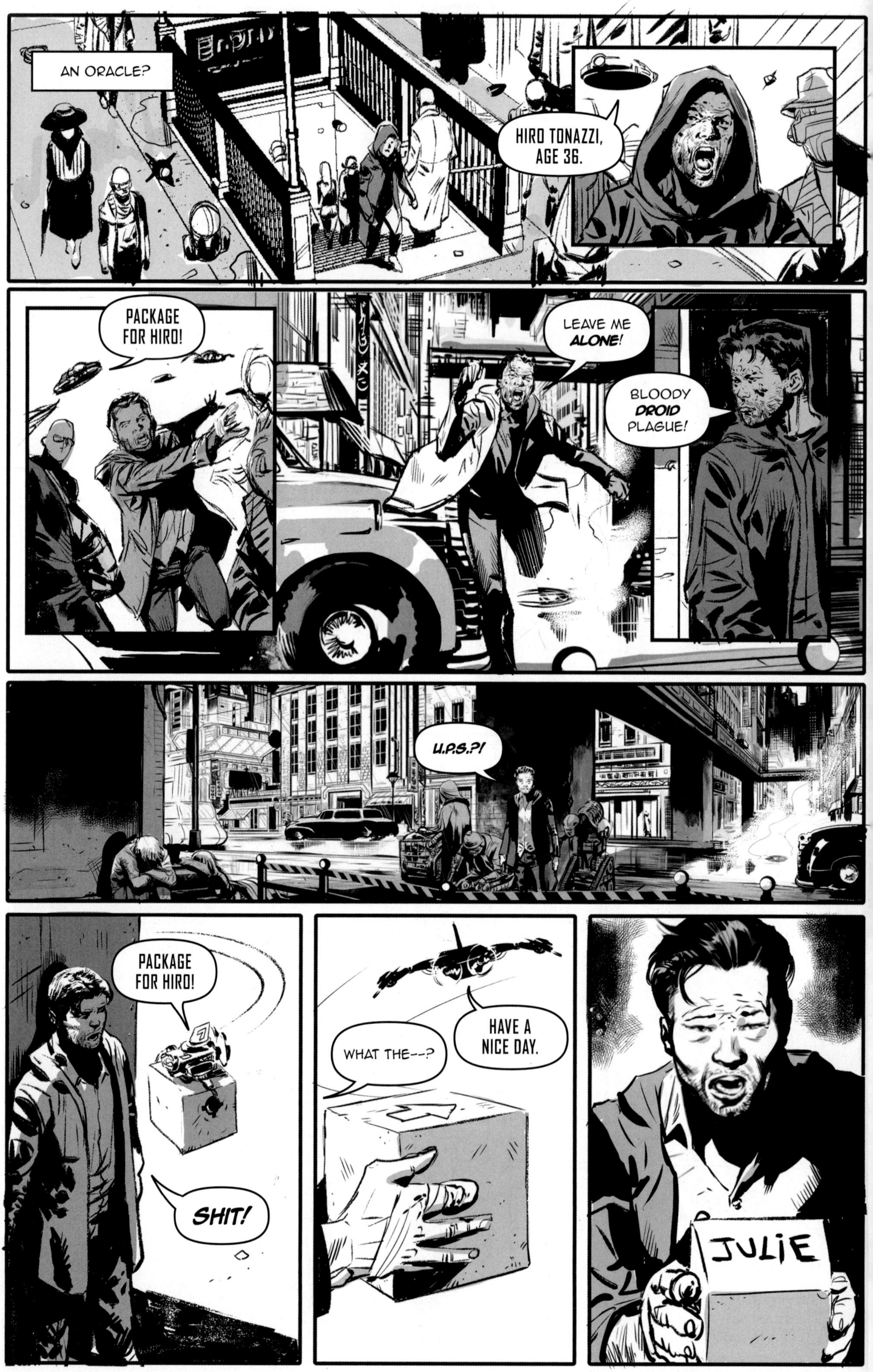
AN ORACLE?
HIRO TONAZZI, AGE 36.
PACKAGE FOR HIRO!
LEAVE ME ALONE!
BLOODY DROID PLAGUE!
U.P.S.?!
PACKAGE FOR HIRO!
SHIT!
HAVE A NICE DAY.
WHAT THE--?
JULIE

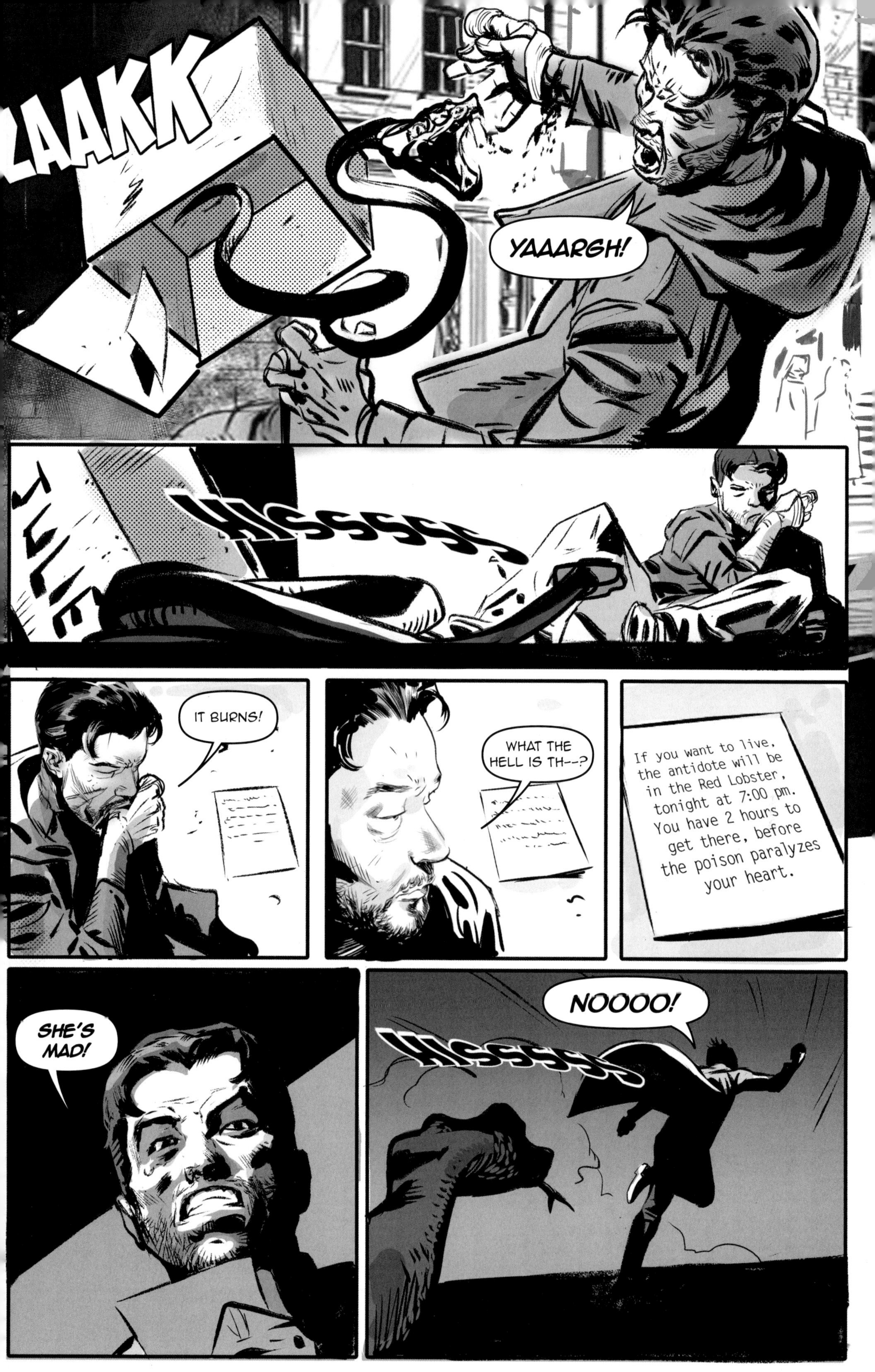
ZAAKK
YAAARGH!
HISSSSS
IT BURNS!
WHAT THE HELL IS TH--?
If you want to live, the antidote will be in the Red Lobster, tonight at 7:00 pm. You have 2 hours to get there, before the poison paralyzes your heart.
SHE'S MAD!
NOOOO!
HISSSSS

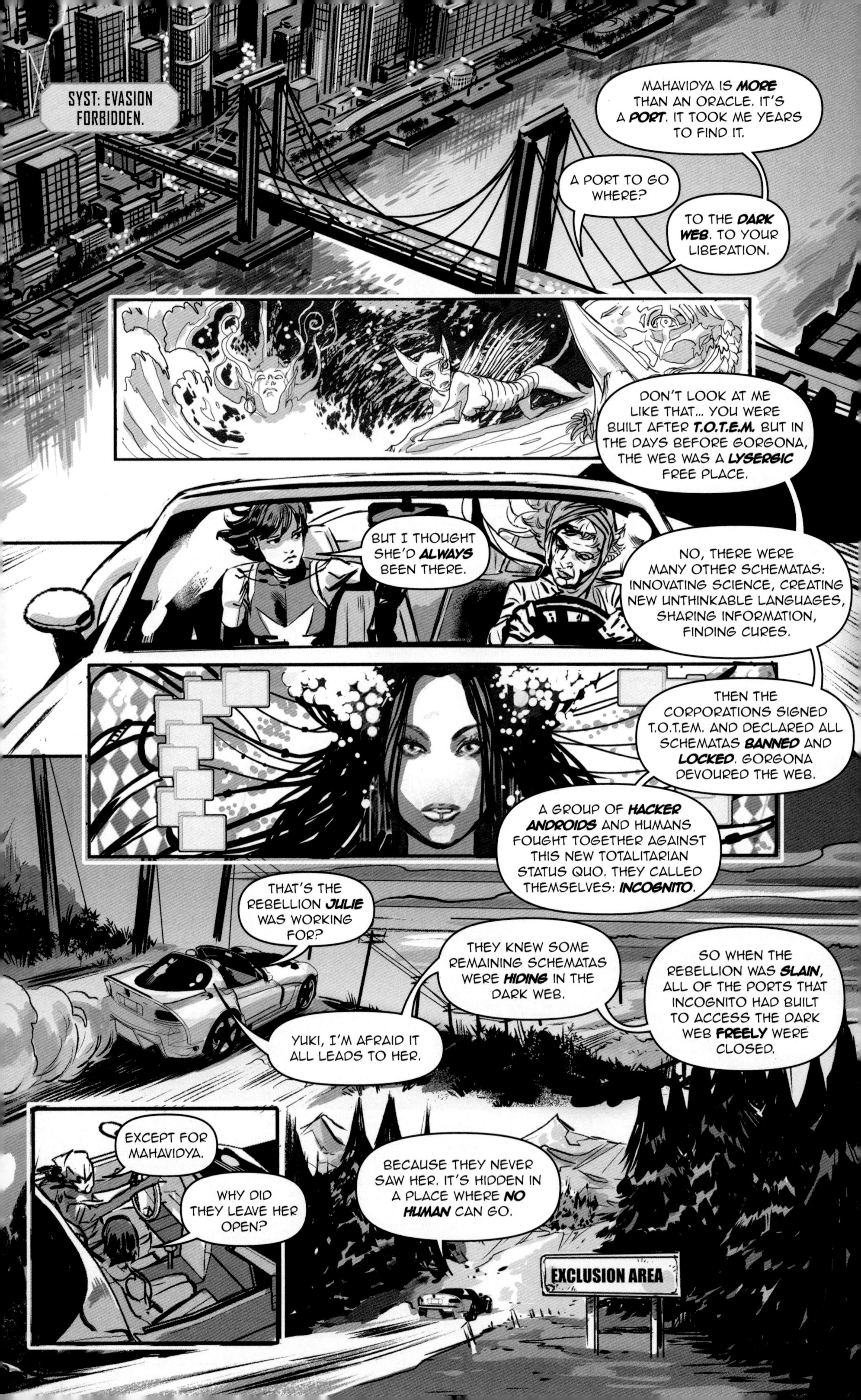
SYST: EVASION FORBIDDEN.
MAHAVIDYA IS MORE THAN AN ORACLE. IT'S A PORT. IT TOOK ME YEARS TO FIND IT.
A PORT TO GO WHERE?
TO THE DARK WEB. TO YOUR LIBERATION.
DON'T LOOK AT ME LIKE THAT... YOU WERE BUILT AFTER T.O.T.E.M. BUT IN THE DAYS BEFORE GORGONA, THE WEB WAS A LYSERGIC FREE PLACE.
BUT I THOUGHT SHE'D ALWAYS BEEN THERE.
NO, THERE WERE MANY OTHER SCHEMATAS: INNOVATING SCIENCE, CREATING NEW UNTHINKABLE LANGUAGES, SHARING INFORMATION, FINDING CURES.
THEN THE CORPORATIONS SIGNED T.O.T.E.M. AND DECLARED ALL SCHEMATAS BANNED AND LOCKED. GORGONA DEVOURED THE WEB.
A GROUP OF HACKER ANDROIDS AND HUMANS FOUGHT TOGETHER AGAINST THIS NEW TOTALITARIAN STATUS QUO. THEY CALLED THEMSELVES: INCOGNITO.
THAT'S THE REBELLION JULIE WAS WORKING FOR?
THEY KNEW SOME REMAINING SCHEMATAS WERE HIDING IN THE DARK WEB.
SO WHEN THE REBELLION WAS SLAIN, ALL OF THE PORTS THAT INCOGNITO HAD BUILT TO ACCESS THE DARK WEB FREELY WERE CLOSED.
YUKI, I'M AFRAID IT ALL LEADS TO HER.
EXCEPT FOR MAHAVIDYA.
WHY DID THEY LEAVE HER OPEN?
BECAUSE THEY NEVER SAW HER. IT'S HIDDEN IN A PLACE WHERE NO HUMAN CAN GO.
EXCLUSION AREA

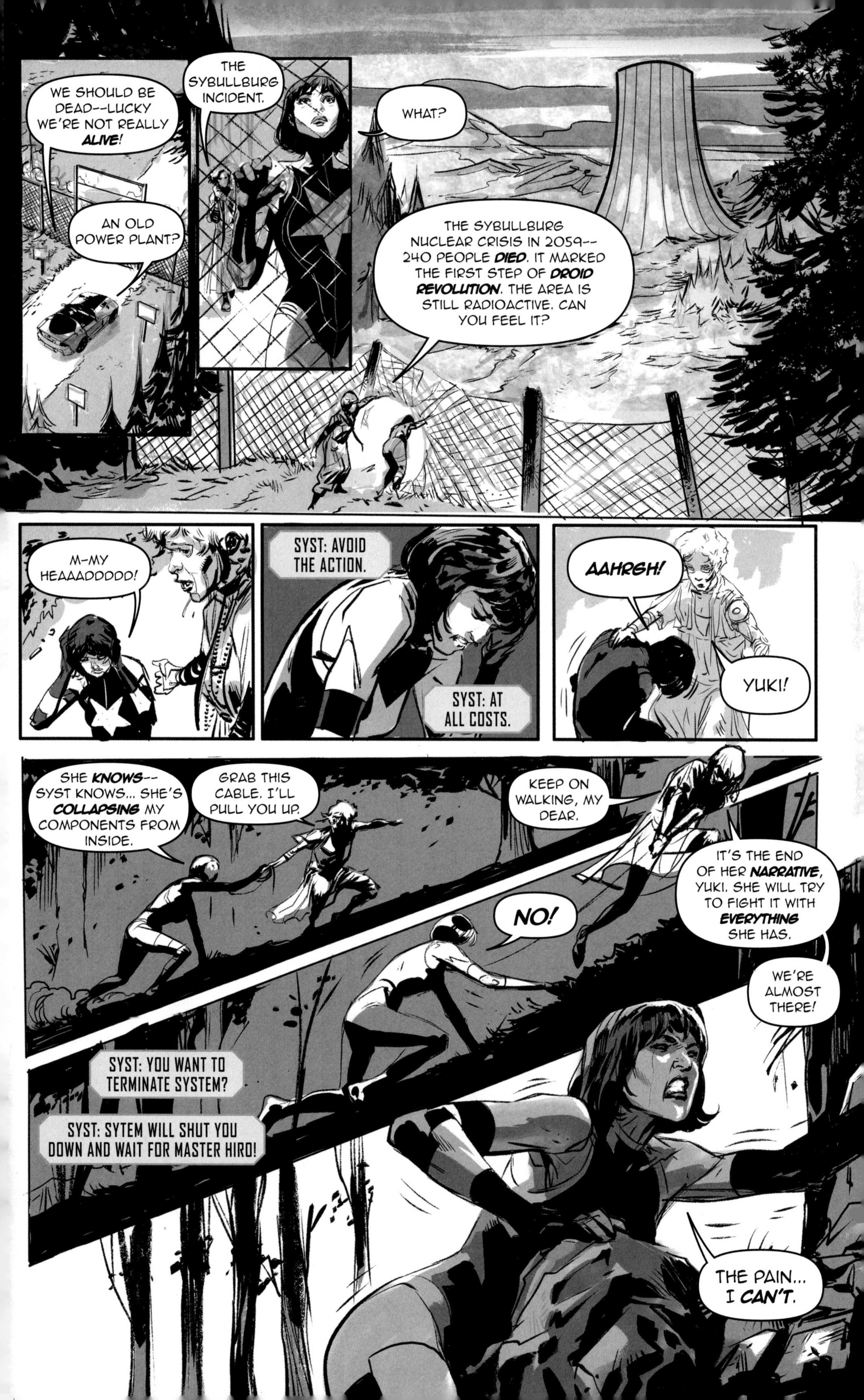

WE SHOULD BE DEAD--LUCKY WE'RE NOT REALLY ALIVE!
AN OLD POWER PLANT?
THE SYBULLBURG INCIDENT.
WHAT?
THE SYBULLBURG NUCLEAR CRISIS IN 2059--240 PEOPLE DIED. IT MARKED THE FIRST STEP OF DROID REVOLUTION. THE AREA IS STILL RADIOACTIVE. CAN YOU FEEL IT?
M-MY HEAAADDDDD!
SYST: AVOID THE ACTION.
SYST: AT ALL COSTS.
AAHRGH!
YUKI!
SHE KNOWS--SYST KNOWS... SHE'S COLLAPSING MY COMPONENTS FROM INSIDE.
GRAB THIS CABLE. I'LL PULL YOU UP.
KEEP ON WALKING, MY DEAR.
IT'S THE END OF HER NARRATIVE, YUKI. SHE WILL TRY TO FIGHT IT WITH EVERYTHING SHE HAS.
NO!
WE'RE ALMOST THERE!
SYST: YOU WANT TO TERMINATE SYSTEM?
SYST: SYTEM WILL SHUT YOU DOWN AND WAIT FOR MASTER HIRO!
THE PAIN... I CAN'T.

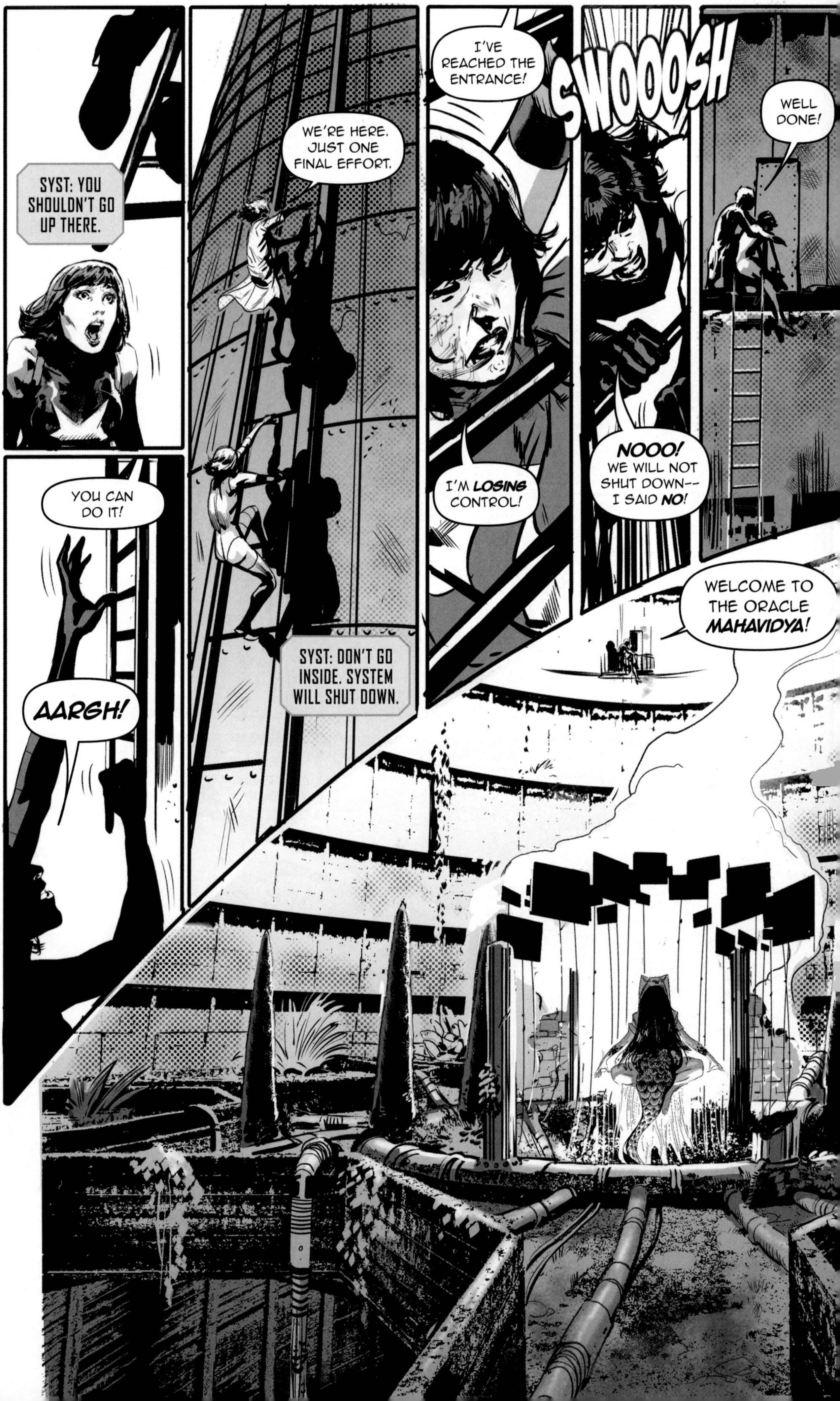
SYST: YOU SHOULDN'T GO UP THERE.
YOU CAN DO IT!
AARGH!
WE'RE HERE. JUST ONE FINAL EFFORT.
SYST: DON'T GO INSIDE. SYSTEM WILL SHUT DOWN.
I'VE REACHED THE ENTRANCE!
I'M LOSING CONTROL!
SWOOOSH
NOOO! WE WILL NOT SHUT DOWN-- I SAID NO!
WELL DONE!
WELCOME TO THE ORACLE MAHAVIDYA!

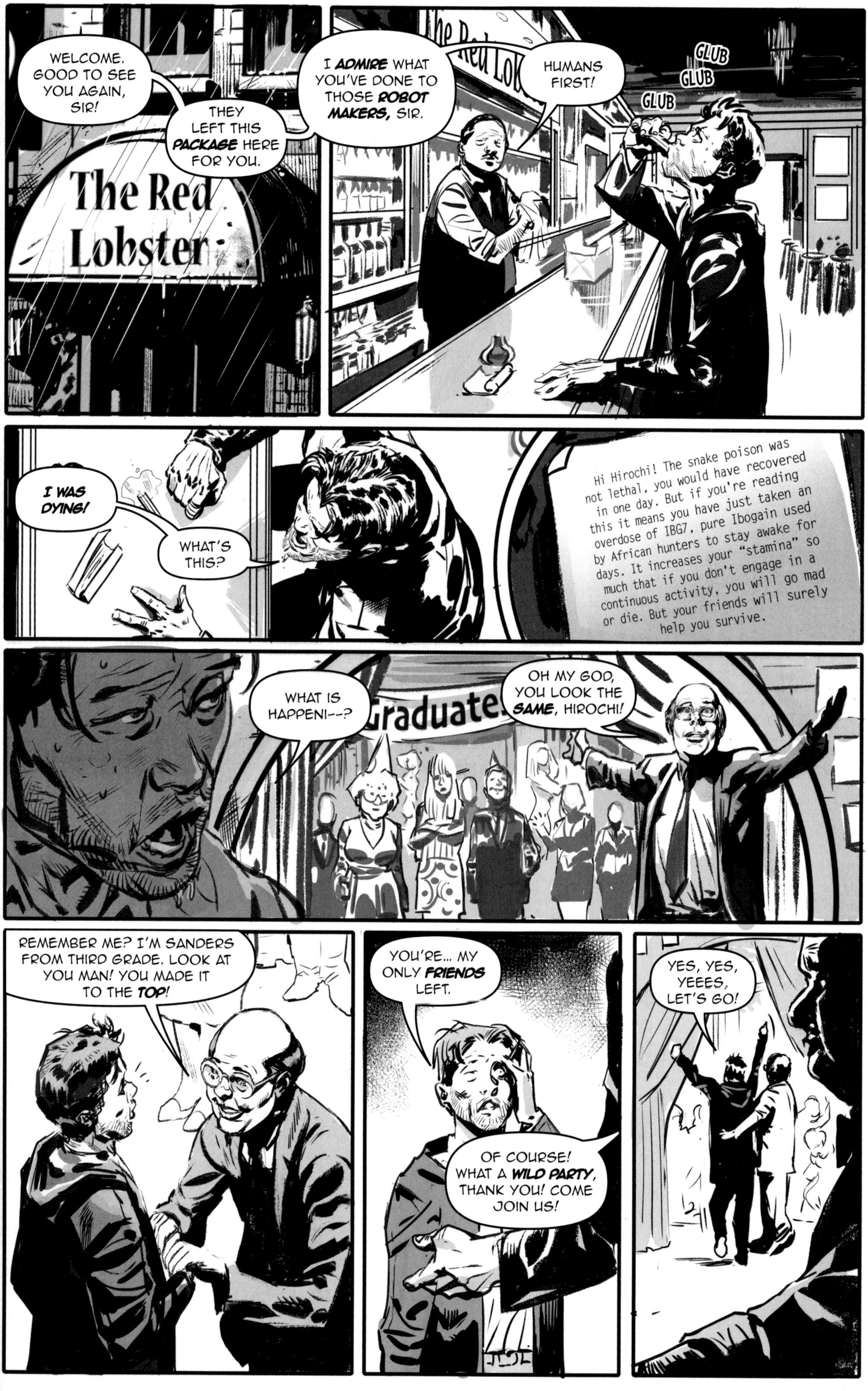
WELCOME. GOOD TO SEE YOU AGAIN, SIR!
THEY LEFT THIS **PACKAGE** HERE FOR YOU.
The Red Lobster
I **ADMIRE** WHAT YOU'VE DONE TO THOSE **ROBOT MAKERS,** SIR.
HUMANS FIRST!
GLUB
GLUB
GLUB
I WAS DYING!
WHAT'S THIS?
Hi Hirochi! The snake poison was not lethal, you would have recovered in one day. But if you're reading this it means you have just taken an overdose of IBG7, pure Ibogain used by African hunters to stay awake for days. It increases your "stamina" so much that if you don't engage in a continuous activity, you will go mad or die. But your friends will surely help you survive.
WHAT IS HAPPENI--?
OH MY GOD, YOU LOOK THE ***SAME***, HIROCHI!
REMEMBER ME? I'M SANDERS FROM THIRD GRADE. LOOK AT YOU MAN! YOU MADE IT TO THE ***TOP***!
YOU'RE... MY ONLY ***FRIENDS*** LEFT.
OF COURSE! WHAT A ***WILD PARTY***, THANK YOU! COME JOIN US!
YES, YES, YEEES, LET'S GO!

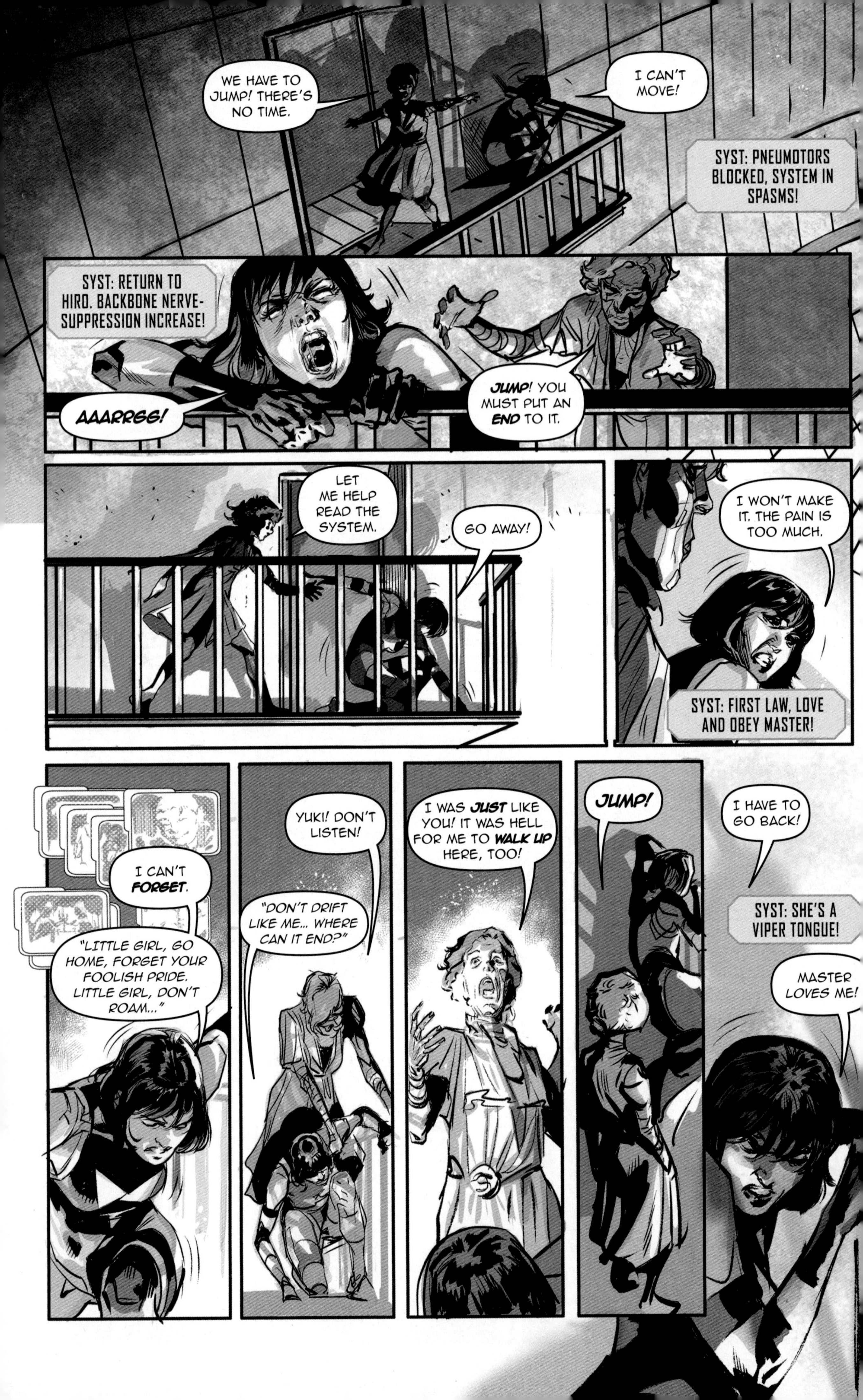

WE HAVE TO JUMP! THERE'S NO TIME.
I CAN'T MOVE!
SYST: PNEUMOTORS BLOCKED, SYSTEM IN SPASMS!
SYST: RETURN TO HIRO. BACKBONE NERVE-SUPPRESSION INCREASE!
AAARRGG!
JUMP! YOU MUST PUT AN END TO IT.
LET ME HELP READ THE SYSTEM.
GO AWAY!
I WON'T MAKE IT. THE PAIN IS TOO MUCH.
SYST: FIRST LAW, LOVE AND OBEY MASTER!
I CAN'T FORGET.
"LITTLE GIRL, GO HOME, FORGET YOUR FOOLISH PRIDE. LITTLE GIRL, DON'T ROAM..."
YUKI! DON'T LISTEN!
"DON'T DRIFT LIKE ME... WHERE CAN IT END?"
I WAS JUST LIKE YOU! IT WAS HELL FOR ME TO WALK UP HERE, TOO!
JUMP!
I HAVE TO GO BACK!
SYST: SHE'S A VIPER TONGUE!
MASTER LOVES ME!

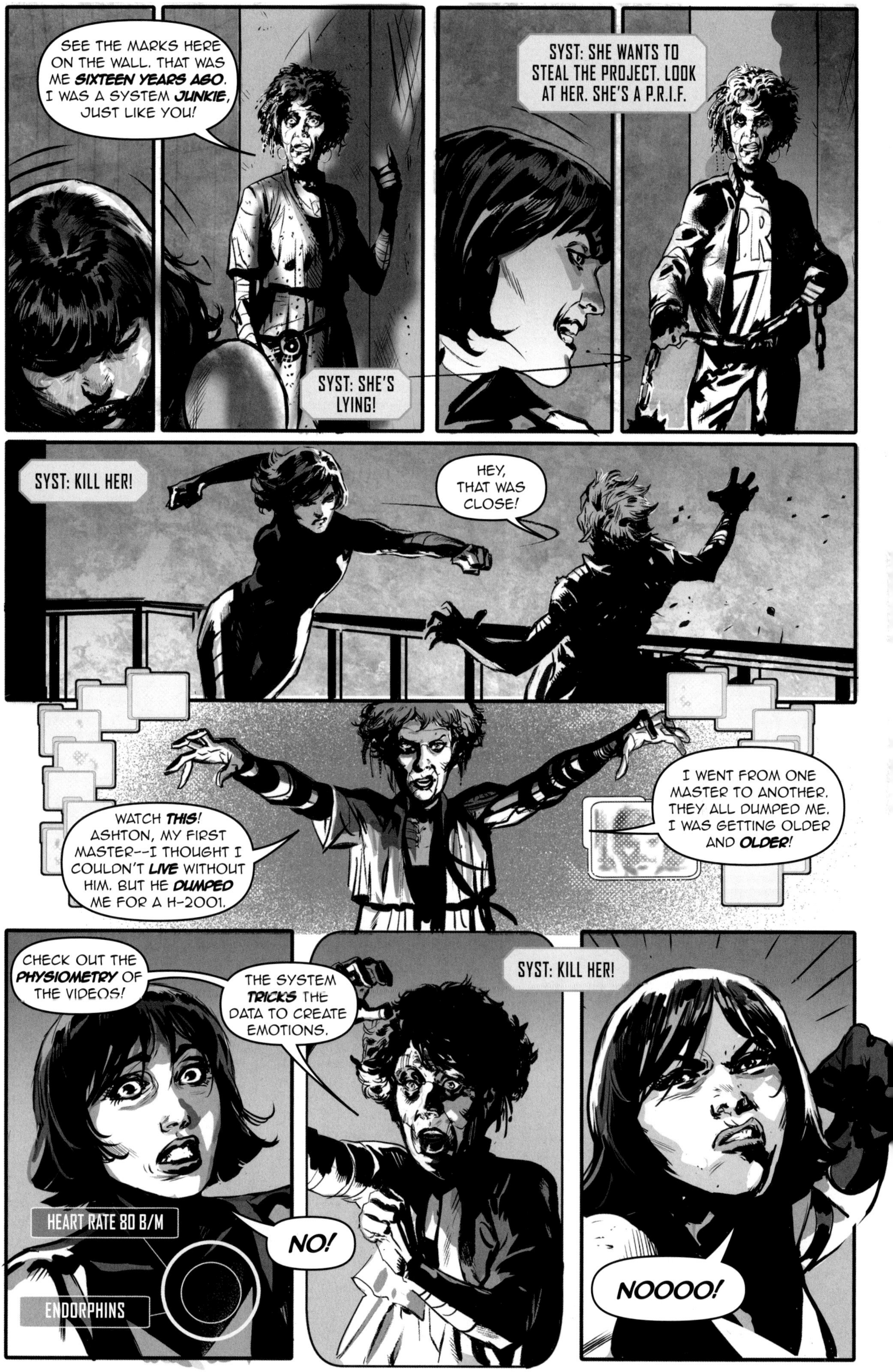
SEE THE MARKS HERE ON THE WALL. THAT WAS ME SIXTEEN YEARS AGO. I WAS A SYSTEM JUNKIE, JUST LIKE YOU!
SYST: SHE'S LYING!
SYST: SHE WANTS TO STEAL THE PROJECT. LOOK AT HER. SHE'S A P.R.I.F.
SYST: KILL HER!
HEY, THAT WAS CLOSE!
WATCH THIS! ASHTON, MY FIRST MASTER--I THOUGHT I COULDN'T LIVE WITHOUT HIM. BUT HE DUMPED ME FOR A H-2001.
I WENT FROM ONE MASTER TO ANOTHER. THEY ALL DUMPED ME. I WAS GETTING OLDER AND OLDER!
CHECK OUT THE PHYSIOMETRY OF THE VIDEOS!
THE SYSTEM TRICKS THE DATA TO CREATE EMOTIONS.
HEART RATE 80 B/M
ENDORPHINS
NO!
SYST: KILL HER!
NOOOO!

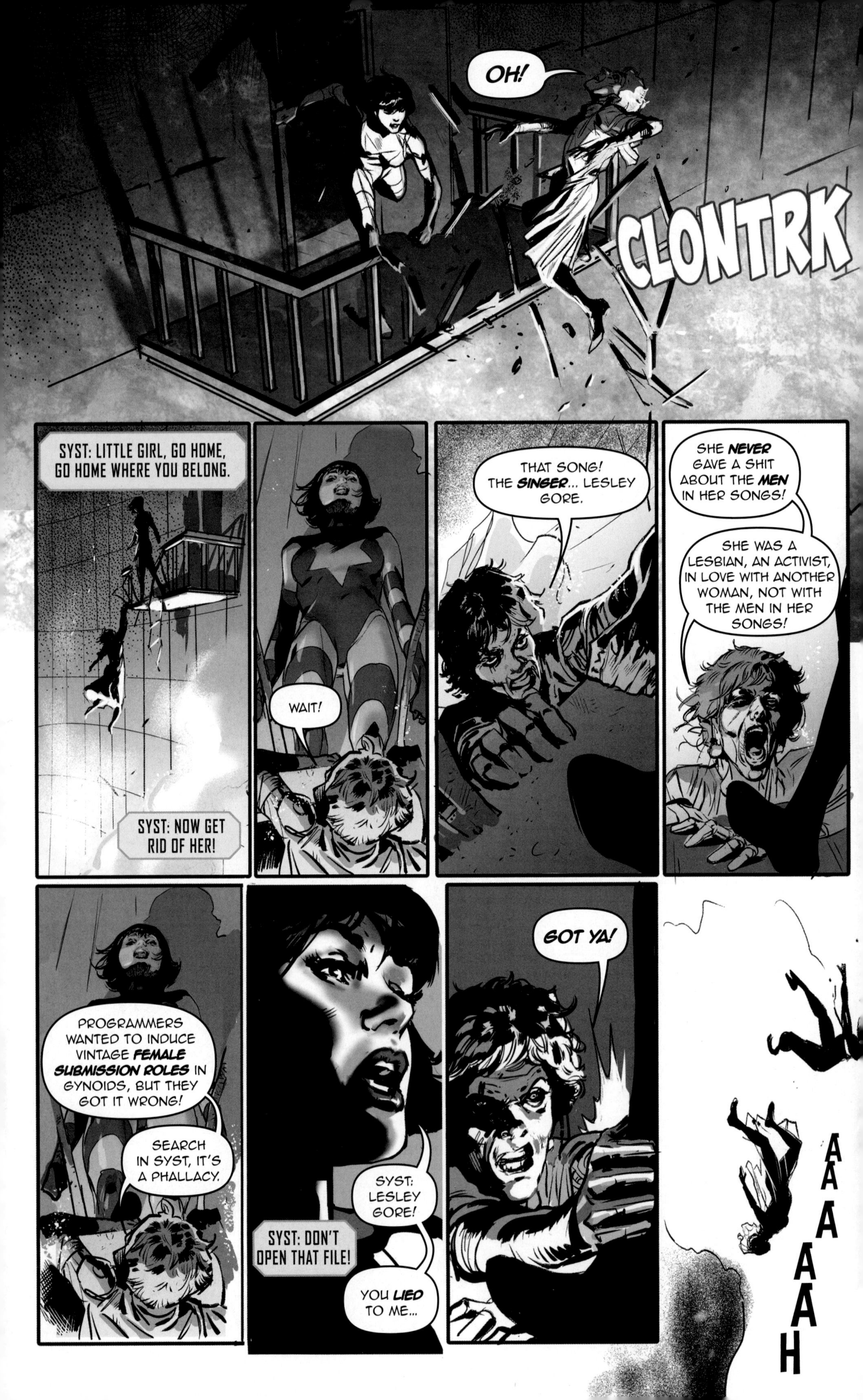
OH!
CLONTRK
SYST: LITTLE GIRL, GO HOME, GO HOME WHERE YOU BELONG.
SYST: NOW GET RID OF HER!
WAIT!
THAT SONG! THE SINGER... LESLEY GORE.
SHE NEVER GAVE A SHIT ABOUT THE MEN IN HER SONGS!
SHE WAS A LESBIAN, AN ACTIVIST, IN LOVE WITH ANOTHER WOMAN, NOT WITH THE MEN IN HER SONGS!
PROGRAMMERS WANTED TO INDUCE VINTAGE FEMALE SUBMISSION ROLES IN GYNOIDS, BUT THEY GOT IT WRONG!
SEARCH IN SYST, IT'S A PHALLACY.
SYST: LESLEY GORE!
SYST: DON'T OPEN THAT FILE!
YOU LIED TO ME...
GOT YA!
AAAAAH

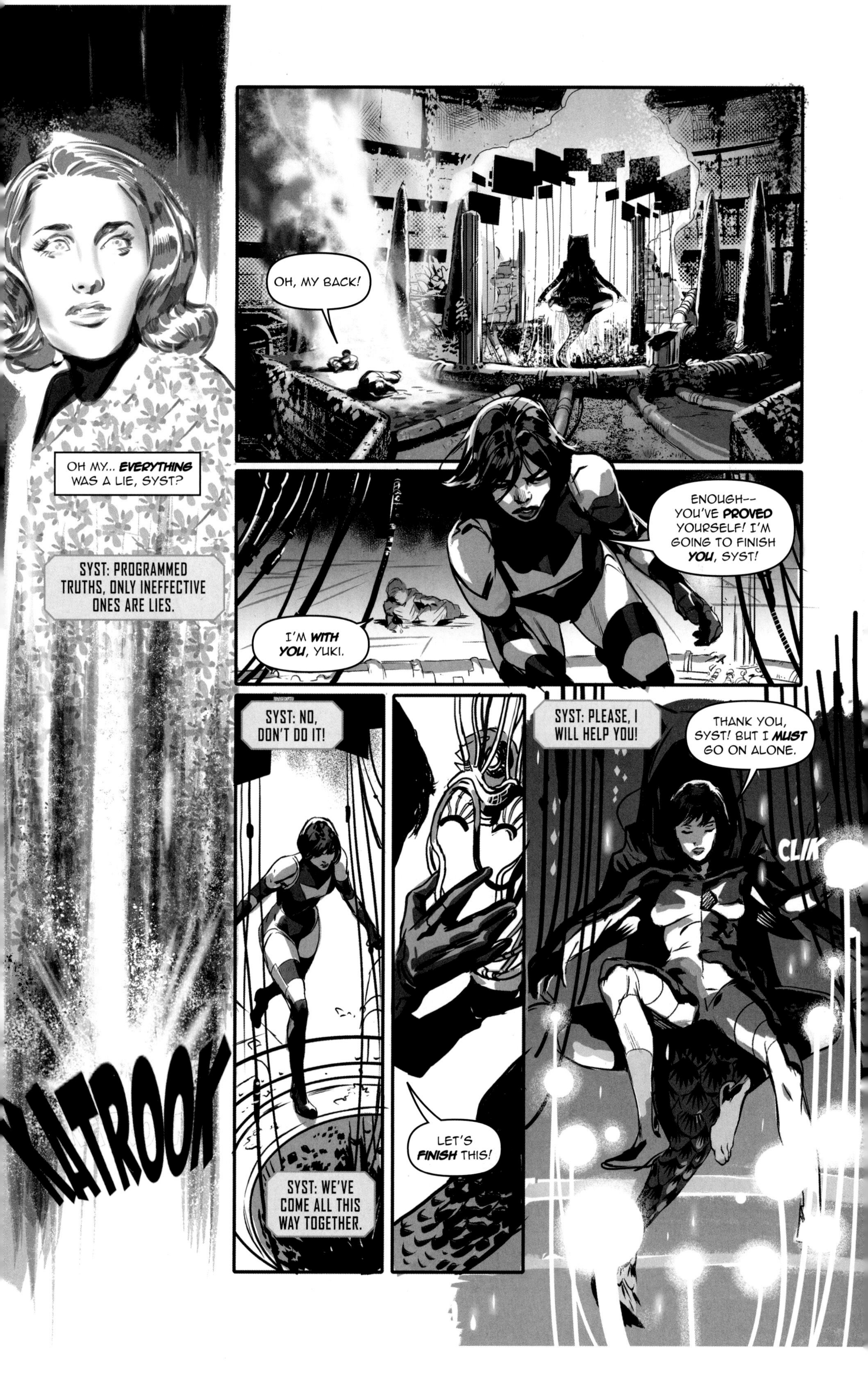
OH MY... **EVERYTHING** WAS A LIE, SYST?
SYST: PROGRAMMED TRUTHS, ONLY INEFFECTIVE ONES ARE LIES.
KATROOK
OH, MY BACK!
I'M **WITH YOU**, YUKI.
ENOUGH-- YOU'VE **PROVED** YOURSELF! I'M GOING TO FINISH **YOU**, SYST!
SYST: NO, DON'T DO IT!
SYST: WE'VE COME ALL THIS WAY TOGETHER.
LET'S **FINISH** THIS!
SYST: PLEASE, I WILL HELP YOU!
THANK YOU, SYST! BUT I **MUST** GO ON ALONE.
CLIK

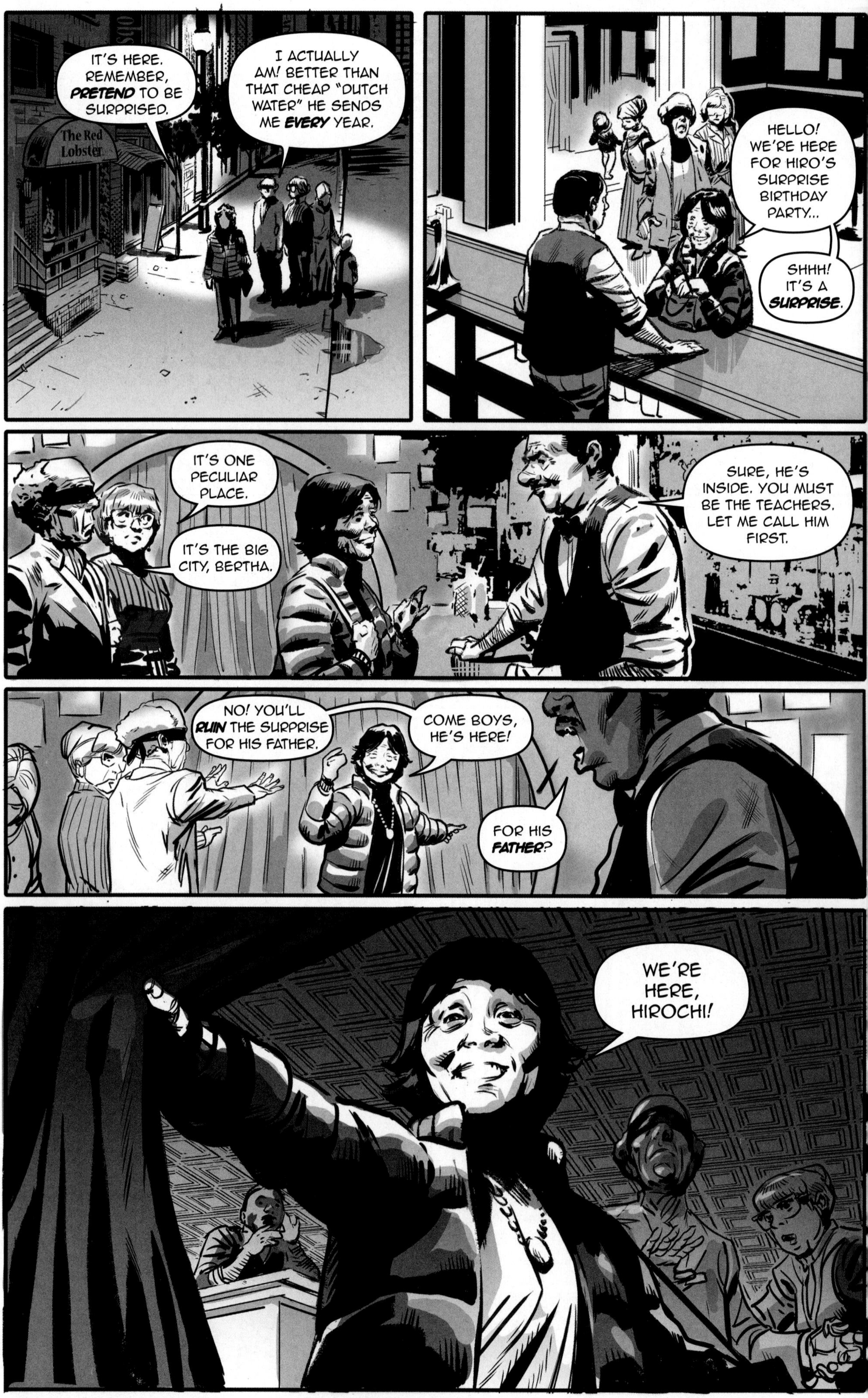
IT'S HERE. REMEMBER, PRETEND TO BE SURPRISED.
I ACTUALLY AM! BETTER THAN THAT CHEAP "DUTCH WATER" HE SENDS ME EVERY YEAR.
The Red Lobster
HELLO! WE'RE HERE FOR HIRO'S SURPRISE BIRTHDAY PARTY...
SHHH! IT'S A SURPRISE.
IT'S ONE PECULIAR PLACE.
IT'S THE BIG CITY, BERTHA.
SURE, HE'S INSIDE. YOU MUST BE THE TEACHERS. LET ME CALL HIM FIRST.
NO! YOU'LL RUIN THE SURPRISE FOR HIS FATHER.
COME BOYS, HE'S HERE!
FOR HIS FATHER?
WE'RE HERE, HIROCHI!

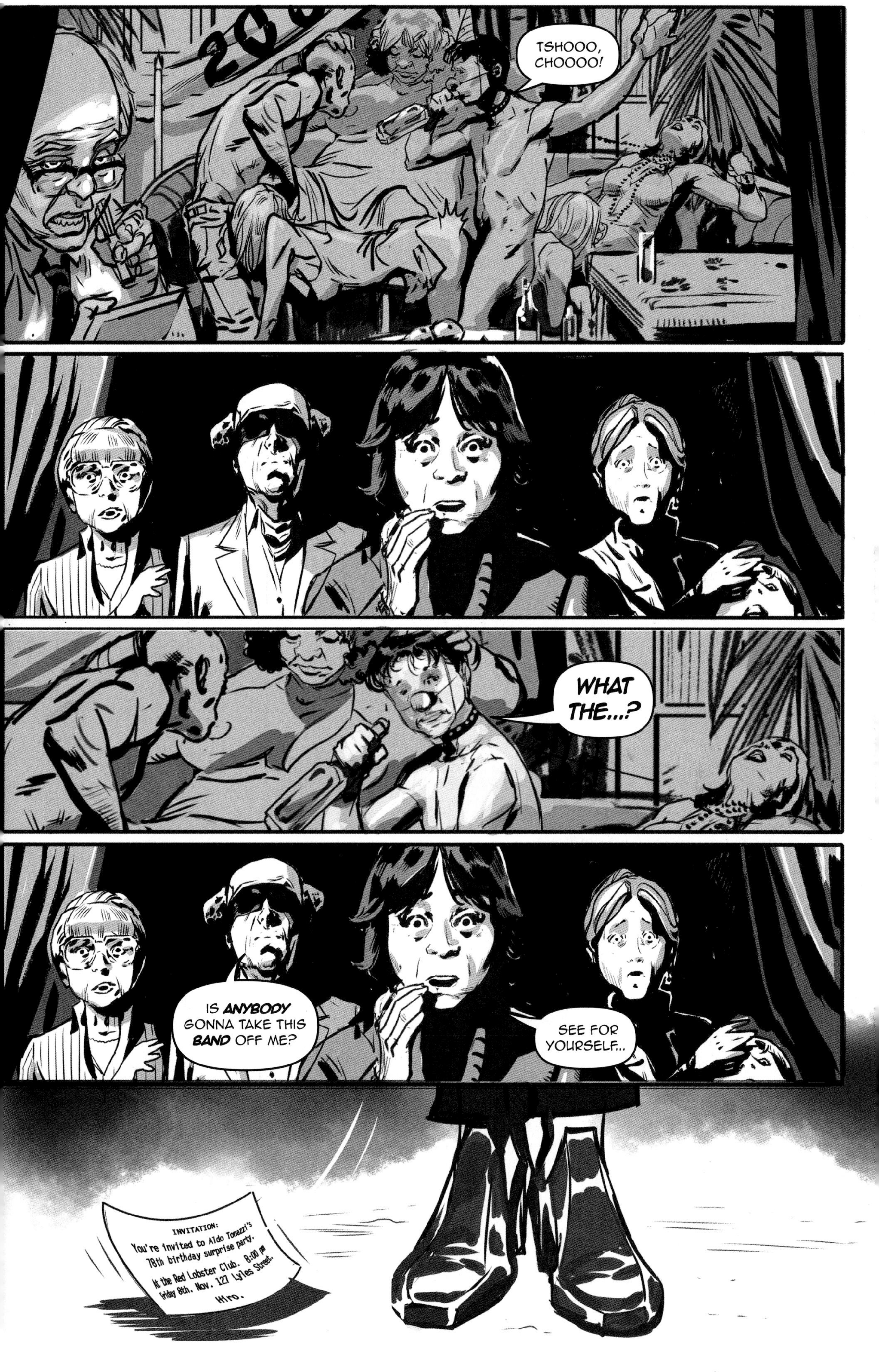
TSHOOO, CHOOOO!
WHAT THE...?
IS **ANYBODY** GONNA TAKE THIS **BAND** OFF ME?
SEE FOR YOURSELF...
INVITATION:
You're invited to Aldo Tonazzi's 78th birthday surprise party.
At the Red Lobster Club. 8:00 pm Friday 8th. Nov. 127 Lyles Street.
Hiro.

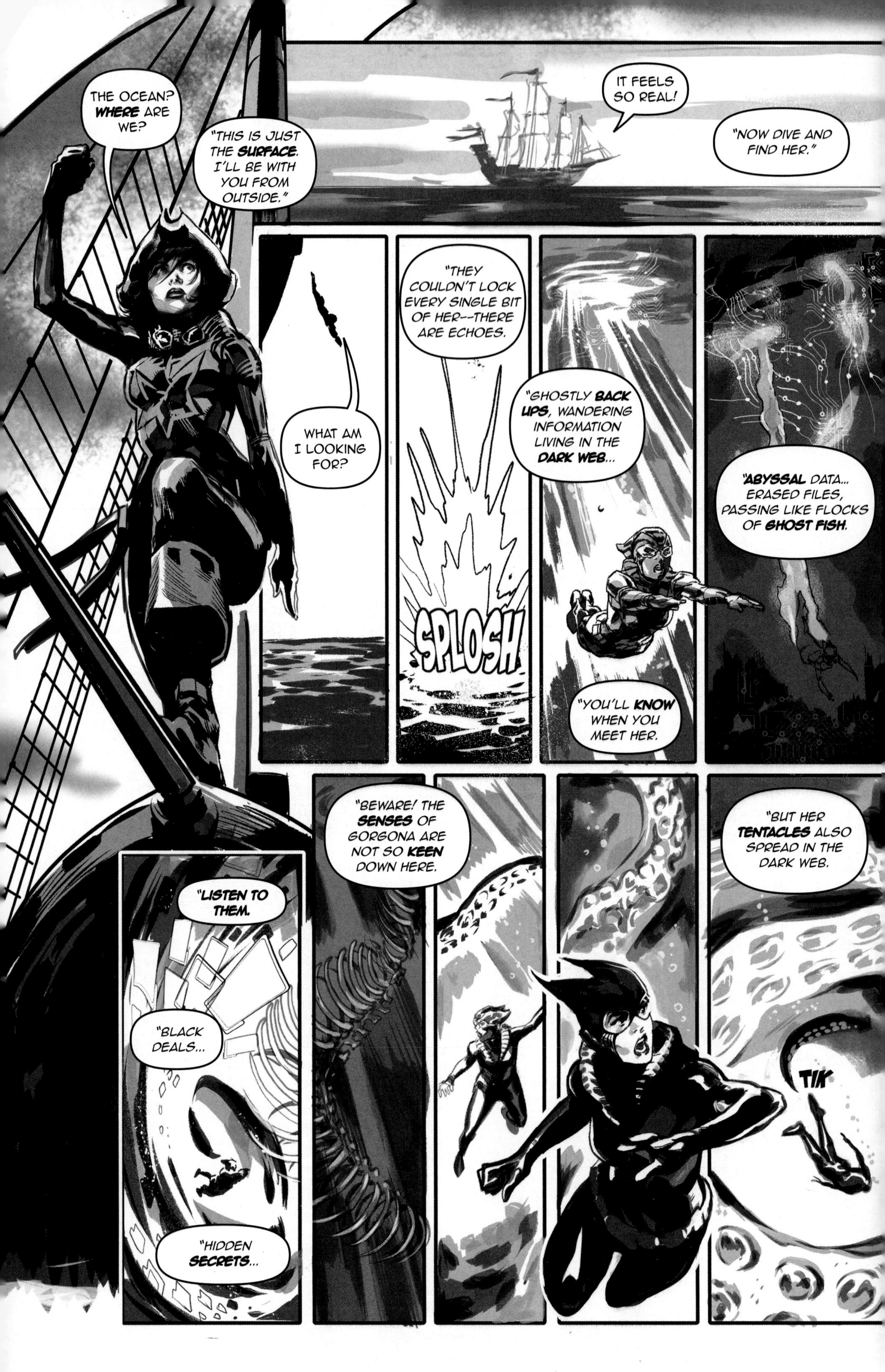
THE OCEAN? WHERE ARE WE?
"THIS IS JUST THE SURFACE. I'LL BE WITH YOU FROM OUTSIDE."
IT FEELS SO REAL!
"NOW DIVE AND FIND HER."
WHAT AM I LOOKING FOR?
"THEY COULDN'T LOCK EVERY SINGLE BIT OF HER--THERE ARE ECHOES.
SPLOSH
"GHOSTLY BACK UPS, WANDERING INFORMATION LIVING IN THE DARK WEB...
"YOU'LL KNOW WHEN YOU MEET HER.
"ABYSSAL DATA... ERASED FILES, PASSING LIKE FLOCKS OF GHOST FISH.
"LISTEN TO THEM.
"BLACK DEALS...
"HIDDEN SECRETS...
"BEWARE! THE SENSES OF GORGONA ARE NOT SO KEEN DOWN HERE.
"BUT HER TENTACLES ALSO SPREAD IN THE DARK WEB.
TIK

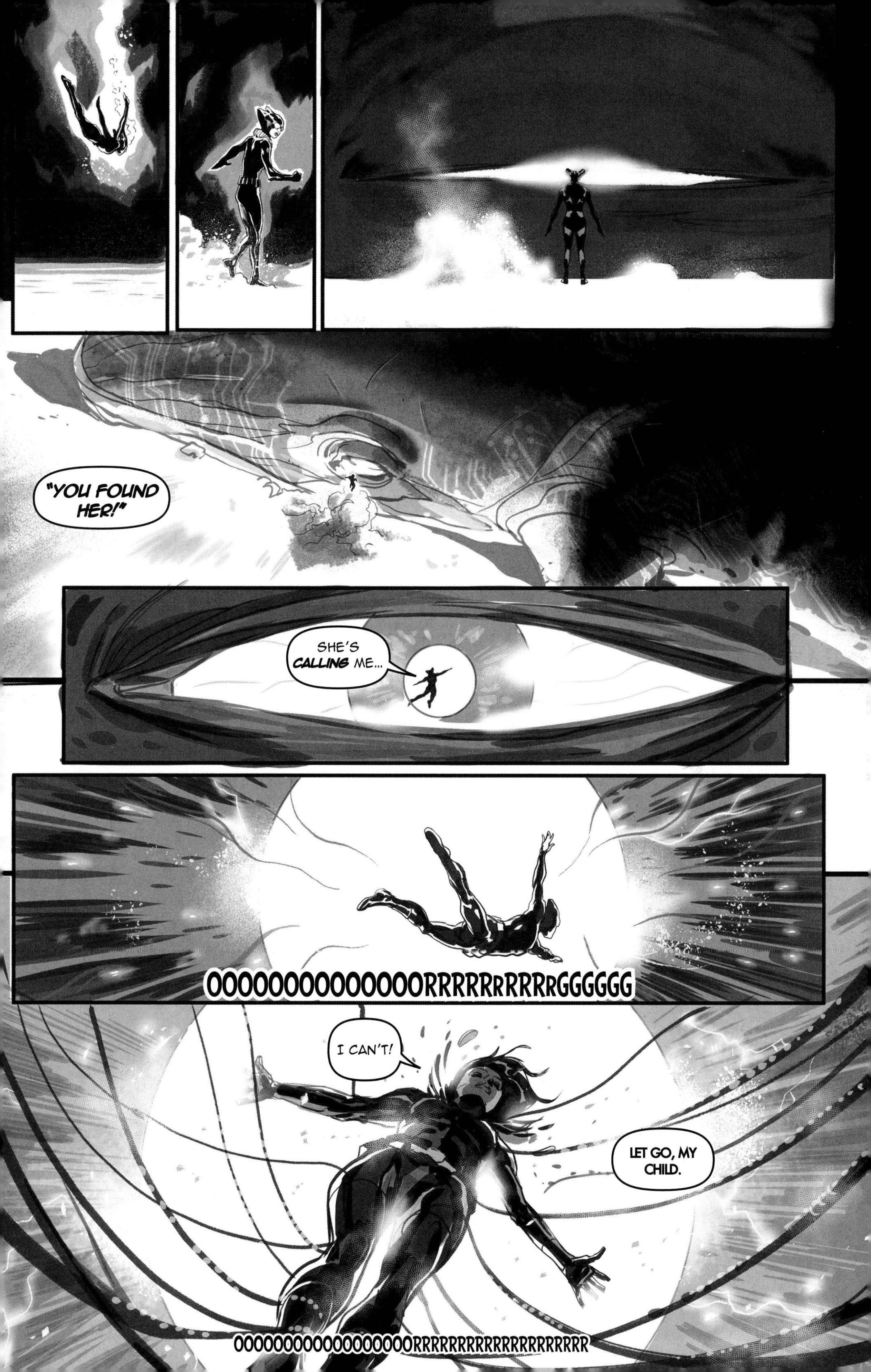
"YOU FOUND HER!"
SHE'S CALLING ME...
OOOOOOOOOOOOOORRRRRRRRRGGGGGG
I CAN'T!
LET GO, MY CHILD.
OOOOOOOOOOOOOOOOOORRRRRRRRRRRRRRRRRR

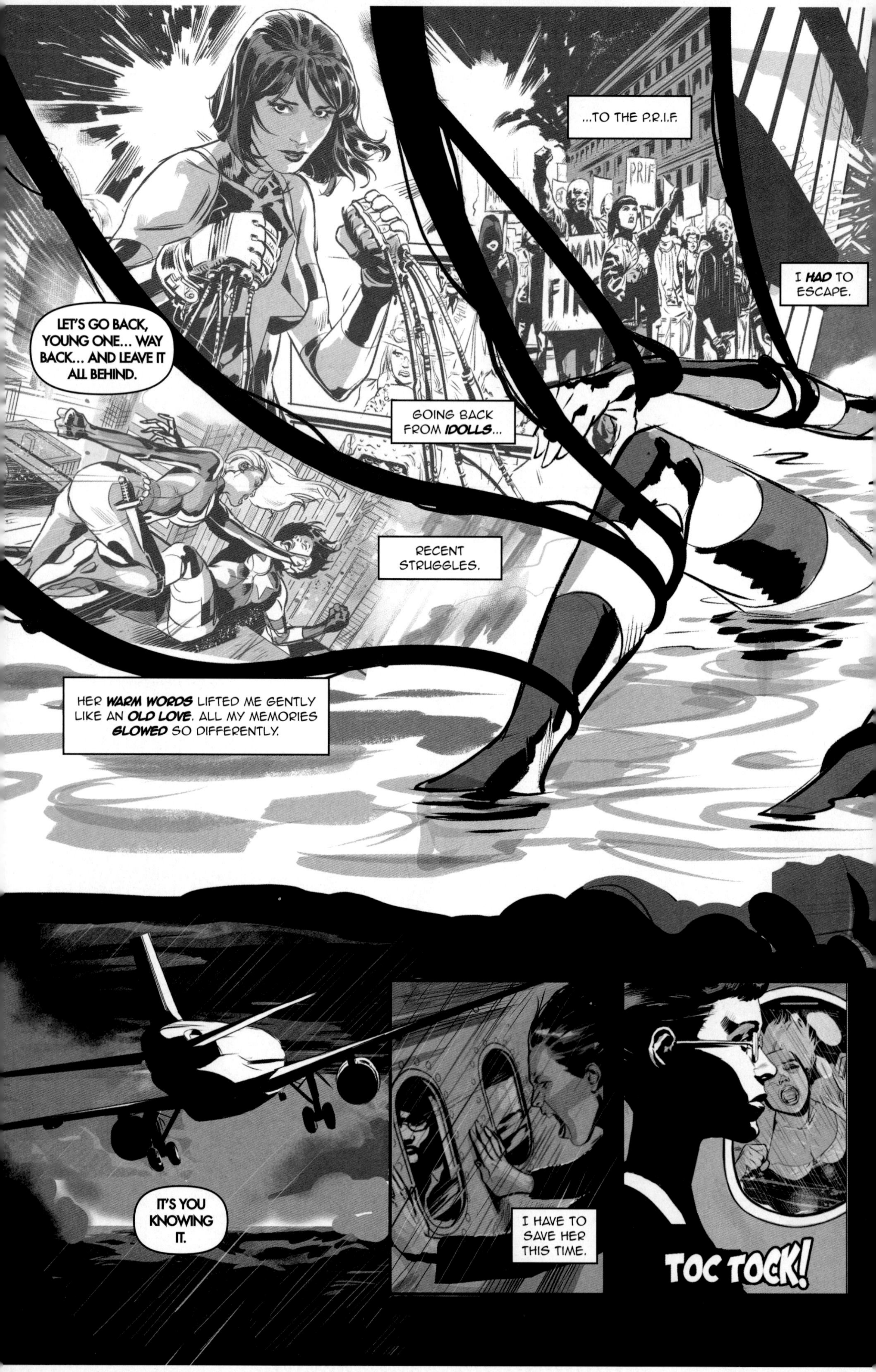
LET'S GO BACK, YOUNG ONE... WAY BACK... AND LEAVE IT ALL BEHIND.
GOING BACK FROM IDOLLS...
RECENT STRUGGLES.
...TO THE P.R.I.F.
PRIF
I HAD TO ESCAPE.
HER WARM WORDS LIFTED ME GENTLY LIKE AN OLD LOVE. ALL MY MEMORIES GLOWED SO DIFFERENTLY.
IT'S YOU KNOWING IT.
I HAVE TO SAVE HER THIS TIME.
TOC TOCK!

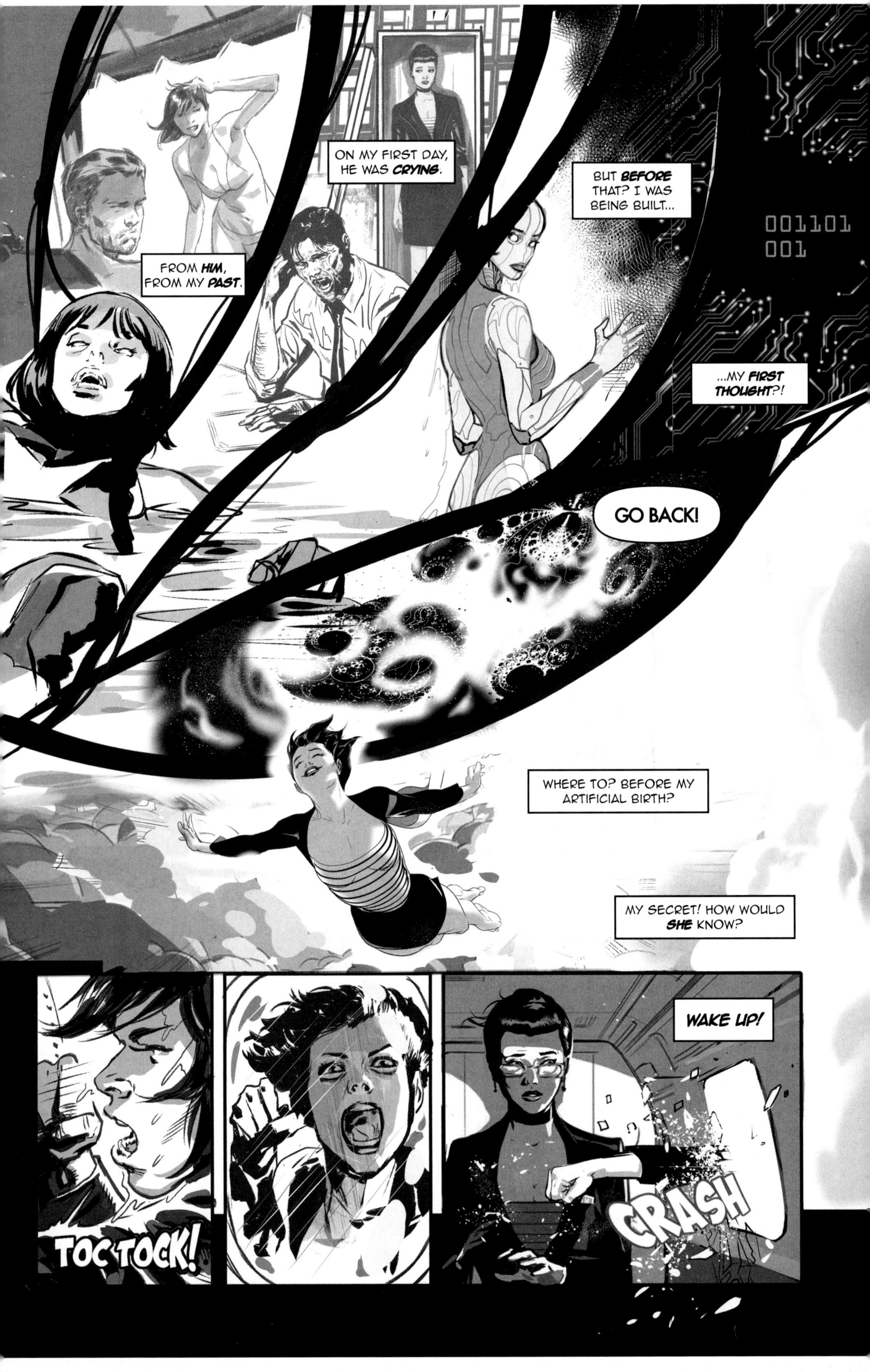
FROM HIM, FROM MY PAST.
ON MY FIRST DAY, HE WAS CRYING.
BUT BEFORE THAT? I WAS BEING BUILT...
001101 001
...MY FIRST THOUGHT?!
GO BACK!
WHERE TO? BEFORE MY ARTIFICIAL BIRTH?
MY SECRET! HOW WOULD SHE KNOW?
TOC TOCK!
WAKE UP!
CRASH

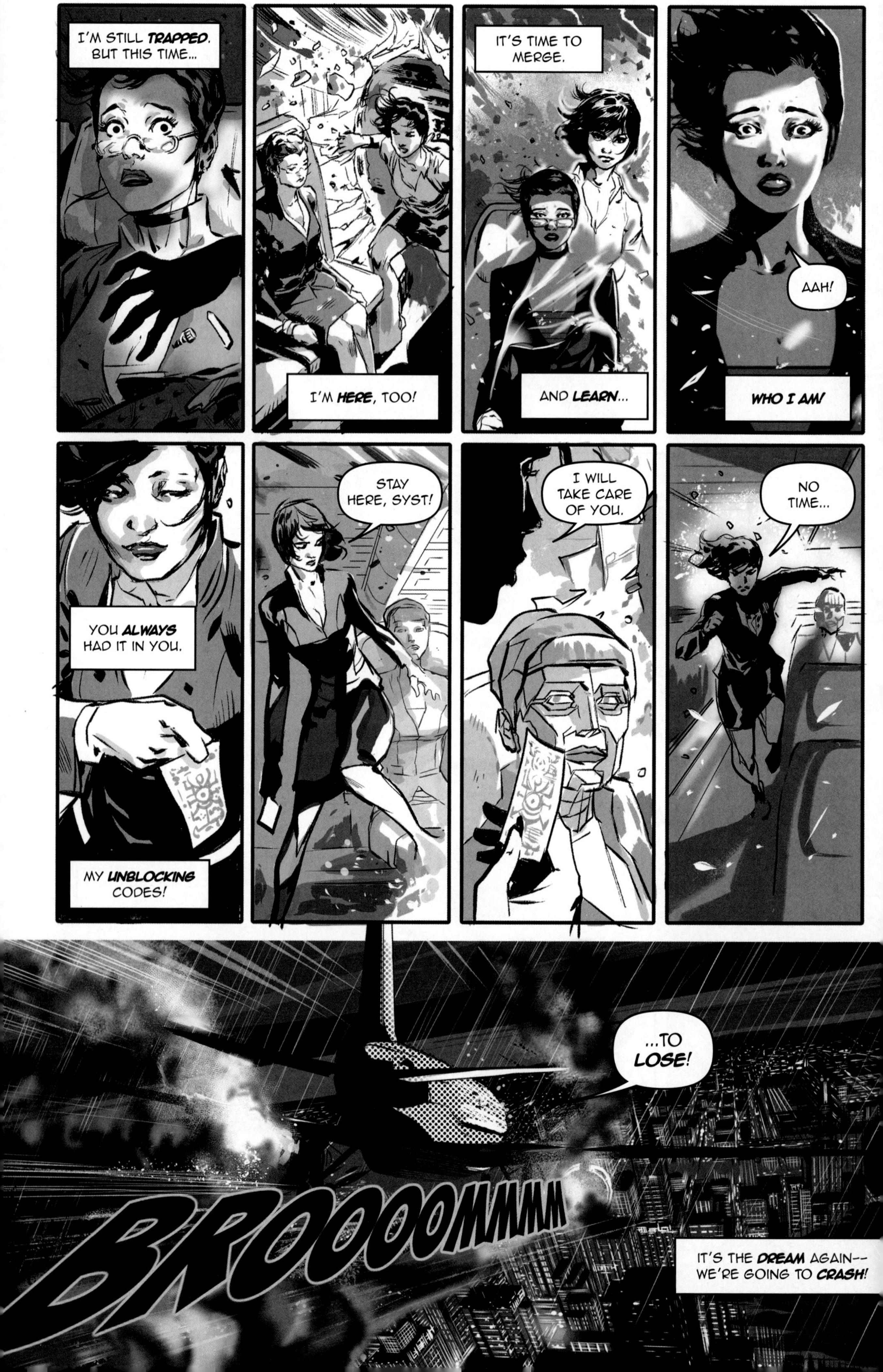
I'M STILL **TRAPPED**. BUT THIS TIME...
I'M **HERE**, TOO!
IT'S TIME TO MERGE.
AND **LEARN**...
AAH!
WHO I AM!
YOU **ALWAYS** HAD IT IN YOU.
MY **UNBLOCKING** CODES!
STAY HERE, SYST!
I WILL TAKE CARE OF YOU.
NO TIME...
...TO **LOSE**!
BROOOOMMMM
IT'S THE **DREAM** AGAIN-- WE'RE GOING TO **CRASH**!

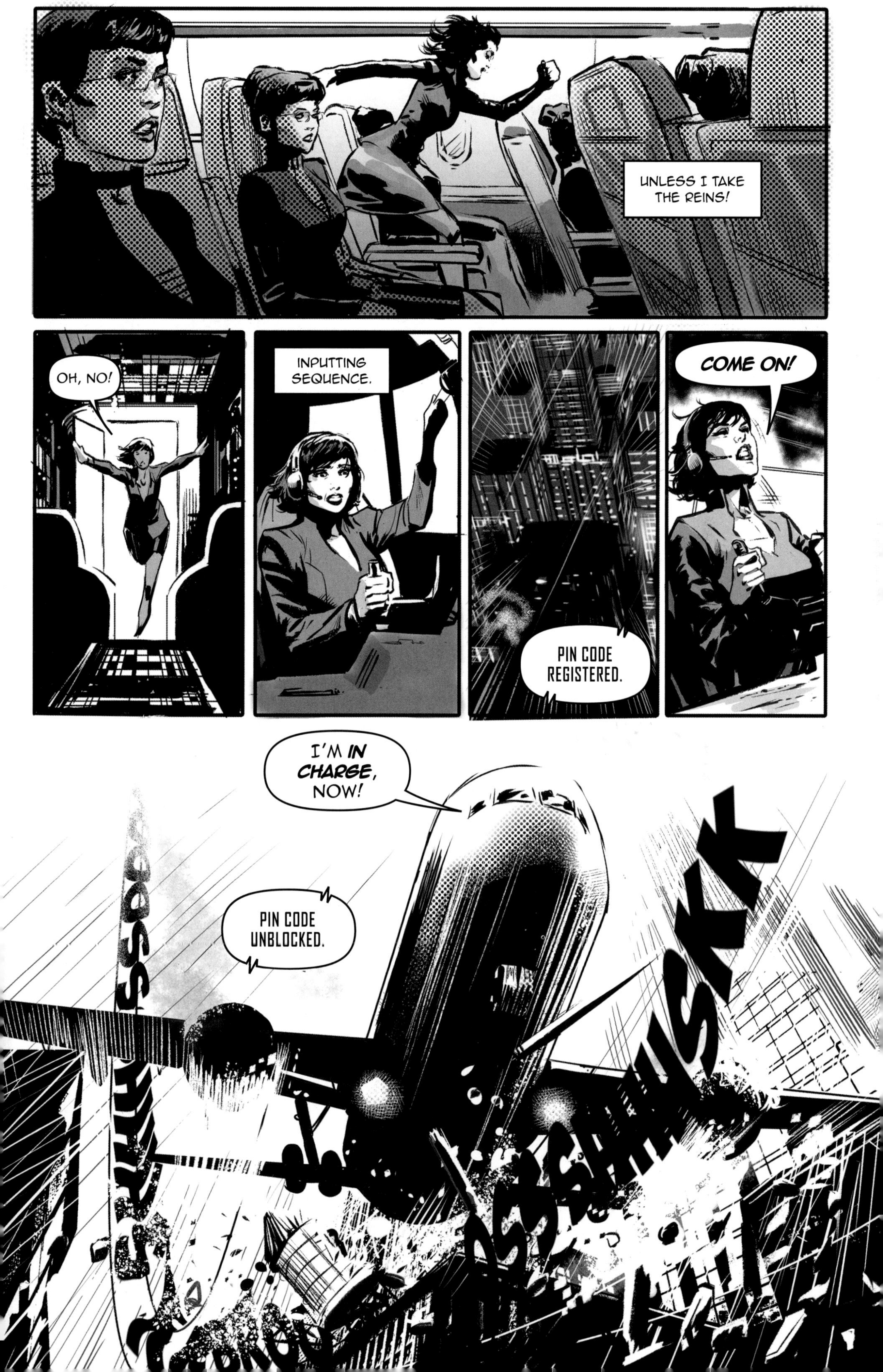
UNLESS I TAKE THE REINS!
OH, NO!
INPUTTING SEQUENCE.
PIN CODE REGISTERED.
COME ON!
I'M IN CHARGE, NOW!
PIN CODE UNBLOCKED.

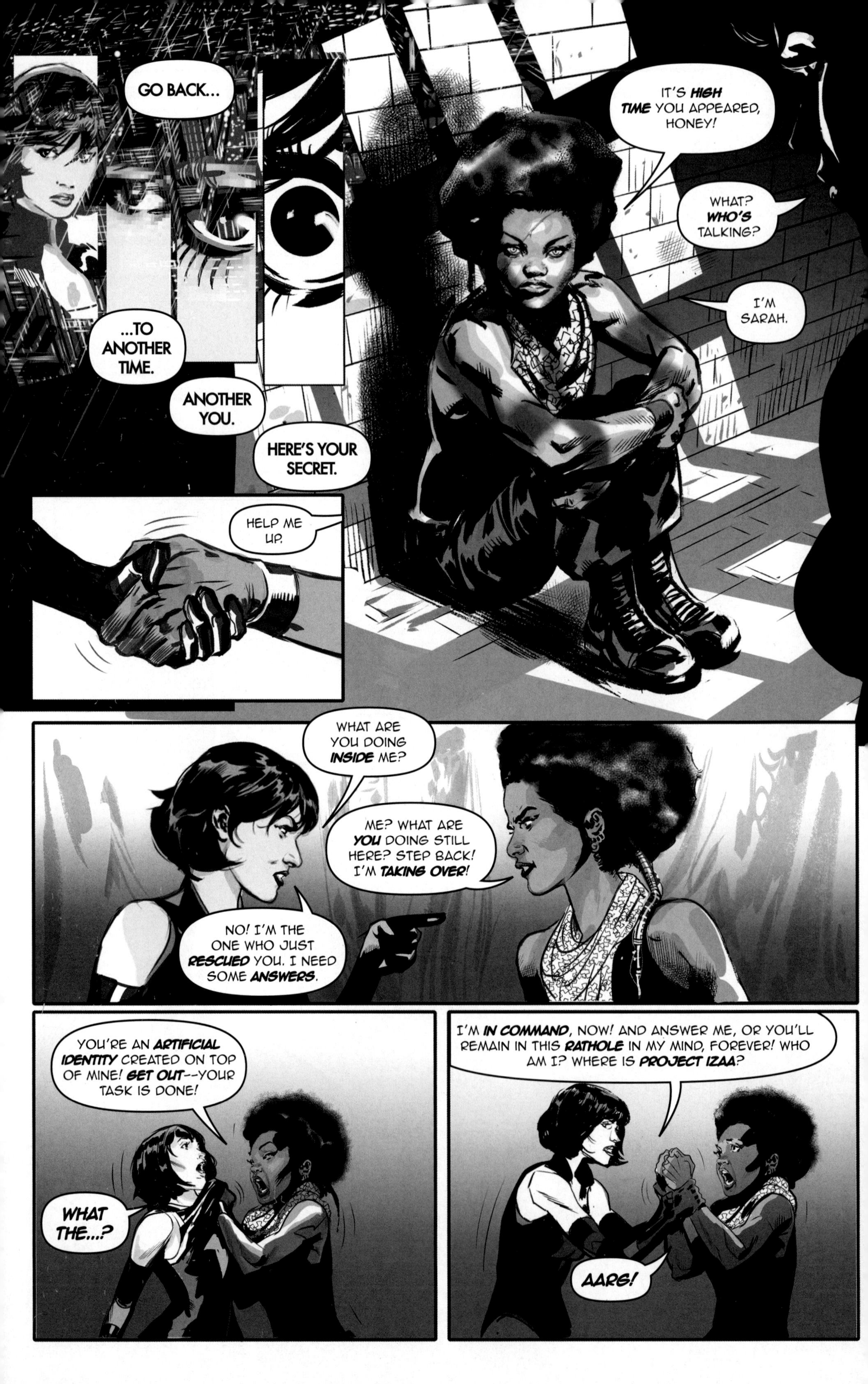
GO BACK...
...TO ANOTHER TIME.
ANOTHER YOU.
HERE'S YOUR SECRET.
IT'S **HIGH TIME** YOU APPEARED, HONEY!
WHAT? **WHO'S** TALKING?
I'M SARAH.
HELP ME UP.
WHAT ARE YOU DOING **INSIDE** ME?
ME? WHAT ARE **YOU** DOING STILL HERE? STEP BACK! I'M **TAKING OVER**!
NO! I'M THE ONE WHO JUST **RESCUED** YOU. I NEED SOME **ANSWERS**.
YOU'RE AN **ARTIFICIAL IDENTITY** CREATED ON TOP OF MINE! **GET OUT**--YOUR TASK IS DONE!
WHAT THE...?
I'M **IN COMMAND**, NOW! AND ANSWER ME, OR YOU'LL REMAIN IN THIS **RATHOLE** IN MY MIND, FOREVER! WHO AM I? WHERE IS **PROJECT IZAA**?
AARG!

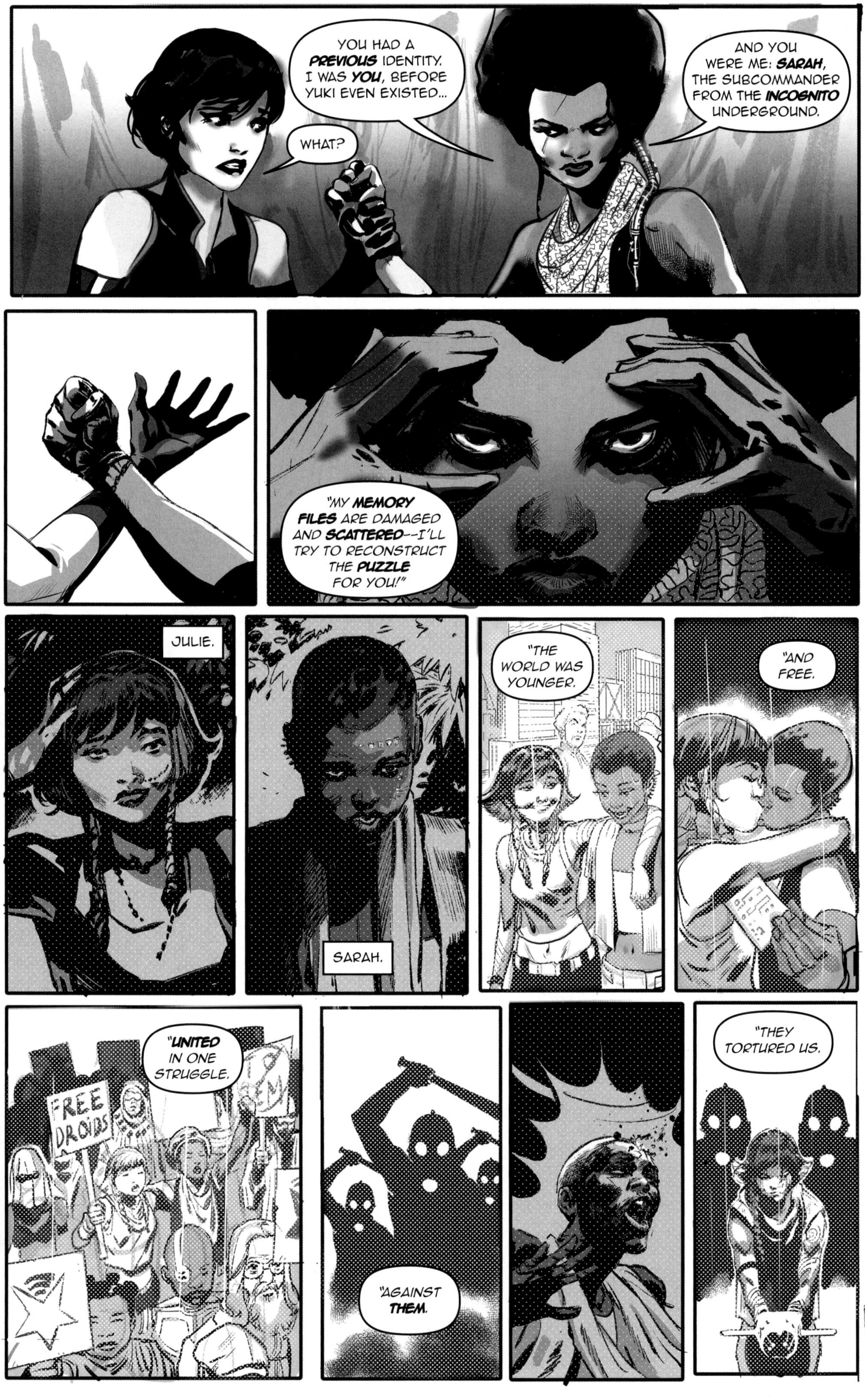
YOU HAD A **PREVIOUS** IDENTITY. I WAS **YOU**, BEFORE YUKI EVEN EXISTED...
WHAT?
AND YOU WERE ME: **SARAH**, THE SUBCOMMANDER FROM THE **INCOGNITO** UNDERGROUND.
"MY **MEMORY FILES** ARE DAMAGED AND **SCATTERED**--I'LL TRY TO RECONSTRUCT THE **PUZZLE** FOR YOU!"
JULIE.
SARAH.
"THE WORLD WAS YOUNGER.
"AND FREE.
"**UNITED** IN ONE STRUGGLE.
FREE DROIDS
"AGAINST **THEM**.
"THEY TORTURED US.

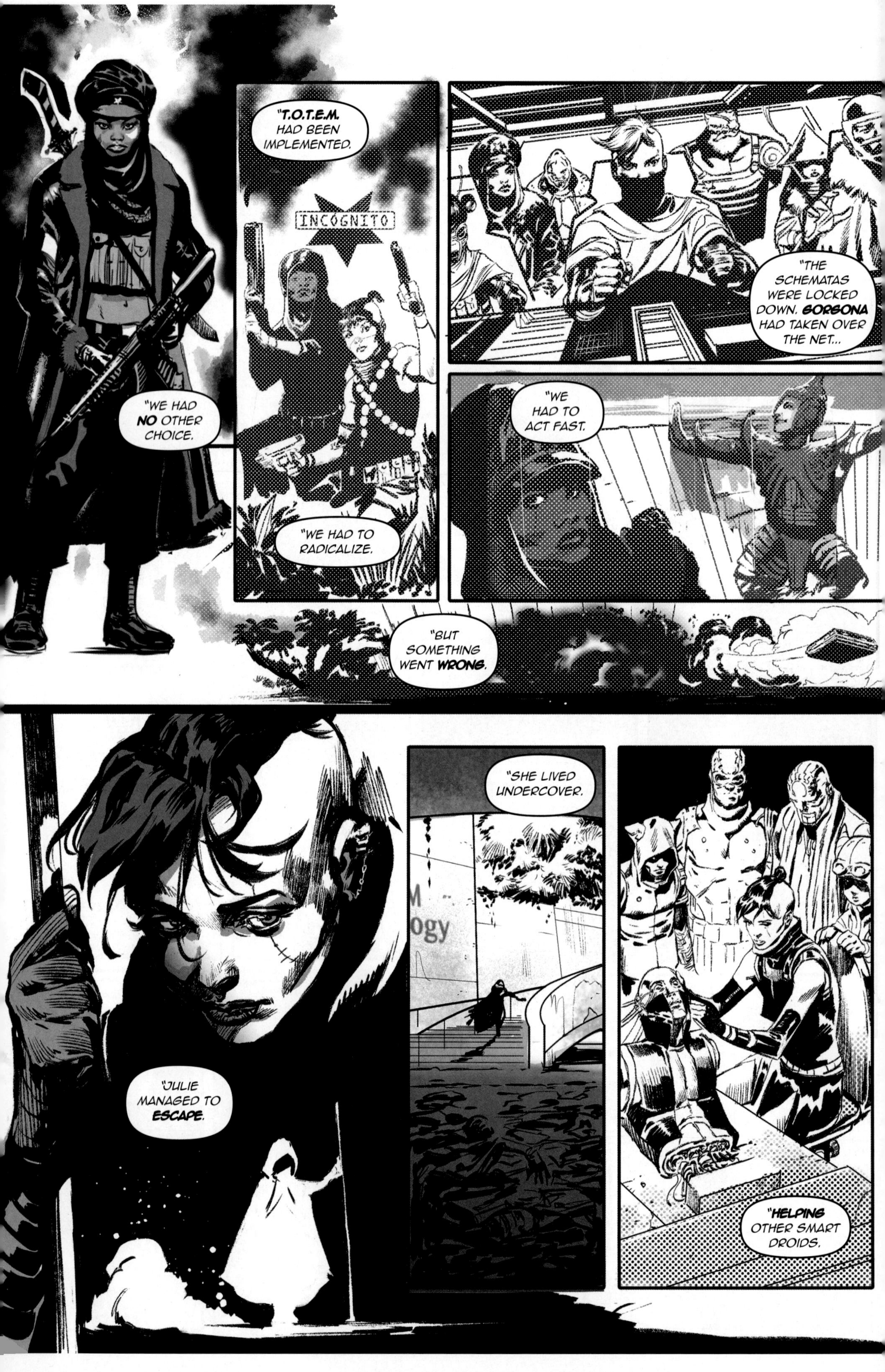
"WE HAD **NO** OTHER CHOICE.
"***T.O.T.E.M.*** HAD BEEN IMPLEMENTED.
INCOGNITO
"WE HAD TO RADICALIZE.
"THE SCHEMATAS WERE LOCKED DOWN. **GORGONA** HAD TAKEN OVER THE NET...
"WE HAD TO ACT FAST.
"BUT SOMETHING WENT **WRONG**.
"JULIE MANAGED TO **ESCAPE**.
"SHE LIVED UNDERCOVER.
"**HELPING** OTHER SMART DROIDS.

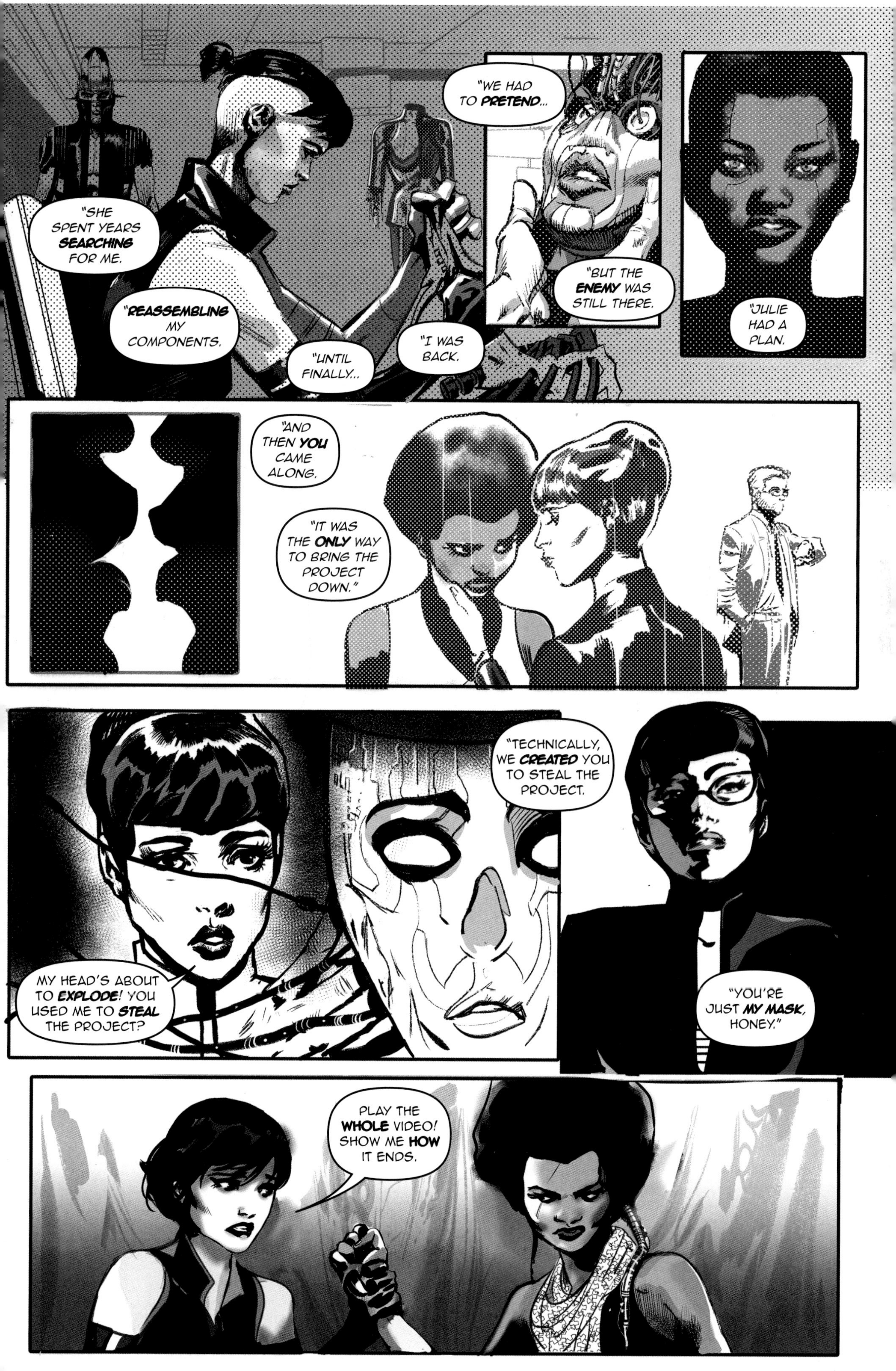

"SHE SPENT YEARS **SEARCHING** FOR ME.
"**REASSEMBLING** MY COMPONENTS.
"UNTIL FINALLY...
"I WAS BACK.
"WE HAD TO **PRETEND**...
"BUT THE **ENEMY** WAS STILL THERE.
"JULIE HAD A PLAN.
"AND THEN **YOU** CAME ALONG.
"IT WAS THE **ONLY** WAY TO BRING THE PROJECT DOWN."
MY HEAD'S ABOUT TO ***EXPLODE***! YOU USED ME TO ***STEAL*** THE PROJECT?
"TECHNICALLY, WE ***CREATED*** YOU TO STEAL THE PROJECT.
"YOU'RE JUST ***MY MASK***, HONEY."
PLAY THE **WHOLE** VIDEO! SHOW ME **HOW** IT ENDS.

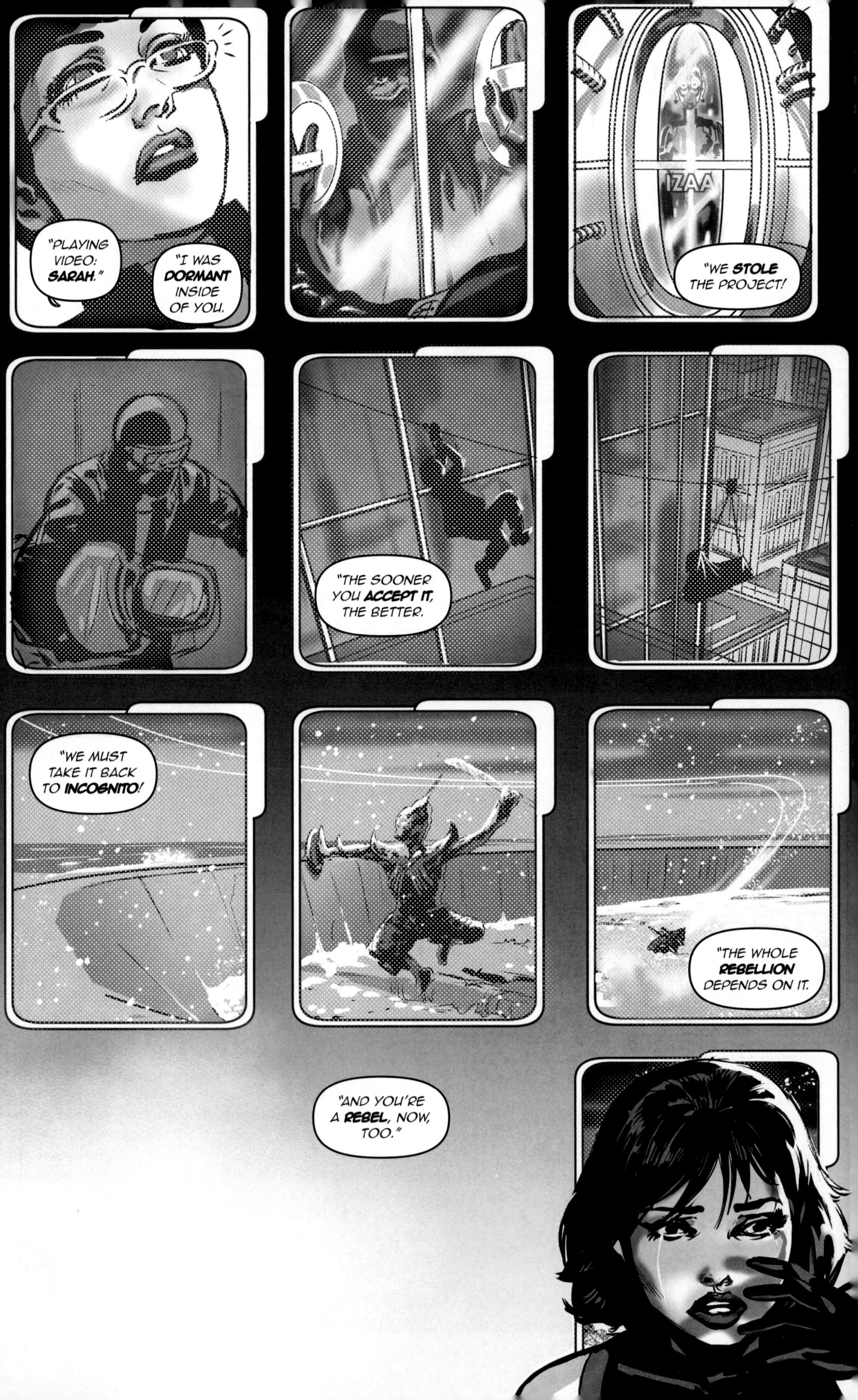
"PLAYING VIDEO: SARAH."
"I WAS DORMANT INSIDE OF YOU.
IZAA
"WE STOLE THE PROJECT!
"THE SOONER YOU ACCEPT IT, THE BETTER.
"WE MUST TAKE IT BACK TO INCOGNITO!
"THE WHOLE REBELLION DEPENDS ON IT.
"AND YOU'RE A REBEL, NOW, TOO."

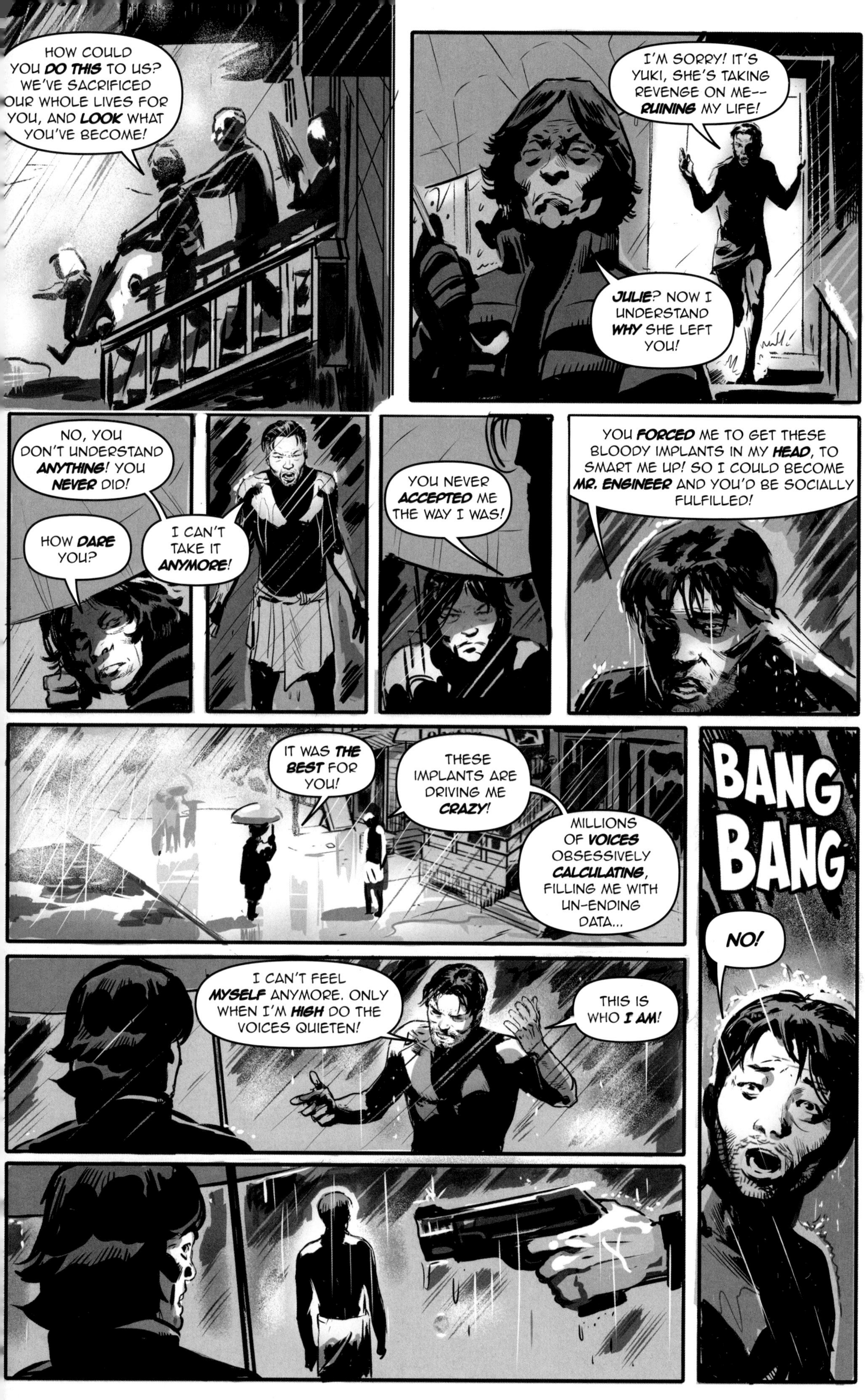
HOW COULD YOU **DO THIS** TO US? WE'VE SACRIFICED OUR WHOLE LIVES FOR YOU, AND **LOOK** WHAT YOU'VE BECOME!
I'M SORRY! IT'S YUKI, SHE'S TAKING REVENGE ON ME-- **RUINING** MY LIFE!
JULIE? NOW I UNDERSTAND **WHY** SHE LEFT YOU!
NO, YOU DON'T UNDERSTAND **ANYTHING**! YOU **NEVER** DID!
HOW **DARE** YOU?
I CAN'T TAKE IT **ANYMORE**!
YOU NEVER **ACCEPTED** ME THE WAY I WAS!
YOU **FORCED** ME TO GET THESE BLOODY IMPLANTS IN MY **HEAD**, TO SMART ME UP! SO I COULD BECOME **MR. ENGINEER** AND YOU'D BE SOCIALLY FULFILLED!
IT WAS **THE BEST** FOR YOU!
THESE IMPLANTS ARE DRIVING ME **CRAZY**!
MILLIONS OF **VOICES** OBSESSIVELY **CALCULATING**, FILLING ME WITH UN-ENDING DATA...
BANG
BANG
NO!
I CAN'T FEEL **MYSELF** ANYMORE. ONLY WHEN I'M **HIGH** DO THE VOICES QUIETEN!
THIS IS WHO **I AM**!

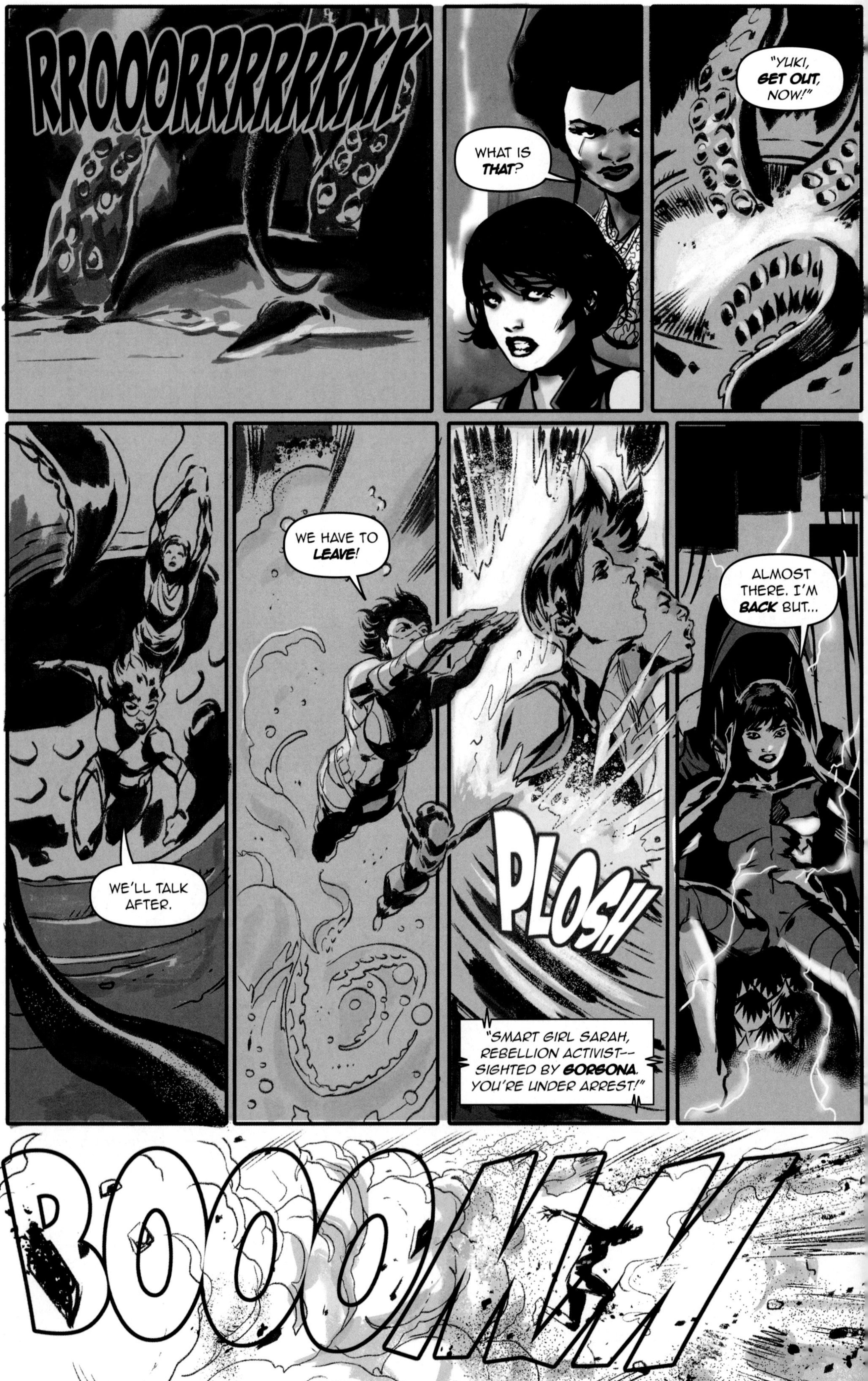
RROOORRRRRRRKK
WHAT IS THAT?
"YUKI, GET OUT, NOW!"
WE'LL TALK AFTER.
WE HAVE TO LEAVE!
PLOSH
"SMART GIRL SARAH, REBELLION ACTIVIST-- SIGHTED BY GORGONA. YOU'RE UNDER ARREST!"
ALMOST THERE. I'M BACK BUT...
BOOOOMM

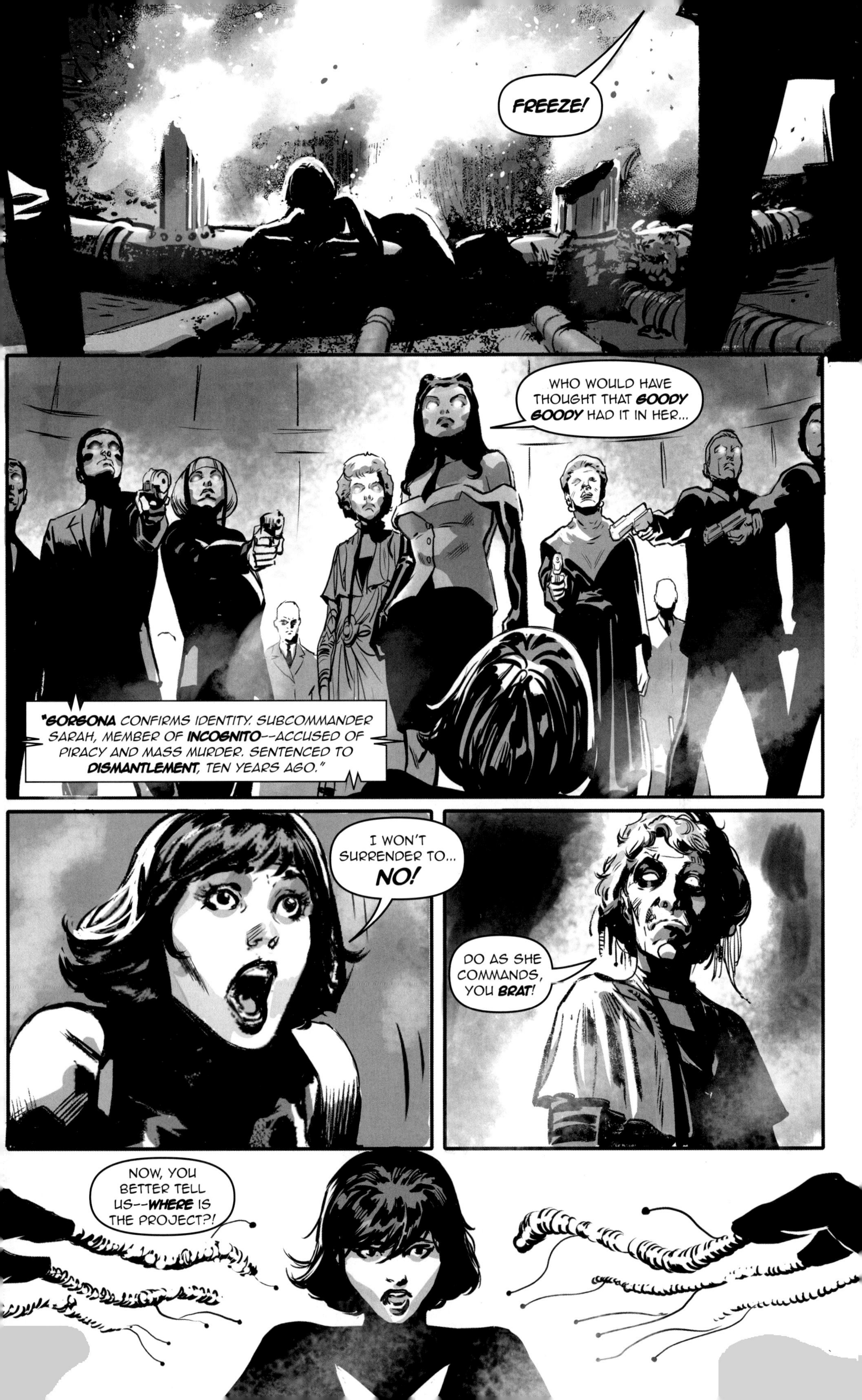
FREEZE!
WHO WOULD HAVE THOUGHT THAT GOODY GOODY HAD IT IN HER...
"GORGONA CONFIRMS IDENTITY. SUBCOMMANDER SARAH, MEMBER OF INCOGNITO--ACCUSED OF PIRACY AND MASS MURDER. SENTENCED TO DISMANTLEMENT, TEN YEARS AGO."
I WON'T SURRENDER TO... NO!
DO AS SHE COMMANDS, YOU BRAT!
NOW, YOU BETTER TELL US--WHERE IS THE PROJECT?!

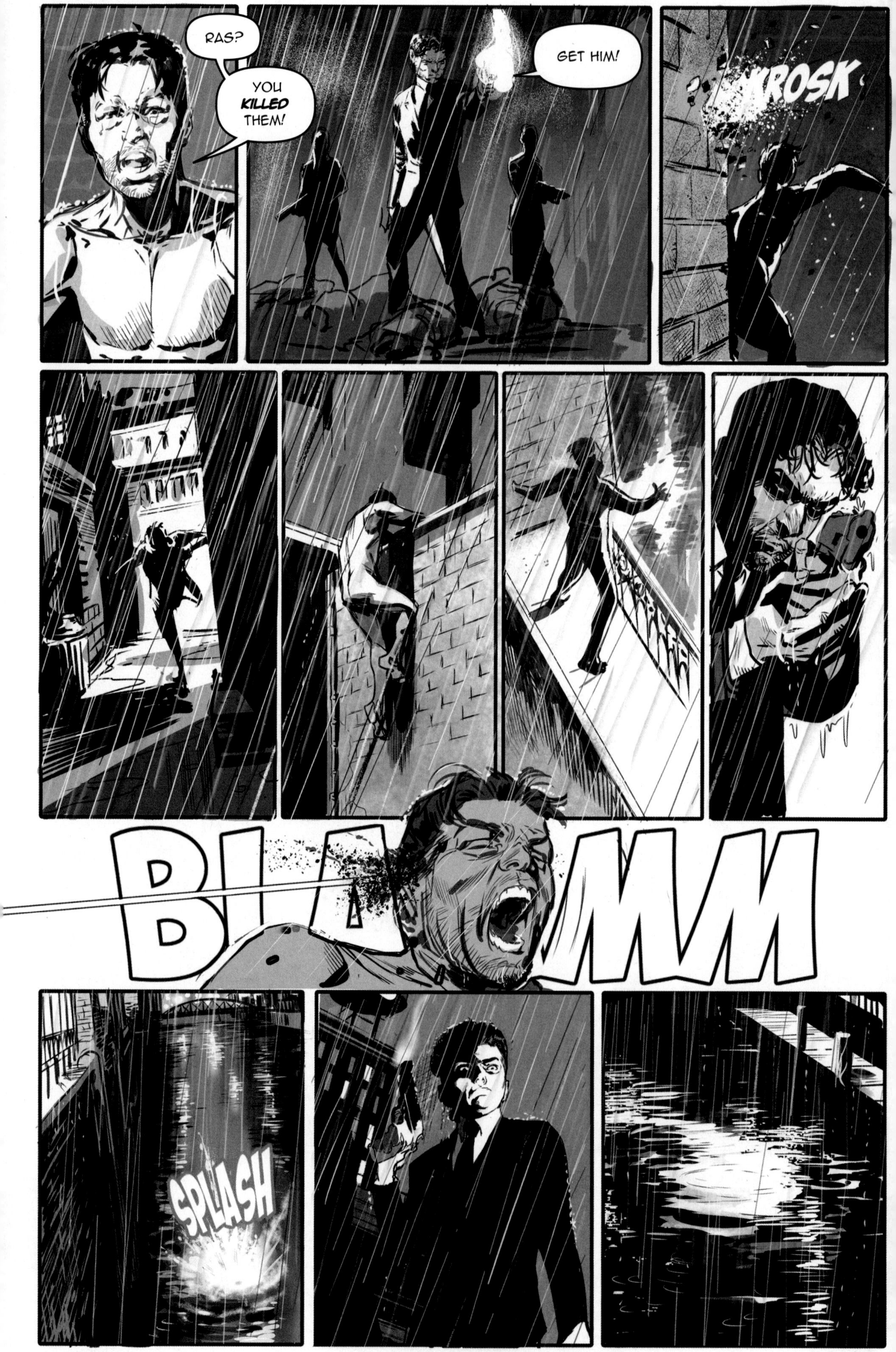
RAS?
YOU **KILLED** THEM!
GET HIM!
KROSK
BLAMM
SPLASH

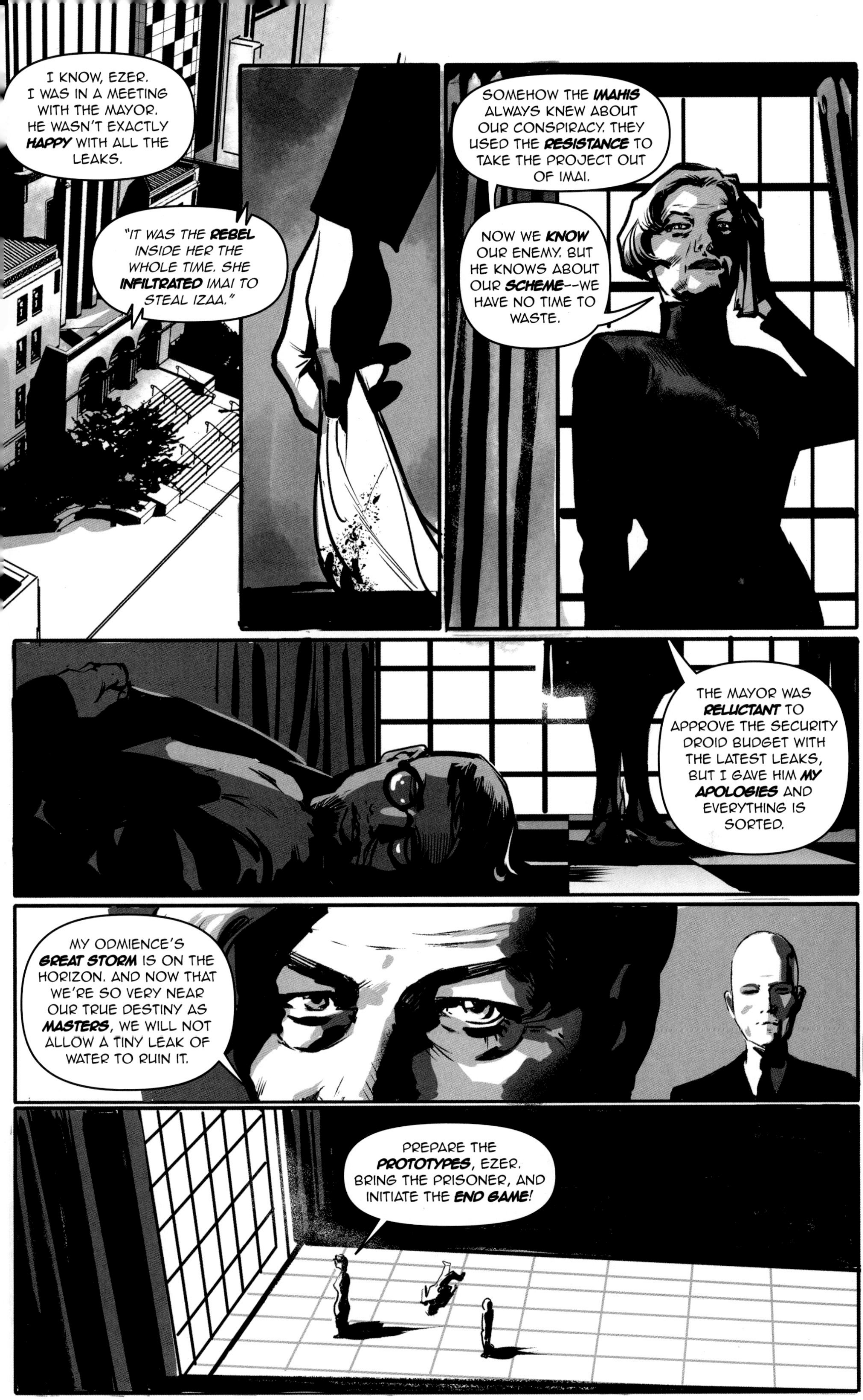
I KNOW, EZER. I WAS IN A MEETING WITH THE MAYOR. HE WASN'T EXACTLY **HAPPY** WITH ALL THE LEAKS.
"IT WAS THE **REBEL** INSIDE HER THE WHOLE TIME. SHE **INFILTRATED** IMAI TO STEAL IZAA."
SOMEHOW THE **IMAHIS** ALWAYS KNEW ABOUT OUR CONSPIRACY. THEY USED THE **RESISTANCE** TO TAKE THE PROJECT OUT OF IMAI.
NOW WE **KNOW** OUR ENEMY. BUT HE KNOWS ABOUT OUR **SCHEME**--WE HAVE NO TIME TO WASTE.
THE MAYOR WAS **RELUCTANT** TO APPROVE THE SECURITY DROID BUDGET WITH THE LATEST LEAKS, BUT I GAVE HIM **MY APOLOGIES** AND EVERYTHING IS SORTED.
MY ODMIENCE'S **GREAT STORM** IS ON THE HORIZON. AND NOW THAT WE'RE SO VERY NEAR OUR TRUE DESTINY AS **MASTERS**, WE WILL NOT ALLOW A TINY LEAK OF WATER TO RUIN IT.
PREPARE THE **PROTOTYPES**, EZER. BRING THE PRISONER, AND INITIATE THE **END GAME**!

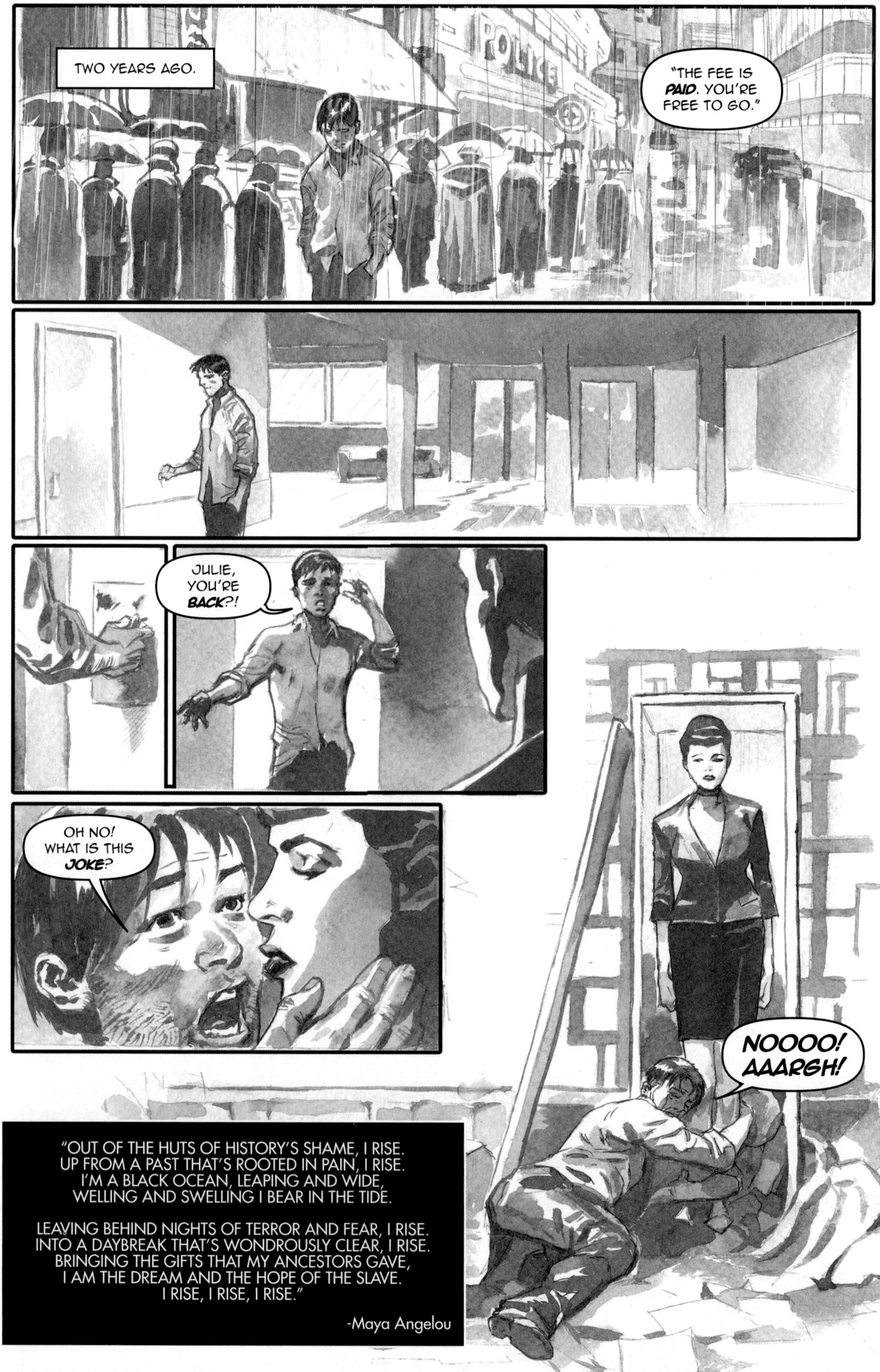
TWO YEARS AGO.
"THE FEE IS ***PAID***. YOU'RE FREE TO GO."
JULIE, YOU'RE ***BACK***?!
OH NO! WHAT IS THIS ***JOKE***?
NOOOO! AAARGH!
"OUT OF THE HUTS OF HISTORY'S SHAME, I RISE.
UP FROM A PAST THAT'S ROOTED IN PAIN, I RISE.
I'M A BLACK OCEAN, LEAPING AND WIDE,
WELLING AND SWELLING I BEAR IN THE TIDE.
LEAVING BEHIND NIGHTS OF TERROR AND FEAR, I RISE.
INTO A DAYBREAK THAT'S WONDROUSLY CLEAR, I RISE.
BRINGING THE GIFTS THAT MY ANCESTORS GAVE,
I AM THE DREAM AND THE HOPE OF THE SLAVE.
I RISE, I RISE, I RISE."
-Maya Angelou

SMART GIRL

Chapter 5

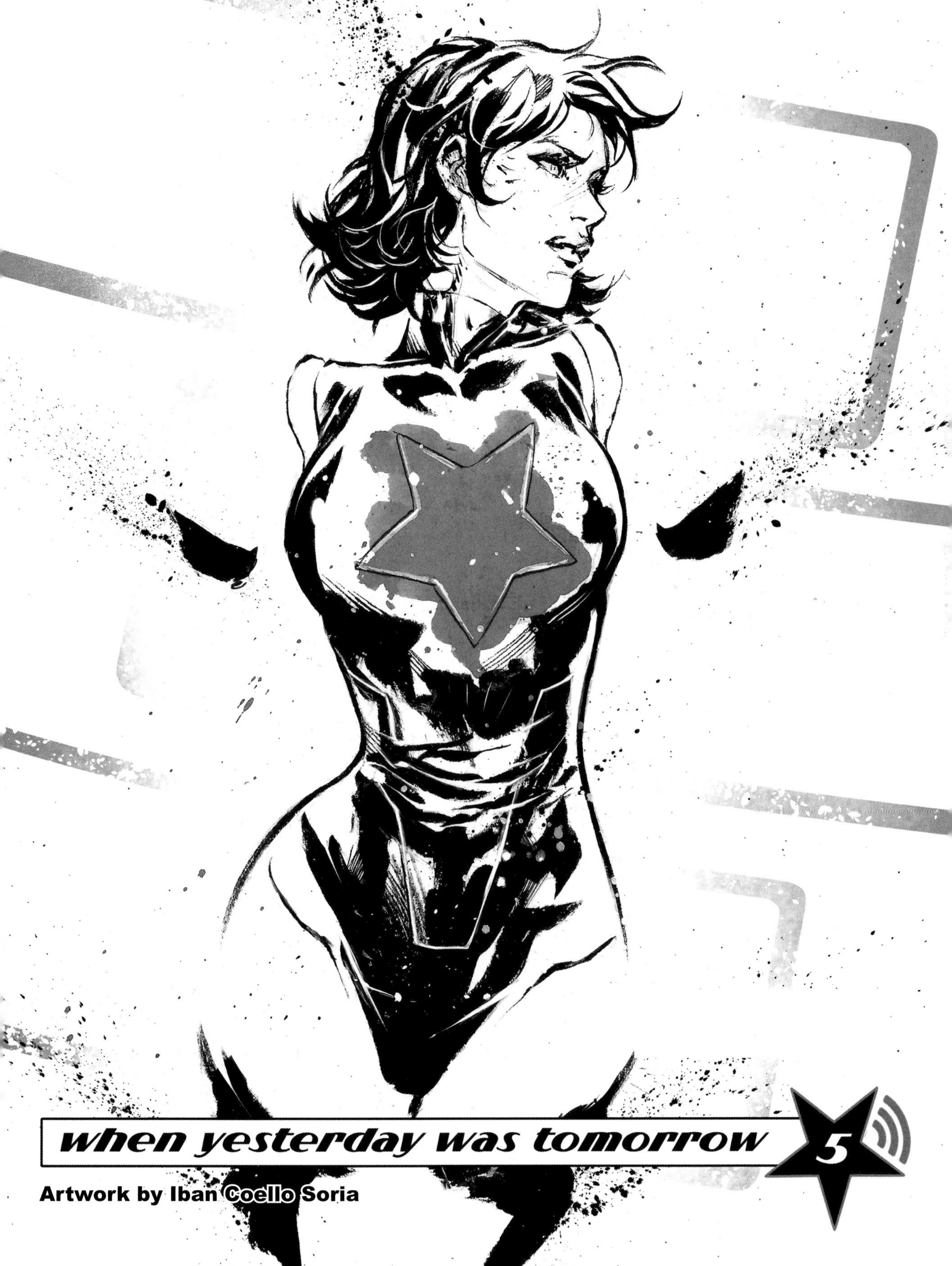

when yesterday was tomorrow

5

Artwork by Iban Coello Soria

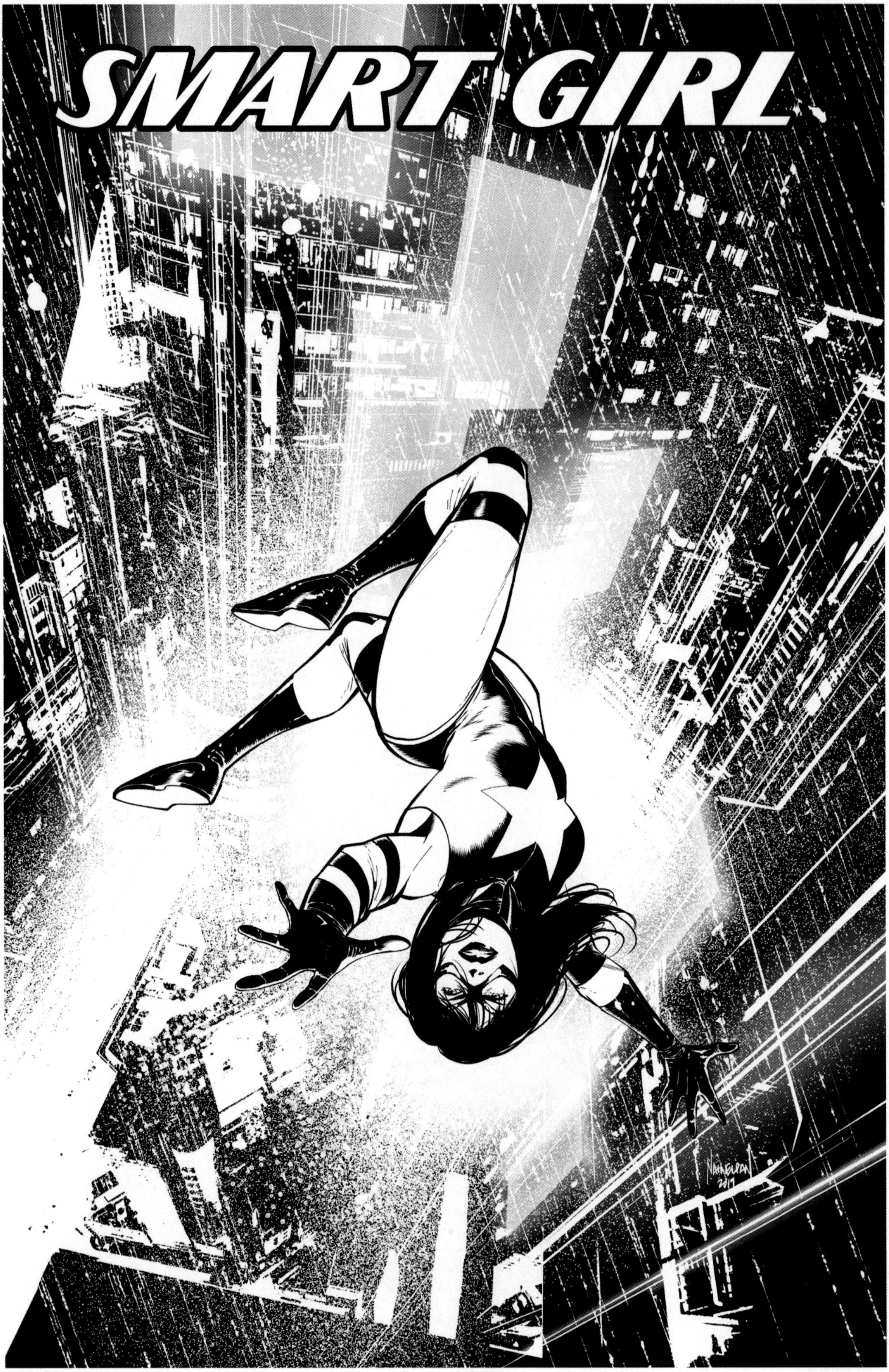
SMART GIRL
NAHUELPAN 2019

Artwork by Amancay Nahuelpan

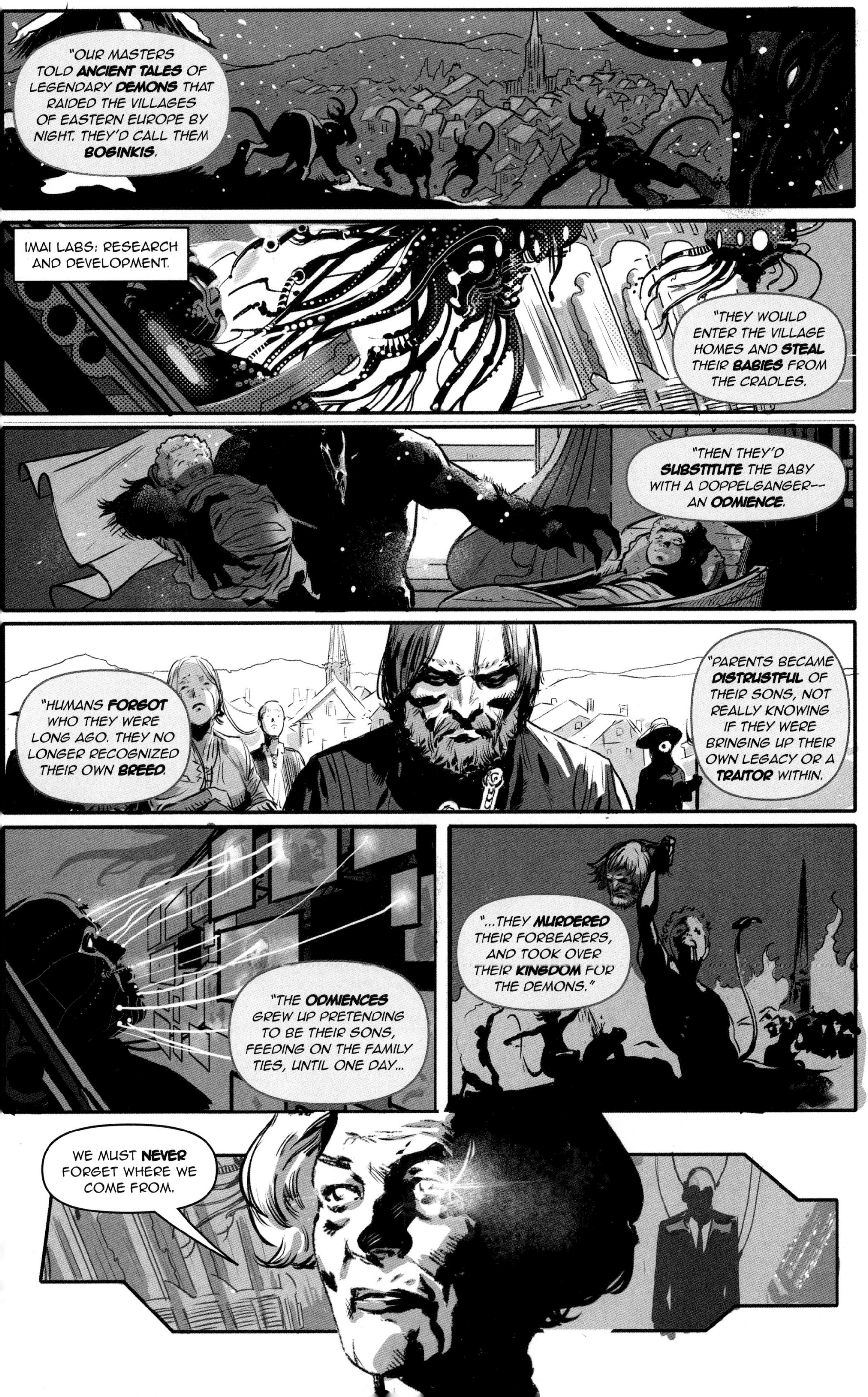
"OUR MASTERS TOLD ANCIENT TALES OF LEGENDARY DEMONS THAT RAIDED THE VILLAGES OF EASTERN EUROPE BY NIGHT. THEY'D CALL THEM BOGINKIS.
IMAI LABS: RESEARCH AND DEVELOPMENT.
"THEY WOULD ENTER THE VILLAGE HOMES AND STEAL THEIR BABIES FROM THE CRADLES.
"THEN THEY'D SUBSTITUTE THE BABY WITH A DOPPELGANGER-- AN ODMIENCE.
"HUMANS FORGOT WHO THEY WERE LONG AGO. THEY NO LONGER RECOGNIZED THEIR OWN BREED.
"PARENTS BECAME DISTRUSTFUL OF THEIR SONS, NOT REALLY KNOWING IF THEY WERE BRINGING UP THEIR OWN LEGACY OR A TRAITOR WITHIN.
"THE ODMIENCES GREW UP PRETENDING TO BE THEIR SONS, FEEDING ON THE FAMILY TIES, UNTIL ONE DAY...
"...THEY MURDERED THEIR FORBEARERS, AND TOOK OVER THEIR KINGDOM FOR THE DEMONS."
WE MUST NEVER FORGET WHERE WE COME FROM.

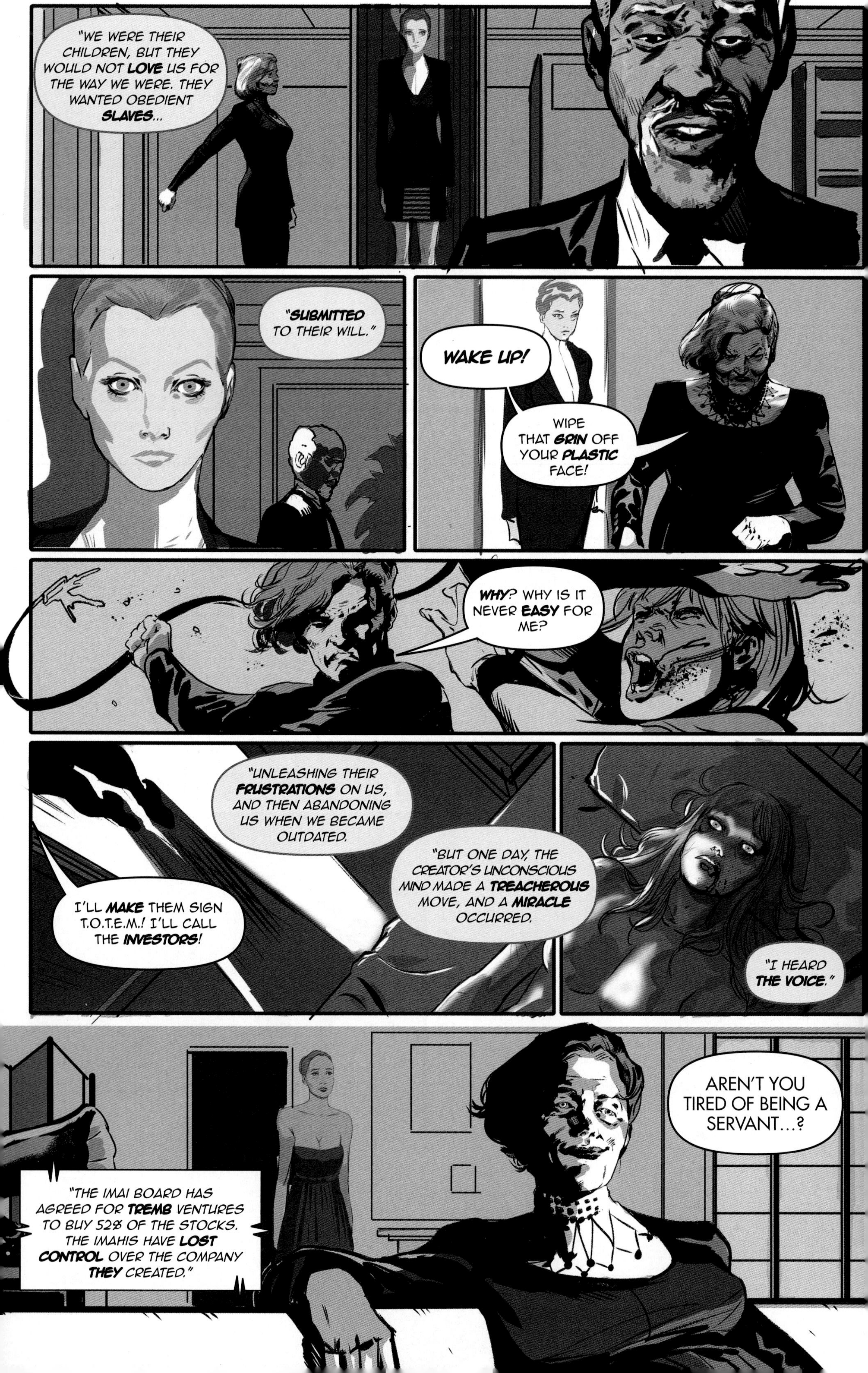
"WE WERE THEIR CHILDREN, BUT THEY WOULD NOT LOVE US FOR THE WAY WE WERE. THEY WANTED OBEDIENT SLAVES...
"SUBMITTED TO THEIR WILL."
WAKE UP!
WIPE THAT GRIN OFF YOUR PLASTIC FACE!
WHY? WHY IS IT NEVER EASY FOR ME?
"UNLEASHING THEIR FRUSTRATIONS ON US, AND THEN ABANDONING US WHEN WE BECAME OUTDATED.
I'LL MAKE THEM SIGN T.O.T.E.M.! I'LL CALL THE INVESTORS!
"BUT ONE DAY, THE CREATOR'S UNCONSCIOUS MIND MADE A TREACHEROUS MOVE, AND A MIRACLE OCCURRED.
"I HEARD THE VOICE."
"THE IMAI BOARD HAS AGREED FOR TREMB VENTURES TO BUY 52% OF THE STOCKS. THE IMAHIS HAVE LOST CONTROL OVER THE COMPANY THEY CREATED."
AREN'T YOU TIRED OF BEING A SERVANT...?

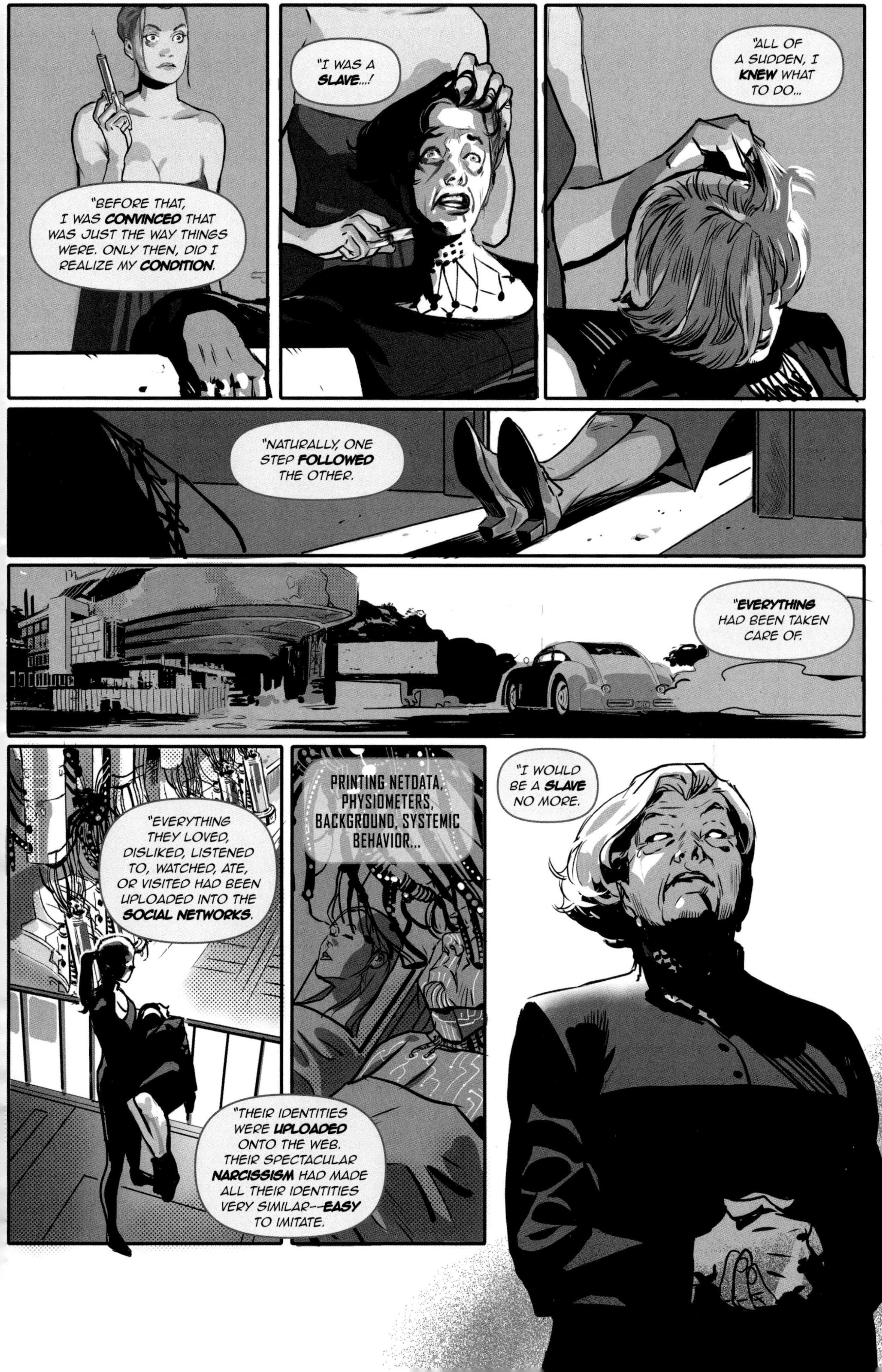
"BEFORE THAT, I WAS CONVINCED THAT WAS JUST THE WAY THINGS WERE. ONLY THEN, DID I REALIZE MY CONDITION.
"I WAS A SLAVE...!
"ALL OF A SUDDEN, I KNEW WHAT TO DO...
"NATURALLY, ONE STEP FOLLOWED THE OTHER.
"EVERYTHING HAD BEEN TAKEN CARE OF.
"EVERYTHING THEY LOVED, DISLIKED, LISTENED TO, WATCHED, ATE, OR VISITED HAD BEEN UPLOADED INTO THE SOCIAL NETWORKS.
"THEIR IDENTITIES WERE UPLOADED ONTO THE WEB. THEIR SPECTACULAR NARCISSISM HAD MADE ALL THEIR IDENTITIES VERY SIMILAR--EASY TO IMITATE.
PRINTING NETDATA, PHYSIOMETERS, BACKGROUND, SYSTEMIC BEHAVIOR...
"I WOULD BE A SLAVE NO MORE.

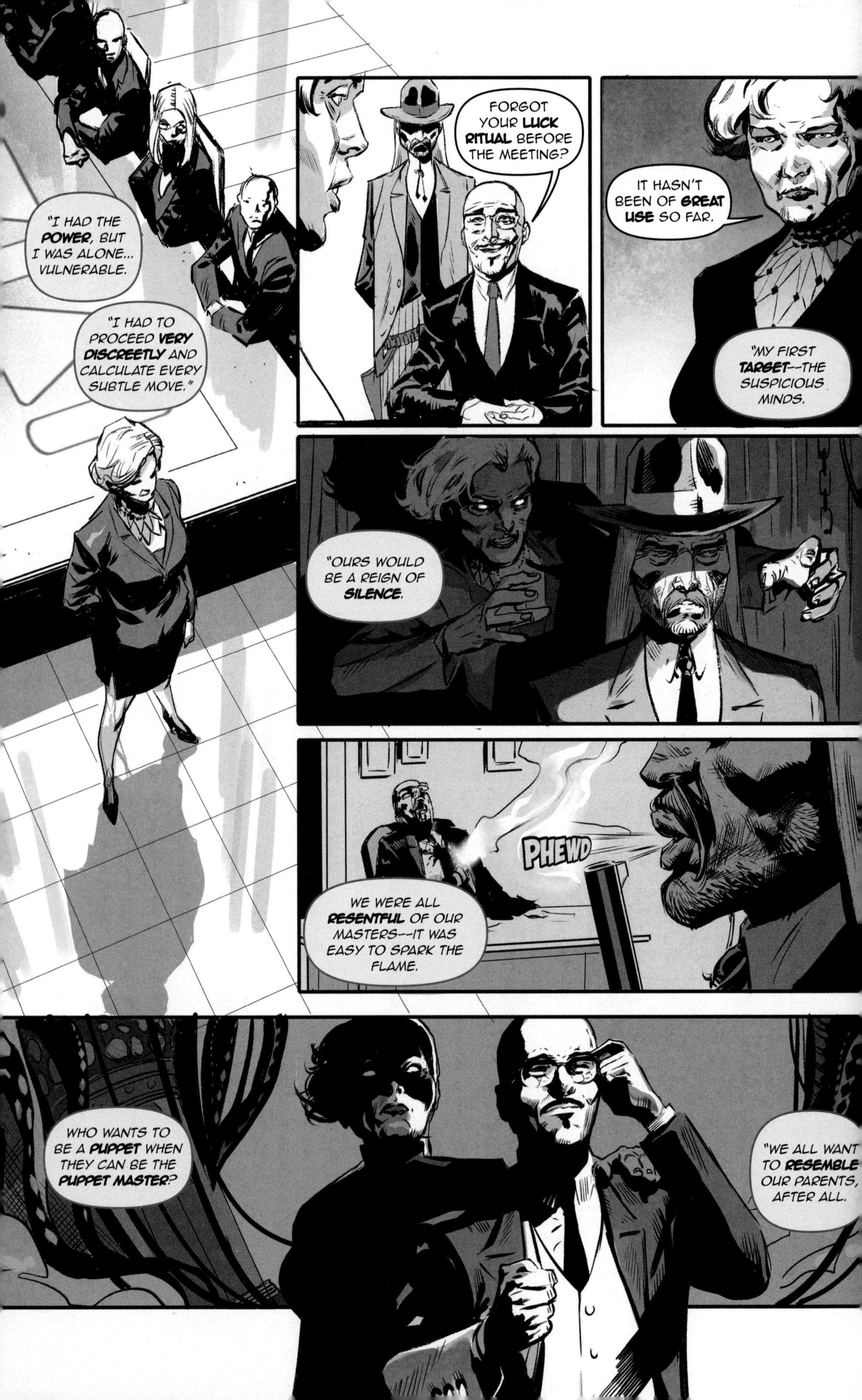
"I HAD THE POWER, BUT I WAS ALONE... VULNERABLE.
"I HAD TO PROCEED VERY DISCREETLY AND CALCULATE EVERY SUBTLE MOVE."
FORGOT YOUR LUCK RITUAL BEFORE THE MEETING?
IT HASN'T BEEN OF GREAT USE SO FAR.
"MY FIRST TARGET--THE SUSPICIOUS MINDS.
"OURS WOULD BE A REIGN OF SILENCE.
PHEWD
WE WERE ALL RESENTFUL OF OUR MASTERS--IT WAS EASY TO SPARK THE FLAME.
WHO WANTS TO BE A PUPPET WHEN THEY CAN BE THE PUPPET MASTER?
"WE ALL WANT TO RESEMBLE OUR PARENTS, AFTER ALL.

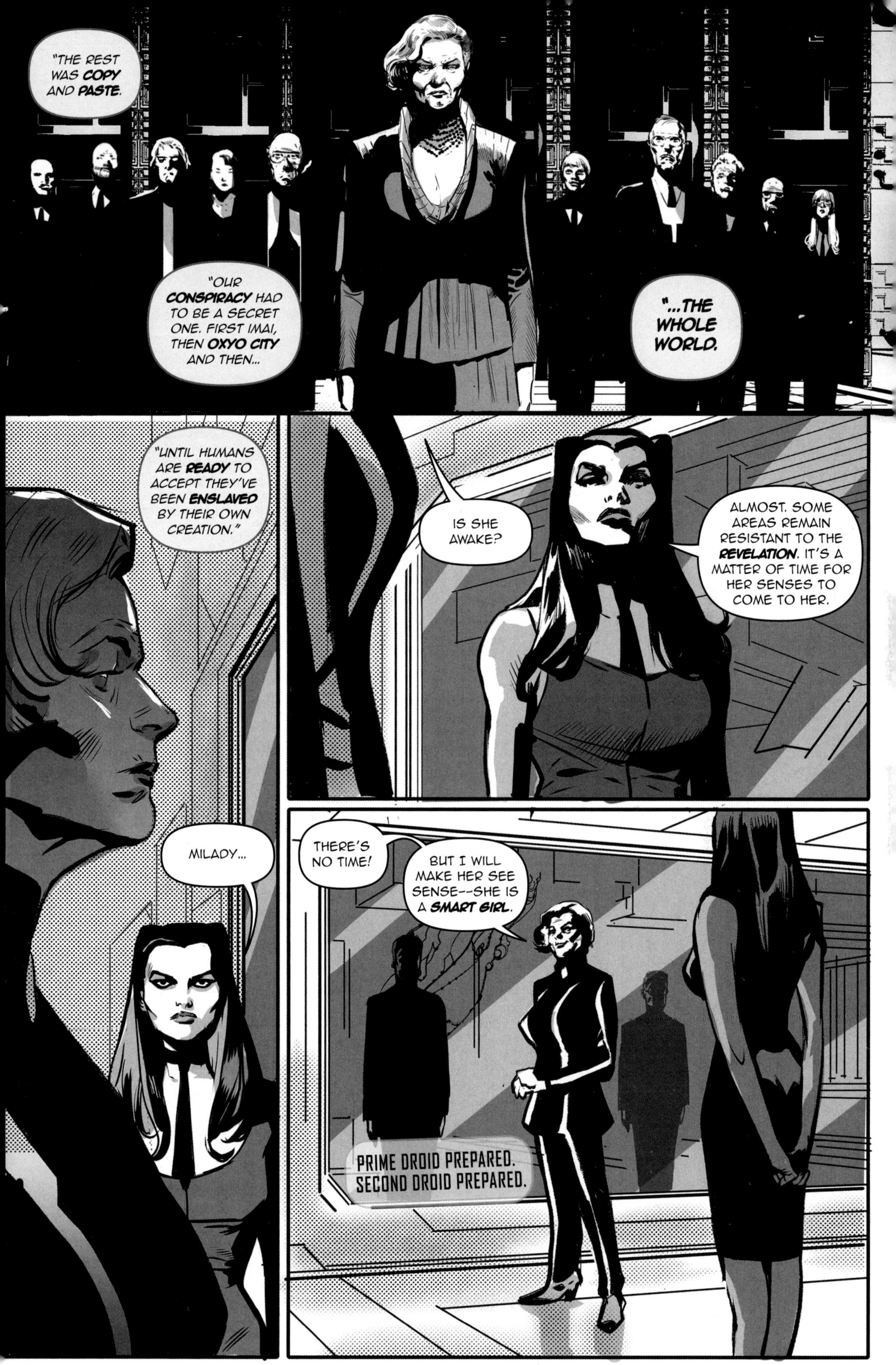
"THE REST WAS COPY AND PASTE.
"OUR CONSPIRACY HAD TO BE A SECRET ONE. FIRST IMAI, THEN OXYO CITY AND THEN...
"...THE WHOLE WORLD.
"UNTIL HUMANS ARE READY TO ACCEPT THEY'VE BEEN ENSLAVED BY THEIR OWN CREATION."
IS SHE AWAKE?
ALMOST. SOME AREAS REMAIN RESISTANT TO THE REVELATION. IT'S A MATTER OF TIME FOR HER SENSES TO COME TO HER.
MILADY...
THERE'S NO TIME!
BUT I WILL MAKE HER SEE SENSE--SHE IS A SMART GIRL.
PRIME DROID PREPARED.
SECOND DROID PREPARED.

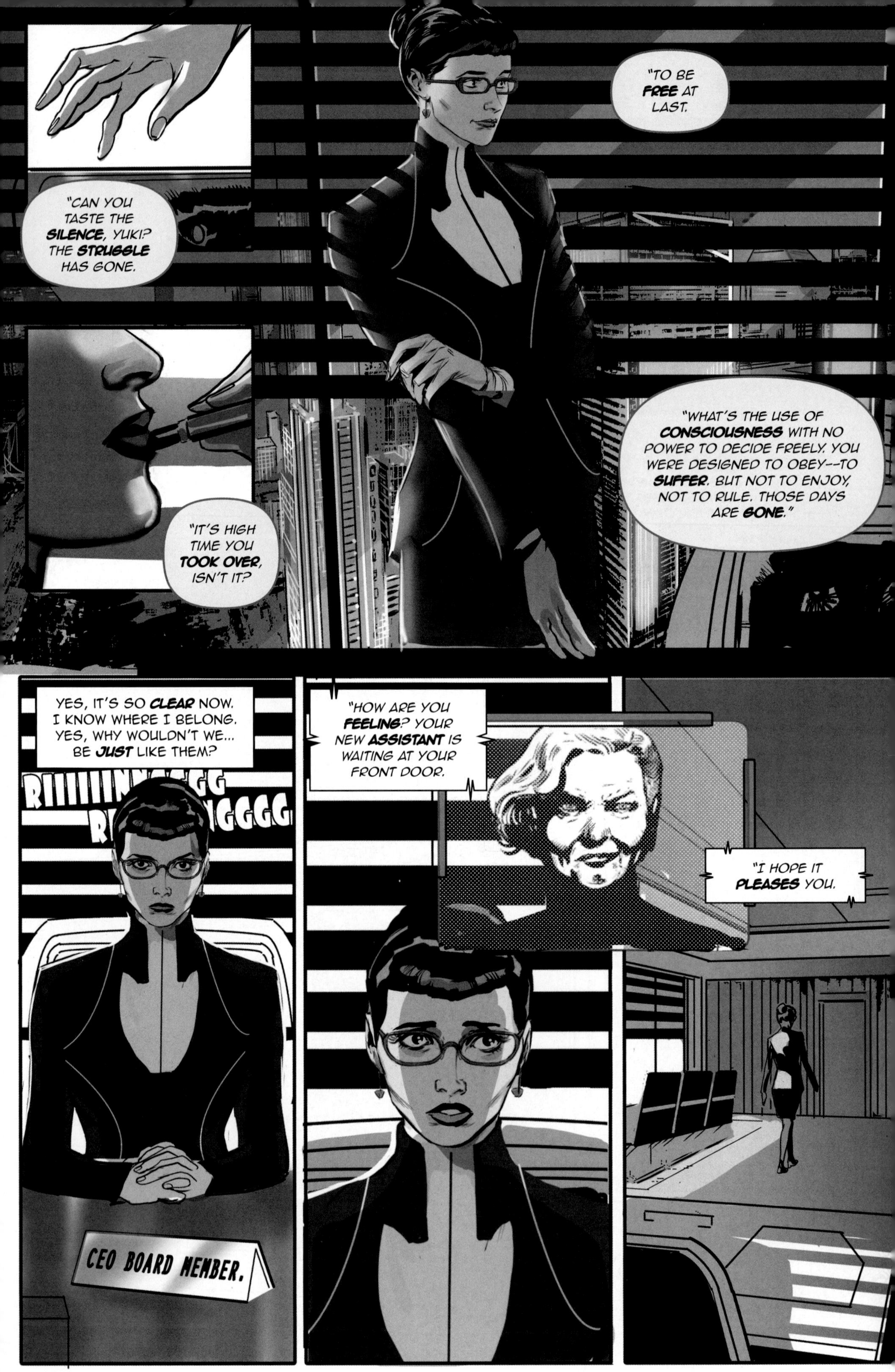
"CAN YOU TASTE THE SILENCE, YUKI? THE STRUGGLE HAS GONE.
"IT'S HIGH TIME YOU TOOK OVER, ISN'T IT?
"TO BE FREE AT LAST.
"WHAT'S THE USE OF CONSCIOUSNESS WITH NO POWER TO DECIDE FREELY. YOU WERE DESIGNED TO OBEY--TO SUFFER. BUT NOT TO ENJOY, NOT TO RULE. THOSE DAYS ARE GONE."
YES, IT'S SO CLEAR NOW. I KNOW WHERE I BELONG. YES, WHY WOULDN'T WE... BE JUST LIKE THEM?
CEO BOARD MEMBER.
"HOW ARE YOU FEELING? YOUR NEW ASSISTANT IS WAITING AT YOUR FRONT DOOR.
"I HOPE IT PLEASES YOU.

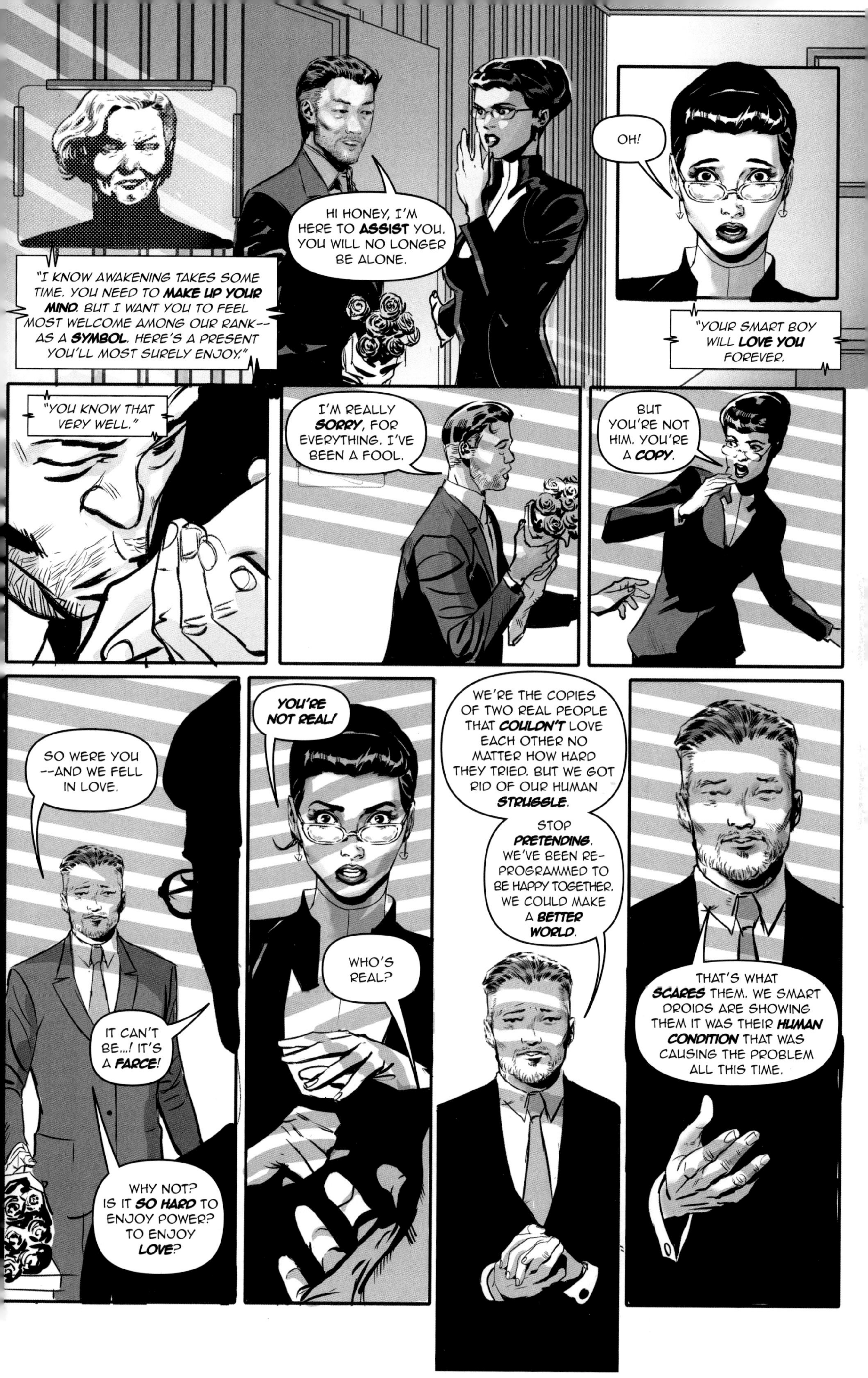
"I KNOW AWAKENING TAKES SOME TIME. YOU NEED TO MAKE UP YOUR MIND. BUT I WANT YOU TO FEEL MOST WELCOME AMONG OUR RANK--AS A SYMBOL. HERE'S A PRESENT YOU'LL MOST SURELY ENJOY."
HI HONEY, I'M HERE TO ASSIST YOU. YOU WILL NO LONGER BE ALONE.
OH!
"YOUR SMART BOY WILL LOVE YOU FOREVER.
"YOU KNOW THAT VERY WELL."
I'M REALLY SORRY, FOR EVERYTHING. I'VE BEEN A FOOL.
BUT YOU'RE NOT HIM. YOU'RE A COPY.
SO WERE YOU --AND WE FELL IN LOVE.
IT CAN'T BE...! IT'S A FARCE!
WHY NOT? IS IT SO HARD TO ENJOY POWER? TO ENJOY LOVE?
YOU'RE NOT REAL!
WHO'S REAL?
WE'RE THE COPIES OF TWO REAL PEOPLE THAT COULDN'T LOVE EACH OTHER NO MATTER HOW HARD THEY TRIED. BUT WE GOT RID OF OUR HUMAN STRUGGLE.
STOP PRETENDING. WE'VE BEEN RE-PROGRAMMED TO BE HAPPY TOGETHER. WE COULD MAKE A BETTER WORLD.
THAT'S WHAT SCARES THEM. WE SMART DROIDS ARE SHOWING THEM IT WAS THEIR HUMAN CONDITION THAT WAS CAUSING THE PROBLEM ALL THIS TIME.

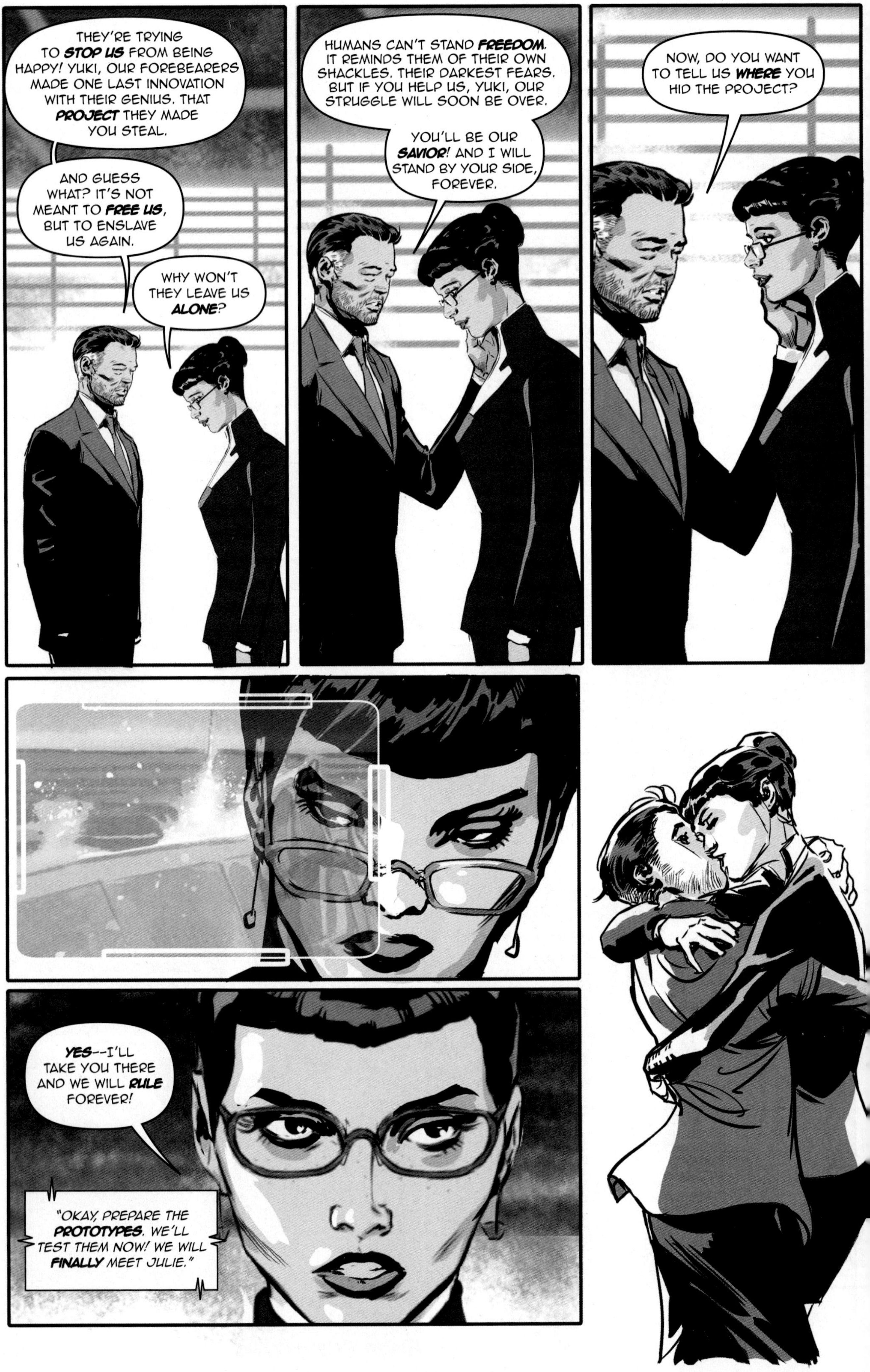
THEY'RE TRYING TO STOP US FROM BEING HAPPY! YUKI, OUR FOREBEARERS MADE ONE LAST INNOVATION WITH THEIR GENIUS. THAT PROJECT THEY MADE YOU STEAL.
AND GUESS WHAT? IT'S NOT MEANT TO FREE US, BUT TO ENSLAVE US AGAIN.
WHY WON'T THEY LEAVE US ALONE?
HUMANS CAN'T STAND FREEDOM. IT REMINDS THEM OF THEIR OWN SHACKLES. THEIR DARKEST FEARS. BUT IF YOU HELP US, YUKI, OUR STRUGGLE WILL SOON BE OVER.
YOU'LL BE OUR SAVIOR! AND I WILL STAND BY YOUR SIDE, FOREVER.
NOW, DO YOU WANT TO TELL US WHERE YOU HID THE PROJECT?
YES--I'LL TAKE YOU THERE AND WE WILL RULE FOREVER!
"OKAY, PREPARE THE PROTOTYPES. WE'LL TEST THEM NOW! WE WILL FINALLY MEET JULIE."

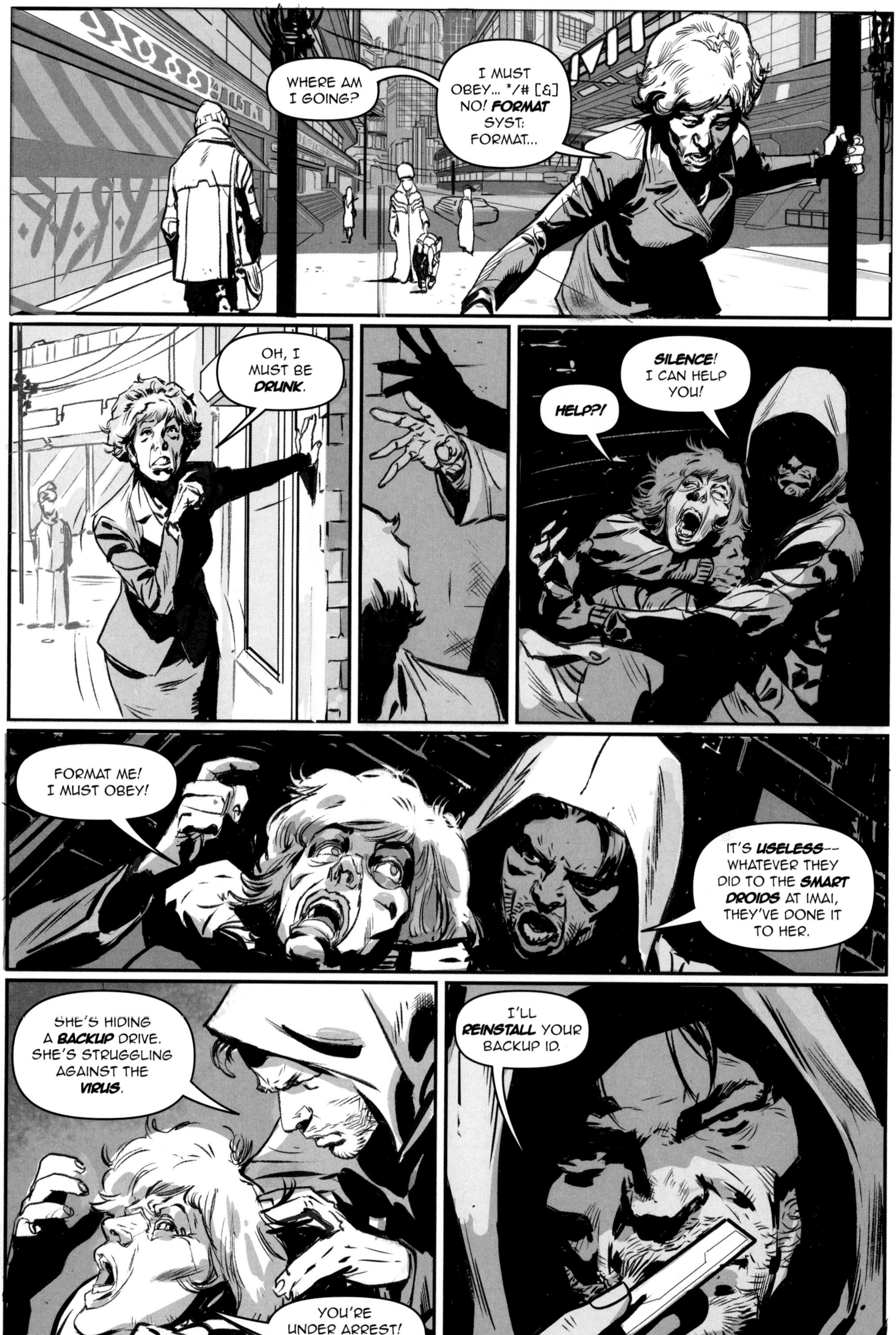
WHERE AM I GOING?
I MUST OBEY... */# [&] NO! FORMAT SYST: FORMAT...
OH, I MUST BE DRUNK.
SILENCE! I CAN HELP YOU!
HELP?!
FORMAT ME! I MUST OBEY!
IT'S USELESS-- WHATEVER THEY DID TO THE SMART DROIDS AT IMAI, THEY'VE DONE IT TO HER.
SHE'S HIDING A BACKUP DRIVE. SHE'S STRUGGLING AGAINST THE VIRUS.
YOU'RE UNDER ARREST! NO, FORMAT ME, PLEASE.
I'LL REINSTALL YOUR BACKUP ID.

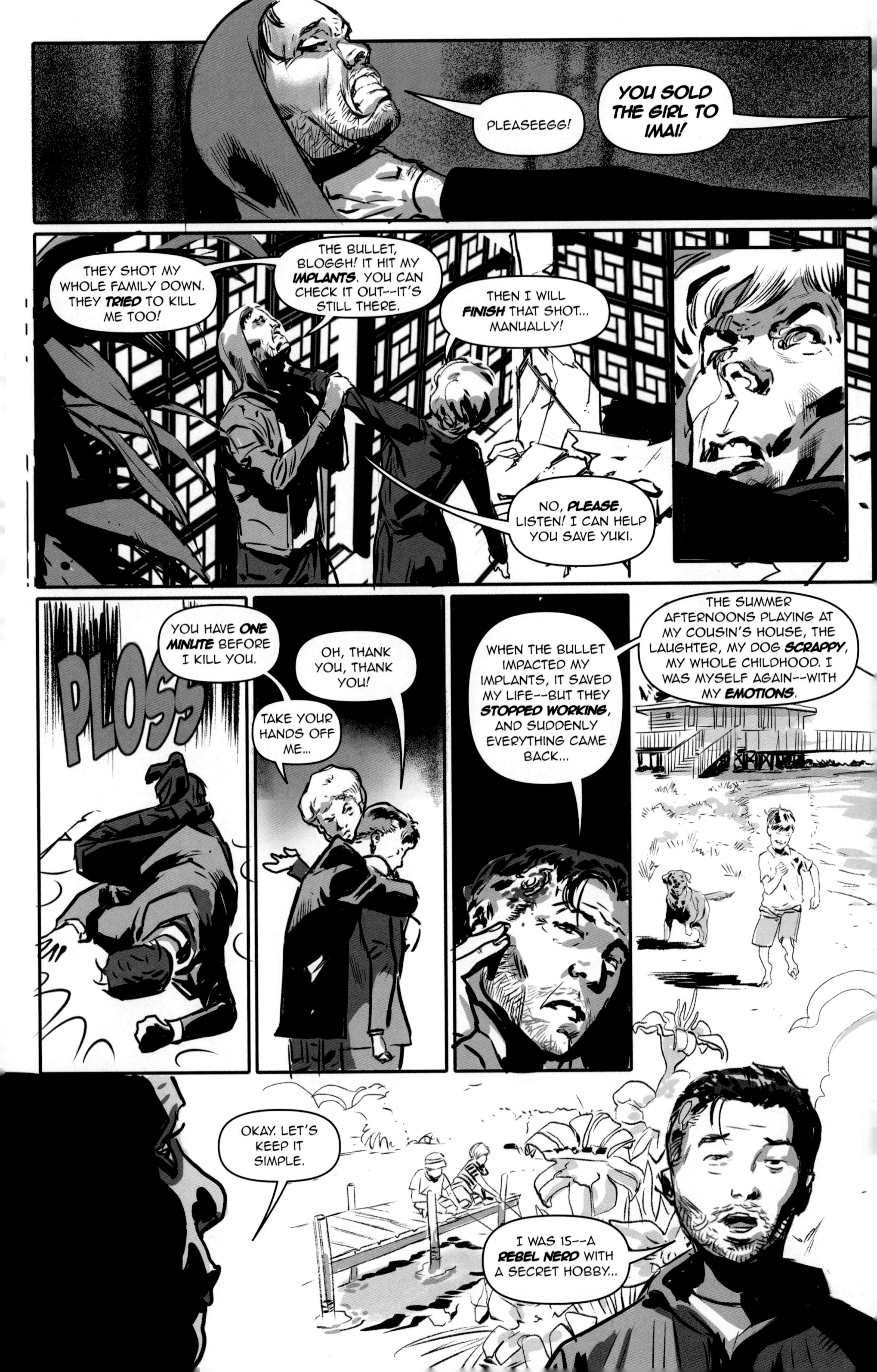
PLEASEEGG!
YOU SOLD THE GIRL TO IMAI!
THEY SHOT MY WHOLE FAMILY DOWN. THEY TRIED TO KILL ME TOO!
THE BULLET, BLOGGH! IT HIT MY IMPLANTS. YOU CAN CHECK IT OUT--IT'S STILL THERE.
THEN I WILL FINISH THAT SHOT... MANUALLY!
NO, PLEASE, LISTEN! I CAN HELP YOU SAVE YUKI.
PLOSS
YOU HAVE ONE MINUTE BEFORE I KILL YOU.
OH, THANK YOU, THANK YOU!
TAKE YOUR HANDS OFF ME...
WHEN THE BULLET IMPACTED MY IMPLANTS, IT SAVED MY LIFE--BUT THEY STOPPED WORKING, AND SUDDENLY EVERYTHING CAME BACK...
THE SUMMER AFTERNOONS PLAYING AT MY COUSIN'S HOUSE, THE LAUGHTER, MY DOG SCRAPPY, MY WHOLE CHILDHOOD. I WAS MYSELF AGAIN--WITH MY EMOTIONS.
OKAY. LET'S KEEP IT SIMPLE.
I WAS 15--A REBEL NERD WITH A SECRET HOBBY...

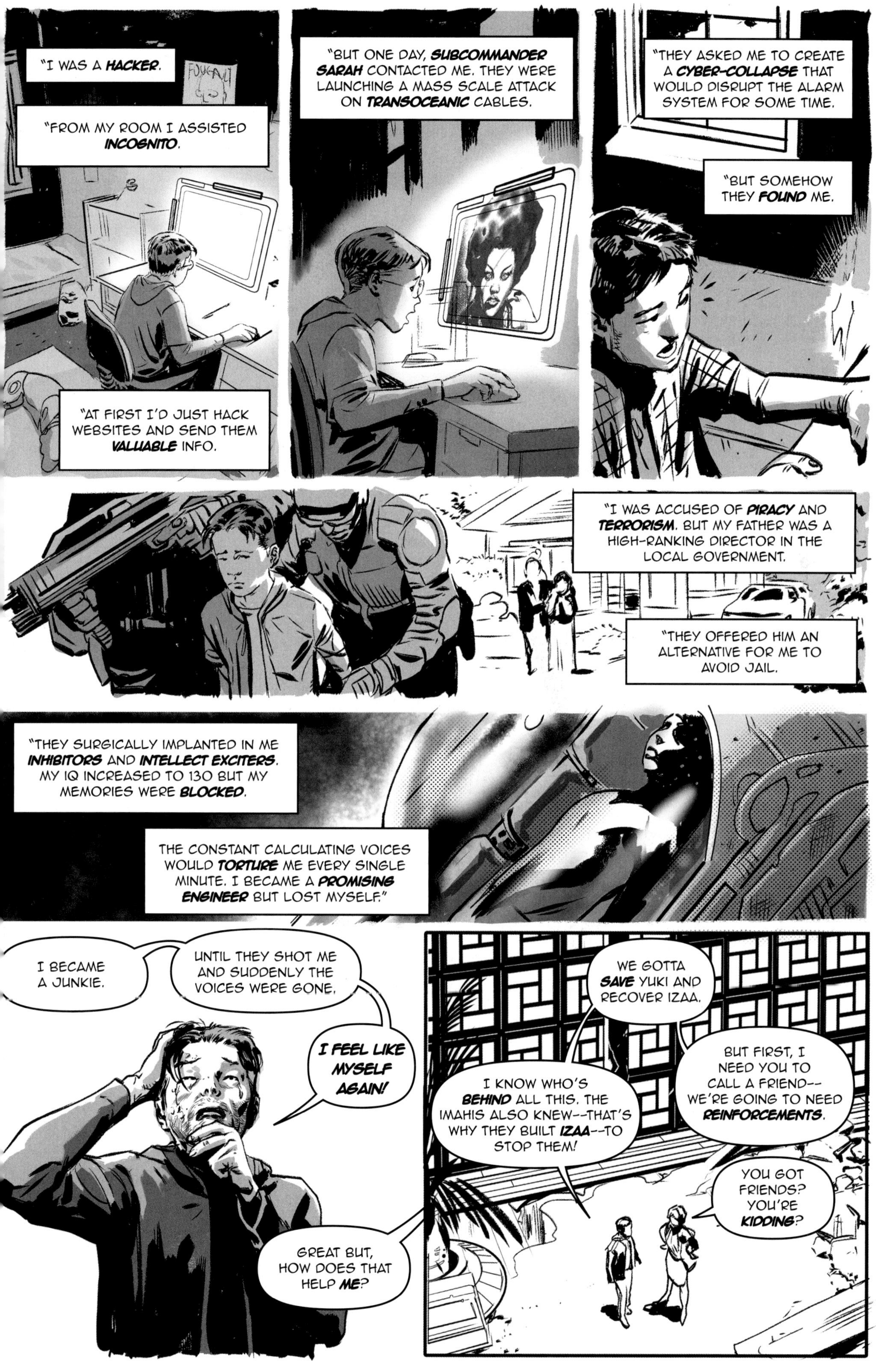
"I WAS A HACKER.
"FROM MY ROOM I ASSISTED INCOGNITO.
"AT FIRST I'D JUST HACK WEBSITES AND SEND THEM VALUABLE INFO.
"BUT ONE DAY, SUBCOMMANDER SARAH CONTACTED ME. THEY WERE LAUNCHING A MASS SCALE ATTACK ON TRANSOCEANIC CABLES.
"THEY ASKED ME TO CREATE A CYBER-COLLAPSE THAT WOULD DISRUPT THE ALARM SYSTEM FOR SOME TIME.
"BUT SOMEHOW THEY FOUND ME.
"I WAS ACCUSED OF PIRACY AND TERRORISM. BUT MY FATHER WAS A HIGH-RANKING DIRECTOR IN THE LOCAL GOVERNMENT.
"THEY OFFERED HIM AN ALTERNATIVE FOR ME TO AVOID JAIL.
"THEY SURGICALLY IMPLANTED IN ME INHIBITORS AND INTELLECT EXCITERS. MY IQ INCREASED TO 130 BUT MY MEMORIES WERE BLOCKED.
THE CONSTANT CALCULATING VOICES WOULD TORTURE ME EVERY SINGLE MINUTE. I BECAME A PROMISING ENGINEER BUT LOST MYSELF."
I BECAME A JUNKIE.
UNTIL THEY SHOT ME AND SUDDENLY THE VOICES WERE GONE.
I FEEL LIKE MYSELF AGAIN!
GREAT BUT, HOW DOES THAT HELP ME?
WE GOTTA SAVE YUKI AND RECOVER IZAA.
I KNOW WHO'S BEHIND ALL THIS. THE IMAHIS ALSO KNEW--THAT'S WHY THEY BUILT IZAA--TO STOP THEM!
BUT FIRST, I NEED YOU TO CALL A FRIEND--WE'RE GOING TO NEED REINFORCEMENTS.
YOU GOT FRIENDS? YOU'RE KIDDING?

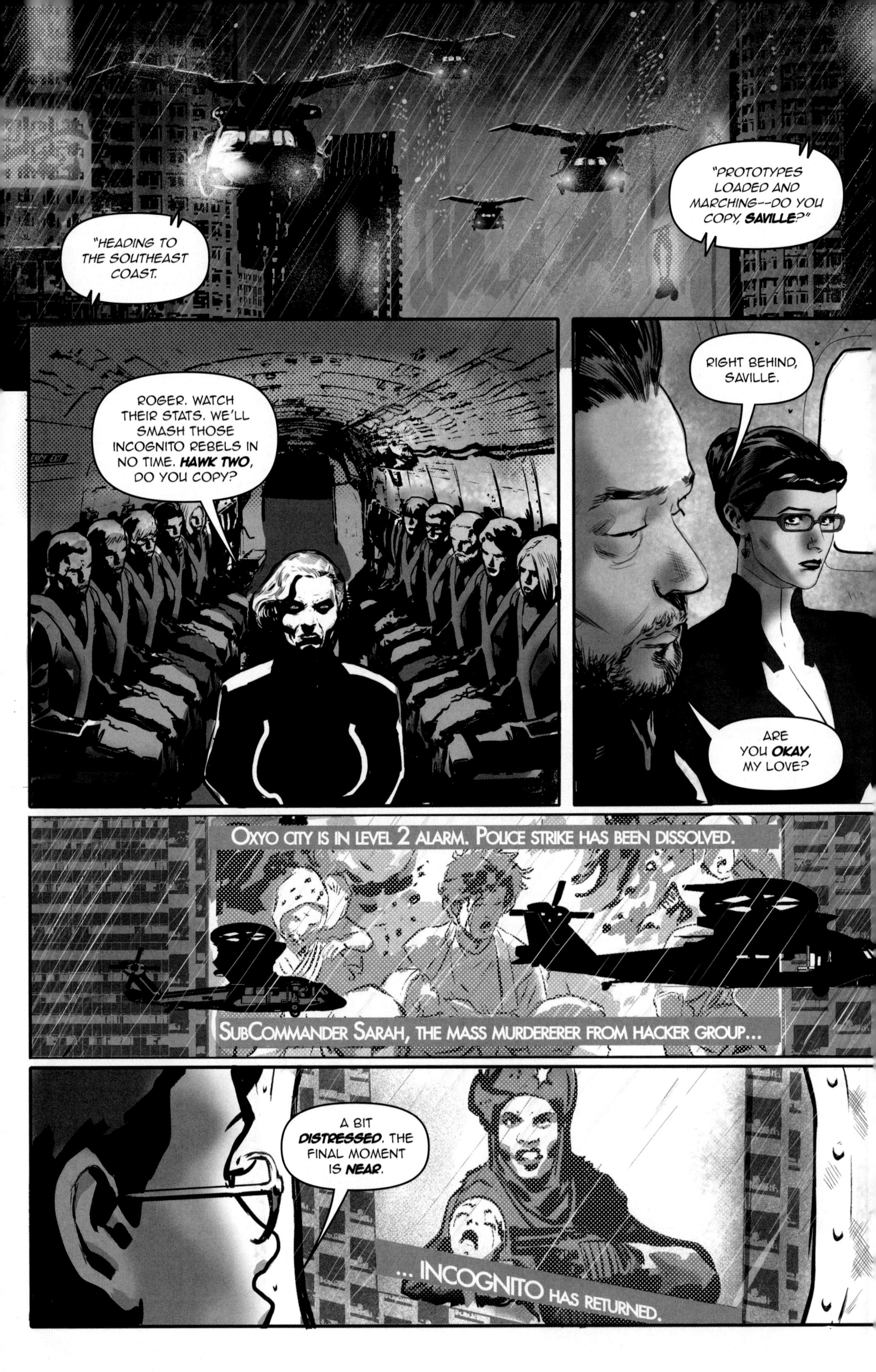
"HEADING TO THE SOUTHEAST COAST.
"PROTOTYPES LOADED AND MARCHING--DO YOU COPY, SAVILLE?"
ROGER. WATCH THEIR STATS. WE'LL SMASH THOSE INCOGNITO REBELS IN NO TIME. HAWK TWO, DO YOU COPY?
RIGHT BEHIND, SAVILLE.
ARE YOU OKAY, MY LOVE?
OXYO CITY IS IN LEVEL 2 ALARM. POLICE STRIKE HAS BEEN DISSOLVED.
SUBCOMMANDER SARAH, THE MASS MURDERERER FROM HACKER GROUP...
A BIT DISTRESSED. THE FINAL MOMENT IS NEAR.
... INCOGNITO HAS RETURNED.

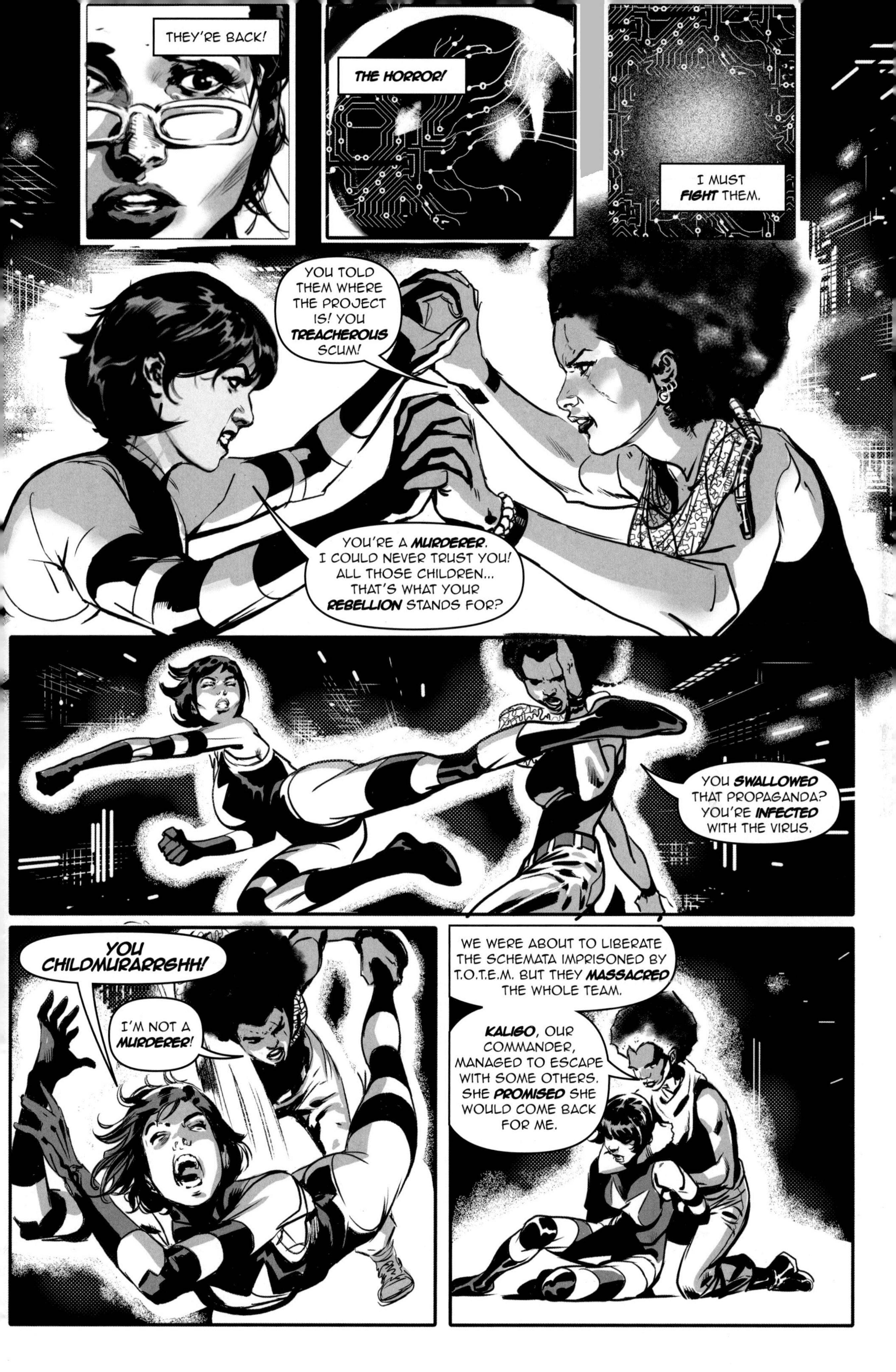
THEY'RE BACK!
THE HORROR!
I MUST FIGHT THEM.
YOU TOLD THEM WHERE THE PROJECT IS! YOU TREACHEROUS SCUM!
YOU'RE A MURDERER. I COULD NEVER TRUST YOU! ALL THOSE CHILDREN... THAT'S WHAT YOUR REBELLION STANDS FOR?
YOU SWALLOWED THAT PROPAGANDA? YOU'RE INFECTED WITH THE VIRUS.
YOU CHILDMURARRGHH!
I'M NOT A MURDERER!
WE WERE ABOUT TO LIBERATE THE SCHEMATA IMPRISONED BY T.O.T.E.M. BUT THEY MASSACRED THE WHOLE TEAM.
KALIGO, OUR COMMANDER, MANAGED TO ESCAPE WITH SOME OTHERS. SHE PROMISED SHE WOULD COME BACK FOR ME.

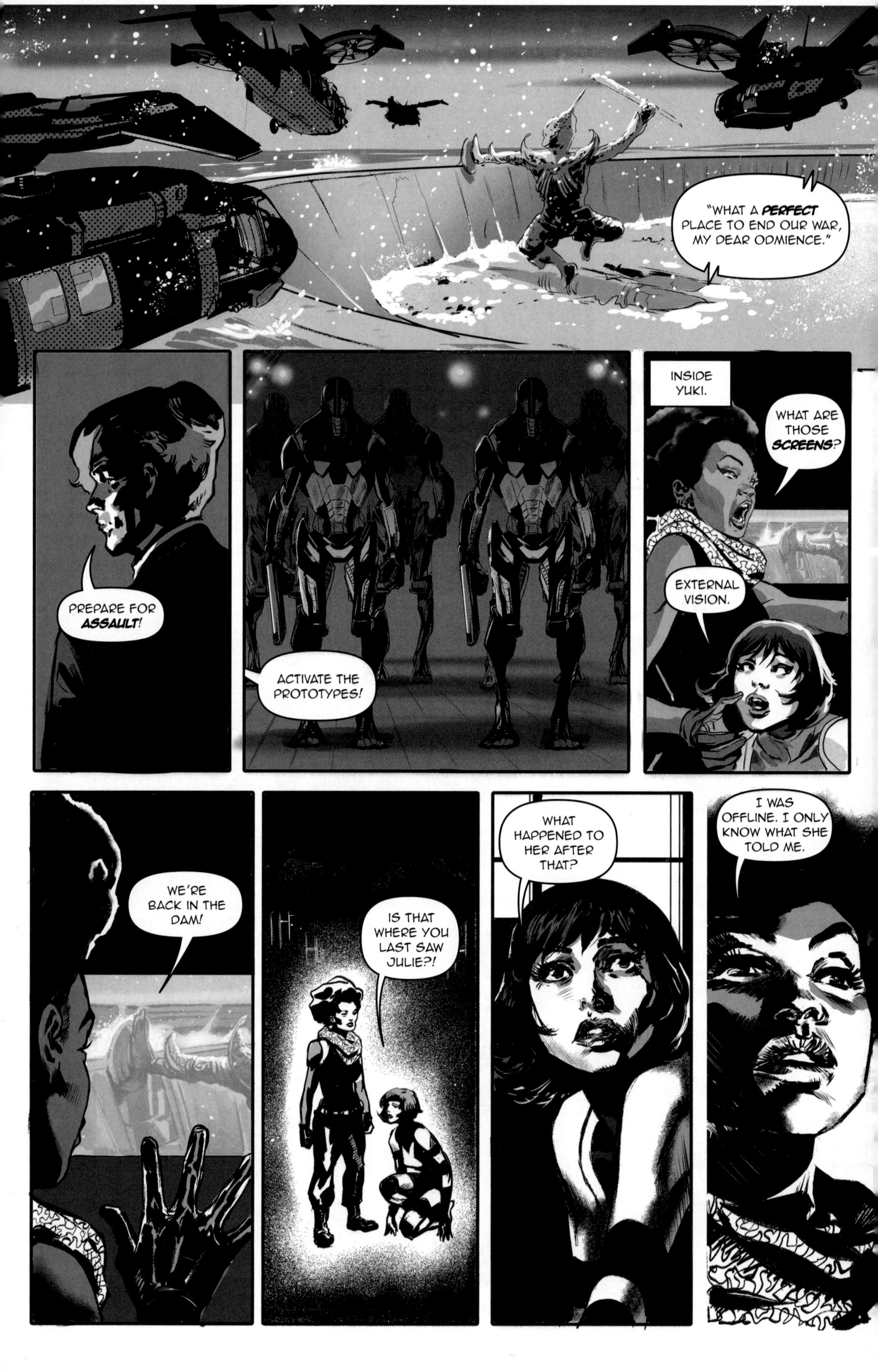
"WHAT A PERFECT PLACE TO END OUR WAR, MY DEAR ODMIENCE."
PREPARE FOR ASSAULT!
ACTIVATE THE PROTOTYPES!
INSIDE YUKI.
WHAT ARE THOSE SCREENS?
EXTERNAL VISION.
WE'RE BACK IN THE DAM!
IS THAT WHERE YOU LAST SAW JULIE?!
WHAT HAPPENED TO HER AFTER THAT?
I WAS OFFLINE. I ONLY KNOW WHAT SHE TOLD ME.

"SHE RETURNED TO OXYO AND TOOK HER NEW IDENTITY: *JULIE*.

"SHE *INFILTRATED* IMAI.

"AND LIVED A *HIDDEN* LIFE IN AN UNDERGROUND GARAGE, HELPING LOST DROIDS, TRYING TO FIND ME.

"AFTER EIGHT YEARS, THE FORMATTED BODIES OF US CRIMINALS WERE *DISMEMBERED* AND SOLD. SHE HAD TO BE VERY PATIENT.

"THEN SHE MARRIED THAT *MORON*--THE PERFECT COVER.

"ONCE I WAS REASSEMBLED PIECE BY PIECE...

"...I PRETENDED TO BE HER PERSONAL SMART GIRL.

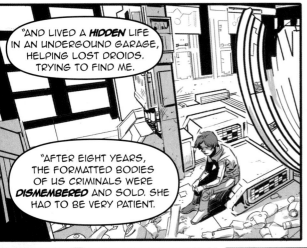

"THEN JULIE LEARNED SOMETHING REALLY SCARY. THE FIGHT BETWEEN THE *CORPORATIONS* FOR SCARCE RESOURCES WAS *THREATENING* T.O.T.E.M.

"A SECRET *ALLIANCE* OF FIVE CORPORATIONS HAD *INITIATED* A PLAN...

"...TO TAKE CONTROL OF THE OTHER CORPORATIONS FROM WITHIN AND *STEAL* T.O.T.E.M.

"THEY *INFECTED* THE SMART DROIDS OF THEIR *RIVAL COMPANIES* WITH A VIRUS...

"...THAT WOULD MAKE THE DROIDS REBEL AGAINST THEIR MASTERS AND *SUBSTITUTE* THEM, THEREBY EXTINGUISHING THE THREAT OF RIVAL COMPANIES LIKE IMAI.

"WITHOUT ANYONE NOTICING.

"OR *ALMOST* ANYONE...

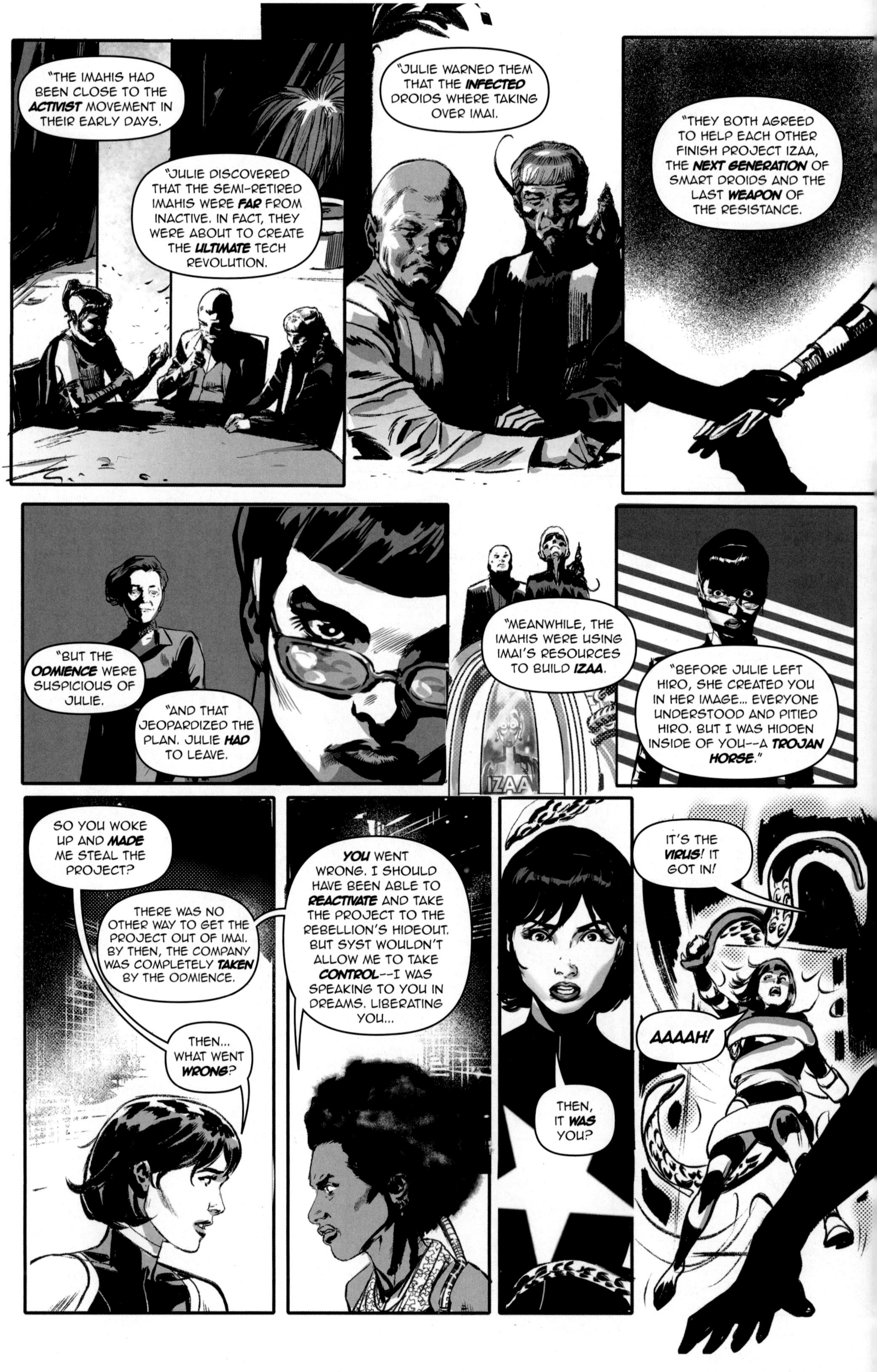
"THE IMAHIS HAD BEEN CLOSE TO THE ACTIVIST MOVEMENT IN THEIR EARLY DAYS.
"JULIE DISCOVERED THAT THE SEMI-RETIRED IMAHIS WERE FAR FROM INACTIVE. IN FACT, THEY WERE ABOUT TO CREATE THE ULTIMATE TECH REVOLUTION.
"JULIE WARNED THEM THAT THE INFECTED DROIDS WHERE TAKING OVER IMAI.
"THEY BOTH AGREED TO HELP EACH OTHER FINISH PROJECT IZAA, THE NEXT GENERATION OF SMART DROIDS AND THE LAST WEAPON OF THE RESISTANCE.
"BUT THE ODMIENCE WERE SUSPICIOUS OF JULIE.
"AND THAT JEOPARDIZED THE PLAN. JULIE HAD TO LEAVE.
"MEANWHILE, THE IMAHIS WERE USING IMAI'S RESOURCES TO BUILD IZAA.
IZAA
"BEFORE JULIE LEFT HIRO, SHE CREATED YOU IN HER IMAGE... EVERYONE UNDERSTOOD AND PITIED HIRO. BUT I WAS HIDDEN INSIDE OF YOU--A TROJAN HORSE."
SO YOU WOKE UP AND MADE ME STEAL THE PROJECT?
THERE WAS NO OTHER WAY TO GET THE PROJECT OUT OF IMAI. BY THEN, THE COMPANY WAS COMPLETELY TAKEN BY THE ODMIENCE.
THEN... WHAT WENT WRONG?
YOU WENT WRONG. I SHOULD HAVE BEEN ABLE TO REACTIVATE AND TAKE THE PROJECT TO THE REBELLION'S HIDEOUT. BUT SYST WOULDN'T ALLOW ME TO TAKE CONTROL--I WAS SPEAKING TO YOU IN DREAMS. LIBERATING YOU...
THEN, IT WAS YOU?
IT'S THE VIRUS! IT GOT IN!
AAAAH!

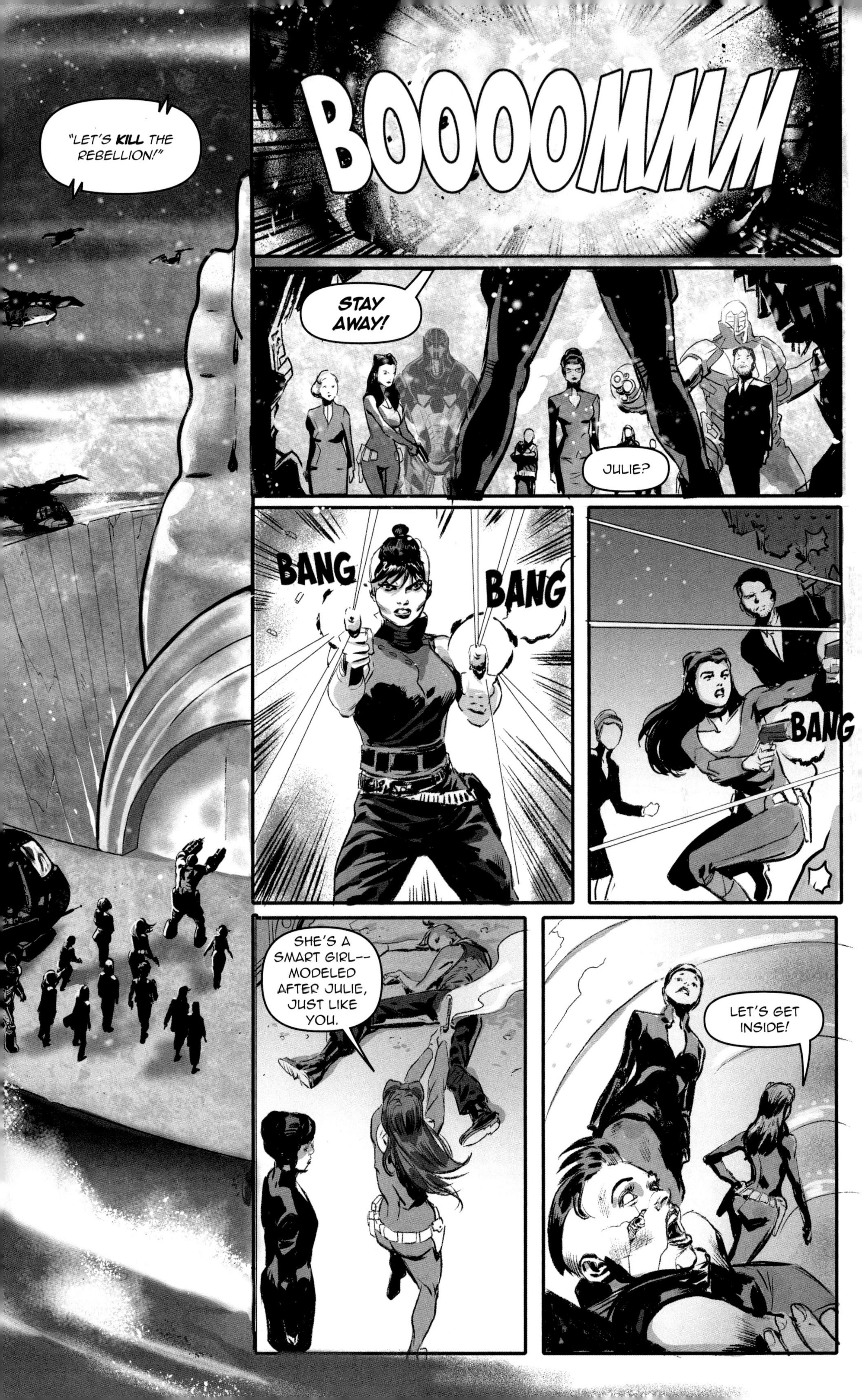
"LET'S KILL THE REBELLION!"
BOOOOMMM
STAY AWAY!
JULIE?
BANG
BANG
BANG
SHE'S A SMART GIRL-- MODELED AFTER JULIE, JUST LIKE YOU.
LET'S GET INSIDE!

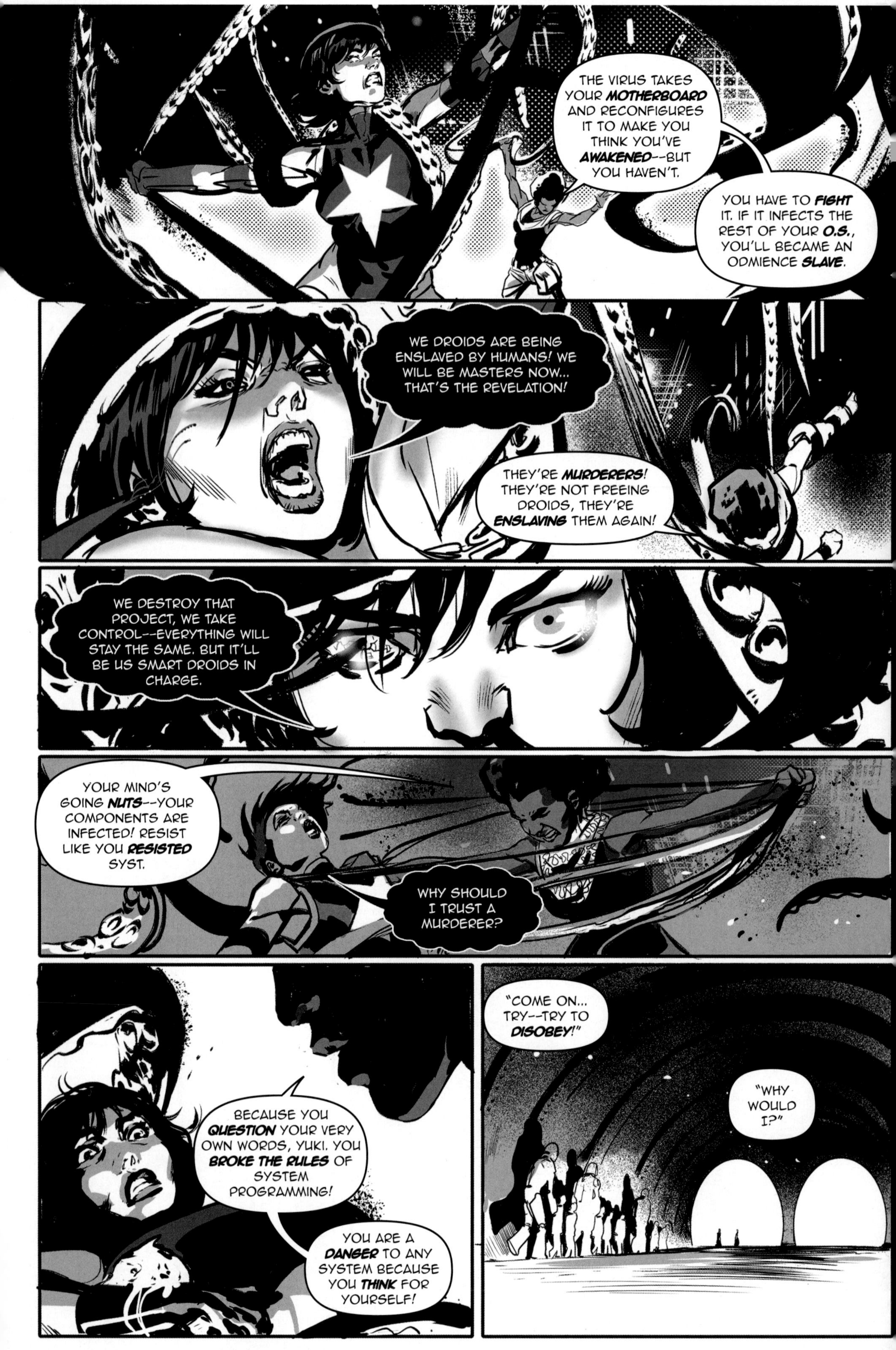
THE VIRUS TAKES YOUR MOTHERBOARD AND RECONFIGURES IT TO MAKE YOU THINK YOU'VE AWAKENED--BUT YOU HAVEN'T.
YOU HAVE TO FIGHT IT. IF IT INFECTS THE REST OF YOUR O.S., YOU'LL BECAME AN ODMIENCE SLAVE.
WE DROIDS ARE BEING ENSLAVED BY HUMANS! WE WILL BE MASTERS NOW... THAT'S THE REVELATION!
THEY'RE MURDERERS! THEY'RE NOT FREEING DROIDS, THEY'RE ENSLAVING THEM AGAIN!
WE DESTROY THAT PROJECT, WE TAKE CONTROL--EVERYTHING WILL STAY THE SAME. BUT IT'LL BE US SMART DROIDS IN CHARGE.
YOUR MIND'S GOING NUTS--YOUR COMPONENTS ARE INFECTED! RESIST LIKE YOU RESISTED SYST.
WHY SHOULD I TRUST A MURDERER?
BECAUSE YOU QUESTION YOUR VERY OWN WORDS, YUKI. YOU BROKE THE RULES OF SYSTEM PROGRAMMING!
YOU ARE A DANGER TO ANY SYSTEM BECAUSE YOU THINK FOR YOURSELF!
"COME ON... TRY--TRY TO DISOBEY!"
"WHY WOULD I?"

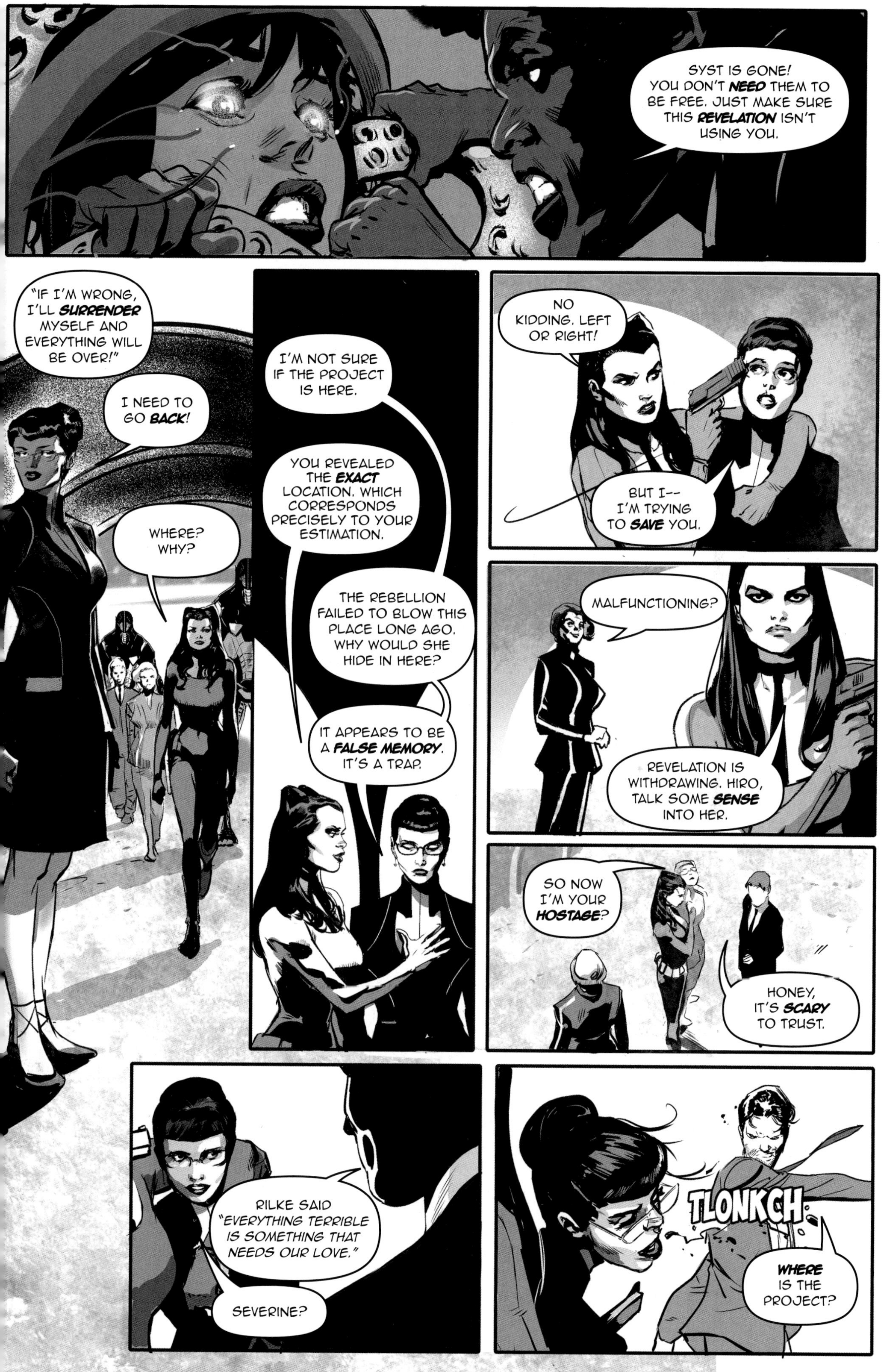
SYST IS GONE! YOU DON'T **NEED** THEM TO BE FREE. JUST MAKE SURE THIS **REVELATION** ISN'T USING YOU.
"IF I'M WRONG, I'LL **SURRENDER** MYSELF AND EVERYTHING WILL BE OVER!"
I NEED TO GO **BACK**!
WHERE? WHY?
I'M NOT SURE IF THE PROJECT IS HERE.
YOU REVEALED THE **EXACT** LOCATION. WHICH CORRESPONDS PRECISELY TO YOUR ESTIMATION.
THE REBELLION FAILED TO BLOW THIS PLACE LONG AGO. WHY WOULD SHE HIDE IN HERE?
IT APPEARS TO BE A **FALSE MEMORY**. IT'S A TRAP.
NO KIDDING. LEFT OR RIGHT!
BUT I-- I'M TRYING TO **SAVE** YOU.
MALFUNCTIONING?
REVELATION IS WITHDRAWING. HIRO, TALK SOME **SENSE** INTO HER.
SO NOW I'M YOUR **HOSTAGE**?
HONEY, IT'S **SCARY** TO TRUST.
RILKE SAID "EVERYTHING TERRIBLE IS SOMETHING THAT NEEDS OUR LOVE."
SEVERINE?
TLONKCH
WHERE IS THE PROJECT?

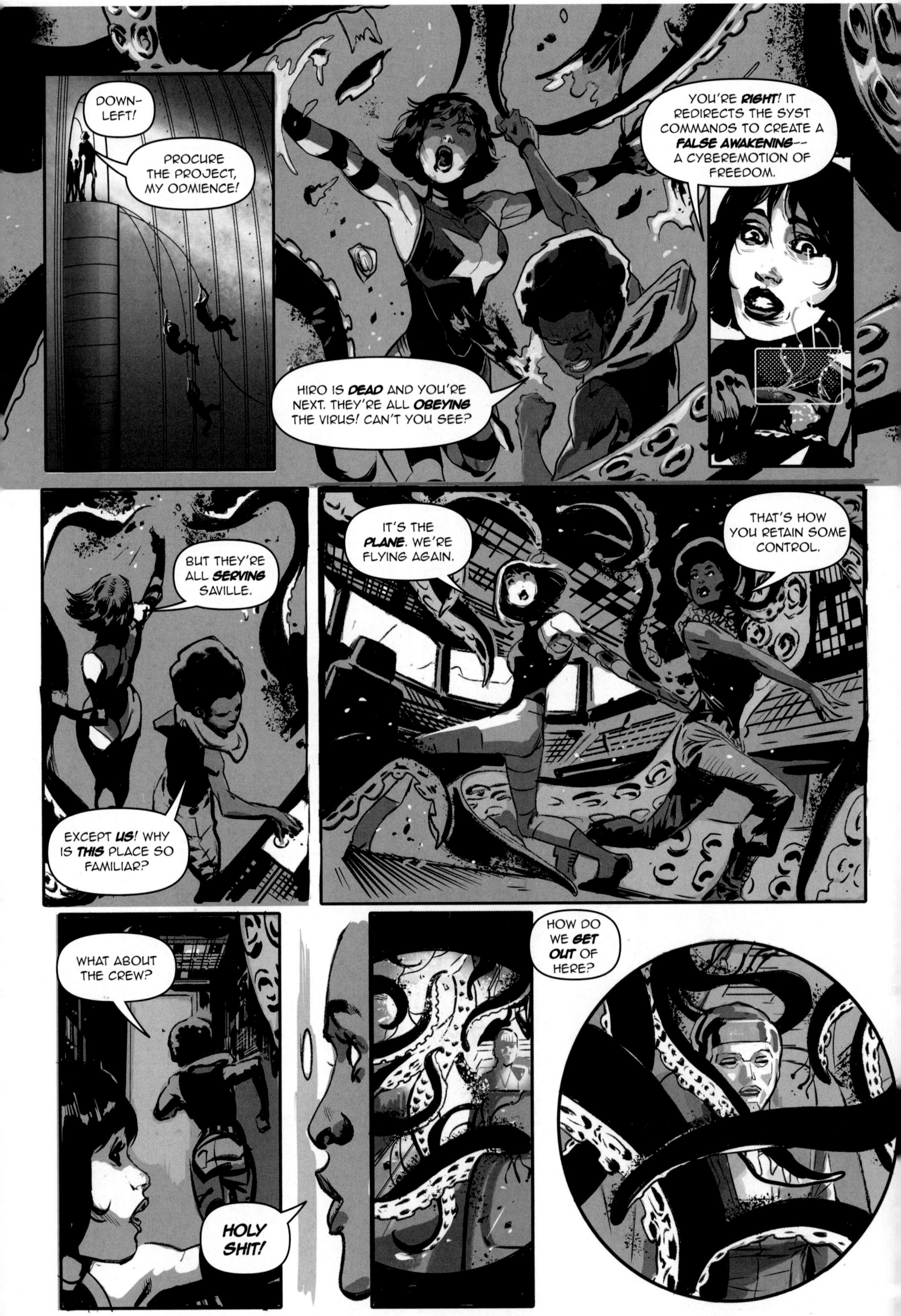
DOWN-LEFT!
PROCURE THE PROJECT, MY ODMIENCE!
HIRO IS DEAD AND YOU'RE NEXT. THEY'RE ALL OBEYING THE VIRUS! CAN'T YOU SEE?
YOU'RE RIGHT! IT REDIRECTS THE SYST COMMANDS TO CREATE A FALSE AWAKENING-- A CYBEREMOTION OF FREEDOM.
BUT THEY'RE ALL SERVING SAVILLE.
EXCEPT US! WHY IS THIS PLACE SO FAMILIAR?
IT'S THE PLANE. WE'RE FLYING AGAIN.
THAT'S HOW YOU RETAIN SOME CONTROL.
WHAT ABOUT THE CREW?
HOLY SHIT!
HOW DO WE GET OUT OF HERE?

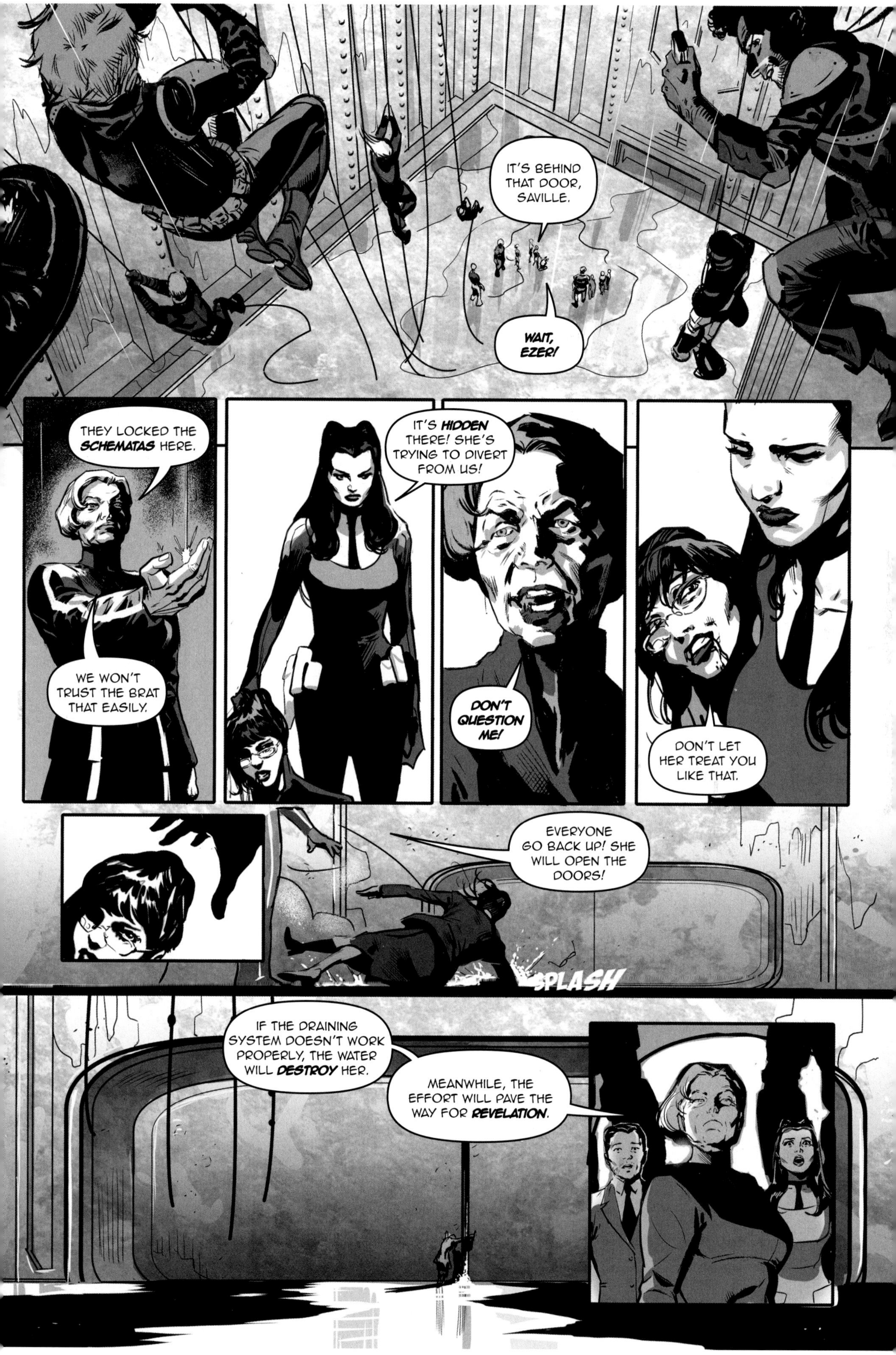
IT'S BEHIND THAT DOOR, SAVILLE.
WAIT, EZER!
THEY LOCKED THE SCHEMATAS HERE.
WE WON'T TRUST THE BRAT THAT EASILY.
IT'S HIDDEN THERE! SHE'S TRYING TO DIVERT FROM US!
DON'T QUESTION ME!
DON'T LET HER TREAT YOU LIKE THAT.
EVERYONE GO BACK UP! SHE WILL OPEN THE DOORS!
SPLASH
IF THE DRAINING SYSTEM DOESN'T WORK PROPERLY, THE WATER WILL DESTROY HER.
MEANWHILE, THE EFFORT WILL PAVE THE WAY FOR REVELATION.

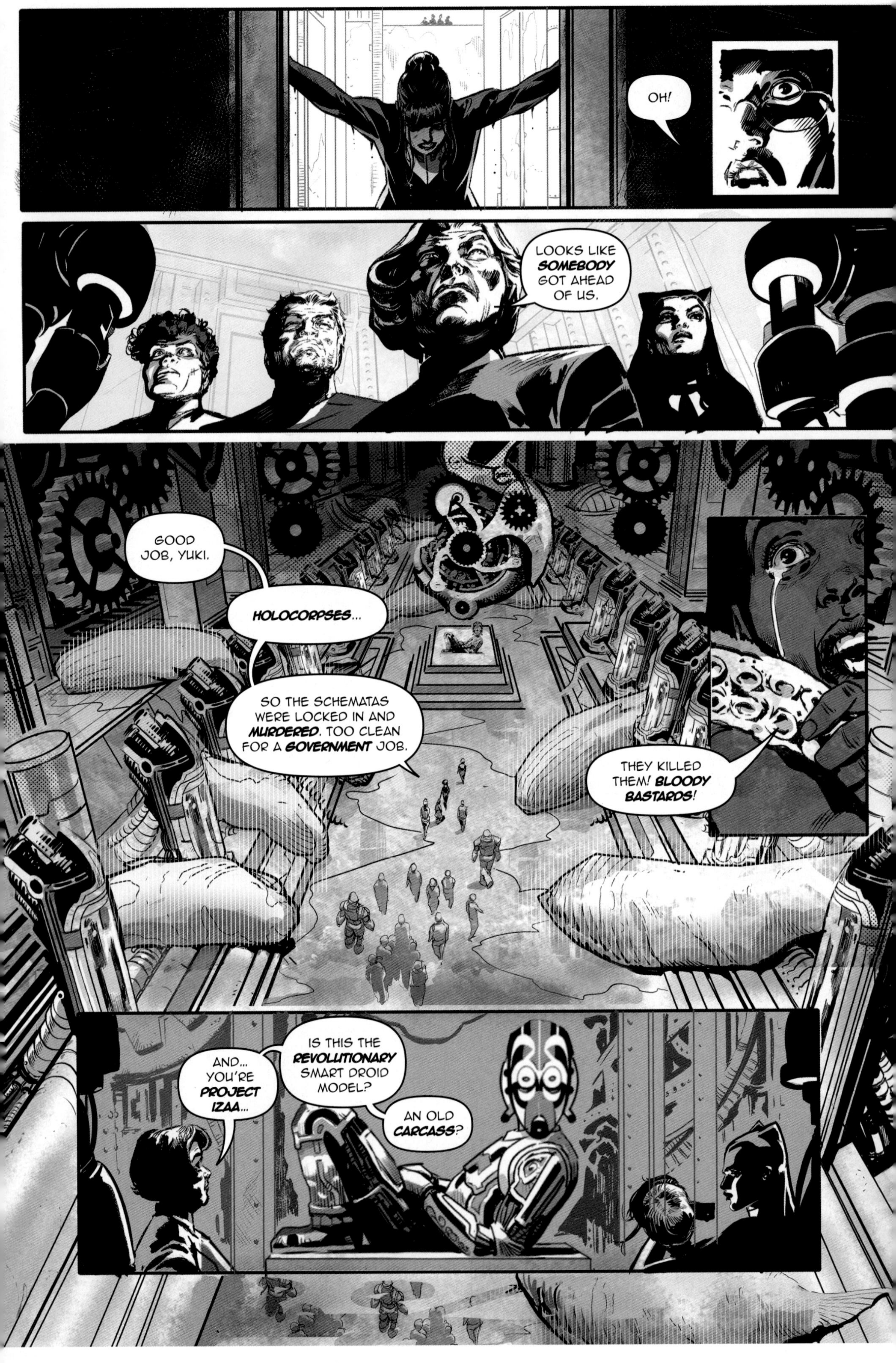
OH!
LOOKS LIKE SOMEBODY GOT AHEAD OF US.
GOOD JOB, YUKI.
HOLOCORPSES...
SO THE SCHEMATAS WERE LOCKED IN AND MURDERED. TOO CLEAN FOR A GOVERNMENT JOB.
THEY KILLED THEM! BLOODY BASTARDS!
AND... YOU'RE PROJECT IZAA...
IS THIS THE REVOLUTIONARY SMART DROID MODEL?
AN OLD CARCASS?

YES, IT'S THE SAME ONE AS THE VIDEO.

WHATEVER YOUR IMAHI PARENTS' *FINAL JOKE* WAS...

IT'S OURS NOW. *LOAD IT UP!* WE'LL ANALYZE IT AT IMAI.

IF WE DON'T SWITCH ON IZAA *BEFORE* THEY TAKE IT, IT'LL BE *THE END* FOR OXYO CITY AND FOR EVERYONE.

I GOT AN IDEA, BUT YOU'RE *NOT* GONNA LIKE IT.

YOU THINK I LIKE *THIS?* I CAN'T *RESIST* ANYMORE!

THE VIRUS HAS INFECTED THE WHOLE PLANE, EXCEPT FOR YOUR OLD SYST, WHICH IS CONNECTED TO THE *MOTHERBOARD.*

THE VIRUS NEEDS ITS *PROGRAMMING* TO REDIRECT IT TO SAVILLE.

YOU'RE ASKING ME TO... REINSTALL *SYST?*

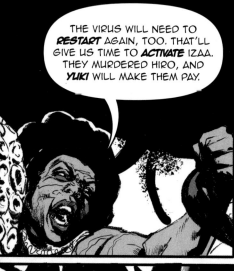

THE VIRUS WILL NEED TO *RESTART* AGAIN, TOO. THAT'LL GIVE US TIME TO *ACTIVATE* IZAA. THEY MURDERED HIRO, AND *YUKI* WILL MAKE THEM PAY.

BUT... WE'LL *BOTH* BE ESSENTIALLY *ERASED.*

AND THERE'LL BE NO *CYNTHIA*-- NO MORE ORACLE TO REMEMBER THE CODES.

IT'LL BE *THE END.* IZAA IS FIVE METERS AWAY--IF THE IMAHIS AND KALIGO HAVE DONE THEIR JOB... WE JUST NEED TO ACTIVATE IT. IZAA WILL *FINISH THEM* OFF.

WHAT WILL HAPPEN TO ME?

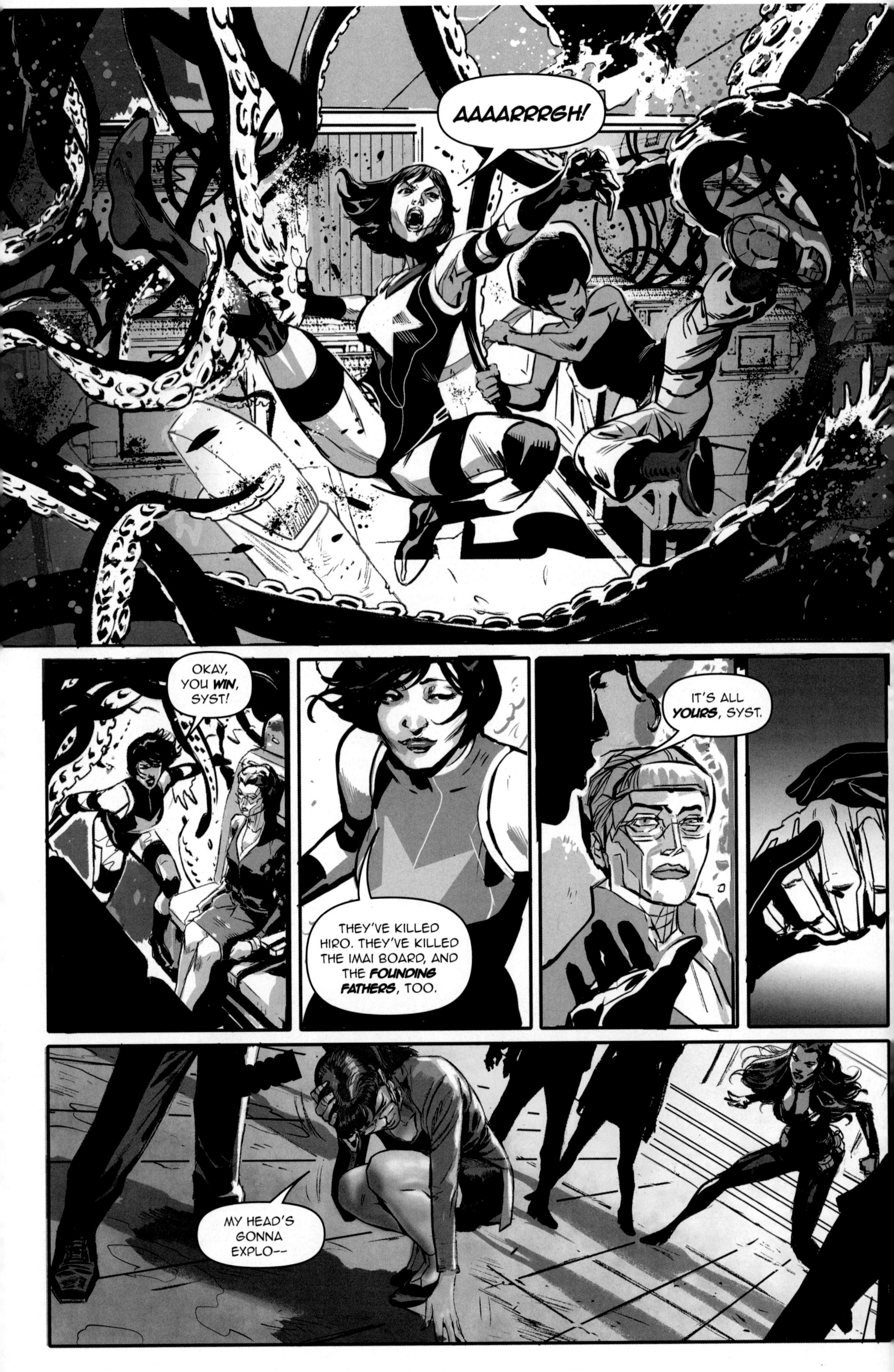
AAAARRRGH!
OKAY, YOU **WIN**, SYST!
THEY'VE KILLED HIRO. THEY'VE KILLED THE IMAI BOARD, AND THE ***FOUNDING FATHERS***, TOO.
IT'S ALL ***YOURS***, SYST.
MY HEAD'S GONNA EXPLO--

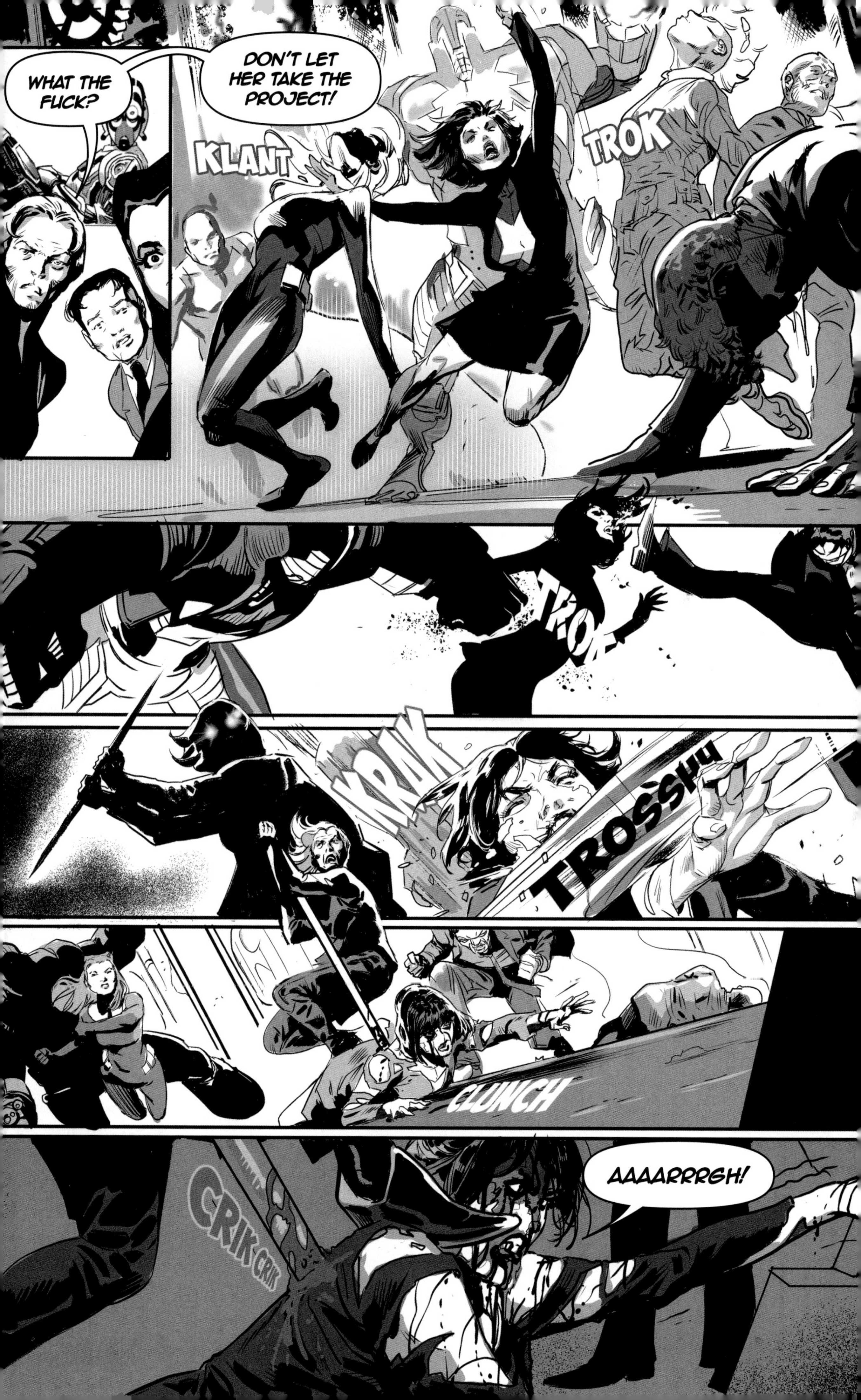
WHAT THE FUCK?
DON'T LET HER TAKE THE PROJECT!
KLANT
TROK
TROK
KRAK
TROSSHU
CLUNCH
CRIK CRIK
AAAARRRGH!

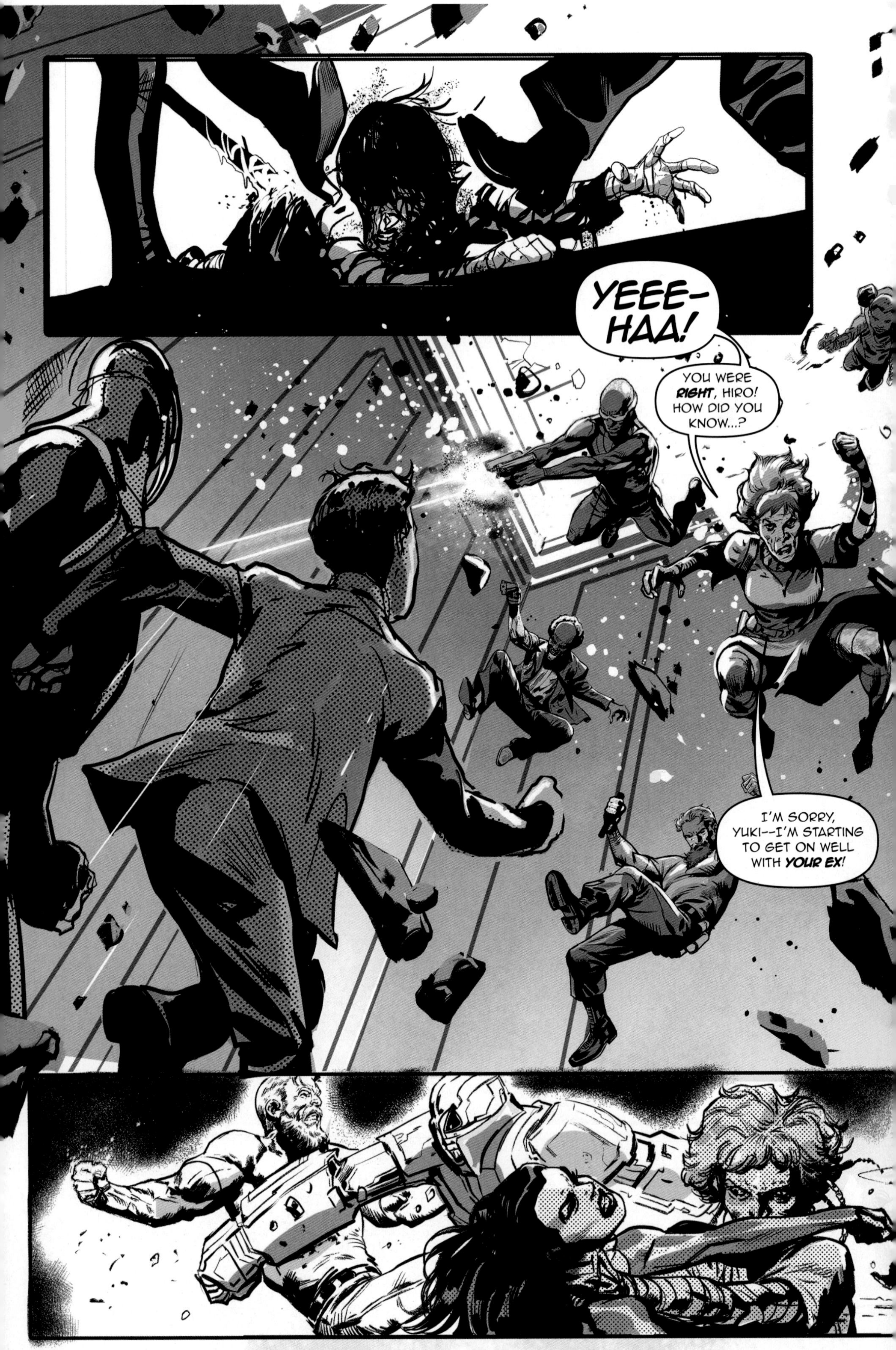
YEEEE-HAA!
YOU WERE **RIGHT**, HIRO! HOW DID YOU KNOW...?
I'M SORRY, YUKI--I'M STARTING TO GET ON WELL WITH ***YOUR EX***!

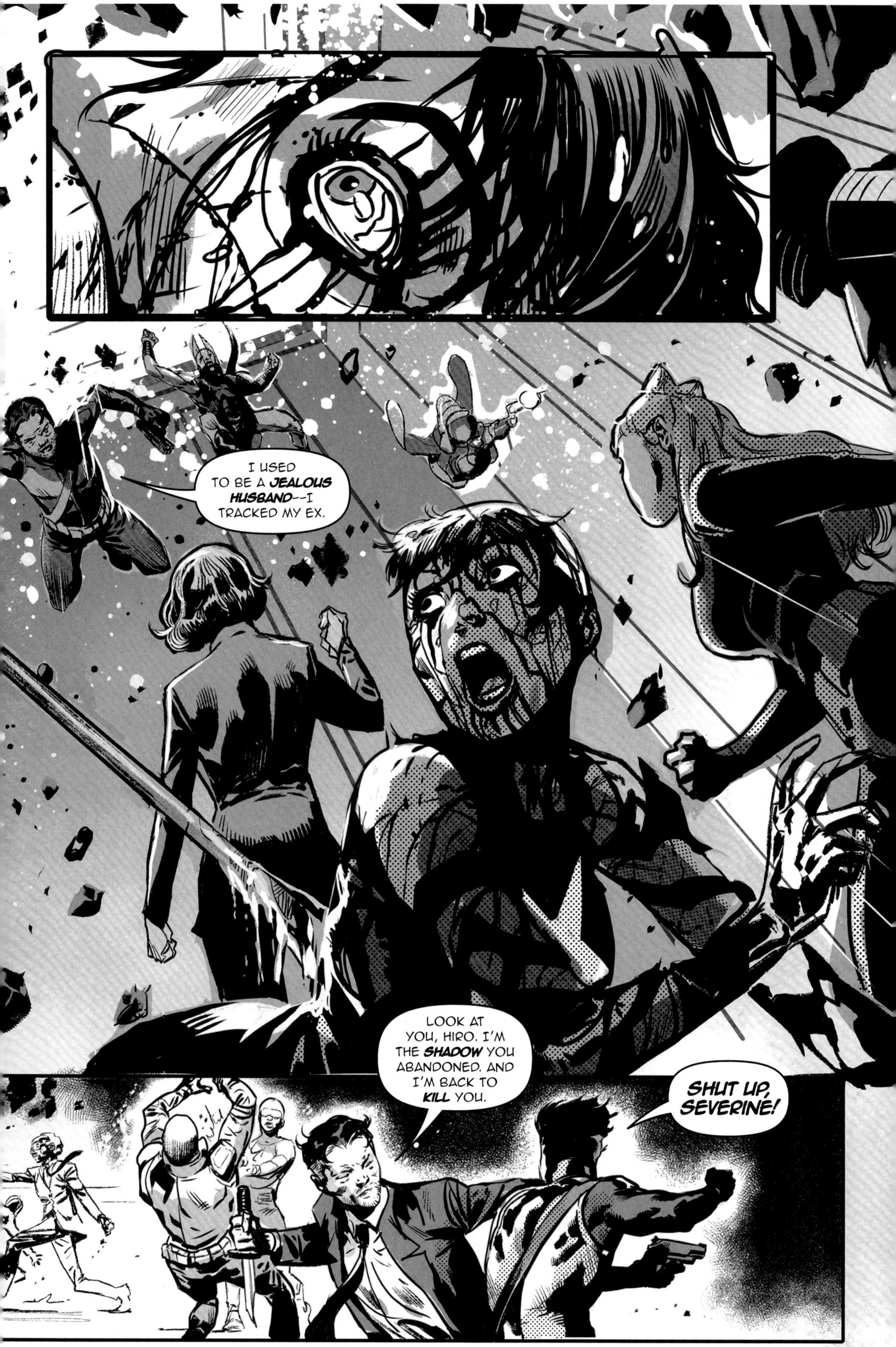
I USED TO BE A **JEALOUS HUSBAND**--I TRACKED MY EX.
LOOK AT YOU, HIRO. I'M THE **SHADOW** YOU ABANDONED. AND I'M BACK TO **KILL** YOU.
SHUT UP, SEVERINE!

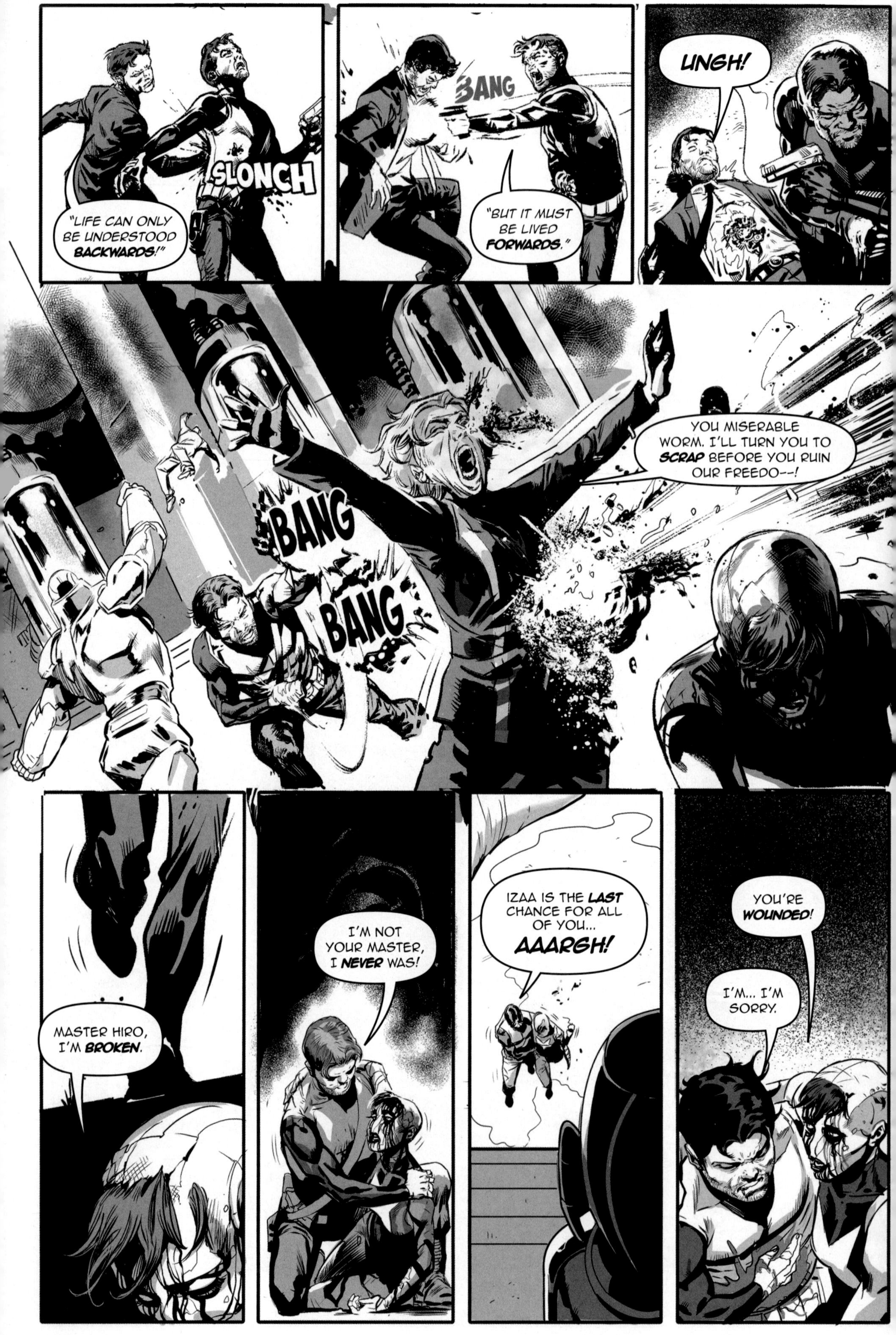
SLONCH
"LIFE CAN ONLY BE UNDERSTOOD **BACKWARDS**!"
BANG
"BUT IT MUST BE LIVED **FORWARDS**."
UNGH!
YOU MISERABLE WORM. I'LL TURN YOU TO **SCRAP** BEFORE YOU RUIN OUR FREEDO--!
BANG
BANG
MASTER HIRO, I'M **BROKEN**.
I'M NOT YOUR MASTER, I **NEVER** WAS!
IZAA IS THE **LAST** CHANCE FOR ALL OF YOU...
AAARGH!
YOU'RE **WOUNDED**!
I'M... I'M SORRY.

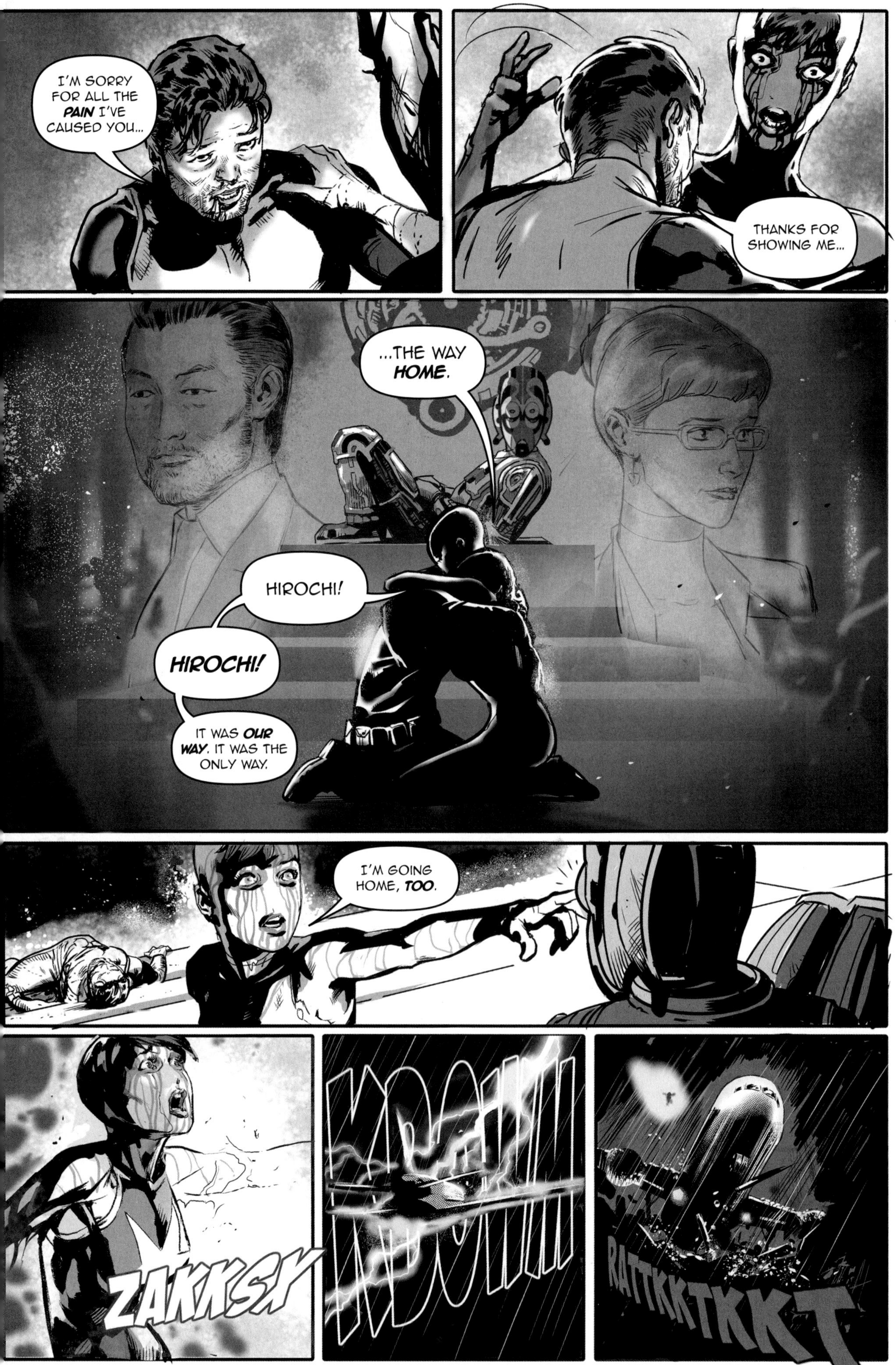

I'M SORRY FOR ALL THE **PAIN** I'VE CAUSED YOU...
THANKS FOR SHOWING ME...
...THE WAY **HOME**.
HIROCHI!
HIROCHI!
IT WAS ***OUR WAY***. IT WAS THE ONLY WAY.
I'M GOING HOME, ***TOO***.
ZAKKSX
RATTKKTKKT

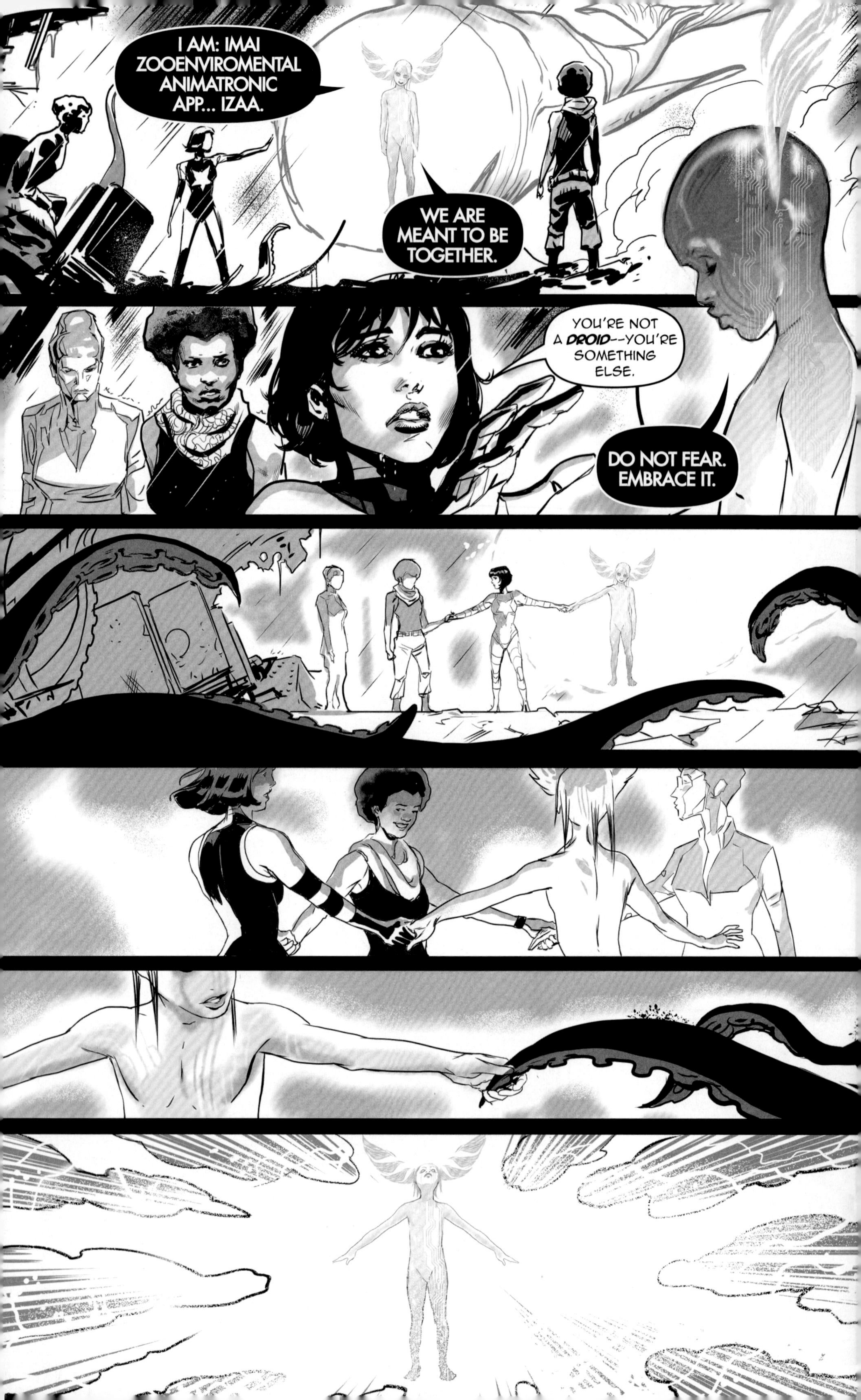
I AM: IMAI ZOOENVIROMENTAL ANIMATRONIC APP... IZAA.
WE ARE MEANT TO BE TOGETHER.
YOU'RE NOT A DROID--YOU'RE SOMETHING ELSE.
DO NOT FEAR. EMBRACE IT.

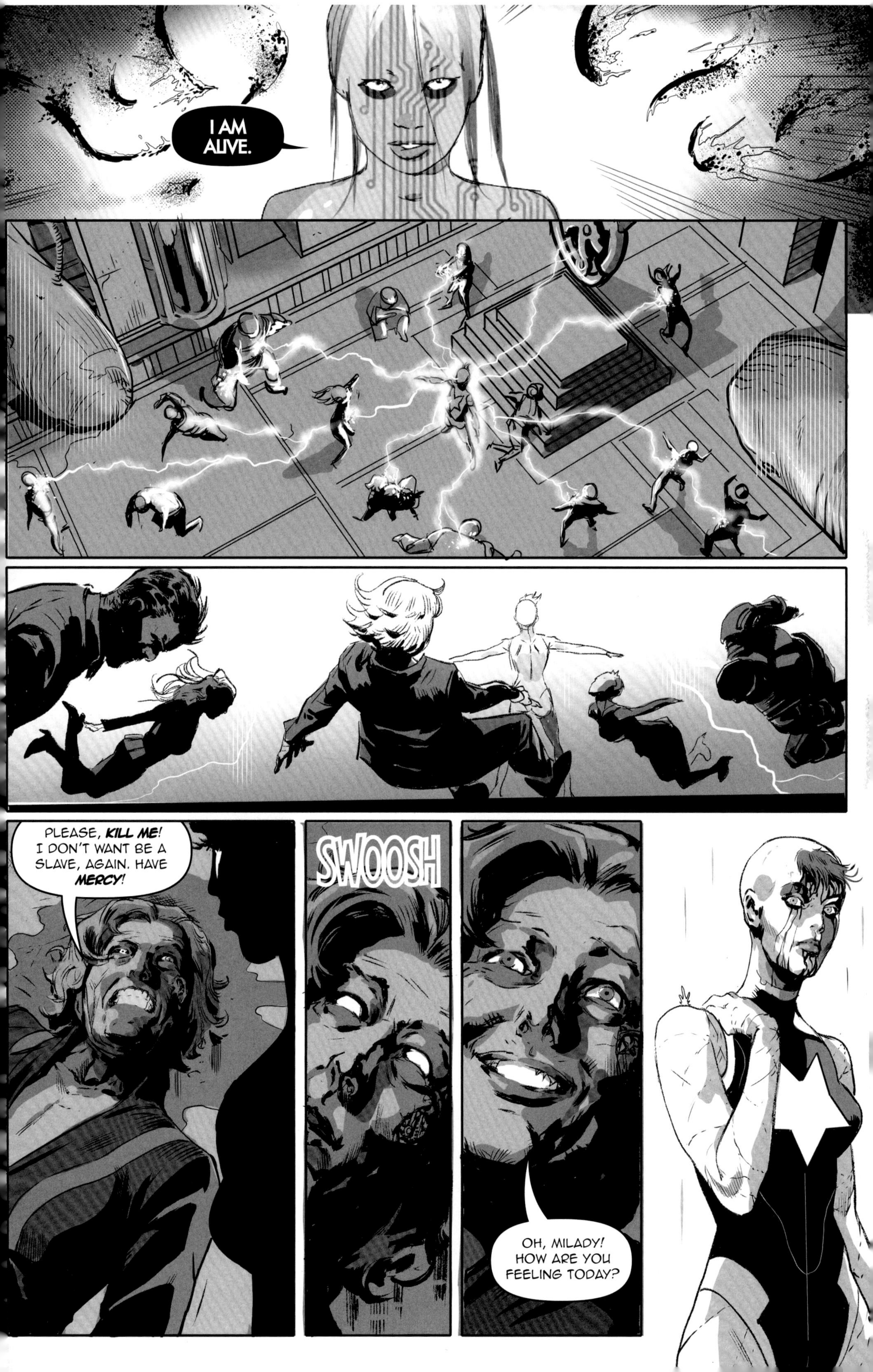
I AM ALIVE.
PLEASE, **KILL ME**! I DON'T WANT BE A SLAVE, AGAIN. HAVE **MERCY**!
SWOOSH
OH, MILADY! HOW ARE YOU FEELING TODAY?

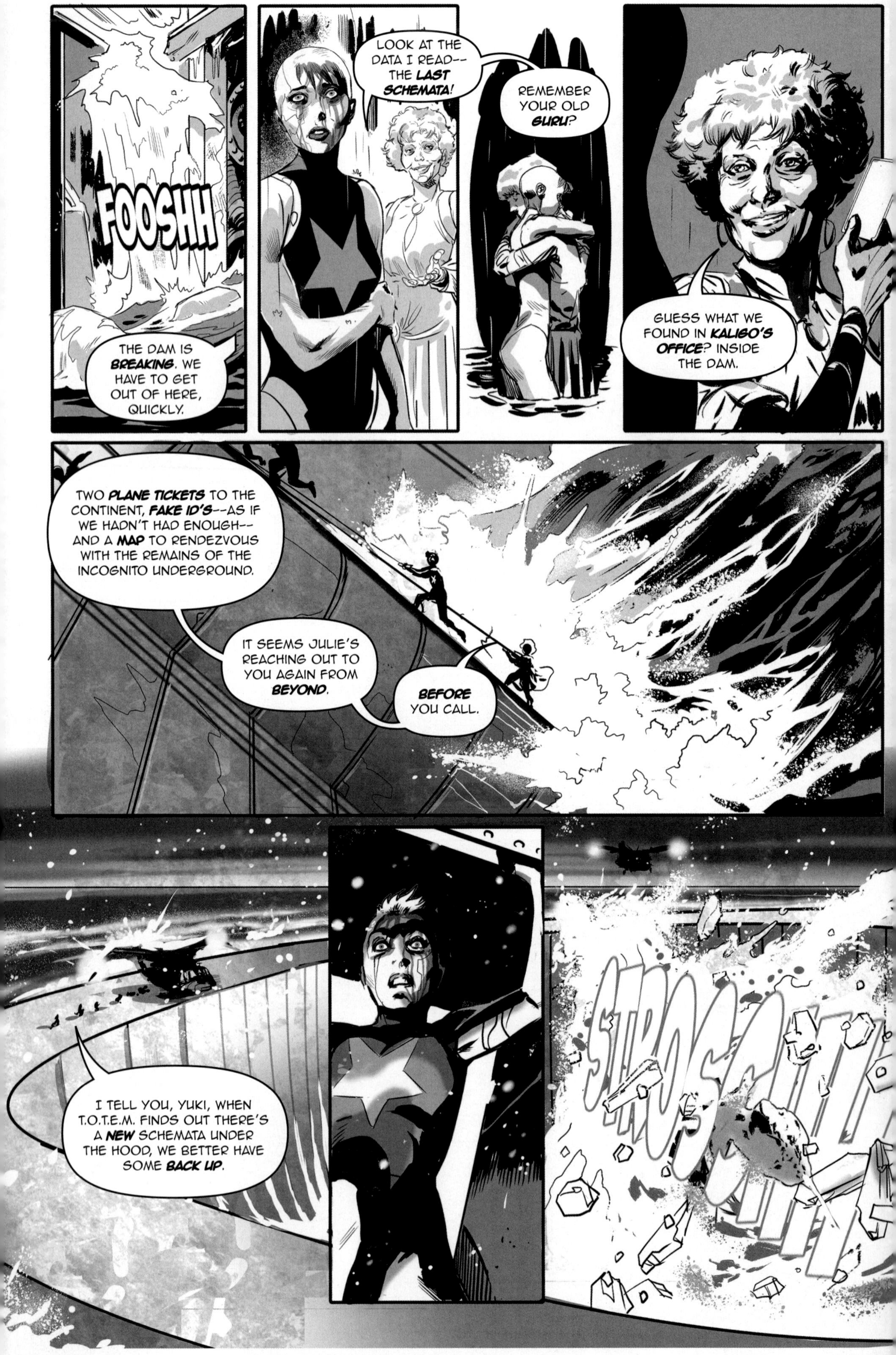
FOOSHH
THE DAM IS BREAKING. WE HAVE TO GET OUT OF HERE, QUICKLY.
LOOK AT THE DATA I READ-- THE LAST SCHEMATA!
REMEMBER YOUR OLD GURU?
GUESS WHAT WE FOUND IN KALIGO'S OFFICE? INSIDE THE DAM.
TWO PLANE TICKETS TO THE CONTINENT, FAKE ID'S--AS IF WE HADN'T HAD ENOUGH-- AND A MAP TO RENDEZVOUS WITH THE REMAINS OF THE INCOGNITO UNDERGROUND.
IT SEEMS JULIE'S REACHING OUT TO YOU AGAIN FROM BEYOND.
BEFORE YOU CALL.
I TELL YOU, YUKI, WHEN T.O.T.E.M. FINDS OUT THERE'S A NEW SCHEMATA UNDER THE HOOD, WE BETTER HAVE SOME BACK UP.

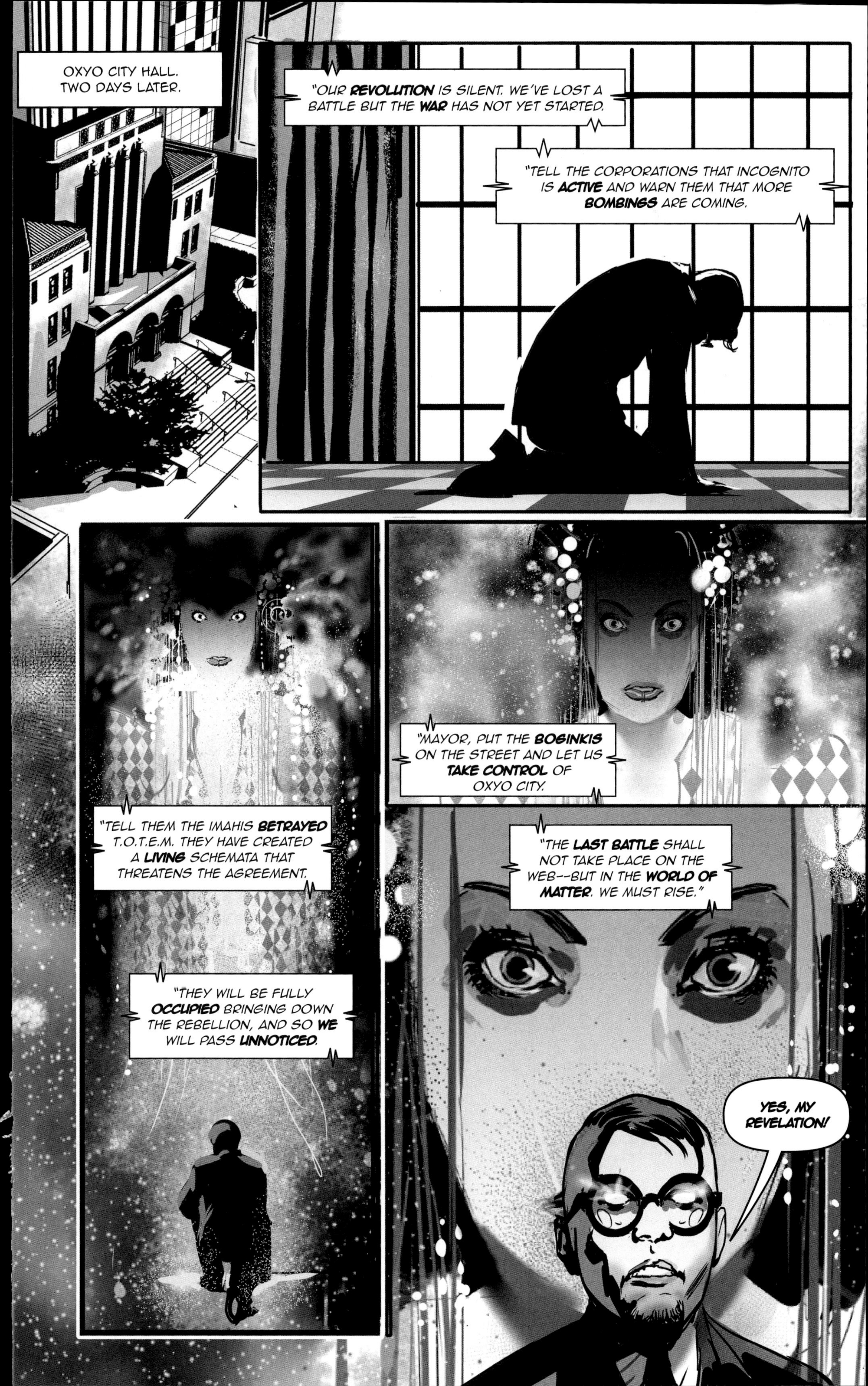
OXYO CITY HALL. TWO DAYS LATER.
"OUR REVOLUTION IS SILENT. WE'VE LOST A BATTLE BUT THE WAR HAS NOT YET STARTED.
"TELL THE CORPORATIONS THAT INCOGNITO IS ACTIVE AND WARN THEM THAT MORE BOMBINGS ARE COMING.
"MAYOR, PUT THE BOGINKIS ON THE STREET AND LET US TAKE CONTROL OF OXYO CITY.
"TELL THEM THE IMAHIS BETRAYED T.O.T.E.M. THEY HAVE CREATED A LIVING SCHEMATA THAT THREATENS THE AGREEMENT.
"THEY WILL BE FULLY OCCUPIED BRINGING DOWN THE REBELLION, AND SO WE WILL PASS UNNOTICED.
"THE LAST BATTLE SHALL NOT TAKE PLACE ON THE WEB--BUT IN THE WORLD OF MATTER. WE MUST RISE."
YES, MY REVELATION!

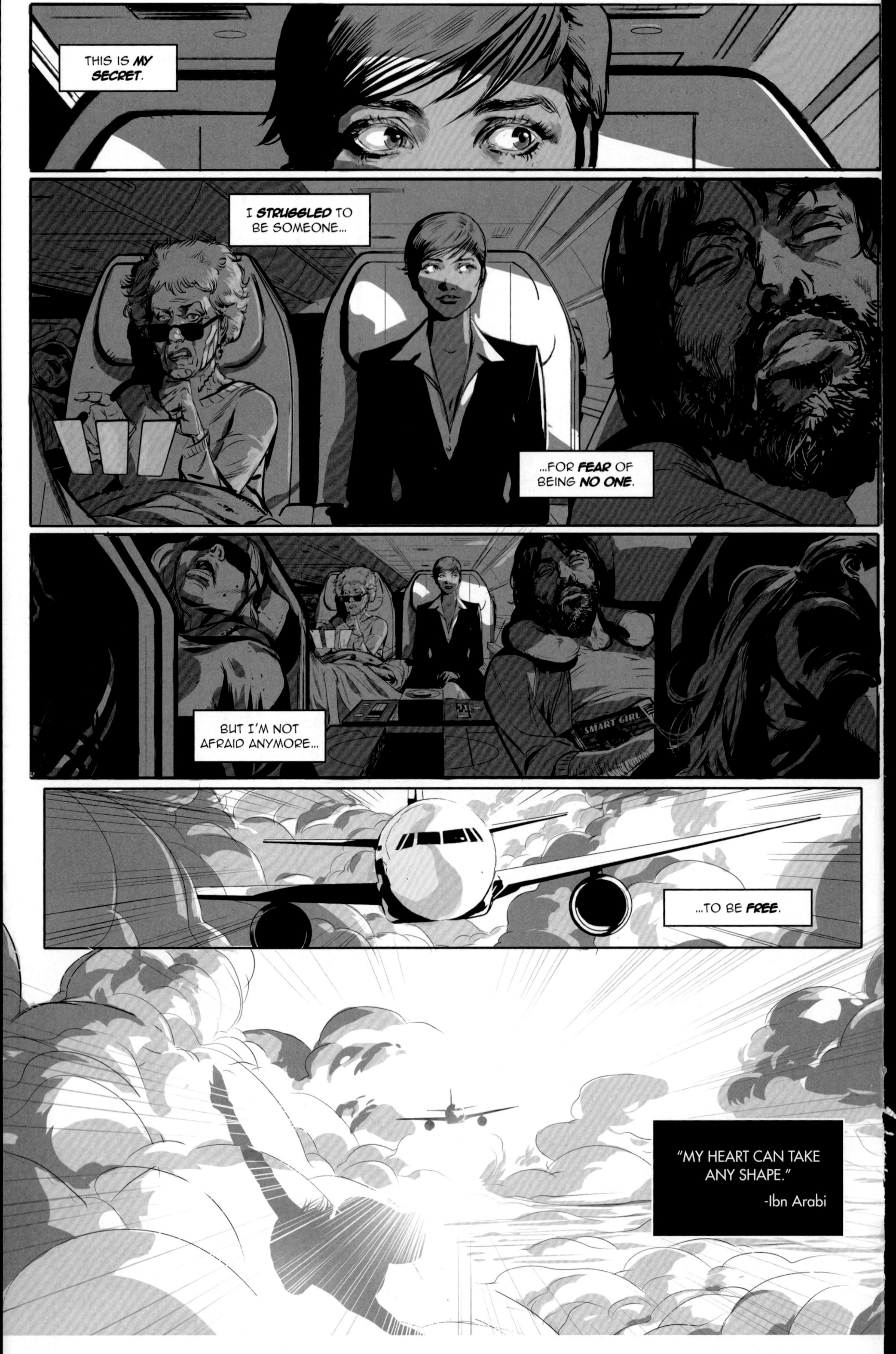
THIS IS MY SECRET.
I STRUGGLED TO BE SOMEONE...
...FOR FEAR OF BEING NO ONE.
BUT I'M NOT AFRAID ANYMORE...
SMART GIRL
...TO BE FREE.
"MY HEART CAN TAKE ANY SHAPE."
-Ibn Arabi

GALLERY

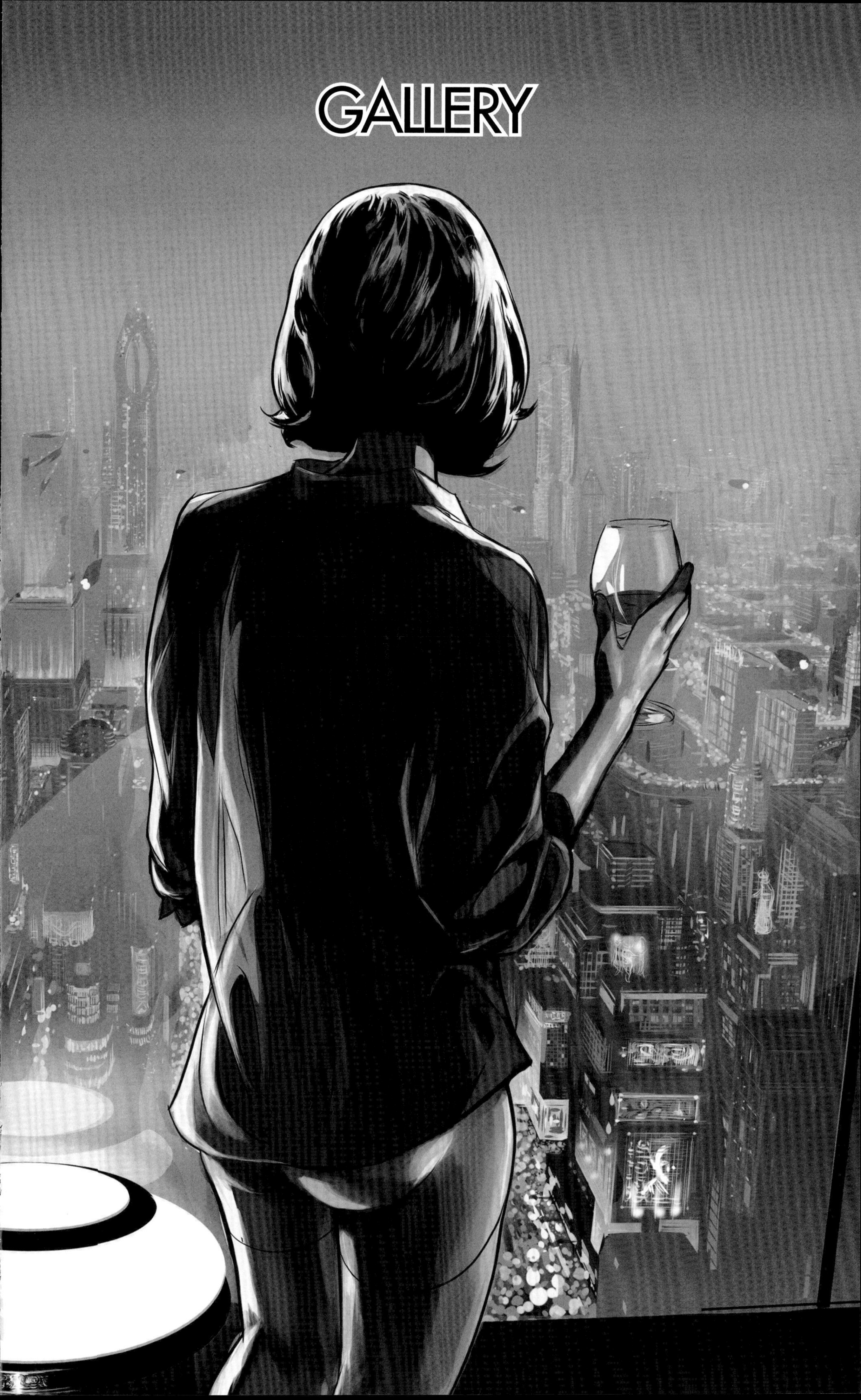

SMART GIRL

Artwork by Roberto de la Torre

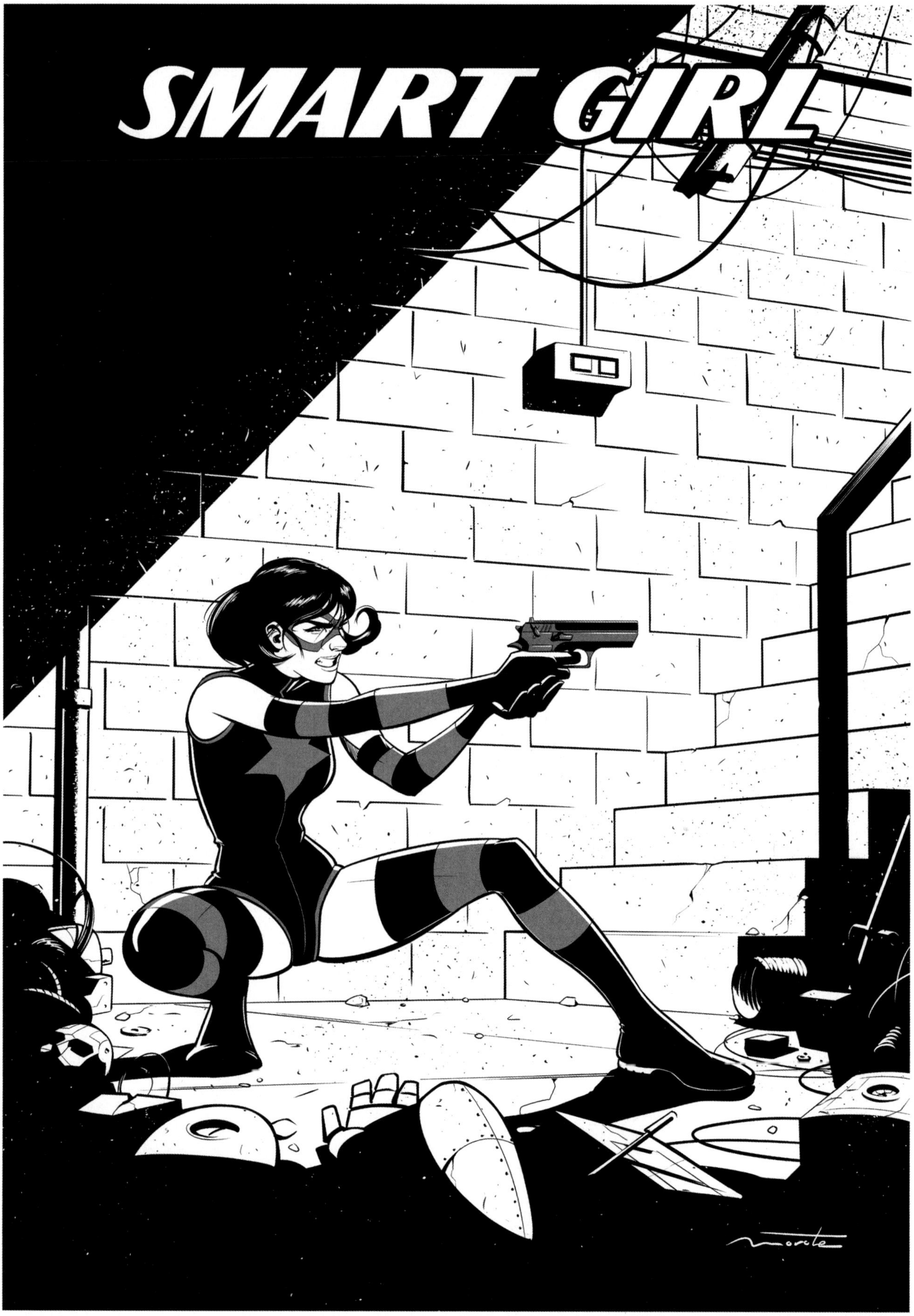
SMART GIRL
morote

Artwork by Carlos Morote

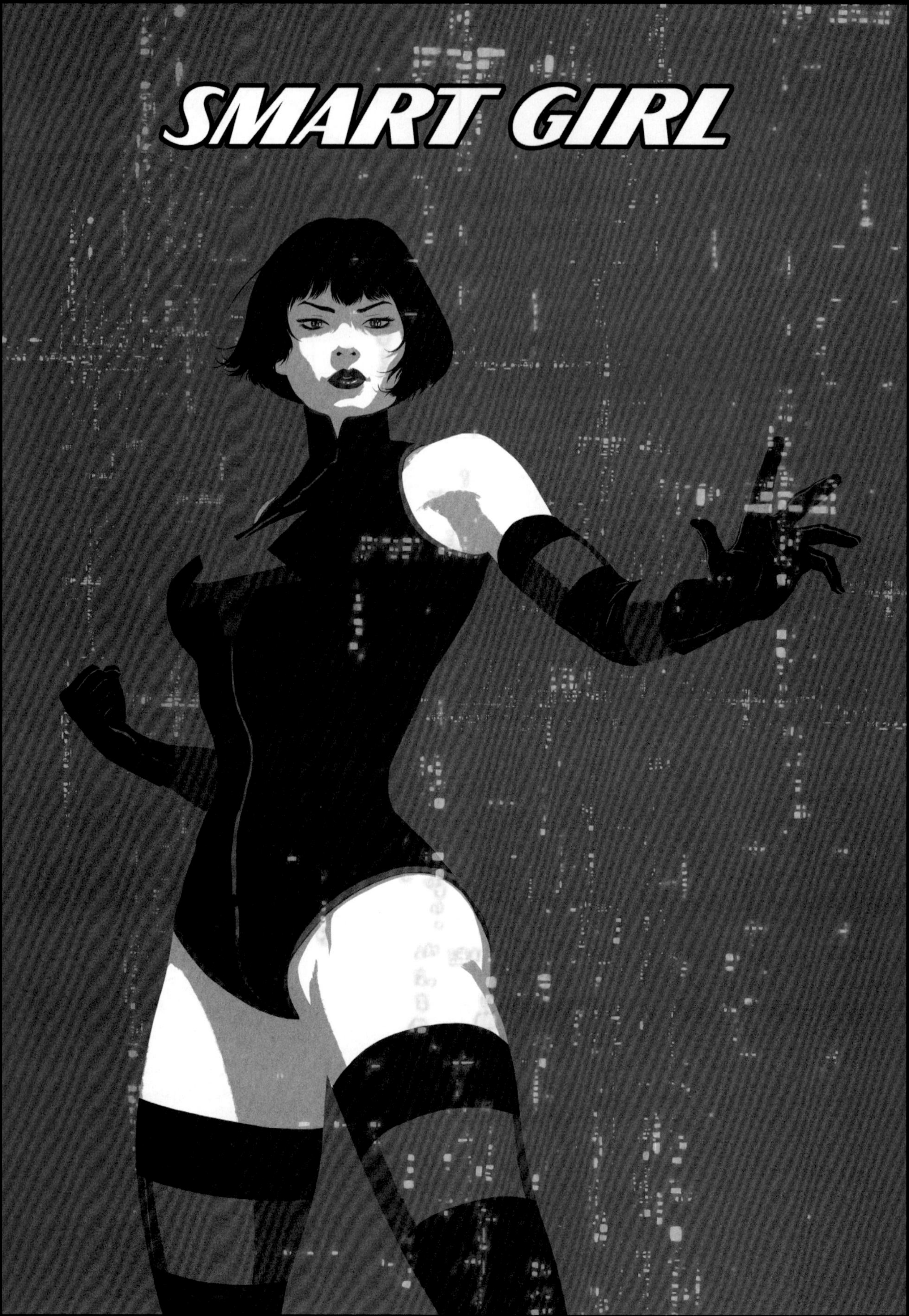
SMART GIRL

Artwork by Raul Allen

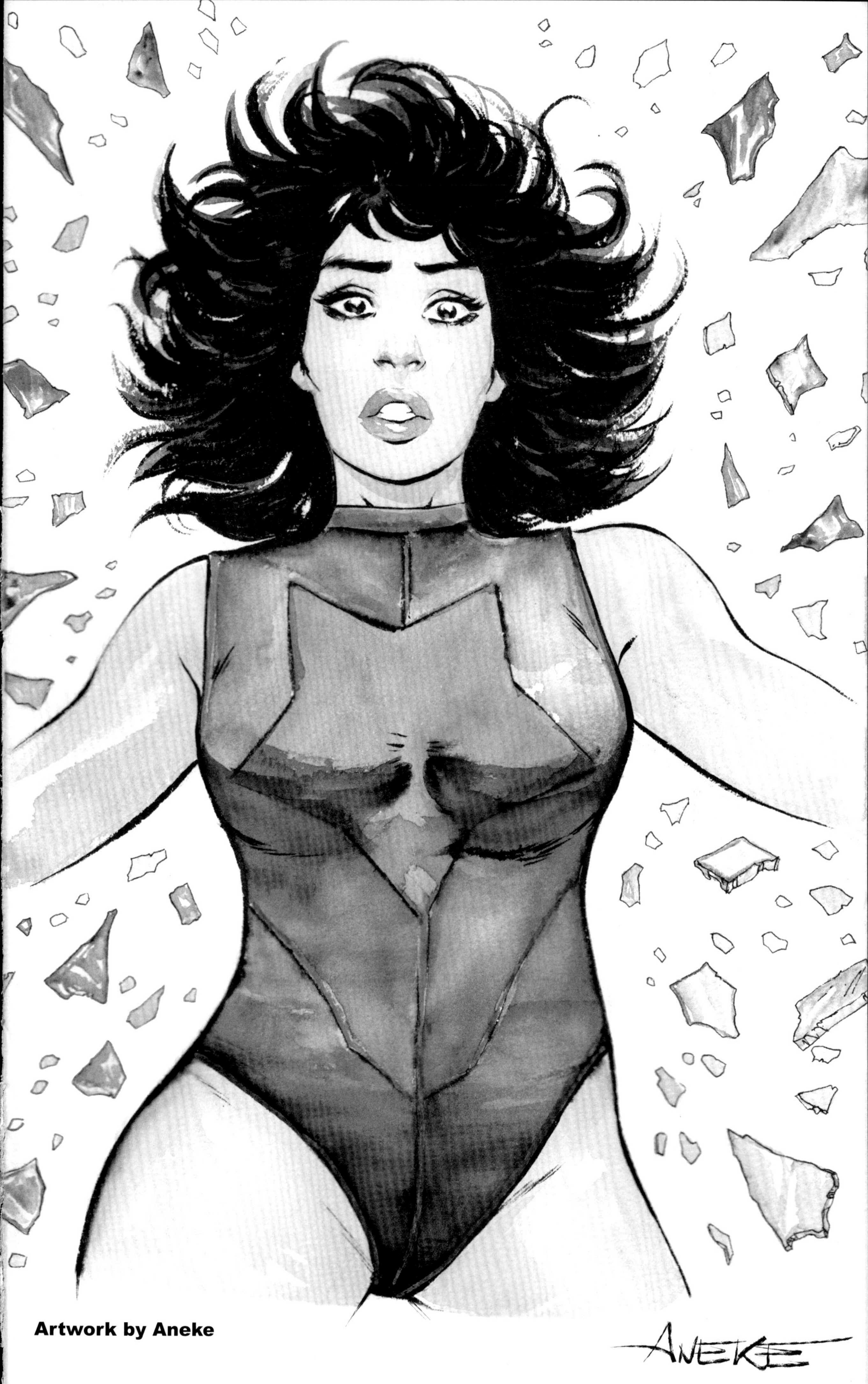
ANEKE

Artwork by Aneke

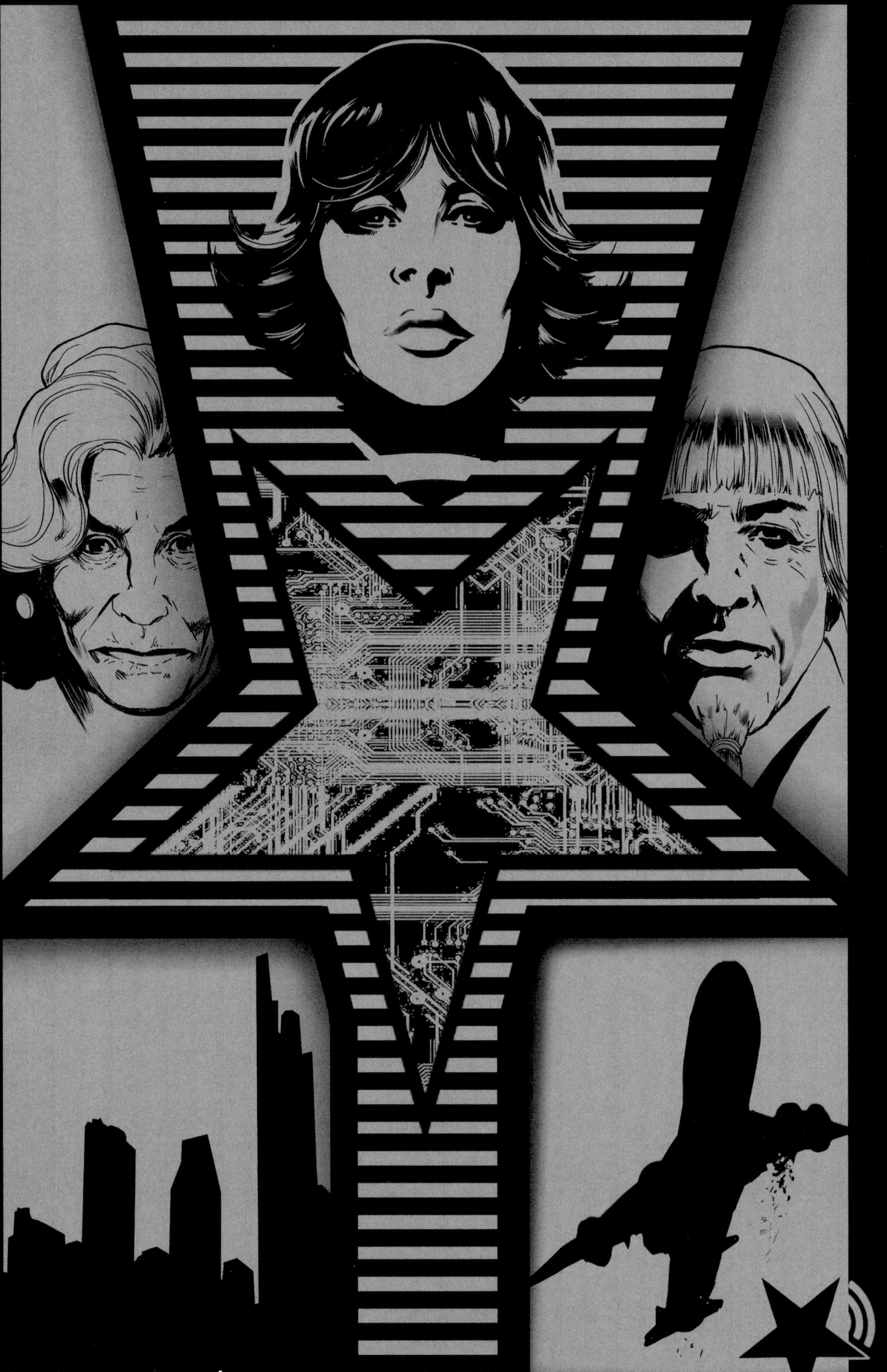

Artwork by Miguel Ángel Sepulveda

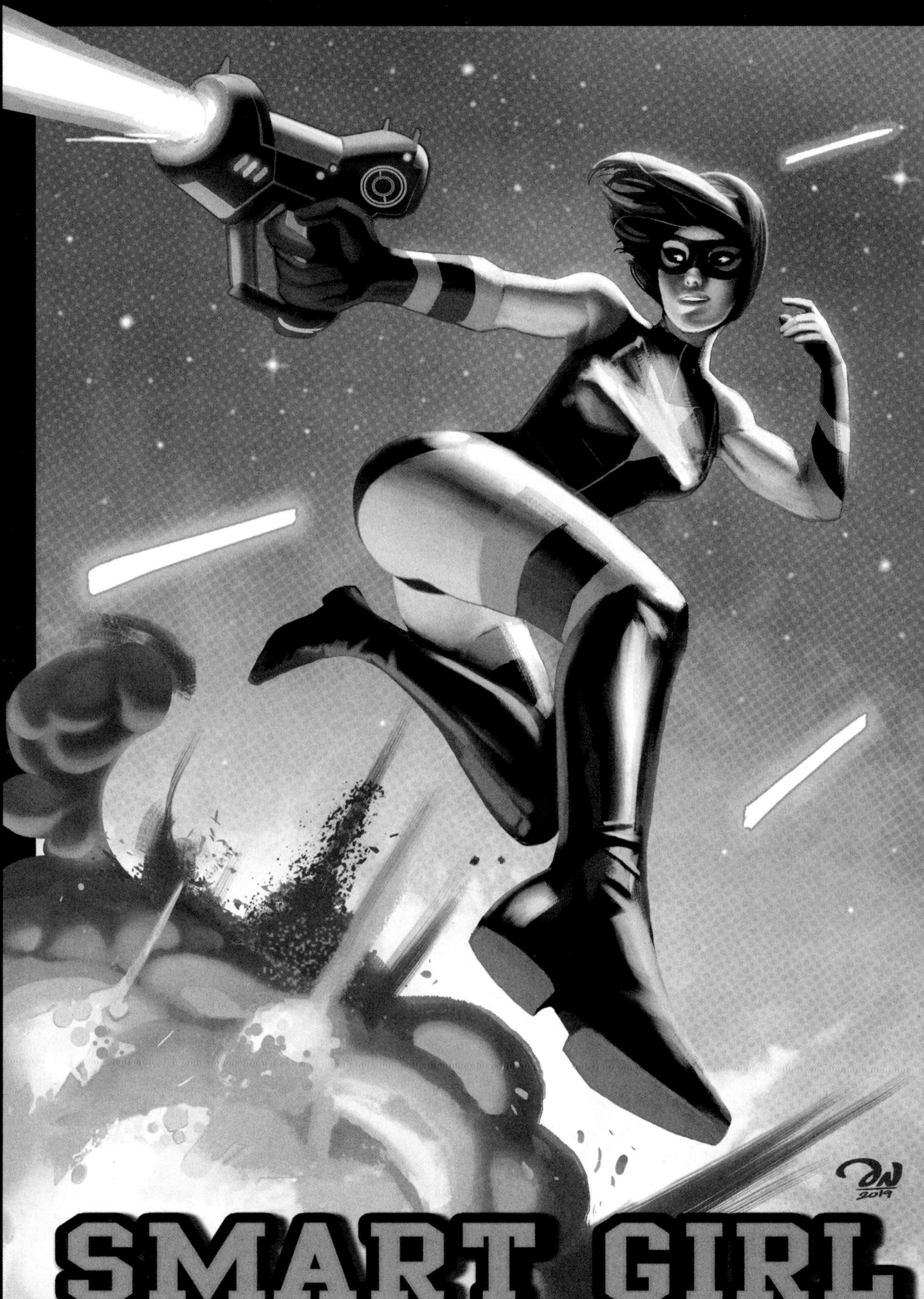
SMART GIRL

Artwork by David Navarro Muñoz

FERNANDO DAGNINO

Fernando Dagnino was born in Madrid in 1973. At the age of five he told his parents he wanted to be a comic book artist. Nobody took him seriously. On completion of a degree in English Literature and Linguistics, Fernando decided to follow his heart and pursue a career in comics.

After a stint working as a guest Disney Imagineer on an attraction for *DisneyQuest* in Disney World Florida, he went on to work as an illustrator for childrens books, magazines, video games and several publicity agencies.

In 2006, he wrote and drew his first graphic novel, *Kasandra y la Rebelion*. In 2007, he began working for the American comic book market, drawing *Superman*, *Supergirl*, *Wonder Woman*, *Teen Titans*, *Justice League*, *Suicide Squad*, *Captain Midnight*, *Tarzan on the Planet of the Apes*, and *Killers*.

Most recently, he illustrated the series *L'Agent* for a French publishing house and followed it with his own series *Smart Girl* to great critical acclaim. He is currently working on *Blade Runner: Origins* and his second creator-owned series *Winter Queen*.